"UN-AMERICAN"
HOLLYWOOD

"UN-AMERICAN" HOLLYWOOD

Politics and Film in the Blacklist Era

EDITED BY FRANK KRUTNIK,
STEVE NEALE, BRIAN NEVE,
AND PETER STANFIELD

RUTGERS UNIVERSITY PRESS
New Brunswick, New Jersey, and London

Library of Congress Cataloging-in-Publication Data

"Un-American" Hollywood: politics and film in the blacklist era / edited by Frank Krutnik . . . [et al.].

    p. cm.

Includes bibliographical references and index.

ISBN 978–0-8135–4197–6 (hardcover : alk. paper)—ISBN 978–0-8135–4198–3 (pbk. : alk. paper)

    1. Motion pictures—Political aspects—United States.   2. Blacklisting of entertainers—United States. I. Krutnik, Frank, 1956–

PN1995.9.P6U5   2007

384.'8097309045—dc22

                        2007006054

A British Cataloging-in-Publication record for this book is available from the British Library.

Visit our Web site: http://rutgerspress.rutgers.edu

Manufactured in the United States of America

Contents

"UN-AMERICAN"
HOLLYWOOD

Introduction

Frank Krutnik, Steve Neale, Brian Neve, and Peter Stanfield

This collection of essays on the films and television programs made by those caught up in the Communist witch hunts of the 1940s and 1950s represents a move to better understand the role of progressive politics within a capitalist media industry. In part, the essayists have written in recognition of the extraordinary if controversial output of the historian of left-wing American culture Paul Buhle and his collaborators Dave Wagner and Patrick McGilligan.[1] Throughout the collection the authors acknowledge Buhle's work on reopening debate on the Hollywood Left and the blacklist, as well as the attention paid to the blacklistees and their films in the left-oriented screen journal *Cineaste*. The insights and information contained here further develop this work and that of Larry Ceplair and Steven Englund in their rigorously researched 1979 history *The Inquisition in Hollywood: Politics in the Film Community, 1930–60*.[2] While Buhle and company aimed to chart the involvement of left film practitioners, especially screenwriters, in an enormously wide range of films, they do not always present convincing arguments about how the political sensibilities of such creative personnel actually impacted, if at all, upon the movies to which they contributed. This present volume, by contrast, attempts a more focused scrutiny of particular case studies and contexts involving the blacklist generation.

"Un-American" Hollywood closes with a reprint of Thom Andersen's seminal 1985 essay "Red Hollywood," together with a new afterword by the author commissioned for this volume. Through his conception of film gris, Andersen called for a more considered approach to the work of the Hollywood Ten and their fellow travelers. Rather than reject the notion propagated by the witch hunters that Communist and ex-Communist filmmakers had insinuated their progressive political ideas into mainstream genre productions, Andersen's analysis confirmed the findings of the House Un-American Activities Committee (HUAC). A number of the contributors in this collection take his essay as their starting point. Working against the received idea that Hollywood always manufactures a politically conservative product, all the contributors set out to show how progressive political ideas and positions were incorporated into certain Hollywood films.

Like the Truman Doctrine, the Marshall Plan, and the 1947 National Security Act, the un-American hearings were a Cold War containment initiative that sought to co-opt allegiance and muzzle dissent. FBI chief J. Edgar Hoover, no stranger to anti-Communist crusades, warned HUAC in March 1947 that the "greatest menace" Communism posed to the United States lay in the ability of its members to influence, to infiltrate, and to corrupt various spheres of American life. "The communist propaganda technique," he asserted, "is designed to promote emotional response with the hope that the victim will be attracted by what he is told the communist way of life holds in store for him. The objective, of course, is to develop discontent and hasten the day when the communists can gather sufficient support and following to overthrow the American way of life."[3] Hollywood, of course, had been promoting emotional response since its inception. Within a paranoid culture that traded in scenarios of subversion and disloyalty, Hollywood's power to reach millions of people, across the United States and across the world, inevitably made it a target of suspicion.

It is significant that nine of the Hollywood Ten, and 58 percent of all film industry personnel called before HUAC, were writers.[4] As originators of a film's conceptual substance, writers provided the most obvious line of attack for interest groups, both within and outside Hollywood, which sought to purge the screen of their particular fantasy of un-Americanism. As Ceplair and Englund note, "Screenwriters were the elite corps of political consciousness in Hollywood in the two decades after 1933, and their leaders were the brains of all the organizations which sprang up in expression of this consciousness. Their time, energy, and money fuelled progressive politics in Hollywood, and their words advertised progressive ideals to the general public."[5] Several of the Hollywood Ten had proven expertise in propagandist entertainment, having worked on wartime films that contained explicitly instructional anti-fascist sentiments.[6] If they could do such a good job planting messages into officially sanctioned projects like *Tender Comrade* (1943), *Sahara* (1943), *Action in the North Atlantic* (1943), *The Cross of Lorraine* (1943), *None Shall Escape* (1944), and *The Master Race* (1944), they were clearly more than capable of injecting subversive sentiments into their postwar films.[7]

According to Hoover, "The communists have developed one of the greatest propaganda machines the world has ever known" and managed "to penetrate and infiltrate many respectable public opinion mediums."[8] But in practice it proved difficult for HUAC to come up with convincing examples of such subversion. Pursuing an unsophisticated approach to questions of cinematic meaning and pleasure, the HUAC investigators proved that they were not good film critics. The Hollywood Left were themselves well aware of the tangible barriers that blocked their influence over film content. In his appeal petition to the U.S. Supreme Court in August 1949, John Howard Lawson, head of the Hollywood branch of the Communist Party, argued that filmmaking in the Hollywood system was far too well supervised to allow anyone to smuggle in subversive content:

> As a matter of undeviating practice in the motion picture industry it is impossible for any screen writer to put anything into a motion picture to which the executive producers object. The content of motion pictures is controlled exclusively by producers; [all aspects of a film] are carefully studied, checked,

edited and filtered by executive producers and persons acting directly under their supervision.[9]

In a 1992 discussion of the blacklist Dan Georgakas suggests that the U.S. Communist Party recognized the difficulty of making radical films within the Hollywood system, advising its members to pursue instead "a democratic and populist ethos that was totally in accord with the New Deal popular culture. Melvyn Douglas, a leading Hollywood liberal, commented years later that the Communists had been followers of the liberals and not vice versa."[10] Blacklisted screenwriter Walter Bernstein substantiates this in his memoir, recalling that when collaborating with director Robert Rossen they "would discuss some leftist point to be made in a scene and then he would go upstairs and present the scene to [Columbia Pictures production head Harry] Cohn. He would return with the radicalism either deleted or softened to an acceptable liberalism."[11]

The blunderbuss tactics of the congressional committee did not encourage cogent analysis of Hollywood films and their ideological maneuvers. But the committee was nonetheless effective in forcing the studios to exert stricter control over the political sympathies of its productions and its employees. Association with radical causes or radical organizations could lead to dismissal, blacklisting, or even, as the case of the Hollywood Ten illustrated, imprisonment. Left politics were by no means obliterated from the screen during this time, but they certainly had to adopt sometimes quite elaborate disguises. Just as the institutional censorship of the Hays Code inspired filmmakers to adopt coded and elliptical strategies of representation, so too political critique was most often insinuated (or interpreted) through displacement, metaphor, or allegory. The most famous examples of this process are the 1950s science fiction films *The Day the Earth Stood Still* (1951) and *Invasion of the Body Snatchers* (1956), or such westerns as *High Noon* (1952), *Johnny Guitar* (1954), and *Silver Lode* (1954). A contrasting example is provided by the socially grounded crime thrillers that Thom Andersen identifies as film gris.[12] These politically inflected tales of criminal transgression attracted several of the Hollywood Left in the late 1940s and early 1950s, perhaps because the generic framework of the crime story allowed them more readily to expose the flaws of contemporary American society.

Throughout all the essays presented in this volume, the writers engage with the problem of making meaning, to use David Bordwell's term.[13] Underlying all the varied approaches presented here is the question of how a particular film or films might be viewed and understood. The meaning of any film or the intentions of a filmmaker are never taken as a given, but are instead understood to be the starting point of the investigation. Allegory, literary criticism and adaptation, art history, genres and cycles, musical cultures, realism, racism, production contexts, scriptwriting, television dramas, all long-serving issues within the study of film, are here examined from perspectives that produce some radically new insights into Hollywood, politics, and film.

Using Ismail Xavier's work on allegory as a basis, Jeff Smith explores how films scripted by the Hollywood Left in the late 1940s and 1950s can be, or have been, interpreted as "disguised" commentaries on HUAC, the McCarthy hearings, and other contemporary political events. The topic of allegory is pertinent here for at least two reasons: first because, as Xavier points out, "allegorical expression is especially prevalent during times of political repression since the disguised nature of allegory allows it to communicate political dissent in a manner that circumvents systems of institutional censorship," and second because historical novels and films in particular "take on allegorical significance insofar as the depiction of past events serves as a means of offering 'disguised comment on the present.'" Films such as *Reign of Terror* (1949), *Quo Vadis* (1951), *Viva Zapata!* (1952), *Julius Caesar* (1953), *The Robe* (1953), *Spartacus* (1960), *El Cid* (1961), and *The Fall of the Roman Empire* (1964) are all especially pertinent here. Smith focuses in particular on *The Robe*. The final version of *The Robe* script was written by and credited to Philip Dunne, a noted Hollywood liberal. Early drafts were written in 1946 by Albert Maltz, one of the Hollywood Ten (see Art Simon's chapter for further consideration of Maltz). Using archival sources and extensive empirical evidence, Smith explores the chronologies governing the production of Lloyd Douglas's novel, first published in 1942, and Twentieth Century Fox's CinemaScope epic. The evolution of the film also involved RKO, the studio that initially owned the property and commissioned Maltz's script, as well as Dunne, producer Darryl Zanuck, and director Henry Koster at Twentieth Century Fox. Smith suggests on the one hand that both the novel and the film were more concerned with fascism than with HUAC, and on the other hand that none of the principal participants understood the film as exhibiting any kind of contemporary political subtext. The same is true of contemporary reviews. Subsequent interpretations of *The Robe* as a blacklist allegory have few if any foundations in the history of the film's production or in its reception by contemporary critics. It may well be that the liberalism that clearly permeates the film is best judged in relation to its overt rather than its covert subject matter: the persecution of early Christians by the Roman Empire rather than the persecution of leftists and liberals by McCarthy and HUAC.

Though Smith is concerned solely with *The Robe,* his mode of analysis can be used to reveal the set of critical presumptions that underlie readings of films that have long been thought of as allegories of the blacklist. Such films as *On the Waterfront* (1954) and *Broken Arrow* (1950) have often been viewed as contemporary commentaries on the witch hunts or in terms of the experience of particular "political" filmmakers. For example, some films are cited as critiques of HUAC and the broader Cold War political agenda. Perhaps the most celebrated are Abraham Polonsky's *Force of Evil* (1948) and Herbert J. Biberman's *Salt of the Earth* (1954), the latter being the only realized project of the Independent Production Corporation (IPC), which was specifically founded in 1951 as a vehicle for blacklisted Hollywood personnel. Interpretations of Polonsky's film, his last as director before his long period on the blacklist, have reflected the growth of work on the phenomenon, as well as critical writing on the symbolic equation drawn between the numbers racket and the capitalist system by director and source novelist Ira Wolfert.

The western and science fiction genres seemed particularly suited to efforts to make contemporary political allusions. Generic elements—from rough justice to lynch mobs, to fears of conformity and alien invasion—are readily interpreted as allegorical. The attack on totalitarianism here, as elsewhere in the period, can be read within the generic codes, or even as a generic code, or be seen as referring outward to public events. While screenwriter Carl Foreman intended the events of *High Noon* as an echo of his own experience of Hollywood politics at the time, the reviewer for the Communist *Daily Worker* commented on the "anti-human theme of nearly all cowboy and detective yarns" and saw the film as "destroying a man's faith in his fellow man."[14]

Issues of mob justice and the denial of civil liberties are also invoked outside of genre in stories such as *Try and Get Me* (*The Sound of Fury*) (1951) and *Storm Center* (1956). Even more iconic significance, in terms of the blacklist, has been loaded onto *On the Waterfront*, a product of the alliance of friendly witnesses Elia Kazan and Budd Schulberg, although the film was rarely interpreted in this way at the time, and no production materials point to any prior intention along these lines. Kazan has subsequently claimed that his own testimony influenced his identification with the Terry Malloy character, but, on the other hand, Budd Schulberg has always stressed the researched, "documentary" aspects of the story, and has sharply decried what he sees as the dominance of the "naming names" reading within the academy.[15] Certainly the overwhelming number of contemporary reviews interpreted this and other supposedly "blacklist" films in terms of their entertainment and artistic values rather than as political parables. As Smith suggests, one should be wary of telling the blacklist story by reference to a group of films whose status owes much to hindsight and little to production or reception evidence of the time.

Allegory is also at stake in Erica Sheen's study of *Christ in Concrete* (1949), an adaptation of Pietro di Donato's novel that was directed in Britain by Edward Dmytryk. As Sheen points out in her essay, allegorical readings—in the form of "close interpretations"—were practiced as much by the OSS (and, as we would point out, by the FBI and its agents) as by contemporary literary critics and by subsequent film studies academics interested in the films produced, directed, or written by the Hollywood Left. When the concept of allegory is applied to *Christ in Concrete*, however, one needs to take into account a range of political influences and contexts: Donati's politics, Italian and Italian American politics, political readings of Italian Neo-Realism and the films of Roberto Rossellini (who was initially slated to direct *Christ in Concrete*), as well as the politics of censorship, the international film industry, and the establishment of a postwar art cinema. While Rossellini's short film *Il Miracolo* (The Miracle, 1948) was the subject of a landmark Supreme Court decision that, for the first time, brought to films in the United States the protection of the First Amendment guarantees of free speech, such liberalism was denied to those, like Dmytryk, with "un-American" political views. It is this paradox, Sheen suggests, that helps explain why "Rossellini's films became canonical texts in the institution of art cinema," while "*Christ in Concrete* remains caught in the limbo of Un-America."

How one might recognize and account for the traces left by politically committed filmmakers is the subject of Frank Krutnik's unique account of the appearance of a print of Diego Rivera's painting *The Flower Carrier* in a number of films that have long been recognized as key examples in any discussion of left-wing influence on the movies. Working as both archaeologist, searching for traces of a hidden history, and detective, reading the clues, Krutnik unravels an extraordinary example of cross-textual patterning. In films such as *In a Lonely Place* (1950), *The Woman on Pier 13* (1949), and *The Prowler* (1951), he discovers that prints of the Rivera painting are "incorporated within the flow of images to emblematize a political critique that could not otherwise be articulated," producing what amounts to "an enigmatic communication from a turbulent past." Krutnik's interpretation of the print's placement within a film's mise-en-scène is contextualized by a consideration of various studios' recycling of set designs and props, and the role of art works as props in general. The close scrutiny of the life and times of Rivera, his struggle to make politically incisive art for the masses, and his significance for left-wing cultural workers in the United States are complemented by a close reading of the ideological significance of *The Flower Carrier* alongside the films in which it appears. Finally, Krutnik complicates the reading of films such as *In a Lonely Place* as allegories of the blacklist by showing how rich the possible interpretations are that govern the placement of the Rivera print, situated, as it is, within "an elaborate *mise-en-scène* of artistic references" alongside the theme of the artist "caught up within a persecutory culture." In Krutnik's view these films are as much about the politics of taste and discrimination as they are about social inequalities.

Scripted by Abraham Polonsky, directed by Robert Rossen, and starring John Garfield, the boxing film *Body and Soul* (1947) has long been regarded as a signature film of the Hollywood Left. As Peter Stanfield considers, however, *Body and Soul* was but one of a large number of films made from the late 1940s to the early 1960s that dealt with the subject of boxing, a surprisingly large number of which attracted liberal and left-wing Jewish filmmakers. The mass popularity of boxing during this period ensured its potency as a discursive forum in which filmmakers could tackle various social and cultural problems—involving, for example, class, masculinity, crime, art, popular culture, ethnicity, and race. Building on the legacy of earlier boxing films such as *Golden Boy* (1939), based on a play by Clifford Odets, *Body and Soul* provided a powerful demonstration of how the sport could be used as a vehicle for exploring and critiquing U.S. social values. At the same time, Stanfield suggests that the boxing movie also carried with it a strong nostalgic pull, hearkening back to the radicalizing crucible of the Depression and to an idealized vision of the urban ghetto as an uncorrupted ethnic community that counterbalances the ruthless, morally degraded U.S. mainstream. Stanfield examines the boxing films of the 1940s and 1950s in relation to the shifting institutional context of the sport, and to its importance within contemporary mass media culture (through newspapers, popular fiction, theater, radio, television, and film). He focuses in particular on the central role that the sport has occupied within the culture of America's ethnic groups, especially with regard to the participation of Jews through the 1920s and 1930s. Even if Jewish involvement diminished thereafter, boxing remained a key part of the cultural heritage of Jewish filmmakers that allowed them to explore the pressures and pitfalls of Americanization.

Though he remains one of the key totemic figures of the blacklist, Joseph Losey's American films of the late 1940s and early 1950s have received scant critical attention relative to his British productions. In this volume, Frank Krutnik examines Losey's *The Prowler* in his inquiry into the Hollywood Left's use of a Diego Rivera image, while Peter Stanfield's chapter on the left's fascination with boxing movies addresses the adaptation of Stanley Elkin's novel *Deadly Summit,* filmed by Losey as *The Big Night* (1951). Doug Dibbern devotes the whole of his chapter, "The Violent Poetry of the Times," to Losey's 1950 film *The Lawless,* which was based on a Daniel Mainwaring script that reworked the headline-capturing events of the Los Angeles zoot suit riots of 1943 and the Sleepy Lagoon murder that preceded them. As with the boxing movie *The Ring* (1952), *The Lawless* is a rare example of a Hollywood film that gives a dramatic focus to Mexican American youth culture. According to Dibbern, the riots and murder had been a final rallying point for the wartime Popular Front before it was shattered by the divisive investigations of HUAC.[16] Dibbern argues that with *The Lawless,* Mainwaring and Losey sought to resuscitate "the discourses surrounding events that had galvanized the left just seven years before." As such, the film dealt both with "how the left might rouse history to fight the growing conservative consensus of the emerging cold war," as well as problems of racial prejudice and discrimination.

Unlike most contributions to this volume, Sean McCann's chapter on jazz and film noir is not overly concerned with the role of filmmakers in the articulation of a progressive sensibility. Instead, he explores the way black popular music is made to embody particular political positions that are highly suggestive of the shifting ideological terrain that Hollywood's left-leaning fraternity was having to cope with in the late 1940s and 1950s. The Popular Front's celebration of jazz as a "people's music" and the postwar shift from jazz as a "language of democratic fraternalism" toward an "emphasis on individual virtuosity and personal freedom" is a process McCann is keen to trace across a number of postwar crime films. In the years following the war, jazz underwent a series of profound cultural shifts in its reception. No longer perceived primarily as a dance music with roots deep in African American music, its championing as an art form by small coteries of dedicated white fans, and the evident musical sophistication of such key purveyors as Duke Ellington, Dizzy Gillespie, Charlie Parker, Ornette Coleman, and Miles Davis united to present jazz, at its best, as a music that equaled anything that had come from Europe, but which in its emphasis on interpretation and improvisation was, indisputably, an American art form. The shifting of the sites of jazz's consumption, from the dives, taverns, and dance palaces to nightclubs, concert halls, and bachelor pads, brings in train a shift in jazz's articulation of a commonality. According to McCann, this process takes on a dreadful force in such celebrated jazz scenes as those found in *Phantom Lady* (1944) and *DOA* (1950), where what is being "depicted in the postwar crime film's anxious or sensational depictions of jazz is not just the peril of sexual and racial transgression, but, by the same token, a nightmarishly exaggerated version of a form of urban sociability underwritten by the unpredictable force of commercial exchange."

The postwar era brought significant stylistic and ideological changes to the Hollywood film. The chapters by Will Straw and Rebecca Prime consider the impact of Hollywood's embrace of the semi-documentary format that Twentieth Century Fox pioneered immediately after the war. These films received substantial critical attention at the time because they were seen to presage broader postwar reorientations in both cinema and U.S. society. Subsequently, however, these films have been overshadowed in critical discussions of 1940s cinema by the voluminous writings on film noir, which nearly always frame the semi-documentary as a more narrowly conformist option because it focused on institutions and systematized procedures rather than individualistic scenarios of crime. In their different ways, the chapters by Prime and Straw seek to reopen the case of the semi-documentary by exploring its political implications and underpinnings.

Will Straw's chapter aims to situate Hollywood's semi-documentary films within the context of contemporaneous critical debates about cinema's role in the postwar era. Scrutinizing the responses of left and liberal cultural critics to these films, Straw shows how they initially welcomed Hollywood's assimilation of documentary techniques. Associated both with authenticity and with social engagement, the documentary—as exemplified by U.S. wartime documentaries, the New Deal films of Pare Lorentz, Willard Van Dyke, Ralph Steiner, and Paul Strand, and the films of the 1930s British Documentary Movement—held the promise of a moral and aesthetic renewal of mainstream cinema. As Straw shows, the New York Communist Party newspaper the *Daily Worker* championed Hollywood's first attempts to introduce documentary techniques into the fiction films, in the belief that they would provide a means of countering the artifice, glamour, and sensationalism of traditional Hollywood fare and help to capture transformed hopes and circumstances of the new era. But while such films as *House on 92nd Street* (1945), *Boomerang!* (1947), *Call Northside 777* (1948), and *The Naked City* (1948) found supporters among progressive critics, the tide turned with Twentieth Century Fox's decision to add *The Iron Curtain* (1948) to its semi-documentary series. Based on a real-life Canadian spy scandal, the film inaugurated Hollywood's cycle of anti-Communist films—several of which would similarly co-opt the conventions of the semi-documentary to authenticate their exposés of the red menace. *The Iron Curtain* clearly exemplifies the conformist image of the semi-documentary that pervades more recent histories. By surveying progressive assessments of the hybridization of fiction and documentary, however, Straw suggests this was by no means always and necessarily the case. Part of the problem with looking at the 1940s semi-documentaries from a twenty-first-century perspective is that it is not always easy to come to terms with their benevolent depiction of social institutions, especially legal authorities (the NYPD, the LAPD, treasury agents, immigration agents, the FBI, and so on). Straw argues that this authoritarian tendency is by no means simply a response to the rightward trend in U.S. society, as it also has roots in the collectivist and administrative vision of government that was popularized through World War II and before that the New Deal. In the early postwar era the liberal left could still maintain faith in the benefits of enlightened expertise, where skilled professionals pooled their resources as a team to achieve more by working together than they ever could alone. Just as wartime films exulted collective over individual action, Straw suggests, the stress upon teamwork and systematic rationality in the semi-documentaries is partly a legacy of the wartime suspicion of sentimental individualism. This utopian corporate liberalism differs from the more authoritarian glorification of police forces, for which Raymond Borde and Etienne Chaumeton chastise the semi-documentaries, although both share a fascination with (and idealization of) the organizational ethic.[17] Overall, Straw convincingly demonstrates that, within an unpredictable era of postwar transition, the Hollywood semi-documentary operated as a site for playing out contending ideologies and discourses relating to concepts of law, individualism, and society.

Where Straw examines the broad context of debate inspired by the semi-documentary, Rebecca Prime explores the political and institutional significance of one especially celebrated police semi-documentary, *The Naked City*. Examining the conception, production, and reception of this landmark entry in the postwar cycle of realist crime thrillers film, Prime illustrates the competing interests, pressures, and politics bearing more generally upon Hollywood films during this period. Directed and co-written by leftists—Jules Dassin and Albert Maltz, respectively—*The Naked City* aimed to assimilate aspects of the neorealist social critique that progressives saw as a potential model for socially engaged Hollywood cinema. Drawing upon archival sources, contemporary reviews, and original interviews with Dassin and screenwriter Malvin Wald, Prime traces the film's troubled production history to show how the politically inflected New York drama that Dassin envisaged was compromised by Hollywood's economic and ideological priorities. In production through the first round of HUAC investigations into Hollywood in 1947, with Maltz interrogated as one of the Hollywood Ten, *The Naked City* was inevitably a touchy proposition for its studio, Universal-International Pictures. As released, the film conformed more closely to the successful semi-documentary thriller format pioneered by Twentieth Century Fox than to the Italian Neo-Realist social dramas that Dassin claimed as his inspiration. Universal eliminated from the release print many of the shots and scenes that drew attention to social inequalities, and Dassin clearly felt betrayed by the reediting and streamlining of his project. The film by no means lacks the potential for social critique, but the latter is certainly more clearly contextualized within the protocols of a generic enterprise. As Prime suggests, by the time *The Naked City* was released the semi-documentary was well entrenched as a mainstream entertainment format that deployed the spectacle of location shooting and other markers of authenticity within the parameters of Hollywood's melodramatic narrative conventions and within a newly energized celebration of social institutions. *The Naked City* inevitably constitutes something of a compromise.

Adrian Scott was the only member of the Hollywood Ten and the wider Hollywood Left who was a producer. Although he did not have the power of independents like David O. Selznick or Samuel Goldwyn or of such studio heads as Darryl Zanuck or Louis B. Mayer, Scott was nonetheless in a unique and relatively influential position. Beginning his career in Hollywood as screenwriter, he became a unit producer at RKO in 1943. Between 1943 and 1947, he produced a series of low-to-medium budget melodramas—among them *Murder, My Sweet* (1944), *Cornered* (1945), *So Well Remembered* (1947), and *Crossfire* (1947)—that established his reputation and that were marked by the participation of two other members of the Hollywood Left, screenwriter John Paxton and director Edward Dmytryk. Using archival sources and documents, and looking in detail at *Cornered* and *So Well Remembered,* Jennifer Langdon-Teclaw explores the interaction between the logistics of the production process, the structures of the studio system, the commercial imperatives of Hollywood, the characteristics of its international markets and partners, and the political views of the films' production personnel. She also highlights Scott's attempts to initiate an exchange program between British and American film workers while working in Britain on *So Well Remembered*. In all cases, what is apparent is that the complex of ever-changing circumstances that impacts on any activity, including film production, always needs to be taken into account when assessing the political role or stance of any one film. What is ironic is that it was the commercial success—the success in Hollywood's terms—of films like *Murder, My Sweet* and *Crossfire* that brought Scott, Dmytryk, Paxton, and their politics to the attention of HUAC.

Art Simon's chapter examines the 1945 RKO short *The House I Live In* in relation to the career and politics of radical screenwriter and activist Albert Maltz. One of the most important figures in the Hollywood Left, Maltz made a significant contribution to U.S. cinema in the wartime and early postwar eras with films such as *This Gun for Hire* (1942), *Destination Tokyo* (1943), *Pride of the Marines* (1945), *Cloak and Dagger* (1946), *The Naked City* (1948), and *Broken Arrow* (1950). As Simon considers, however, Maltz's accomplishments extended far beyond his work for the screen. He was a "citizen-writer" who engaged in a range of left cultural practices, working in 1930s left-wing theater, writing proletarian novels and short stories, contributing essays to leftist journals, and even establishing journals himself. An active member of the Communist Party since the mid-1930s, Maltz found himself an easy target for HUAC in the late 1940s. As a member of the Hollywood Ten, he was jailed for contempt of Congress and subsequently blacklisted, making a partial return to screenwriting in the late 1960s. Before being attacked by HUAC, Maltz had come under fire from his comrades on the left for his 1946 *New Masses* article "What Shall We Ask of Writers?" which argued that art should not be shackled by narrowly didactic political aims. Facing a firestorm of criticism from Communist Party intellectuals in *New Masses* and the *Daily Worker* for his ideological treason, Maltz subsequently retracted his views (for further discussion of the Maltz controversy, see Thom Andersen's article "Red Hollywood," reprinted in this volume).

Simon's scrupulously researched essay makes a strong case for *The House I Live In* as a central text of the Popular Front. A tireless campaigner against minority prejudice, Maltz seized upon the opportunity of working with Frank Sinatra, then at the height of his tremendous success as a bobbysox idol, to craft a heartfelt warning against the dangers of anti-Semitism. Buoyed by Sinatra's charismatic presence, the film articulates an ethical Americanism of ethnic and religious plurality that resounds with the voices of Thomas Paine, Thomas Jefferson, and Abraham Lincoln. Through its defense of immigrants, its championing of religious tolerance, and its democratic inclusiveness, the film represented a strategic extension of the Popular Front cultural agenda at a time of intensifying domestic anti-Semitism. Along with *Pride of the Marines*, released the same year, *The House I Live In* marks the culmination of Maltz's efforts to fight anti-Semitism, which date back to his involvement with The League of American Writers and his co-founding of the magazine *Equality* in the late 1930s. Having already suffered anti-Semitism in his youth, Maltz proved its victim once more when he was hauled before the red-baiting, Jew-hating inquisitors of HUAC. Where the RKO film defines the United States as a house that welcomes all races and religions, the Americanism of the House Committee proved to be far less accommodating.

Brian Neve has produced an account of Robert Rossen's work as a scriptwriter for Warner Bros. during the 1930s and 1940s, a period marked by his ten-year membership in the Communist Party. Remembered now for his directorial work on *Body and Soul, All the King's Men,* and *The Hustler,* Rossen produced an extraordinary body of work as a scriptwriter, including *Marked Woman* (1937), *They Won't Forget* (1937), *Dust Be My Destiny* (1939), *The Roaring Twenties* (1939), *The Sea Wolf* (1941), *Out of the Fog* (1941), *Blues in the Night* (1941), *Edge of Darkness* (1943), *A Walk in the Sun* (1945), *The Strange Love of Martha Ivers* (1946), and *Desert Fury* (1947). Regardless of their generic provenance—gangster movie, war film, women's picture, literary adaptation, musical—the films all show a remarkable interest in social politics. Neve isolates three key themes in Rossen's scripts: "Class and the experiences of proletarian lives; social and other constructions of the 'gangster' and racketeer, and anti-fascism." Rossen's work exemplifies the Popular Front strategy of using formulaic fictions as a vehicle for social critique. Neve's investigation of the production history of these films reveals negotiations that went on behind the scenes as the social concerns of particular filmmakers were balanced (at best) or muted altogether by the counter-drive to individualize and romanticize characters' social experiences. Neve considers *Martha Ivers* as something of an exemplary script in its dramatization of social concerns, in which "public life" is presented as a mere "front, thinly disguising the determining material forces. The distortion of personality, the 'strange love,' is matched by an equal distortion of social organization." Neve concludes by showing how Rossen continued to develop this theme in the films he directed before being blacklisted. Like Kazan he would eventually name names, but his early death in 1966 meant he would not receive the same opprobrium as Kazan, nor would his films receive the same level of critical scrutiny—though, as Neve shows, they certainly merit equal attention.

Responding to new work on the blacklist and film history, the Writers' Guild of America has raised awareness of the work of blacklisted writers by correcting writing credits that have long been distorted by the use of pseudonyms and fronts.

While scholarship has filled in many of the lacunae relating to accurate feature film credits, work on the effects of blacklisting on television credits is still in its infancy. Steve Neale has pioneered work in this area, and his chapter here explores the relationship between blacklisted American writers and the companies that emerged in Britain in the fifties to serve the new commercial television network. While we have known for some time that blacklisted writers worked on commercial television series made in Britain during this time, notably *The Adventures of Robin Hood,* the extent of their involvement, and the precise working arrangements and credits, have been difficult to establish.

Using the archive collections of key writers and interviews with those involved (notably script editor Albert Ruben), Neale uncovers the story of blacklistee contributions to the series of swashbuckling costume dramas that commenced with *Robin Hood* (1955–60). Following the latter's success in Britain and America through the late fifties, the formula was subsequently adapted to filmed series such as *The Adventures of Sir Lancelot* (1955–57), *The Buccaneers* (1956–57), and *Sword of Freedom* (1957). As Neale explains, these were all produced by American exile Hannah Weinstein for her company, Sapphire Films, with funding and distribution through ATV and ITP in the UK and Official Films in the United States. Before the Supreme Court ruled in 1958 that the State Department did not have authority to deny people passports because of their "beliefs and associations," Ring Lardner Jr. and Ian McLellan Hunter wrote *Robin Hood* scripts from New York. These filmed adventure dramas helped to differentiate ITV from the more staid notions of public service broadcasting associated with its lone rival, the BBC, but were also, as Neale points out, transnational cultural products that were seen in America and beyond. Neale uses archive sources to establish for the first time the pseudonyms and fronts used by the writers in the various series. Such work is extremely valuable not only in mapping resistance to the blacklist, but also in filling in gaps of knowledge concerning these popular and significant television series. The work opens up further possibilities for relating the formulas and themes of individual episodes, and each series as a whole, to the individual and group ideologies of experienced Hollywood screenwriters whose work was available to television because of the blacklist.

The institutional mechanisms of the blacklist began to crumble in the late fifties, with Dalton Trumbo's efforts in particular contributing to its demise. Trumbo's Academy Award for *The Brave One* in 1957, under the assumed name of Robert Rich, helped demonstrate the absurdity of the blacklist, given the widespread use of fronts and the vibrant black market in scripts—many of which were made for independent producers such as the King Brothers and released through United Artists, which was never a signatory to the blacklist. For some, however, the blacklist continued into the late sixties: Abraham Polonsky, for example, found it difficult to secure legitimate work until the late flowering of his directing career with *Tell Them Willie Boy Is Here* (1969) and *Romance of a Horse Thief* (1971). Dalton Trumbo plays a role in Mark Shiel's chapter, since he was one of the writers of *FTA* (*F*** the Army*, 1972), a film that powerfully articulated the growth of opposition to the war in Vietnam, even within the military itself. The upsurge in liberal and left protests against the war through the late sixties and early seventies climaxed in 1972 with the presidential candidacy of George McGovern, who ran as the most liberal major-party presidential candidate in American history. With the final collapse of the remaining elements of the blacklist, a number of previously blacklisted writers and directors were able to make a contribution to this new burst of cultural protest. As Shiel argues, however, the New Left had different concerns. Whereas the Communist Left had contributed to patriotic World War II anti-fascism, during the Vietnam War the politics of the New Left was characterized by pacifism and dissent.

Shiel emphasizes the importance of *FTA*, produced and directed by Francine Parker in collaboration with Hollywood actors and activists Jane Fonda and Donald Sutherland, even though the film was only briefly released and then disappeared, save for bootleg copies. Shiel explains how the film worked as an agit-prop documentary, mixing shots of dissenting GIs, shots of Fonda and other celebrities in the audience, and excerpts from the traveling vaudeville shows that were performed in a number of cities in the Pacific adjacent to U.S. military bases. Reflecting the post-1968 radicalization of the U.S. left, Shiel suggests, the film was released at a time when McGovern was engaged with his ultimately doomed presidential campaign to deny Richard Nixon reelection. Shiel recounts how the film links Old and New Lefts at the point where Donald Sutherland, alone on stage, passionately reads an extended passage from Dalton Trumbo's pacifist World War I novel, *Johnny Got His Gun* (1939). Trumbo also used Sutherland as an actor when he was able to make his one and only film as director, adapting *Johnny Got His Gun* (1971) from his own script and novel. As Shiel adds, this unusual period in American cultural politics also saw the post-blacklist reappearance of key writers from the Old Left, including Waldo Salt (*Midnight Cowboy*, 1969), Albert Maltz (*Two Mules for Sister Sara*, 1970), and Ring Lardner Jr. (*M*A*S*H*, 1970).

The present volume republishes Thom Andersen's 1985 article "Red Hollywood," a key work of scholarship relating to the blacklist and the Hollywood Left. Having long been out of print, Andersen's article appears here as a significant point of reference in mapping earlier approaches to the topic. Andersen also has written an afterword for this volume that revisits and extends his original themes and arguments.

There are two main strands to Andersen's original article. His first contribution was to review the disparate literature on the blacklist and on the work of those filmmakers who lost their livelihoods owing to their association with the Communist Party. Earlier scholars and polemicists often lacked sympathy for the iconic Hollywood Ten and others who were blacklisted or greylisted, and also exhibited distain for Hollywood and American film culture. Andersen's review combines a strong commitment to and knowledge of American film and a thorough understanding of the history of American radicalism as he gives a sympathetic yet critical reading of works from different ideological and scholarly backgrounds. Among these are Larry Ceplair and Steven Englund's *The Inquisition in Hollywood*, Nancy

Lynn Schwartz's *The Hollywood Writers' Wars,* and Victor Navasky's *Naming Names,* each a substantial work published in or just after 1980 that greatly advanced knowledge and understanding of the phenomenon.

As Andersen argued, Ceplair and Englund were the first writers to document in depth the political and historical background of the Hollywood blacklist, examining in particular the changing nature of the Communist Party, the Popular Front alliance with liberals that blossomed in the late thirties and in a different form during World War II, the union and Guild struggles that prefigured the postwar conflicts, and the rise of anti-Communist groups and of HUAC itself. While appreciating the value of Navasky's empirically based study of the "naming names" issue, Andersen found the moral polarities of this work to be overly simple, arguing that he failed adequately to explore the political motives of both those who resisted and those who cooperated. The issues always appeared more morally clear-cut to the great majority of resisters who were still committed to the Party. For example, the Communist screenwriter Paul Jarrico argued that "for those who were generally pissed off at the party but reluctant to name names, the choice must have been difficult. For a person like me, a true blue red, the choice was easy."[18]

The other and more original strand of Andersen's article challenged the then-common depreciation of the artistic and political merit of the work of the Hollywood Left. He wrote persuasively on postwar crime films, coining the term film gris to describe a group of films released between 1947 and 1951 that provided opportunities for left-wing and liberal filmmakers to articulate critical perspectives on postwar American values and on the political and economic system. Mapping fruitful areas of research for later scholars, Andersen's analysis also drew attention to the role of leftists in early thirties film and in wartime propaganda, and to the centrality of John Garfield in key films of the postwar era. In collaboration with filmmaker/theorist Noël Burch, Andersen made the 1995 video *Red Hollywood,* which powerfully demonstrated the influence on film of left-wing artists from the thirties to the fifties and beyond. Andersen's initial essay was sympathetic to the Hollywood Left, while also being critical of partial and partisan approaches. He provided, for example, a balanced account of the conflict between Albert Maltz and the Party in 1946, citing the importance of Maltz's later view that "no one I knew in the CP would have stayed in the Party had they known then what they found out later."[19]

Andersen's afterword revisits the literature on the Hollywood Left and the blacklist, as well as his earlier discussion of left politics and crime films. His updated literature survey examines in particular the work of Paul Buhle and his collaborators. In a series of books published between 1997 and 2003, Buhle captured and recorded invaluable interview material and drew attention to the sheer amount of film work influenced by the left. Andersen is critical of aspects of this work while accepting its importance. In the new piece he also explores the claims made for individual films, examining more recent currents of thought that include the writing of Ronald and Allis Radosh, who view the leftists more problematically, in terms of their direct or indirect relationship with Stalinism and the Soviet Union.[20] Andersen also refers to Michael Denning's key work on the Popular Front, and raises questions, further explored in contributions to this book, about the implications of the blacklist for the possible development in postwar America of the styles and practices of the European neorealist movement.[21]

Besides the light it sheds on the work and significance of the blacklist generation, this book is also timely because its topic resonates with more contemporary events in the United States. Since the administration of George W. Bush launched its war on terror, it has become commonplace for liberal and left-wing commentators to evoke the repressions of the early Cold War era as a warning from history against the consequences of the current clampdown on political debate and civil rights. The concept of un-Americanism, so vital to the HUAC crusade, was resoundingly revived in the emotional rhetoric that followed al-Qaeda's September 2001 attacks on the United States. A few months after those events, the Bush administration introduced into law the USA Patriot Act, which the American Civil Liberties Union described as "an overnight revision of the nation's surveillance laws that vastly expanded the government's authority to spy on its own citizens, while simultaneously reducing checks and balances on those powers like judicial oversight, public accountability, and the ability to challenge government searches in court."[22] While the U.S. government, in alliance with Britain, was quick to capitalize upon the national mood of shock and incomprehension by sending troops into Afghanistan and Iraq, neither the U.S. media nor the official political opposition was able to mount any effective critique of such crusading adventurism.

The parallels between the post-9/11 culture of repression and that of the early Cold War era provide the subtext for the highly successful 2005 film *Good Night, and Good Luck,* which deals with the battle between television journalist Edward R. Murrow (David Strathairn) and Senator Joseph McCarthy, the prime figurehead of the postwar anti-Communist movement. Directed and co-written by actor George Clooney—one in a long line of high-profile Hollywood liberals that includes Fredric March, Humphrey Bogart, Frank Sinatra, Warren Beatty, Barbra Streisand, Jane Fonda, Robert Redford, Sean Penn, and the double act of Susan Sarandon and Tim Robbins—the film champions Murrow's determined stand against the rabble-rousing McCarthy as a model of responsible and ethical media enquiry.[23] Clooney has emphasized in numerous interviews that Murrow's principled pursuit of truth is sorely lacking today because the U.S. media has been cowed into submission by the emotive and Manichean agenda of the war on terror. During the publicity junket for *Goodnight, and Good Luck,* Clooney told *The Guardian* of the flak he routinely received for his avowedly left-liberal politics:[24]

> I was at a party the other night and it was all these hardcore Republicans and these guys are like, 'Why do you hate your country?' I said, 'I love my country.' They said, 'Why, at a time of war, would you criticise it then?' And I said, 'My country right or wrong means women don't vote, black people sit in the back of buses and we're still in Vietnam. My country right or wrong means we

don't have the New Deal.' I mean, what, are you crazy? My country, right or wrong? It's not your right, it's your duty. And then I said, 'Where was I wrong, schmuck?' In 2003 I was saying, where are the ties [between Iraq] and al-Qaida? Where are the ties to 9/11? I knew it; where the fuck were these Democrats who said, 'We were misled'? That's the kind of thing that drives me crazy: 'We were misled.' Fuck you, you weren't misled. You were afraid of being called unpatriotic.[25]

By hijacking the terms and the terrain of patriotic Americanism, Clooney suggests, the right has made it very difficult for dissenting liberal voices to escape the slur of disloyalty. Something quite similar happened to the film radicals when they were summoned before HUAC. As part of their defense, the Hollywood Ten repeatedly tried to counter the committee's narrowly right-wing loyalty program by invoking the more inclusive and more ethical traditions of Americanism exemplified by the U.S. Constitution and the Bill of Rights. But at the hearings in September 1947, John Howard Lawson, Albert Maltz, Adrian Scott, and company were strenuously gaveled down by the chairman, J. Parnell Thomas, their reasoned statements mostly going unheard. The merest whiff of an association with Communism, or with radical causes, immediately branded these Hollywood personnel as treacherous servants of an enemy power. Such repression was arguably more dangerous, and more long-lasting, than the causes they openly or secretly espoused. While there are clearly great differences between the cultures of the early Cold War era and the contemporary war on terror, they both reveal intense, politically charged battles over what Americanism means and who it is for. They also reveal highly charged struggles over the social role of the mass media, including cinema, that pivot around the question of whether they should aim for unquestioning and affirmative entertainment or should aspire to serve as guardians of truth, liberty, and conscience.

1

Are You Now or Have You Ever Been a Christian?

THE STRANGE HISTORY OF *THE ROBE* AS POLITICAL ALLEGORY

Jeff Smith

In an essay in *Danse Macabre*, best-selling author Stephen King writes, "If horror movies have redeeming social merit, it is because of that ability to form liaisons between the real and unreal—to provide subtexts. And because of their mass appeal, these subtexts are often culture-wide."[1] For King, the value of these subtexts is that they endow popular fictions with a social and cultural significance that allows them to tap into the deeply held fears and anxieties of their readers. It is through these subtexts that the horror film has commented on a host of social and political issues, including scientism, racism, consumerism, conformism, and, of course, Communism.

Although King only acknowledges it implicitly, these subtexts are also important to the extent that they find expression in the rhetorical form of allegory as patterns of metaphorical substitution that bridge the gap between the real and unreal, past and present. Both in the horror film and in other film genres, allegory has been a privileged mode of interpretation in relation to films made during the blacklist period. As such, it seems appropriate to investigate the use of allegorical interpretation as it has been applied by film historians and critics to Hollywood films of the 1950s. Through this analysis, I hope to reveal the particular biases and assumptions of blacklist allegories as well as the extent to which this type of interpretation has informed the reception of 1950s films. More specifically, I wish to address several questions about the validity of allegorical readings of the blacklist. Is there a basis for such allegorical interpretations? What is the place of authorial intention and audience reception in the encoding and decoding of blacklist allegories? What does this reading strategy tell us about the politics of the films' makers? Does this reading strategy privilege certain meanings of the text over others of equal significance?

In an essay on the nature of historical allegory in film, Ismail Xavier discusses two traits of allegory that help to explain why it serves as a favored mode of interpretation at particular historical moments. First, Xavier notes that allegorical expression is especially prevalent during times of political repression since the disguised nature of allegory allows it to communicate political dissent in a manner that circumvents systems of institutional censorship. Second, Xavier also notes that history itself is used as a form of allegorical expression within the genre of the historical film. Describing these as "pragmatic allegories," Xavier suggests that historical novels and films take on allegorical significance insofar as the depiction of past events serves as a means of offering "disguised comment on the present."[2]

Both these points help account for the prevalence of allegorical interpretation in films made during the Hollywood blacklist. The blacklist certainly seems to fit Xavier's first criterion in that it is generally understood as a form of political censorship designed to silence both radical leftists and liberals, both of whom had hoped to use the cinema as a means of exploring social issues during the immediate postwar period. Moreover, Xavier's notion of "pragmatic allegories" also explains how certain historical films have been read as allegories of both the Hollywood blacklist and the Cold War politics that helped create it. Not surprisingly, a diverse group of historical films have been subjected to this type of interpretive strategy, including *Reign of Terror* (1949), *Quo Vadis* (1951), *Viva Zapata!* (1952), *Julius Caesar* (1953), *The Robe* (1953), *Spartacus* (1960), and *El Cid* (1961).[3] In these films, the political and religious conflicts associated with the French Revolution, the Mexican Revolution, ancient Rome, and eleventh-century Spain are used to offer disguised commentary on the contemporary debate regarding the threat of Communism to American political institutions.

Xavier also notes two particular strategies employed in encoding a text as allegorical. The first involves the creation of national allegories through the use of an individual who stands in for a larger social class or political group and who embodies particular traits associated with a particular national imaginary. The second involves creating a sort of one-to-one correspondence between particular features of the text and the specific circumstances of the text's historical context. These strategies may be used separately or they may be combined as they are in allegorical readings of L. Frank Baum's *The Wizard of Oz* (1903). According to this interpretation, *Oz* is a metaphorical reworking of early-twentieth-century debates about the gold standard as the basis of the American economy. Baum's story is figuratively linked to these issues through the name "Oz" as a commonly understood abbreviation for ounce and through the "yellow brick road" as a metaphoric representation of the gold standard itself. Moreover, the characters themselves are seen to symbolize particular historical personages or political interest groups. The Wizard stands for President William McKinley, while the Cowardly Lion represents his rival, William Jennings Bryan. Likewise, the Tin Woodsman and the Scarecrow stand in for industrial laborers and farmers, respectively. As this example indicates, such allegorical interpretations are frequently tied to their particular historical moment. Philip L. Gianos points out that this metaphorical dimension of *Oz*'s narrative was probably lost on most viewers of the film adaptation produced in 1939 and is almost certainly absent in the experience of contemporary viewers of the film.[4]

As a particular type of interpretation, allegorical readings of historical films also share a great deal with the practice of film interpretation more generally.

1.   The Emperor Tiberius gives Marcellus Gallio the order to investigate the activities of early Christians.

As David Bordwell has argued, interpretations of films are often produced by mapping specific features of the text according to semantic fields furnished by a particular theoretical paradigm, by a facet of the film's historical context, or even by the analyst's own individual agenda.[5] In the case of historical allegory, the superordinate semantic field that organizes all the other interpretive elements is the binary opposition between past and present. Using this master opposition, the analyst simply maps the points of correspondence between specific features of the text and the particular facets of the film's present historical context that they seem to symbolize. Unlike other kinds of interpretation, though, the emphasis on historical context as a frame of reference places a certain check on the text's interpretive potential.

In this essay, I organize my discussion of allegory around *The Robe* as a particular case study of blacklist interpretation. While the film shares the outwardly conservative tone of other biblical epics, *The Robe* has received attention from several scholars, who see it as an implicit critique both of the blacklist and of dominant American Cold War ideology. John Belton, for example, argues that the film "casts Caligula as a witchhunting, McCarthyesque figure and the Christians as persecuted victims of his demonic attempts to purge the Roman empire of potential subversives."[6] Belton's reading is echoed by Bruce Babington and Peter William Evans, who note the historical parallelism inscribed in the coincidence of *The Robe*'s production with the second round of hearings conducted in Hollywood by the House Un-American Activities Committee (HUAC) in 1951. Further, Babington and Evans call attention to the contemporary resonance of Tiberius's order to Marcellus to collect information on the early Christians. Says Tiberius, "I want names, Tribune, names of all the disciples, of every man and woman who subscribe to this treason."[7] Both these readings of *The Robe* depend on a pattern of binary oppositions that are similar to the one listed in Table 1.

In making their case for an allegorical reading of *The Robe*, however, both Belton and Babington and Evans make reference to screenwriter Philip Dunne's background as a noted Hollywood liberal. Dunne was one of the founding members of

Table 1   Binary Oppositions: *The Robe* as
Anti-HUAC Allegory

Past	Present
Ancient Rome	United States
Christians	Communists
Roman tribunals	HUAC
Persecution	Censorship
Crucifixions	Blacklisting

the Committee for the First Amendment, a group of Hollywood liberals that protested on behalf of the nineteen "unfriendly" witnesses who were scheduled to appear before HUAC in October of 1947. By referencing Dunne's political credentials, these scholars introduce the possibility that *The Robe*'s use of allegory constitutes an intentionalist discourse by, ever so subtly, suggesting that the homologies between past and present may have been planted by Dunne as part of the screenwriting process. This in itself should not be surprising, however, since, as Ismail Xavier notes, allegorical discourse is often understood within a framework of intention-utterance-interpretation that presumes that the text contains indices of allegorical intention.[8] Belton pushes the point of intention even further, however, by calling attention to Dunne's claim that he rewrote an existing script by a blacklisted writer. By prefacing this observation with the claim that Hollywood's radical left used the biblical epic to "make a case for the Hollywood Ten and the evils of repressive government," Belton gives at least some credit for *The Robe*'s allegorical meanings to the unnamed writer in Dunne's autobiography.[9]

Dunne's account of *The Robe*'s production history, and the corresponding role of a blacklisted writer in that history, is almost too good to resist. The readings of the film based on this account suggest that one of those persons silenced by HUAC had nonetheless found a disguised way to critique government repression. More important, by endowing the unnamed screenwriter with a kind of subversive agency, these accounts further suggest that the radical left tweaked the collective noses of Hollywood by using its norms and conventions of representation in a manner that counters the ostensible interests of those who instituted the blacklist in the first place.

There is just one problem with this account, though. While it is true that early drafts of *The Robe* were written by a member of the Hollywood Ten, Albert Maltz, the screenwriter completed work on *The Robe* in September of 1946, more than a year before his HUAC testimony and the subsequent issuance of the Waldorf Statement by the studios. This chronology, therefore, turns common sense causation on its head insofar as it places the imputed effect of the blacklist—the screenplay and film that is seen as a reaction to it—before its supposed cause. As such, it raises an important question about *The Robe*: Can we still see the film as blacklist allegory?

If the earlier allegorical interpretations of Belton and the others are to hold up, then the following interrelated assumptions that implicitly support these readings must prove to be true:

1. Since Albert Maltz wrote the screenplay prior to the institution of the blacklist, he must be consciously or unconsciously responding to the broader political pressures of his era, the same pressures that ultimately led to the Hollywood blacklist in 1947.
2. Albert Maltz must be the sole—or at least the primary—source for these allegorical meanings. If other persons, especially those whose politics are less radical than Maltz's, contribute to the film's allegorical subtext, then the argument that Maltz was using the screenplay as a political forum is weakened.
3. Albert Maltz's contributions to the screenplay must have survived the processes of revision and translation to the screen. Even though Belton acknowledges the work of Philip Dunne, there is a tacit assumption that Maltz's political message survived the revision process relatively unscathed. Since these earlier interpretations only examine the finished product, they assume that *The Robe* as it appeared on screen is more or less the same as *The Robe* of Maltz's early drafts of the screenplay.

To test these three assumptions, let us examine them against the historical records that detail *The Robe*'s production.

One way to salvage the historical narrative sketched out by Dunne and others might be to reread the role of intention to suggest that Maltz presciently offers a cautionary tale about the Red Scare by situating his adaptation of the Lloyd Douglas novel within an allegorical framework. Certainly, one might make a prima facie case for such a possibility, since by 1946 there had been some indications of an impending shift in American politics. Winston Churchill had given his famous "Iron Curtain" speech in July of 1946 and problems within the Screen Writers Guild and the Hollywood Writers Mobilization had signaled a rift between liberals and radicals within the industry.[10] Besides the immediate postwar context, there already had been several state and federal government actions taken to limit the influence of Communism on American life. HUAC had been investigating Communism on and off since 1938. In 1940, Congress passed the Smith Act, an anti-sedition law that outlawed the advocacy of government overthrow. Furthermore, the Tenney Committee conducted investigations of Communists in Hollywood during the early 1940s and the right-wing Motion Picture Alliance for American Ideals was established in 1944.

While one cannot entirely dismiss the possibility that Maltz's screenplay was a response to events that foreshadowed the eventual blacklist, there are several things that complicate this account. First of all, a problem with the "foreshadowing theory" is evident in the subplot involving Marcellus's efforts to gather the names

Table 2   Binary Oppositions: *The Robe* as Anti-Fascist Allegory

Past	Present
Ancient Rome	Fascist Italy
Christians	Communists
Roman tribunals	Brownshirts
Underground caverns	"Underground" Italian resistance
Crucifixions	Firing squads

of early Christians. This subplot is cited by Babington and Evans as some of the clearest evidence in *The Robe* of allegorical intention. Unaware of the chronology of *The Robe*'s production, these critics attribute the import of this subplot to screenwriter Philip Dunne and assume that he consciously strove to draw parallels between Tiberius's charge to gather the names of early Christians with HUAC's investigations of Communists in the late 1940s and early 1950s.

Yet this subplot appears to be wholly Maltz's invention rather than Dunne's. Perhaps more importantly, the notion of "naming names" would have far less political resonance when it was introduced to the screenplay in 1945 than it would have just two years later. Indeed, the issue of informing would not really become a major theme of blacklist allegories until 1951, the same year of Larry Parks's infamous appearance before HUAC where he pleaded with the committee to avoid the stigma of being a stoolpigeon. In a now notorious exchange, Parks begged, "Don't present me with the choice of either being in contempt of this Committee and going to jail or forcing me to really crawl through the mud to be an informer. For what purpose?"[11] Parks's question will linger over several films interpreted as allegories of informing, such as Alfred Hitchcock's *I Confess* (1952) and Elia Kazan's *On the Waterfront* (1954), but the specific practice of clearing oneself before the committee could not have been anticipated by Maltz back in 1945. While it is true that Maltz's screenplay might still be seen as an augury of things to come, the subplot of "naming names" cited by Babington and Evans cannot be read retrospectively as evidence of authorial intention.

Another problem with the zeitgeist theory is that it ignores other allegorical readings of *The Robe* that are more directly related to the historical context surrounding Maltz's work on the screenplay. For example, since Maltz's first draft was completed during the final stages of World War II, one might just as easily read the film as an allegorical critique of Italian fascism and its hopes of restoring Italy to the glory of the Roman empire. This analogy also depends on the juxtaposition of past and present, but it puts Fascist Italy in place of the United States in terms of the binarisms established by the pattern of substitution (see Table 2). There are several factors that might support this type of allegorical interpretation. For one thing, anti-fascism was a major political cause for the Hollywood Ten. As members of the Popular Front, many of them participated in the activities of political inter-est groups, such as the Hollywood Anti-Nazi League. Moreover, in their failed defense during the HUAC investigations, several members of the Hollywood Ten compared the committee's ostensible interest in censorship with similar types of actions taken by fascist governments. In his prepared statement, Dalton Trumbo likened the investigation to the Reichstag fire, saying, "For those who remember German history in the autumn of 1932 there is the smell of smoke in this very room."[12] For another, in his subsequent screenwriting work, Maltz gained notori-ety for his exploration of the perils of fascism. Shortly after his work on *The Robe*, Maltz would coauthor the screenplay for *Cloak and Dagger* (1946), a film that was, according to Bernard F. Dick, "simultaneously an attack on fascism, a tribute to the Italian Communist resistance, an exaggerated account of Germany's attempt to manufacture an atomic bomb, and a plea that the atomic age would not get off to as bad a start as Hiroshima seemed to indicate."[13] After *Cloak and Dagger*, Maltz wrote the screenplay for *Crossfire* (1947), a film that received Oscar nominations and was marketed to audiences as a social problem film dealing with the issues of anti-Semitism and domestic fascism. Last, although it is a small point, in *The Robe*, Maltz's early descriptions of Rome's majesty are suggestive of Fascist Italy's inter-est in monumental political symbolism. Consider page 2 of Maltz's first draft: "As Caligula's voice continues, CAMERA SLOWLY MOVES UP TO the doorway and FOCUSES ON a carved stone Roman Eagle. The claws of the Eagle are holding the 'fasces with the ax.' Rays of carved lightning emanate from the fasces." It is worth noting here that Maltz's description makes explicit reference to the etymological root of "fascism," namely the fasces. In ancient Rome, the fasces was a bundle of rods that contained an axe and served as a symbol of power when displayed for Roman magistrates. The combination of the fasces with the Roman Eagle and carved lighting takes on contemporary resonance here as implicit references to the Iron Eagle of Nazi symbolism and the awesome force of the German blitzkrieg or "lightning war." For all these various reasons, one is tempted to conclude that Maltz's intentions were not to use *The Robe* as a critique of American anti-Communism, but rather as a critique of Italian Fascism.

In sum, while it is virtually impossible to disprove the claim that Albert Maltz was consciously or unconsciously acknowledging the possibility of political repres-sion after the war, it seems far more likely that his early drafts of *The Robe* were a response to more proximate historical circumstances, namely the rise of Italian Fascism prior to World War II. For this reason, one might reject Maltz as the source of *The Robe*'s allegorical subtext *tout court*. Yet *The Robe*'s status as blacklist allegory does not depend solely on Maltz's participation. Although it lacks the narrative appeal of Belton's account, which casts Maltz in the role of court jester thumbing his nose at Washington's power structures, it is possible—perhaps even likely—that others, such as author Lloyd Douglas, screenwriter Philip Dunne, director Henry Koster, and producer Darryl Zanuck, contributed to the allegorical meanings of *The Robe*. It is this issue—the role of adaptation and revision—that I take up in the next two sections of this essay.

In addition to the previously cited problems of chronology and causation, another problem emerges with respect to these accounts of *The Robe* as blacklist allegory, namely the problem of adaptation. While some of these earlier interpretations either implicitly or explicitly acknowledge that *The Robe* is an adaptation of a preexisting source, they quite explicitly suggest that writers personally invested in the blacklist utilized this material to fashion a critique of early 1950s political repression. Indeed, any implicit claims for Maltz and Dunne's authorial agency depend on the tacit premise that they were the primary sources for *The Robe's* blacklist subtext.

Yet at least some of the elements that critics have cited in support of *The Robe* as blacklist allegory were already present in Douglas's novel, which was published in 1942. In fact, Douglas refers quite specifically to blacklisting early on in the novel when Senator Gallio's wife, Cornelia, expresses fears that the family will be socially blacklisted if her husband continues his outspoken criticism of the government. Beyond this reference to blacklisting, however, the novel contains several moments that characterize early Christians as a perceived threat to the Roman government. For example, Caligula's speech in the final scene of the film, which refers to Christians as "seditionists," comes directly from Douglas's novel. Similarly, in Chapter 10, in a report to Tiberius about Jesus' crucifixion, Senator Gallio describes Christians as a "small but turbulent revolutionary party." Later, in Chapter 21, in a dialogue with Diana, Tiberius characterizes the Jesus movement as having in it "the seeds of revolution," and further suggests that it has aspirations of overthrowing the Roman Empire, albeit not by force. Finally, and most tellingly, a radical egalitarian spirit is strongly evident in the plan Stephanos recounts to Demetrius late in Douglas's novel:

> "The whole plan was unsound," he explained disconsolately. "Simon announced that any Christian might sell his property and bring the proceeds to the Ecclesia with the promise that his living would be provided for."
>
> "No matter how much or how little he had?" queried Demetrius.
>
> "Right! If you owned a farm or a vineyard, you sold it—probably at a sacrifice—and brought Simon the money. If you had nothing but a few chickens, and a donkey, you came with the money you'd got from that. And all would live together in brotherly love."[14]

While the plan itself is hardly a strict application of Marxist theory, its notion of communal property and provisions would undoubtedly seem vaguely "communistic" to HUAC investigators just a few years later. In its own way, it is not unlike the "Share and share alike" line from *Tender Comrade* that Lela Rogers found so objectionable as a "friendly witness" testifying before HUAC in 1947.[15]

When comparing the film to the novel, it becomes clear that determining the intentions of *The Robe's* screenwriters is problematized by the process of adaptation. If the elements that support the allegorical readings of *The Robe* are already present in Douglas's novel, then it is difficult to wholly subscribe to a theory that it was Maltz's or Dunne's intention to warn viewers of the evils of repressive government. This is especially true when one considers that a third party, producer Frank Ross, *assigned* the task of adapting the novel to Maltz and then later to Dunne. Because the decision to work on *The Robe* was not entirely in their control, Maltz and Dunne could scarcely have the foresight to know that a film version of *The Robe* would be a potential vehicle for political commentary by the 1950s.

Besides the problem of adaptation, a third problem with the earlier accounts of *The Robe* as blacklist allegory emerges in the issue of screenplay revision. As we all know, a typical Hollywood screenplay undergoes several stages of revision in the process of making it to the screen. Often, a writer completes several drafts of a screenplay only to have it handed over to other writers, who then take the producer's notes and do their own pass on the project. The new screenwriters may be used to do a polish job, to punch up the dialogue, to solve particular story problems, or even to write a completely new draft based on the previous writer's material. Once the screenplay is made into a shooting script, the actors and directors still may make other changes on the set during the process of the film's actual production. In fact, while much of this work goes uncredited, it is not uncommon to have as many as a dozen different people contributing to the final shape of a screenplay as it is brought to the screen.

Here again, while Belton's interpretation of *The Robe* as blacklist allegory acknowledges Philip Dunne's role as the credited screenwriter for the film, he implicitly assumes that Dunne's work more or less preserved Maltz's original vision, and that his own contributions to the screenplay did little to add to the film's political subtext. Indeed, if it were shown that several of the allegorical elements were contributed by Dunne rather than Maltz, it would considerably weaken the narrative of political subversion that animates this particular interpretation of the film.

Despite the strange timing of Maltz's work on *The Robe,* his scripts contain several apparent references to the blacklist, many of which were cut from the screenplay during the revision process. For instance, while Caligula's final speech makes reference both to Christian sedition and to Spartacus, who by 1953 was viewed as a kind of Marxist hero, the same scene in the screenplay includes three additional references to Christian sedition that were cut from the final film, including Marcellus's denial that he is a seditionist or that he is personally engaged in a plot to overthrow the state.[16] (Instead, Marcellus says that Christians as a group are not engaged in such a plot.) Moreover, in a scene in which Marcellus is being transported back to Rome to face trial, Maltz includes a line of dialogue that appears to be precisely the kind of "subversive propaganda" that made HUAC appoint itself media watchdog. In the scene, a young boy brings dinner to Marcellus's cabin, but is asked by the guard whether the prisoner had already received a tray of food. When the boy protests that he is simply following the captain's orders, the guard responds, "What a fine world it'd be if there *were* no captains."[17] Although the line itself is a throwaway, its egalitarian sentiment and its apparent reference to a classless society make it similar to the examples of Communist propaganda that HUAC's "friendly witnesses" attested to in 1947.

2.   Marcellus and Abidor, the informant. In Maltz's screenplay, the scroll beneath Marcellus's hand is the place where the Tribune records his list of names.

Likewise, although the film includes Tiberius's charge to find the names of Christians as well as Abidor's role as informant, it cuts several scenes that further develop the "naming names" motif. For example, in scene 204 of Maltz's screenplay, Marcellus pays Abidor a coin for every name the latter gives him to add to his list.[18] Scenes 221–222 show Marcellus writing the names of early Christians on a parchment scroll. Maltz's description even includes an insert in which the audience sees four names listed at the bottom of the scroll.[19] Finally, scene 244 of Maltz's screenplay shows Marcellus burning his scroll in a campfire outside his tent:

CAMERA MOVES IN STILL CLOSER. As the flames eat at the paper, it writhes with the heat, and, for a moment, turns toward the camera. We catch a glimpse of part of the list of names

Reuben. . . . Weaver

James. . . . . Fisherman

And then the names turn black under the flames.[20]

In examining the differences between Maltz's early drafts and Dunne's finished screenplay, there are at least two ways in which we might account for these particular changes. One possibility is that some lines and scenes were undoubtedly cut due to considerations of length. Maltz's screenplay ran 277 pages, and much of Dunne's work on the project involved drastically cutting and reshaping Maltz's material. In comparison, Dunne's final draft of *The Robe* ran only 141 pages in length.[21] That, however, does not adequately explain why these specific elements were cut nor does it eliminate the possibility that these changes were made on political grounds. Indeed, if one ascribes agency to *The Robe*'s production team in shaping the meanings of the text, then one must grant the possibility that either Dunne or the producers cut these elements to obscure the script's political subtext rather than to clarify and illuminate it. According to this scenario, elements that may have seemed harmless when the script was completed in 1946 might be viewed as politically problematic as the film entered its production phase in 1952.

This explanation, however, depends on the premise that Dunne or the producers construed Maltz's work as a possible blacklist allegory. Indeed, one could hardly seek to hide the film's political subtext unless one understood that political subtext in the first place. Yet, while this initially appears to be a plausible hypothesis, the historical record seems to indicate that neither of the film's producers actually understood the film in this way. Correspondence between Maltz and producer Frank Ross shows that RKO criticized the screenplay for overemphasizing the mysticism of early Christianity and for downplaying Christianity as a way of life.[22] If RKO understood the film as a metaphor for anti-Communist repression, then we would surmise from their advice that they desired a more materialist and less metaphysical depiction of Christianity. If this were true, then the studio would be complicit with Maltz's political critique even if they disavowed such awareness for political or public relations reasons. Since this seems unlikely, it seems more reasonable to conclude that RKO simply failed to notice any anti-Communist subtext.

Moreover, even after the blacklist was established, Twentieth Century Fox seemed no more cognizant of The Robe's political subtext than RKO was. A conference memo from Darryl Zanuck to Dunne and Frank Ross compares The Robe to David and Bathsheba and asks, "Are we again permitting 'talk'—an overabundance of talk—to motivate our climax?"[23] As a means of engendering some suspense in The Robe's "talky" third act, Zanuck proposes that Caligula should appoint Gallio, Marcellus's father, as the "head of a committee of the Senators to investigate the case of a traitor. Thus Gallio is forced into position of 'trying' his own son."[24] Zanuck's suggestion to provide a filial pressure on Marcellus would not only complement the legal and political pressures depicted in the narrative, but it would also have the effect of enhancing the parallel between ancient Rome and contemporary America. By placing Marcellus's fate in the hands of his father, Zanuck sought to blame the persecution of Christians on a bureaucratic government committee rather than a power-mad, dictatorial emperor. Although this conference memo raises the unlikely possibility that Zanuck himself sought to use The Robe as a vehicle for criticizing American political repression, he did not follow through and use his power as producer to push his agenda further.[25] Nothing resembling this subplot survives in Dunne's subsequent drafts of the script nor in the finished film.

If neither Ross nor Zanuck's notes imply any political intent on their part, is it possible that screenwriter Philip Dunne was responsible for these specific cuts? Although my conclusions on this question are tentative, it does not appear that Dunne deliberately sought to becloud The Robe's political subtext. Several of the elements cited above were taken over by Dunne in his drafts of the screenplay and were only cut during the very late stages of the revision process. For example, in his working script dated June 26, 1952, that runs more than a hundred pages shorter than Maltz's draft, Dunne cuts the aforementioned line about "captains," but reworks the insert of Marcellus's scroll so that the camera shows him adding Miriam's name to the list in a "shaky sprawling hand."[26] Similarly, Dunne reworked some of the scenes Maltz had written between Marcellus and Abidor, but in a manner that preserves the characterization of the latter as a greedy informant. Scene 98, for example, shows Abidor dictating names for Marcellus's scroll:

Abidor

Benjamin and his wife, farmer
Marcellus dips his pen in the ink and writes.

Abidor

Justus, the weaver. It is said he is the leader.
CLOSE SHOT—Insert
The list, as Marcellus writes the names.

Abidor's voice

Hariph, the potter. His daughter, Rachel—

Although these sequences appear in Dunne's late drafts of *The Robe,* they were eliminated by the time the shooting script was completed, thereby making the reasons for their exclusion much more difficult to discern.

A more pertinent question, perhaps, is whether or not Dunne actually understood *The Robe* as a blacklist allegory, and unfortunately the historical record here raises more questions than it answers. While Dunne does not specifically address *The Robe*'s political subtext in his autobiography, there is some evidence that he might have seen the film as a Cold War allegory. George Custen notes that in 1949 Dunne tried to interest Darryl Zanuck in adapting a *New Yorker* article about William W. Remington, a Department of Commerce official charged with being a Communist. Later, Dunne pitched the idea of adapting George Orwell's *1984* to Zanuck by saying, "We could make another *The Robe,* set in the future instead of the past."[27] The problem, as Custen points out, is that Dunne saw these projects as being anti-totalitarian, as much against Communism as they were against HUAC. This seems particularly pertinent to the idea of adapting *1984* since it is just as easy to see the novel as an indictment of Stalinism as of American anti-Communism. In fact, when one considers the anti-Stalinist allegory of Orwell's *Animal Farm,* one might be inclined to prefer the former reading rather than the latter. If this is the case, then Dunne's intentions would accord more with Maria Wyke's reading of *The Robe* as a film that defends Christianity as a weapon in the war against Communism. According to this view, *The Robe* is an allegory about the persecution of Christians by present-day Communist governments rather than a film that defends the Communists interrogated by HUAC. Since the issue of Dunne's intentions gives rise to two seemingly opposed interpretations, one is tempted to ignore the issue altogether as hopelessly clouded and confused.

If this complicated chronology and the role of the source novel have problematized an allegorical interpretation based on Maltz's intentions, is there another way we might understand *The Robe* as allegory? The obvious candidate for

3.   As Maria Wyke points out, the technological novelty of CinemaScope was the focal point of contemporaneous reviews of *The Robe*.

an alternative explanation lies in reception theory. According to this line of argument, the process of encoding allegorical utterances has little or no bearing on the meanings created in the process of decoding these structures. Historical, social, and cultural contexts create the conditions for such reading strategies, which in the case of historical films and fictions involve the understanding of analogies between past and present. As I indicated near the start of this chapter, one can readily adduce this kind of allegorical interpretation in the long-term reception of *The Robe* among film scholars. But are traces of this allegorical framework evident in the contemporaneous reception of the film? While it is always difficult to assert and prove a negative proposition (e.g., that reviews of *The Robe* do *not* show the traces of allegorical interpretation), my answer to this question is a qualified no. Rather, as Maria Wyke points out, the technological novelty of CinemaScope overwhelmed the contemporaneous reception of *The Robe,* such that reviews offer virtually no consideration of the film's subtexts.[28] This appears to be true even in publications that one might expect to read the film as a form of political commentary. The review in *Commonweal,* a journal edited by John Cogley, one of the most important early historians of the blacklist, is typical. In the review's first three paragraphs, Philip T. Hartung discusses the decision to make *The Robe* in CinemaScope. This is followed by a brief plot synopsis and an assessment of the film's performances. The review concludes by praising the tastefulness and dignity of its depiction of Christ, but also complains that the film is not as stirring as it might be and that this is likely to be due to director Henry Koster's unfamiliarity with the new technology.[29] This avoidance of political subtext is evident despite the fact that the same issue of *Commonweal* begins with a discussion of European reactions to McCarthyism and concludes with a book review that addresses the relationship between Communism and religious institutions.

Besides the inattention to subtext, the contemporaneous reception of *The Robe* also effaced Maltz's contribution to the film in press accounts of its production. Early reports on the film (circa 1945) note the participation of Maltz, who replaced the first screenwriter on the project, Ernest Vajda.[30] After Maltz completed his work on the script, *The Robe* remained in preproduction limbo until 1948 when producer Frank Ross announced that RKO was finally ready to make the picture with Victor Fleming and Gregory Peck as the film's director and star, respectively. Ross also announced that he had hired Maxwell Anderson and Andrew Solt to do the screenplay adaptation despite the fact that he already had Maltz's completed script.[31] The project met another roadblock, though, when RKO canceled the production less than a month later, citing the project's $4.5 million budget as too large an expenditure for the studio. After some legal wrangling between Ross and RKO, *The Robe* landed at Twentieth Century Fox when Darryl Zanuck bought out RKO's interest in the project. In a 1952 article detailing the producer's ten-year struggle to bring *The Robe* to the screen, Ross claims that he was not able to hire a top-notch screenwriter during the early 1940s because "most of the good ones were in the service."[32] Ross goes on to say that several lesser-known screenwriters worked on the project until he wrote a scenario himself and hired Philip Dunne to "do a polishing job."[33] This press report corroborates the account of the production offered in Dunne's autobiography and it further points to Ross's role in preventing Maltz from gaining screen credit. In Ross's statements to the press, Maltz had gone from an artistic collaborator in 1945 to one of a group of lesser-knowns in 1952, this despite the fact that Maltz had written *This Gun for Hire* (1942), *Destination, Tokyo* (1943), *Pride of the Marines* (1945), and Ross's own Oscar-winning short, *The House I Live In* (1945).

While the paucity of contemporaneous evidence regarding blacklist interpretations poses one problem for a reception studies model, another more significant problem emerges when one considers the long-term reception of *The Robe* and the theoretical issue of "misreading." In her influential study of historical reception, *Interpreting Films,* Janet Staiger briefly considers the problem of misreading as one of the possible interpretive stances taken by spectators. For Staiger, the issue of misreading is a potential liability for her model of reception studies insofar as it opens up the theoretical possibility of an unconstrained pluralism of interpretations. Staiger, however, dismisses the potential problem of infinite semiosis by drawing a distinction between the *"philosophical possibility* of reading anything any way" and the *"historical fact* that the range of interpretations is constrained by numerous factors such as language, ideologies, personal goals for the experience, conditions of reception, self-identities related to class, race, gender, age, and ethnicity, and so forth—including the contemporary critical methods readers have been taught."[34] For Staiger, then, every reading, even a misreading, is potentially valuable to reception studies as "an important datum in evidence gathering and hypothesis making."[35]

Yet the possibility of "misreading" seems to run slightly counter to another doctrinal commitment for Staiger, namely that such misreadings still function as part of the horizon of expectations created for any individual spectator. Noting that every text has its own history of reception, Staiger argues that this history of successive interpretations functions as a background that "sets up assumptions about a text's meaning and thus influences its current interpretation."[36] Citing

Tony Bennett, who in turn cites Pierre Macherey, Staiger argues that each of these interpretations becomes a kind of textual encrustation, not unlike the layers of secretion that form a seashell or the layers of sedimentary rock that indicate a fossil's geological history.

Taken at face value, Staiger's account goes a long way toward explaining my own interpretive position vis-à-vis *The Robe*. In tracing the history of *The Robe's* reception, it is undoubtedly true that these previous interpretations, particularly those of Belton and Babington and Evans, have influenced my approach to the film. Yet Staiger's model of textual encrustation suggests that my own interpretation simply "sluices over" these previous accounts as just another layer of interpretation resting atop the others. And if we accept this model of the accretion of interpretations, my own reading of *The Robe* is no more right or wrong than the others.

But this conclusion defies common sense. How can one interpretation supported by the available historical evidence be equally valid as another interpretation that is unsupported by the available historical evidence? These two interpretations are not merely different; they are, in fact, incompatible. Given Staiger's context-activated model of reception, it might be fair to say that my interpretation of *The Robe* has changed because the context for its reception has changed as well. But this simply begs a larger sort of "chicken and egg" question: what accounts for the change in context that produces the change in interpretation? In this instance, one can clearly specify the reasons for the change in context, namely more detailed and specific information about both *The Robe's* history of production and the attendant impossibility of clear-cut authorial intention posited in earlier interpretations.

Perhaps more important than the reasons themselves is their origin outside of both the text itself and any specific act of interpretation. This poses a theoretical dilemma for Staiger, who asserts that "meaning is 'in' the contextual event of each reading, not 'in' one reading event rather than another."[37] While I generally agree with Staiger's emphasis on context, her model suggests that a text's meaning inheres solely in particular interpretive acts. Yet doesn't it logically follow that if factors outside the act of reading cause changes in its context that they also cause changes in the text's meaning as well? And if this is true, doesn't it also follow that a text's meaning is affected by elements that exist outside of both the text and specific act of its reception? Or to put it another way, surely the fact that Albert Maltz completed his work in 1946 changes the context for the reception of *The Robe*, but does it not also exist as a historical fact apart from that reception context?

Staiger's model of historical reception has been influential within film studies, but it is hardly the only model available to film historians. In contrast to Staiger's model of "textual encrustation," there are other variants of reception theory that conceive of historical reception as a set of discursive practices. As Jason Mittell points out in his discussion of television genres, these discursive practices can include processes of definition, interpretation, and evaluation.[38] Using the "discursive practices" model, the historical reception of *The Robe* might be broken down into a series of discursive clusters that are correlated with a set of successive reading formations. These discursive clusters might be charted as follows:

> The Robe as anti-Fascist allegory (Maltz's original screenplay)
> The Robe as potential blacklist allegory (Dunne's drafts, Zanuck's conference memo)
> The Robe as technological novelty (contemporaneous reviews, histories of widescreen cinema, Wyke's *Projecting the Past*)
> The Robe as actual blacklist allegory (Belton's *American Cinema/American Culture*, post-1970s blacklist film criticism)
> The Robe as both potential and actual blacklist allegory (my own interpretation as outlined in this essay)

The "discursive practices" model initially appears to be an improvement over Staiger's model in that the former encompasses a much wider variety of reading formations and contextual factors than the latter, which—in *Interpreting Films,* at least—seems resolutely focused on contemporaneous magazine and newspaper reviews as the most important index of historical reception. However, it is not clear to me that the "discursive practices" model resolves the problem of "misreading" acknowledged by Staiger. This is because the very problem of "misreading" is predicated on implicit standards of definition, interpretation, and evaluation that remain external to the discursive practices themselves. Here again we confront the same problem that plagued Staiger's model, namely that there is nothing within the "discursive practices" model that would enable film scholars to evaluate the validity of one interpretation over another.

To illustrate this point further, consider Mittell's discussion of television's relation to Hollywood studio animation.[39] In tracing the history of generic discourses related to television cartoons, Mittell offers a fascinating account of the way in which the animated shorts that were created for a broad, heterogeneous motion picture audience became "ghettoized" as Saturday morning television aimed at children. Moreover, Mittell's analysis further traces the way in which this definition of Saturday morning television was expanded in the 1990s by the twin developments of prime-time animation and cable networks aimed at a "12 and under" demographic. In a case study of Turner Entertainment's Cartoon Network, Mittell shows the way in which the company's corporate holdings served to shape their definition of studio animation to include Warner Bros., MGM, and Hanna-Barbera cartoons, but to exclude cartoons by Disney and Walter Lantz. Mittell rather convincingly demonstrates the way that particular industrial factors serve to discursively construct the very definition of "cartoon" as something virtually indistinguishable from Cartoon Network's own brand identity.

Yet Mittell's model of generic discourses offers nothing to suggest that Cartoon Network's definition of cartoon is somehow inadequate. Although Mittell clearly reveals its narrowness and limitations, his model suggests that Cartoon Network's definition of cartoon is neither better nor worse than that provided by, say, Michael

Barrier in *Hollywood Cartoons,* an admittedly much more complete and exhaustive study of studio animation than that proffered by the television industry.[40] The fact that Barrier's definition of cartoons is based on extensive primary research, interviews, and the study of archival resources does little to recommend it over the definition provided by Cartoon Network. Barrier is no less engaged in a set of discursive practices than the television industry itself. (Indeed, this is particularly evident in the narrative emphasis that Barrier places on Walt Disney in his history of studio animation.)

In the same way that Mittell's analysis of television genres permits no external standard of genre definition, the "discursive practices" model of historical reception does not permit any standard of interpretation against which rival allegorical readings may be measured. Since any reading of *The Robe* is constituted through a set of discursive practices, my own interpretation of the film is merely different from those provided by Belton, Wyke, and Babington and Evans. More important, since primary historical research is also constituted through discursive practices, the evidence gleaned from such research does nothing to confirm or disconfirm the validity of a particular interpretive stance. To suggest that any reading does not accord with the "facts" is to impose some independently verifiable, objective standard of interpretation on historical data when the data itself can only be understood through a set of discursive practices that are embedded within the craft of historical research and historical writing. According to this view, historical documents are simply another kind of text, whose meanings are not immanent, but rather are constructed through discursive practices of definition, interpretation, and evaluation. Thus, if any reception theorist desires to let the historical data supporting a particular interpretation "speak for itself," one falls victim to the very same problem of textualist assumptions that the model of discursive practices is intended to correct in the first place. Viewed in this way, the "discursive practices" model of historical reception offers little to recommend it over Staiger's model of "textual encrustation." Both models evade the problem of misreadings in that they both seem to preclude the possibility that an interpretation might be disconfirmed.

Does all this mean we must reject an allegorical interpretation of *The Robe?* Actually, I think not. Indeed, the strongest evidence to support this model of allegorical interpretation comes not from the possible or deliberate references to anti-Communist repression in the screenplay, but to Maltz's implicit conception of Rome as an empire founded on political repression that disregarded constitutional checks and balances to hold power. In his notes for *The Robe,* Maltz cited several passages from a book entitled *The Ancient World.* A passage describing the empire's treatment of conquered territories reads:

> Rome strictly *isolated* the subject communities from one another. She dissolved all tribal confederacies; she took skillful advantage of the grades of inferiority that she had created among her dependents to *foment jealousies* and to play off one class of communities against another. Likewise, within each city, she set

class against class, on the whole favoring an aristocratic organization. In politics as in war, the policy of her statesmen was *"Divide and Conquer."* (emphasis in original text)[41]

With such a conception of Rome as an underlying element of *The Robe,* one can readily understand how it might take on specific political resonance as something that paralleled the anti-Communists' policies regulating the American left between 1947 and 1953.

It is worth noting, though, that the very vagueness of Maltz's notes and research enable a number of possible interpretations of *The Robe's* subtext. By equating Rome's persecution of Christians with a more generalized notion of political repression, Maltz's dramatic concept was flexible and capacious enough to support myriad readings depending on whom one identifies as oppressor and oppressed. Thus, while it is logical to see Maltz's script as an indictment of Italian Fascism when it was written in 1945, the changes in the political landscape after World War II make it equally logical to see the 1953 film as either a defense of the Hollywood Ten or as a critique of religious repression in Communist countries.

In sum, although *The Robe* certainly makes sense as a Cold War parable, that interpretation is supported more by the adaptability of Maltz's scenario than it is by anything in the film's production. More important, perhaps the most useful model for understanding *The Robe's* allegorical dimensions is that of a text situated in relation to its historical context. While this assertion may seem terribly old fashioned in an era awash in reception studies of film, a "text-context" model seems to have two distinct advantages over its competitors: 1) it is the only model that explains *The Robe's* allegorical meanings within its shifting historical relations; and 2) it is the only model broad enough to encompass issues both of authorial intention *and* of historical reception. While these elements prove to be quite muddled in examining the allegorical dimensions of *The Robe,* this is not to say that these elements are irrelevant in all types of allegorical interpretation. On the contrary, it would be a major mistake to rule out authorial intention and historical reception *tout court.* Both these aspects of a film's historical context may be relevant when and where they can be concretely demonstrated and verified. The problem here is not that authorial intention and historical reception are always unknowable, but rather that they *sometimes* remain unknown, even after considerable historical investigation. As such, it is important to consider both authorial intent and audience reception as part of a text's historical context, but neither should be viewed as wholly determinate factors in a film's allegorical meaning. Instead, as my case study of *The Robe* has demonstrated, an examination of primary documents may complicate a text's possible meanings as much as it may illuminate them. A "text-context" model of allegorical interpretation weighs all these possible factors, but relies on the historian and critic's judgment about when and where they might be relevant.

While film critics may have been reticent to discuss an allegorical subtext in *The Robe* at the time of the film's release, the equation of early Christians and

Communists began to enter public discourse only a few years later. In the anti-Communist classic *The Naked Communist* (1958), W. Cleon Skousen poses the question quite succinctly in asking in a chapter title, "Did the Early Christians Practice Communism?" In the analysis that follows, Skousen suggests that some students in the United States believe that early Christians practiced a form of "brotherhood," a communism that involved the sharing of property and resources within the community. Skousen adds that this belief is given additional weight by the fact that the "Pilgrim Fathers . . . undertook to practice Communism immediately after their arrival in the New World."[42] After initially considering this argument, Skousen quickly dismisses this characterization of early Christians on two grounds. First, Skousen argues that all such social experiments are doomed to fail as unnatural and immoral, and points to Governor William Bradford's rejection of "brotherhood Communism" as proof that the Plymouth Colony evolved to a more sustainable system of socioeconomic principles. Second, Skousen quotes scriptures, especially the parable of the Talents, to show that early Christians may have shared wealth and resources, but that they did not legally hold common property. Instead, the communitarian philosophy of early Christians served as a means of solving common problems, but stopped short of a more radical redistribution of wealth. Skousen concludes, "When carefully analyzed, this was simply free enterprise capitalism *with a heart!*"[43]

To be sure, Skousen's defense of free-market capitalism as a Christian tenet is more likely to have been a response to the emergence of experimental Christian communities, especially among the followers of the Niebuhrs and of Henry F. Ward, than it is a response to the 1950s biblical epic.[44] Still, Skousen's comments on early Christianity indicate a possible reading formation for *The Robe* that might well have contributed to the long-term reception of the film, especially the linkage of Communism and Christianity that appears in the work of Belton and Babington and Evans. Indeed, viewed in this context, the reading of *The Robe* as a blacklist allegory is only a modest extrapolation and extension of the very question posed by Skousen.

Yet most of the elements cited in support of an allegorical reading of *The Robe* turn out to be far more complicated than first thought. For example, it is true that the film was coauthored by a blacklisted writer, but that writer's participation in the project occurred before the blacklist was even instituted. It is also true that *The Robe* contains certain textual elements that appear to be references to the blacklist, but the early drafts of the screenplay contain several more concrete references that were gradually eliminated in the revision process. Finally, while Philip Dunne's liberalism and his early defense of the Hollywood Ten may well have encouraged him to see *The Robe* as a scenario of Cold War repression, it appears that he saw the film as being as much a critique of Stalinist totalitarianism as it was a critique of anti-Communism.

Given the conflicting, contradictory, and perhaps willfully ignorant readings of the screenplay that circulated among the film's production team, it seems likely that the blacklist interpretation of *The Robe* emerged as a consequence of the text's shifting relationship to its historical context. Indeed, the very flexibility of *The Robe*'s scenario may well have encouraged Maltz himself to reconsider his script's implications in the period immediately following his being blacklisted. In a 1948 speech on censorship, Maltz described HUAC's activities as the most recent in a long history of efforts to restrict and suppress personal freedom. Maltz then followed this assertion with a long series of examples that began, "Are you or are you not a Christian, you who commit treason against the Roman State by your belief in Jesus Christ?"[45] As this quote suggests, Maltz probably never intended *The Robe* to be an allegory of the blacklist, but he may well have been the first person to interpret it that way.

2 Un-American

DMYTRYK, ROSSELLINI, AND *CHRIST IN CONCRETE*

Erica Sheen

Richard Maltby begins his influential account of the relation between Hollywood and the House Un-American Activities Committee with an assertion of its centrality to our understanding of the relation between American film and politics. "No adequate history of the Cold War in America can be written without reference to the blacklist and other agencies of cultural repression that were generated by those encounters," he claims. "But those events are now well documented, and their history has been written more than once. What remains to be said?"[1]

In answering this question he identifies what he describes as "the mutually supportive melodramas Hollywood and the Committee wove around their encounter in 1947": "the interaction between the Committee and Hollywood is above all an interaction on the level of rhetorical style and political aesthetics."[2] He follows this analysis with an account of the "generic evolution" that articulated this interaction in the years between the committee's establishment during the years of the New Deal to 1947, the year it first turned its sights on Hollywood: the spy and private eye thriller; the semi-documentary *policier*; political melodrama; film noir. His essay exemplified an approach that has continued to dominate discussions of Hollywood and HUAC. To put it another way, the questions we ask of this period of Hollywood history have to a considerable extent been dictated by HUAC itself: questions about the presence of Communists in the American film industry, and of Communist "content" in their films. From that perspective, it is perhaps surprising that film scholarship has been so "friendly" in its response. According to Dan Georgakas, recent work has "renewed and reshaped the old arguments." It has confirmed the fact that "the Hollywood Reds were well-entrenched in the studio system and many were highly regarded by the studio bosses." But it has not made so much headway with the question of content: "What remains at issue is to what degree their political views were reflected in the Hollywood films on which they worked."[3] For Georgakas, as for Maltby, then, there is a remainder, something structural but resistant to the very terms of our enquiry. It should not, I think, be surprising that this is the case. Focusing our understanding of Hollywood and HUAC on questions of presence and content is to apply paradigms of authorship and genre that were critical by-products of the cultural transformation to which HUAC contributed,[4] and will as a result have limited critical purchase on its causes.

What might break this critical impasse would be the discovery of something outside the circle; something not easily assimilated into its cycle of repetitions. Such a remainder can be found in a film that is arguably one of the most important productions of the period, Edward Dmytryk's "lost" film of Italian American novelist Pietro di Donato's *Christ in Concrete* (1949).

The facts of Dmytryk's involvement with HUAC are well documented, and I do not intend to repeat them here. Nor do I intend to offer a textual reading of the film itself, since to do so would simply re-inscribe it within the hermeneutic circle of authorship and genre. *Christ in Concrete* was made in England after Dmytryk's conviction for contempt of Congress and before his imprisonment in 1950 and subsequent decision to testify before HUAC in 1951. It thus occupies an extremely distinctive position in the ideological struggle that would come to be identified as the Cold War, and it is that position which I will be seeking to characterize in this discussion. Since the title was considered blasphemous by its English distributors, it was released initially as *Give Us This Day* and then, in the United States, as *Salt to the Devil*.[5] It was presented to critical acclaim at the Venice Festival in August 1950 while Dmytryk himself was in prison, but then suppressed by the American Legion on its release in the United States. As Dmytryk describes it,

> *Give Us This Day* had opened to exceptional reviews, but on the following day, the theatres were visited by Legionnaires who informed the managers that continuation of the run would bring a boycott not only of my film but of all others for the foreseeable future. Exhibitors are no smarter than the next man, but they are no dumber either. With a few exceptions, they closed shop, and in effect, my film never saw the light of day in the United States.[6]

This implies that the film's lack of presence in subsequent film history was the direct result of this suppression, but that is not in fact the case. After its theatrical release, the copyright unusually reverted to the novelist, so there was no one within the film industry with a financial interest in reviving the film. As a consequence, when di Donato tried to negotiate a TV broadcast in the late 1960s, he found that there was no American copy available. I will pursue the implications of this situation at a later stage, but note here two points. First, its emergence now as a DVD has been instigated by the di Donato family as current rights holders, and it is their perspective that it is presented in this production, frequently at Dmytryk's expense. Second, the film constitutes a quite special case of what is a fairly standard situation for films of that period in that it owes its survival to TV—in this case, *Italian* TV. According to the British Film Institute's on-line biography of Dmytryk, the film is "rarely shown, except for a yearly screening on Italian television," a revealing if accidental racism that goes some way toward establishing the terms of my argument. It is the film's Italian connection—the status in Italian American culture of Pietro Di Donato's novel, its affinity to the emerging aesthetic of Italian Neo-Realism, its address to Italian American international relations in 1947–48—that helps us see how it might change the frames of reference we use to discuss the relation between American film and politics, in particular, how it challenges Maltby's assertion that Hollywood politics are "different in kind from those practiced in Washington."[7]

In what is currently one of the few available critical discussions of the film, Peter Bondanella refers to it as "one of the first Hollywood representations of Italian Americans that reflects the influence of Italian cinema—specifically, the post-war neo-realist film." But he insists that it is closer to film noir than to neorealism because it uses a flashback structure—"all more typical of American film noir under the influence of German Expressionism." He draws attention to the fact that the opening of the film was reedited for Italian audiences, and refers to this procedure as a kind of censorship: "The Italian print *suppressed* the initial opening scenes of the work, transforming the picture into a more clearly chronological movie."[8] In his insistence on a generically American identity, Bondanella might be said to pursue the agenda of Americanization to which HUAC was implicitly committed. Of course, in an American context, the procedure to which Bondanella refers is a standard feature of distribution, and has been applied with little critical compunction to films traveling in the opposite direction. From this perspective, the Italian reediting of Dmytryk's film is a somewhat uncanny inversion of Roberto Rossellini's difficulties with the distribution of *Stromboli* (1949) in America, where RKO insisted on the insertion of a voiceover explaining its ambiguous ending. *Stromboli* was made and released at exactly the same time as *Christ in Concrete*, and exhibited at the Venice Festival in the same year. I describe the relation between the two as uncanny—*unheimlich*—because these two films are held together in a process of mirroring which helps us understand that what was at stake in the confrontation between Hollywood and HUAC was not merely questions of presence and meaning, but a conception of filmmaking as a form of constitutional participation in the political process.

Christ in Concrete and *Stromboli*—though here we should note its full title, *Stromboli terra di Dio* (Land of God)—examine the two sides of the central contemporary question for the Italian American community: America's claim to the status of "terrestrial paradise" for the postwar immigrant.[9] In Rossellini's film, Karin, a European woman (not Italian, but married to an Italian) tries to make a home with her fisherman husband on the volcanic island of Stromboli, but is unable to overcome her alienation as a stranger and seeks in desperation to escape to America. In Dmytryk's film, an Italian woman agrees to come to America to marry an Italian American bricklayer husband on the condition that he provides her with a house. If *Stromboli*—however we read its ending—suggests that Italians must reconcile themselves to Italy, *terra di Dio*, its culture and its values, *Christ in Concrete* shows what awaits them if they leave their homes in search of the terrestrial paradise. The story of the failure of Geremio and Annunziata's marriage and of Geremio's terrible death—buried alive in concrete when the construction he is working on collapses—is that of immigrants building the American dream with their very hands, but being destroyed by the terms on which they have to make the money they need to afford it.

Writing a report of the 1950 Venice Festival published in *Hollywood Quarterly* in 1951, Tullio Kezich discussed both films. To begin, he recorded the fact that the International Grand Prize was awarded to André Cayatte's *Justice est faite*, but then pointed out that

> everyone admits that even though many noteworthy films were shown at Venice in 1950, none was so far ahead of the others as to unqualifiedly deserve top honors. In awarding the Grand Prize, the judges, including critics and well-known personalities of the Italian cultural world, had to arrive at a compromise which, like all compromises, did not completely satisfy anybody. And it is perhaps significant to note that the Italian motion picture critics awarded their 1950 annual prize to a film that was not in the competition: Edward Dmytryk's *Give Us This Day*.[10]

This innuendo—"it is perhaps significant"—is fraught with the pressure of what it does not say. By the time of the festival, Dmytryk was in prison; by the time the review appeared, he had recanted and testified to HUAC. Both Kezich's position as a commentator on this "significance," and *Hollywood Quarterly*'s as the medium through which it is communicated, are themselves significant. *Hollywood Quarterly* describes Kezich as "at twenty three one of Italy's more perceptive movie critics [. . .] also writing a book on the American 'western,'" thus placing him in a very particular, and very complex, historical position of reception. Stephen Gundle records that "when in 1954 Giuseppe Turroni went in pursuit of the [Italian] film-going public for the magazine *Rassegna del film* he met a twenty-three year old student enrolled with the PCI who admitted preferring westerns and adventure films to Visconti's *La terra trema* [. . .], which was 'too intellectual and difficult.'"[11] I do not mean to imply that Tullio Kezich was a Communist, though the very question is born of a Cold War–induced misrecognition of the meaning of political affiliation. To make such an identification in 1950 would simply be to align the young writer with the ideas of a legitimate political party that had until 1948 been heading for a resounding popular victory, a party that remained at the heart of Italian cultural life throughout the 1950s and beyond, the party that most publicly advanced the cause of contemporary cinema.

In fact, *Hollywood Quarterly* represented a similar position of reception within the American industry. First published in 1946 as a collaboration between UCLA and the Hollywood Writers Mobilization, a radical group under the leadership of John Howard Lawson, its aims were identified in a programmatic statement in *Public Opinion Quarterly* which asserted as an "insistent fact" that "the idea that movies are essentially a medium of communication, with a high degree of universality" and identified the "common objectives of the arts and sciences as related to radio, motion picture and television" as "to provide a professional recognition of their full possibilities as powerful tools of communication."[12] In 1946, only a year before the HUAC hearings began, no one in Hollywood had qualms about being associated with such a program. Only the year before, Walt Disney had published a piece in *Public Opinion Quarterly* arguing the educative potential of "Mickey as Professor." The question of universality was perceived to have implications above all for the generic formulae that had dominated and limited the industry's communicative potential, both at home and abroad and whose cultural and economic value was now seriously under question. As Robert Shaw put it,

> The industry worries about the foreign market [England, France, Russia, Czechoslovakia and Latin America]. Will the people of those countries, tempered in so many of them by the grim realities of war, pay at the box office to see an endless parade of slick glamour pictures, a monotonous repetition of the Cinderella boy-meets-girl formula? Will Americans continue to see such pictures at the present rate . . .? In a recent symposium on 1946 trends in film making, a majority said the best hope of the film industry is for better stories, fresher material, a more honest and perhaps more documentary approach to the issues confronting common men and women.[13]

In support of such a position Shaw records that Harry Warner of Warner Bros. at a recent Nobel anniversary dinner "spoke for his industry in saying that the motion picture, as the nearest approach to an international language, 'is faced with the responsibility of helping to create the conditions of international good will that are the essential foundations of world peace.' "[14]

This position unmistakably echoes the critical register associated with Italian Neo-Realism; thus Rossellini, speaking against an entertainment cinema that is not "at least partially capable of attaining the truth," asserted that "to give anything its true value means to have understood its authentic and universal meaning."[15] By 1950, however, critics were already beginning to see Rossellini as someone who had turned his back on this political commitment. Later in his review, Kezich turns his attention to *Stromboli,* which he describes as *not* one of Italian cinema's "best works." After recording the difference between the Italian and American versions, he concedes that it is "worth seeing for a magnificent Ingrid Bergman," but concludes that "unlike [. . .] *Città Aperta* and *Paisà*, it contains no valid message of universal appeal."[16] His comments anticipate the terms of subsequent discussions of Rossellini's politics, but in the context of the reading I am seeking to develop here, they help us situate the crisis in relations between Italy and the terrestrial paradise in 1947–49 as the precise context for the return to Italy and Italian values presented in Rossellini's film, and for the departure from America and American values in Dmytryk's.

Within a year of the founding of the *Hollywood Quarterly*, the international language of film had become unreadable. In May 1947, only a year after Harry Warner "spoke for his industry," his brother Jack did the same, but to very different effect. As Richard Maltby records, Warner testified to HUAC in secret session confirming the covert presence of Communist propaganda in film: "Some of these lines have innuendos and double meanings, and things like that, and you have to take eight or ten Harvard law courses to find out what they mean."[17] The association of a sophisticated textual hermeneutic with Communist infiltration is important. Jon Lewis's comment on this—"the logical extension of such an argument—that the mass audience would be unable to recognise such subtle political content and were thus unlikely to be poisoned by such propaganda—never seemed to cross their minds"—is sensible, but misses the point.[18] A feature of this moment in the public understanding of a culture of cinema radically reconfigured both by HUAC and by the breakdown of vertical integration is the emergence of a model of textual interpretation (with its associated apparatus of authorship and genre) that would contrast definitively with the utopian ideal of communication and universality that had burgeoned before the assault of HUAC. In fact, it is arguable that Jack Warner should have referred to Yale, not Harvard, and to English literature, not to law. From the early 1940s onward, Yale's English faculty, with its commitment to the New Critical discipline of "close reading," had been producing the core personnel of the OSS (Office of Strategic Operations), which would emerge from the early years of the Cold War, in particular from its experience of covert operations in Italy, as the basis of the modern CIA.[19] William Epstein has shown the association between particular acts of scholarly production—CID (Central Information Division) chief Wilmarth Lewis's formidable footnoting system for the forty-eight-volume edition of the letters of Horace Walpole for Yale University Press—and the very concept of "intelligence" as a mode of practical political agency rather than abstract intellectual ability.[20] As Lewis's historical methods gave way to the more fashionable influences of I. A. Richards and William Empson, the emphasis moved away from the minute delineation of historical context to techniques of textual interrogation—"close reading"—dedicated to the exposure of hidden meanings and ambiguity. At the heart of this culture of "intelligence" was James Jesus Angleton, child of a notably international American family (Mexican mother; childhood in Milan), who followed education at a British public school with English at Yale, became a devotee of New Criticism, published a student journal devoted to literary modernism, and invited William Empson to come to the campus to speak. Angleton followed Yale with Harvard Law School, so he may well be the particular close reader Warner had in mind.

If the affinity between literary close reading and Cold War political hermeneutics has been recognized, its relevance for the critical reception of film as text in a postwar culture of cinema has not. My aim here is to suggest the ways in which a particular film, positioned at the intersection of the institutional, industrial, economic, political, and international frames of reference that began to take shape within the two- or three-year period following the end of hostilities in Europe, can help us close-read the "significance" that emerges from this intersection. We might perhaps have perceived the potential for this particular hermeneutic activity in what has been taken to be the crucial determinant in Dmytryk's position as a member of the Hollywood Ten: the fact that he was the only director among a group of screenwriters. Jack Warner observed that it was the "intellectual" writers who were the most avid supporters of Communism.[21] The implications of this hermeneutic of suspicion manifest themselves in the curiously contradictory discourse of exposure that pervades Dmytryk's later account of his HUAC experiences, a discourse that reflects crucially on the way we understand the transfer of intelligence from page to screen. On one hand, Dmytryk comments on the fact that, as a director, he was disadvantaged by HUAC in a way that writers were not, precisely because a director is visible, and writers could work under cover. On the other, he asserts that he alone saw that the Ten's HUAC performance in September 1947 was "suicidal": "The rest of the crew basked in the bright spotlight of what they considered a victory. . . . If that seems perverse, even dim-witted, behavior for a bunch of intelligent writers you must understand that communism rules by revelation." [22] The hermeneutic tension between covert operation and revelation—and the resulting need for us constantly to read between Dmytryk's own lines—becomes particularly articulate as a way of approaching the problem of meaning that pervades an understanding of *Christ in Concrete*.

I suggested earlier that the film occupies an extremely distinctive position in the ideological struggle that would come to be identified as the "Cold War." It is in fact the sole occupant of a somewhat Borgesian category:[23] it is the only film made by the only director in a group consisting otherwise exclusively of writers, after the first wave of HUAC interrogations and before the second, in a situation in which, as Dalton Trumbo pointed out, no one in 1947 knew what the penalty would be but everyone in 1951 did.[24] It thus constitutes a highly particular articulation of the subtext of HUAC's political program. David Kalat of All Day Entertainment simplifies the film into "an unmistakable gesture of provocation and defiance": because "no effort was made to conceal the participation of any of its most controversial names," he see it as "a middle finger aimed straight at HUAC."[25]

Predictably, Dmytryk's memoir presents the situation very differently. It is certainly true that he doesn't conceal the fact that he chose to work with blacklisted colleagues Ben Barzman and Sam Wanamaker, though he does suggest that he did so because they were, for obvious reasons, available. But he does conceal—or at least fails to reveal—the relation he thereby entered into with Pietro di Donato and Roberto Rossellini. He records that he was approached by Rod Geiger and asked if he would like to direct the film. Providing us with an excellent opportunity to observe the emergence of the post-vertical integration producer, Dmytryk first describes Geiger somewhat dismissively as an opportunistic "wildcat," but subsequently and with admiration as an "independent" producer, a "true entrepreneur," and a "peerless promoter." According to Dmytryk, Geiger had worked for an American distributor of foreign films before the war. Then, as a member of the Signal Corps, he worked in public relations for the U.S. Army in Italy (designing VD posters for toilets), and in this capacity was able to help Rossellini get hold of army film stock to make *Roma città aperta*. Aided by Rossellini's grateful recognition in a co-producer credit, he followed this success by funding and distributing *Paisà*, and was now looking to develop his career as a producer. As Dmytryk describes it,

> He bought a sprawling first novel written by a Brooklyn bricklayer, Pietro di Donato, and hired a New York playwright to transform it into a screenplay. Then he came to Hollywood. He reached me through a friend, and I called on him in his suite at the Hollywood Plaza Hotel. I had never heard of Geiger, and wildcat producers were a glut in Hollywood; I entertained no false hopes.

> I had read di Donato's short story "Christ in Concrete" many years before
> when it had appeared in the original *Esquire* magazine. It had been a prize
> winner, and it would make a great sequence, but a sequence doesn't make a
> picture, and a short story blown up into a novel is often a disaster. Geiger how-
> ever had no qualms.[26]

There are some curious gaps here. Is it likely that someone with Dmytryk's interests didn't know who had produced and distributed Rossellini's films? Is it likely
that he didn't know that the production originally began with Rossellini as director,
and proceeded quite a long way on that basis?[27] Is it likely he didn't know that
Pietro di Donato was something more than just a "Brooklyn bricklayer"?

Di Donato was well known as an Italian American radical. In 1927, he had participated in the rally in New York's Union Square on the night of the execution of
the anarchists Nicola Sacco and Bartolomeo Vanzetti, and joined the Communist
Party immediately afterward. First published in 1939, his "proletarian" novel *Christ
in Concrete* stood as a benchmark for the beleaguered tradition of Italian American
radicalism in the difficult years that followed. Recent scholarship has described the
Italian American Communist community as "a piece of the Italian American experience that has been gouged out and hidden away," and has identified the political
machinery by which it was systematically "eradicated."[28] In 1950, the year in which
Christ in Concrete and Rossellini's *Il Miracolo* (1948) were both suppressed, that community received its death blow in the strategically manipulated overthrow of one
of its few remaining great public figures, Vito Marcantonio. A congressman of
"extraordinary status within Italian Harlem and enormous popularity throughout
New York's Little Italies and to some extent among the larger population of Italian
Americans throughout the United States," Marcantonio was systematically ousted
by an electoral alliance between the Democratic, Republican and Liberal Parties.[29]

As the immediate context for a film of Di Donato's novel, the suppression of
Italian American radicalism must be seen as a domestic counterpart to international events that coincided precisely with the period of the film's production.
From this perspective, Dmytryk's film emerges as something more articulate than
an erect middle finger: it constituted a direct address to an international situation
that only a year or two previously had so confidently been identified as the basis of
a concept of film as a universal language. In 1947, as HUAC rolled into action in
Hollywood, the U.S. government initiated a policy of direct intervention in Italian
domestic politics with the express purpose of preventing the imminent success of
the electoral alliance between the PCI (Partito Comunista Italiano) and PSI (Partito Socialista Italiano) in the 1948 parliamentary elections. Establishing an alliance
with the DC (Democrazia Cristiana), whose own interests in exploiting the economic potential of the American preoccupation with Communism made it a willing partner,[30] Washington embarked on a program of "psychological" warfare
against Italy under the leadership of James Jesus Angleton.[31] Under pressure to
prove its "American" credentials, the Italian American community was encouraged
to draw the attention of relatives in Italy to the need to resist Communism if they

wished to continue to receive the benefits of their association with the terrestrial paradise. A mass letter-writing campaign, orchestrated by the distribution of postage-paid sample letters, argued the evils of Communist domination, but also threatened the loss of American aid. Shortwave radio broadcasts featuring American politicians recited the horrors of life under Communist dictatorship; the Voice of America presented appeals from representative figures of both the Hollywood and Italian American communities, including Frank Sinatra, an active member of leftist organizations until a savage media campaign forced him to renounce his radical affiliations and join the campaign against Italian Communism in 1948.[32]

Washington's vision of Europe in 1947–48 was thus as much an endgame strategy in its own domestic program of Americanization as an opening gambit in a new phase of globalization. Geir Lundestad has urged the importance of a perspective on the Cold War that approaches it not as a "bipolar clash"[33] but stresses "other powers," variation of circumstance, and "local actors."[34] My aim here is to identify the production of *Christ in Concrete*—its earliest stages with Rossellini, its completion by Dmytryk, its suppression and even its subsequent disappearance—on precisely those terms, as a "local actor" in this complex dynamic. What the anti-Communist campaigns, both at home and abroad, achieved in these early years was suppression, not so much of a Soviet-led program of Communist infiltration but of the *possibility* of a radicalism that was not yet in any real sense dominated by the Soviet Union, a radicalism that had the potential to respond, as Antonio Gramsci had responded in Italy, to the varied social and economic conditions of postwar Europe, even of postwar America. Indeed, the rhetoric of bipolar clash was the means by which this suppression was achieved, more than the end to which it was directed. If we look back at Robert Shaw's vision of Hollywood's "new horizons," or the "significance" that hovers somewhere in the air between Los Angeles and Venice in Kezich's review, we can sense the extent to which such a conception of filmmaking, or at least of its potential, was shared in Hollywood, and the extent to which Hollywood had begun to imagine the idea of an international, or rather perhaps transnational, film community as the place where this potential could become, in Lukàcsian terms, *concrete*. When Bernardo Bertolucci describes the culture of film that would emerge from the mutual address of Hollywood and European "art" cinema in the 1950s and 1960s as "a densely populated mid-Atlantic bar or rallying place,"[35] his metaphor makes it clear that we have to think of this address not merely in terms of quotas, co-productions, and box office, but also as a form of shared virtual space. Steve Neale has identified "art," as in art cinema, as "the space in which an indigenous cinema can develop and make its critical and economic mark,"[36] but for a few brief years, that space was not yet, and perhaps more significantly, not *necessarily*, oppositionally structured. The crucial first two or three years in the development of what we now refer to as art cinema was thus founded not just on forms of economic interdependence between industries, but also on shared political ideals between two communities—even, one might say, *within* what those two communities themselves could imagine as at least potentially a single community.

Notwithstanding his recognition of the negative impact of the industrial aspect of the American system of production, Roberto Rossellini's account of his early dealings with Hollywood is shot through with a sense of that potential, and a sense that his "return" to Italy was born of personal and political necessities that closed it down. Statements such as "I believe cinema is a new art and has the potential for making new discoveries"[37] align him with a Gramscian vision of the regenerative social role of film, but they also gloss his recognition that America offered opportunities for the realization of that potential that were inhibited by Alcide de Gasperi's DC; as he put it, "it is too easy to forget that on the other side of the Atlantic there is a public composed of connoisseurs, of specialists, which is extremely important. That public comes to see films which have something new to say."[38] He refers to the "concrete offers" he received from David Selznick in 1945–46, and to his perception of the potential such offers had to open up for him a "career"—"had my goal been a 'career.'" Explaining why he chose to stay in Italy rather than accept these offers, he pointed out that "in Italy there is hardly enough work already and I was afraid of betraying my friends and the people who usually worked with me."[39] And here—in a mirror image of Edward Dmytryk's very different experience of friendship and betrayal—we can see the basis of the decision to withdraw from *Christ in Concrete*, a decision that led paradoxically to his collaboration with Ingrid Bergman and the anti-Communist Howard Hughes's post–Dore Schary RKO on *Stromboli* just as Dmytryk began work on *Christ in Concrete* in Methodist J. Arthur Rank's Denham studios with a bunch of Communist activists. This is a mirror image of Wellesian complexity, a mirror image that deep-focuses the personal, professional, industrial, and institutional contradictions of the address between America and Italy, politics and cinema, and of the individual acts of filmmaking that carry its hidden and double meanings. Geoffrey Nowell-Smith has described the kind of cinema Rossellini sought to achieve as an "other cinema": "what held it together was not a shared aesthetic but the political will to create an 'other' cinema for Italy in the immediate post-war context."[40] I do not mean to suggest that this 'other' cinema was in any simple sense a historically possible cinema in America. But it was inextricably embedded within it, and has remained there despite HUAC.

The assault on Hollywood, encapsulated here in the production history of *Christ in Concrete*, led to one of those curious paradoxes of liberty and oppression that periodically articulate the distinctive American concept of freedom. In January 1951 Rossellini's film *Il Miracolo*, part of the *Ways of Love* trilogy, was banned from performance in New York at the instigation of City Commissioner Edward McCaffrey. When distributor Joseph Burstyn obtained an injunction against the ban, the New York Board of Regents revoked the film's license. In the debate that followed, McCaffrey's accusation of blasphemy revealed inevitable political overtones. Despite the film's sympathetic reception at the Vatican, Francis Cardinal Spellman of New York denounced it as a Communist plot aimed at "dividing religion against religion": "Divide and conquer is the technique of the greatest enemy of civilization, atheistic communism."[41] Burstyn appealed the decision, the Supreme Court revoked the ban, and film was finally brought under the protection of the First

1.   Edward Dmytryk, center, on the set of *Christ in Concrete*. On his left is publicity director John Ware and on his right is Lea Padovanni, who plays Annunziata. Courtesy of The British Film Institute.

Amendment. It is truly ironic that the constitutional protection denied to Dmytryk was now effectively granted to Rossellini. Curiously, commentary on *Burstyn v. Wilson* has not sought to pursue this juxtaposition. Ellen Draper sees the case as symptomatic of a "deep disagreement about the proper role of film in society" but does not associate that disagreement in any way with HUAC. Indeed, she systematically sets aside precisely the kind of questions about that disagreement that I have sought to raise in this discussion:

> Except for [Elaine Powdermaker's] *Hollywood the Dream Factory* and John Howard Lawson's Marxist tract *Film in the Battle of Ideas*, I can find no American books considering the nature of film, let alone film censorship from this period. . . . During the fifties . . . the public discussion of movie censorship took place almost exclusively in periodicals and newspapers: the very arena of the discussion in the 1950s indicates the factionalism, uncertainty and inconclusiveness of the debate about movie censorship.[42]

For Draper, the fact that *Burstyn v. Wilson* limited its decision to the particular circumstances of a particular film means that it failed to define film as a "medium." But that, I would argue, is precisely what it did. In extending to the individual film a protection that had hitherto been refused to the filmmaker, it positioned it as an ambiguous text to be closely read rather than an act of political freedom of speech. It thus instituted the rehabilitation of un-American filmmaking into a profitable business for the American film industry, and with it a formalist conception of art cinema that remains fundamental even in contemporary film scholarship. In 1956,

Variety published foreign-film box office receipts for the first time.[43] That same year, the *Yale Law Journal* presented an anonymous exposure of the way committee interrogations use "vague authorizing resolutions" to allow "the members of a committee or its staff to select individuals of one political stripe for public humiliation." In an examination of the authorizing resolution for the House Un-American Activities Committee, we learn that "the word 'un-American' is nowhere defined."[44] The conversion of "atheistic communism" to "foreign grosses" is a way of providing such a definition, albeit one that clearly demonstrates the extent to which to define is to assimilate. I suggested earlier that *Christ in Concrete*'s disappearance from film history owed less to the actions of the American Legion than to the fact there was no one in the industry, like Joseph Burstyn, with a financial interest in ensuring that audiences had the opportunity to see it. But to say this would simply overlook the fact that the unusual conditions applying to the rights to *Christ in Concrete* are themselves a direct expression of Dmytryk's exclusion from participation in the political process of filmmaking. Rossellini's films became canonical texts in the institution of art cinema; *Christ in Concrete* remains caught in the limbo of Un-America.

3 "A Living Part of the Class Struggle"

DIEGO RIVERA'S *THE FLOWER CARRIER*
AND THE HOLLYWOOD LEFT

Frank Krutnik

This chapter explores a curious visual legacy of the Hollywood Left. *The Flower Carrier*, a 1935 easel work by the flamboyant Mexican muralist and Communist Diego Rivera, is prominently displayed in several films released during the period in which Hollywood was under intensive scrutiny from HUAC.[1] The recurrence of *The Flower Carrier* across *The Woman on Pier 13* (1949), *In a Lonely Place* (1950), *The Prowler* (1951), and several other films amounts to an enigmatic communication from a turbulent past. In a mysterious and provocative instance of countertextual inscription, this painting is incorporated within the flow of images to emblematize a political critique that could not otherwise be articulated. The films themselves also carry explicit political resonance, even if their methods and agendas contrast sharply. *In a Lonely Place* is often read as an allegorical treatment of the culture of suspicion that prevailed in Hollywood during the HUAC era. *The Prowler* is a tough, socially grounded crime film that critiques the skewed postwar culture of materialist aspiration; it was the product of a left-wing director and writers who would soon become blacklist exiles. As Thom Andersen suggests, such politically inflected tales of criminal transgression were attractive to the Hollywood Left in the late 1940s and early 1950s, perhaps because the familiar generic framework of the crime story provided an effective yet contained vehicle for exposing the flaws of contemporary American society.[2] *The Woman on Pier 13*, by contrast, uses the materials of the crime film from a divergent political perspective. But although it was a notorious entry in the cycle of Hollywood anti-Communist thrillers produced in the late 1940s and early 1950s, *The Woman on Pier 13* nonetheless mobilizes Rivera's painting as a blatant signifier of left-wing affiliation.

As I show, Rivera's artwork intersects in diverse ways with the respective fictional worlds of each film. Moreover, the recurrence of the image across a number of films within the same period establishes a cross-textual discursive network that, intentionally or not, is waiting to be decoded. The characters within the films clearly have different motives for selecting the picture than the filmmakers do. But who is actually responsible for inserting the picture within each film? Were their intentions explicitly political, or more innocent? Who were they hoping to address?

Were they in communication with one another? Were they using one single copy of *The Flower Carrier*, or are numerous reproductions involved? This instance of cross-textual communication raises many such questions, but definitive answers remain elusive. Even so, the filmic examples I discuss below provide a glimpse of one particularly tantalizing and hitherto forgotten textual byproduct of this period of political conflict and repression. I know of five films from the 1947–51 period that make use of *The Flower Carrier*. In order of release:[3]

- *Bury Me Dead*. Production of this PRC/Eagle Lion Film began on April 7, 1947, and it was released on October 18, 1947.[4]
- *Where There's Life*. Produced and distributed by Paramount Pictures, the film was in production from March 27 to May 22, 1946, and was released on November 21, 1947.[5]
- *The Woman on Pier 13* (aka *I Married a Communist, Beautiful But Dangerous*). Produced and distributed by RKO Radio Pictures, the film was in production from April 24 to late May 1949. It opened in Los Angeles on October 7, 1949, and in San Francisco five days later, but was not generally released until June 3, 1950.
- *In a Lonely Place*. Santana Pictures, Inc. made the film, for distribution through Columbia Pictures Corporation. In production from October 25 to December 1, 1949, the film opened in New York City on May 17, 1950, and was released in August 1950.
- *The Prowler*. Horizon Pictures made the film, with distribution through United Artists. Production began in early April 1950, and the film was released on May 25, 1951.

It is important to note that different companies produced these films. This discounts the possibility that *The Flower Carrier* was, like other artworks, part of a batch of prints purchased by one studio for standard set dressing. For example, besides sharing wall space with *The Flower Carrier* in the Columbia release *In a Lonely Place*, Vincent Van Gogh's 1888 painting *La Mousmé* also decorates a character's bedroom in the 1949 Columbia production *The Reckless Moment*.[6] Columbia was a pretty thrifty outfit in this respect: Pierre-Auguste Renoir's 1879 painting *La Fille du déjeuner* can be found in both *The Reckless Moment* and *In a Lonely Place*, and it also crops up in the 1953 Columbia film, *The Big Heat*.[7] Where *La Mousmé* and *La Fille du déjeuner* were clearly part of the set decorator's repertoire at Columbia, *In a Lonely Place* is thus far the only Columbia release I have found that uses *The Flower Carrier* during this time. The Rivera painting has a relatively minor, though nonetheless intriguing, role to play in *Bury Me Dead* and *Where There's Life*, but I will demonstrate below that the other three films render it a vibrant and meaningful part of their mise-en-scène.[8]

The repeated use of this painting raises fascinating questions about the nature of the political meanings that the Hollywood Left were accused of injecting into their films. In a 1938 letter to *Partisan Review*, Leon Trotsky celebrated the revolutionary force of Diego Rivera's mural art with the following euphoric eulogy:

> Do you wish to see with your own eyes the hidden springs of the social revolution? Look at the frescoes of Rivera. Do you wish to know what revolutionary art is like? Look at the frescoes of Rivera. . . . You have before you, not simply a "painting," an object of passive esthetic contemplation, but a living part of the class struggle.[9]

The Flower Carrier itself operates as a "living part of the class struggle" by depicting a scenario of exploited labor that is readily amenable to interpretation as a political statement. As such, it has the capacity to politicize representational contexts that are not themselves ostensibly political, particularly in associating the exploitative scenario of the painting with women who are troubled by the actuality or prospect of domesticity. Recognition of the painting also invokes a broader awareness of Diego's Rivera's continual identification with radical politics—a crucial component of both his art and his celebrity. Because Rivera's status as a political artist is crucial to the employment of *The Flower Carrier* within these films, it is worth examining his career and significance in more detail before proceeding to the painting itself.

By the late 1940s, Diego Rivera, a committed if undisciplined Communist, was widely known in the United States both as an artist and as a figure of political controversy.[10] He was most renowned for explicitly political works of public art that had incited scandalous collisions with the forces of censorship. Like other Mexican artists, Rivera was swept up in the revolutionary fervor that gripped the country following the overthrow of dictator Porfirio Díaz in 1910. Under the patronage of Minister of Education José Vasconcelos, Rivera was one of several artists—along with José Orozco, David Alfaro Siqueiros, and Xavier Guerrero—who, in the early 1920s, were offered opportunities to paint large-scale murals in public buildings. After the divisive conflicts of the 1910s, Vasconcelos embarked upon an ambitious project of cultural unification that aimed to bring together Mexico's diverse regions and classes. The program of monumental public art played a vital role in helping to create a new secular myth of the Mexican Revolution.[11] As Ida Rodriguez-Prampolini puts it, Rivera and his fellow muralists were inspired by the problem "of how to convey to a largely illiterate population the history of its own political struggles as well as how to introduce them to new revolutionary truths."[12] The radical agenda of these artists was outlined in the manifesto of the Syndicate of Technical Workers, Painters and Sculptors, which Rivera helped to found in 1922. Largely written by Siqueiros, the manifesto called for a Mexican art that "surges from the people; it is collective, and our own aesthetic aim is to socialize artistic expression, to destroy bourgeois individualism."[13]

Rivera experienced a political and artistic epiphany on returning to Mexico in 1921, after a lengthy period in Europe. During his twelve years in Paris, Rivera had been intoxicated by the artistic and political enticements of the cosmopolitan city.

Working through a range of traditional and modernist forms, Rivera established himself as a charismatic figure in the art scene, winning acclaim for his Cubist works. However, the Russian Revolution inspired Rivera to turn away from Cubism in search of a more politically engaged artistic practice—which he would later find in his mural work. According to his engagingly fanciful autobiography, Rivera grew disenchanted with Cubism because it lost its political vitality by accumulating "a tangle of conventions." After the First World War, he claims,

> I foresaw a new society in which the bourgeoisie would vanish and their taste, served by the subtleties of cubism, futurism, dadaism, constructivism, surrealism, and the like, would no longer monopolize the function of art. The society of the future would be a mass society. . . . A new kind of art would . . . be needed, one which appealed not to the viewers' sense of form and color directly, but through exciting subject matter. The new art, also, would not be a museum or gallery art but an art that people would have access to in places they frequented in their daily life—post offices, schools, theaters, railroad stations, public buildings. And so, logically, albeit theoretically, I arrived at mural painting.[14]

Jettisoning the traditional subjects of European monumental art in favor of scenes from Mexico's history and culture, Rivera's murals provide lovingly detailed evocations of "its land, its workers, its customs, and its popular way of life."[15] These nationalist epics flaunt Rivera's commitment to revolutionary principles by celebrating the struggles of oppressed workers and native peoples, and by satirizing the capitalist excesses of Mexico's northern neighbor. Furthermore, in revisiting the pre-Columbian heritage, the murals critique the European colonial influence to map an alternative set of continuities between past, present, and future. In their graphical simplicity and vibrant coloration, they similarly resist the elitist abstraction of the European avant-garde, aiming instead for popular accessibility and emotional impact.

Moving back to Mexico from Europe, Rivera spurned the revolution in artistic form for the promise of social revolution. He joined the Mexican Communist Party (PCM) in 1922 but was expelled from the organization in 1929 ostensibly because he collaborated with the bourgeois government in accepting a mural commission for the Palacio Nacional. Although Rivera tried to rejoin the PCM on several occasions, his flamboyant approach to politics ignited many other conflicts with the Party—and he would not be accepted back into the fold until September 1954. Exiled from the Communist Party, Rivera became an increasingly outspoken critic of the Stalin regime—especially its tactics in the Spanish Civil War, the Moscow trials, and the Molotov-Ribbentrop pact.[16] Although it would ultimately end in a bitter feud, Rivera also developed a personal and political alliance with the exiled Leon Trotsky—which further alienated him from the Mexican Communist Party.[17]

Soon after Rivera's expulsion from the PCM, Dwight D. Morrow Jr., the U.S. ambassador to Mexico, hired him to paint a mural in the Cortes Palace in

Cuernavaca. This was the first of several large-scale assignments Rivera would accept from wealthy and influential North American patrons, who attempted to co-opt his art for their own cultural agendas. In 1930 he was offered the first of several mural commissions in the United States, to paint the fresco *California Allegory* in the Luncheon Club of San Francisco's Pacific Stock Exchange. Further murals followed in San Francisco, Detroit, and New York, and his paintings also became popular attractions in North American art galleries—most significantly, in a hugely successful retrospective at New York's Museum of Modern Art in 1931.[18]

Rivera seized eagerly upon such opportunities because they enabled him to take his revolutionary art north of the border, using capitalist funding to create anti-capitalist public art.[19] He told a reporter for New York's *Herald Tribune* that after leaving the Mexican Communist Party there was "one thing left for me, to prove that my theory [of revolutionary art] would be accepted in an industrial nation, where capitalists rule. . . . I had come [to the United States] as a spy, in disguise."[20] Art, Rivera declared in a 1932 article, is "one of the most efficient subversive agents."[21] For their part, corporate sponsors clamored for his services as a means of publicizing their other-directed liberalism, at a time when the global recession was undermining faith in the capitalist system. As Frida Kahlo's biographer Hayden Herrera puts it, the implication was that "anyone who footed the bill for Rivera's Marxist messages must have the public good rather than private gain in mind."[22]

Nevertheless, Rivera's radical use of the mural form inevitably collided with the interests of his corporate clients, and with other conservative factions. His 1932 murals in the Detroit Institute of Arts, sponsored by the Ford Motor Company, were attacked not just for their Marxist reading of the Ford empire but also for what were considered their sacrilegious images.[23] Despite a lobbying effort to have the murals whitewashed, the paintings survived. Rivera's subsequent mural, at the Rockefeller Center, would not prove so fortunate. Grandiloquently titled "Man at the Crossroads Looking with Hope and High Vision to the Choosing of a New and Better Future," this most controversial and confrontational of his North American projects featured a blatantly communistic statement about class relations. Rivera was ejected from the project for refusing to remove the figure of Lenin, and the murals were covered over—and later destroyed.[24] The incident became a public sensation. While cementing Rivera's status as the *enfant terrible* of the art world, the furor effectively killed off his chances of securing further large-scale commissions in the United States. For example, soon after the battle over the Rockefeller assignment General Motors withdrew Rivera's commission for a mural in their building at the 1933 World's Fair.[25] The scandal of the Rockefeller mural ensured that by 1933 Rivera was one of the most highly publicized artists in U.S. history. As Linda Downs puts it, he was "hailed by the intellectual left and the art community and scorned by conservatives and the corporate patrons who had once sought him out."[26]

Instead of serving as propaganda for the corporate liberalism of the U.S. establishment, the Rockefeller assignment had exactly the opposite effect: the desecration of the mural exposed the repressive bounds within which artistic expression was permitted. The CPUSA officially denounced Nelson Rockefeller's dismissal of Rivera from the project, comparing it to "the vicious deeds of Hitler."[27] But Rivera and the other Mexican muralists would nonetheless continue to exert influence over Depression-era U.S. culture through the New Deal mural programs of the Public Works of Art Project (1933–34) and the Federal Arts Project (1935–43); his paintings would also remain popular with the North American public through the 1940s. Even so, his reputation diminished among U.S. art critics as they shifted their allegiances from realism and social engagement to the European experimentalism (Cubism, surrealism, etc.) that Rivera himself had earlier forsaken and to abstract expressionism.[28]

The Mexican muralists may have scorned the privatized realm of easel art,[29] but Rivera produced many such works, including numerous portrait commissions, as a means of subsidizing both his mural projects and his lifestyle—as a celebrity, as a collector of pre-Columbian art. Pete Hamill notes that by the 1940s, Rivera had become something of a brand name within Mexican bourgeois culture: owning a painting by the famous Rivera, or hiring him for a portrait, was a supreme marker of cultural distinction.[30]

The Flower Carrier differs from Rivera's society portraits, however, as it was designed for public exhibition. In 1935 Rivera was commissioned by Albert M. Bender to produce a work for the San Francisco Museum of Art. An art patron, collector, and insurance agent, Bender had helped establish San Francisco's mural program in the late 1920s and had played a significant role in enabling Rivera's entry into the United States.[31] To fulfill the commission, Rivera supplied *The Flower Carrier* (Figure 1).[32] Images of flowers are found throughout Rivera's work, taking on a range of significances. Frequently symbolizing the vibrant natural beauty of Mexico, the exotic flowers he chooses are often explicitly associated with its pre-Columbian heritage. The calla lily in particular became something of a Rivera trademark, recurring across such paintings as *Flower Day* (1925), *Flower Festival* (1925), *Flower Seller* (1941), *Flower Seller* (1942), *Calla Lily Vendor* (1943), *Nude with a Flower* (1943), *Portrait of Natasha Zakolkowa Gelman* (1943), and *Nude with Calla Lilies* (1944). In all these instances, flowers are especially connected with women. *The Flower Carrier*, however, depicts a man and a woman, both dark-skinned, who bear a more troubled relationship with the natural world.

This study of a burden carrier (*cargador*) proved a popular entry in the Museum's collection, being shown through the 1940s and early 1950s at exhibitions in Boston (1941), Toronto (1944), San Francisco (1945), Mexico City (1949), Venice (1950), Paris (1952), Stockholm (1952), and London (1953).[33] The presence of the image in several films of the late 1940s and early 1950s in itself implies that this may have been one of Rivera's most popular and most recognizable paintings in the United States. The painting presents a striking image of a Mexican peasant laborer who is borne down by the weight of a huge basket of flowers on his back. The woman helps to steady the basket as he begins to lift himself up from the ground. For these two native figures, flowers have ceased to connote the beauty of nature

1. The *Flower Carrier* [formerly *The Flower Vendor*] by Diego Rivera (1935). San Francisco Museum of Modern Art. Albert M. Bender Collection, gift of Albert M. Bender in memory of Caroline Walter. © 2007, Banco de Mexico Diego Rivera & Frida Kahlo Museums Trust, Mexico D.F. / DACS 2007

because they have been transformed into commodities. Although each individual flower weighs very little, when collected together as produce for the marketplace they constitute a crushing burden for the peasant worker. The graphical directness of the image makes its point with compassion and understatement, without detracting from the theme of economic subjection and exploitation. The painting's overt political emphasis distinguishes it from Rivera's private and corporate commissions, and it may well be the case that he was inspired by the public exhibition context of the art museum to deliver a work that was more in keeping with the political agenda of his murals.

Within the Hollywood films I discuss here, Rivera's image has been appropriated as an artistic adornment for the bourgeois home. And, in the process, it bears a potential doubleness. Unlike the paintings found in such 1940s crime films as *Laura* (1944), *The Woman in the Window* (1945), and *Scarlet Street* (1945), *The Flower Carrier* is deployed not as an original artwork—a privately owned and potentially valuable property—but as a mechanically produced and mass-circulated print. It can be comfortably located within the parameters of bourgeois taste culture, as a colorful, exotically "primitive" image by a famous modern painter that displays the refined sensibilities of the purchaser. At the same time, however, for those in the know the painting may mobilize a more radical set of political associations that create alternative reading possibilities. Moreover, although Rivera's image is displayed in private living spaces *within* the films, the very nature of cinema itself as a *public* medium means that, as Rivera himself wanted, audiences are able to encounter *The Flower Carrier* within the context of daily life rather than the institutional environment of the museum or gallery.

Proclaiming its hostility toward left politics in no uncertain terms, *The Woman on Pier 13* nonetheless spells out the status of *The Flower Carrier* as a communistic artwork. The film owes its very existence to the Hollywood Left, being one of several anti-Communist tracts produces by the Hollywood studios as a means of parading their loyal Americanism in the face of the HUAC inquisition. While none of these films was a commercial success, they were regarded as a necessary public relations exercise. Blacklisted director Joseph Losey claims that RKO used *The Woman on Pier 13*, originally titled *I Married a Communist*, as "a touchstone for establishing who was not 'a red': you offered *I Married a Communist* to anybody you thought was a Communist, and if they turned it down, they were."[34] Set in San Francisco—where Rivera began his North American murals, and where *The Flower Carrier* itself is housed—the film's background story involves Communist infiltration of waterfront unions, inspired by the strikes that had shut down San Francisco's docks in 1934 and 1948.[35]

Brad Collins (Robert Ryan) is the vice president of a shipping company, but his current respectability conceals a guilty secret. Under his real name, Frank Johnson, Collins had been a Communist agitator in the troubled years of the Depression, when one of the labor disputes he organized led to a man's death. The plot begins when fashion photographer Christine Norman (Janis Carter), the girlfriend from his Communist past, spots Collins in a bar with his new wife, Nan (Laraine Day). A blonde siren who lures unsuspecting young men into the Communist Party, Christine still holds a torch for her former lover. Spurred on by jealousy, she informs Party leader Vanning (Thomas Gomez) about Johnson's new life—and Vanning proceeds to blackmail Collins into sabotaging his company's negotiations with the waterfront unions. In a scenario familiar from gangster films such as *Little Caesar* (1931), the Party will not allow Collins to escape his obligations to them ("You can't quit—they won't let you," Brad protests). As is typical of Hollywood's anti-Communist films, the film depicts the Party as a criminal gang that is set on destroying the American way of life. Demanding unswerving allegiance from its members, the Party expects them to renounce individual liberties, emotions, and pleasures. As the menacing Vanning warns Christine: "You've been given important responsibilities in the Party. They're not to be endangered by personal entanglements."

A print of the Rivera painting occupies a prominent place on one wall of Christine's apartment, which is the locale for several key scenes in the film (see Figure 2). The composition of shots frequently offers the painting a central role in the visual

2. *The Woman on Pier 13*.

field, playing up its affiliation with Christine in particular. One major scene, for example, involves a heated exchange between Christine and Nan's brother Don (John Agar). The victim of Christine's charms, the politically naive Don begins to spout Communist doctrine without realizing that she is manipulating him on behalf of the Party. Figures 3 and 4 are taken from the scene in which Don confronts Christine after he has learned of her political loyalties. The scene opens with a long shot that presents an expansive view of the apartment, with *The Flower Carrier* clearly visible on the right-hand side of the screen. Christine comes through the door on the left and then moves over toward the painting. The camera pans right to follow her as she walks, and she places her coat and bag on the chair in front of it. The camera reframing places the Rivera painting in the center of the image, and also introduces us to the presence of Don in the right-hand foreground. As Christine moves toward Don, he begins to accuse her of loving him less than she loves "the commie party."

During their altercation, Christine lets slip that Brad is also working for the Party. To prevent Don from exposing his brother-in-law, Vanning orders his assassination. Suspecting foul play, Nan begins to investigate Don's death and confronts Christine in her apartment—in a scene that accords unusual prominence to *The Flower Carrier* (Figure 5). Christine taunts Nan with her knowledge of Brad's guilty past: "The great Bradley Collins is really Frank Johnson, a member of the Communist Party—and working for the party right now. . . ." Showing Nan material from Brad's Party file, she declares mockingly: "Charming, weren't we! Young love

3. *The Woman on Pier 13.*

4. *The Woman on Pier 13.*

5. *The Woman on Pier 13.*

among the lower classes. Two young Communists out to save the world." However, Christine herself will soon follow Don to the grave, as Vanning pushes the
increasingly unstable woman out of a window.[36] Given its association both with the
Communist radical Diego Rivera and with San Francisco, it hardly seems accidental that *The Flower Carrier* is permitted a key role in such scenes. By associating the
painting with the wayward Christine, the film renders it an explicit signifier of
"Communist art." At the same time, the painting also suggests a more intense affiliation with Christine that chimes with the way it is employed in *The Prowler* and *In
a Lonely Place*. Like Susan Gilvray and Laurel Grey, Christine is a woman who
ultimately lacks authority and agency: despite her seeming self-confidence she is
brutalized, and ultimately killed, by the manipulative Vanning. It could very well
be some clued-in anti-Communist who chose Rivera's painting for the film, but the
inclusion of *The Flower Carrier* may conceivably have a more resistant significance.
Joseph Losey claims that an extremely reluctant Nicholas Ray was one of several
directors offered this film project and that he had worked on the script, rehearsed
the actors, and even built the sets.[37] Though Ray's biographer Bernard Eisenschitz
disputes the extent of Ray's involvement with the film, it is nonetheless intriguing
that Losey specifically mentions Ray's influence on the design of the sets.[38]

The Prowler, one of Thom Andersen's prime examples of film gris, is shaped by
key figures from the blacklist generation. Joseph Losey, who would soon face
political exile in Britain, directed the film, and it was scripted by the blacklisted Dalton Trumbo, using the soon-to-be-blacklisted Hugo Butler as his front.[39] As one of

the Hollywood Ten, Trumbo could not receive an official screen credit but, in a coded defiance of the blacklist, Losey managed to smuggle him into the film by casting him as the voice of radio disc jockey John Gilvray, who is heard several times through the movie.[40] In a strange twist of fate, Hugo Butler and his wife, Jean Rouverol, fled to Mexico to escape subpoenas from HUAC—and they soon found themselves living next door to Diego Rivera.[41]

One of numerous reworkings of the *Double Indemnity* formula of adultery and murder, *The Prowler* focuses on characters whose lives are blighted by a culture of greed and competition.[42] Webb Garwood (Van Heflin) is an embittered, self-serving police patrolman who embarks on a scheme to murder John Gilvray (Sherry Hall) so that he can obtain both his widow, Susan (Evelyn Keyes), and his money. A rootless individual who is constantly performing, Garwood conceals his true intentions to pass himself off as a decent and respectable citizen. He hates being a cop, for example, because it makes him a servant of the people, yet he is quick to exploit the uniform to his own advantage. He even uses it to get away with murder, convincing everyone that he's a "square guy" after he shoots Gilvray as a suspected prowler. Garwood's respectable façade veils a monstrous, all-consuming class envy. The film suggests, however, that this derives not from merely individual failings but is nurtured by a mercenary and materialistic society. Losey later claimed that this was "a film about false values. About the means justifying the end and the end justifying the means. '100,000 bucks, a Cadillac and a blonde' were the *sine qua non* of American life at the time and it didn't matter how you got them— whether you stole the girl from somebody else, stole the money and got the Cadillac from corruption."[43]

A hard-hitting expose of the perils of ambition, *The Prowler* was a rather sensational item at the time. The Production Code Administration (PCA) objected to the film's sordid tone, deriving especially from scenarios of adultery and extramarital pregnancy. "According to Spiegel," reported Ezra Goodman in the *Daily News* on March 7, 1950, "the picture presented a number of censorship problems, the foremost one being that the woman commits adultery and is not explicitly punished at the end. 'But we fought it and won,' says Spiegel. 'The woman sort of atones for it by suffering.'"[44] PCA chief Joseph Breen "objected to the low moral tone of the film and insisted that details of the adulterous affair and the pregnancy be kept to a minimum in the script. . . . Breen [eventually] accepted the script but was consulted throughout the production by assistant director Robert Aldrich on scenes in which moral tone was in question, including acceptable visible signs of the pregnancy."[45] Reviewers in both the trade and mainstream press frequently pointed to the scandalous nature of the plot. "For fans who like their screen fare on the sordid side," *Boxoffice* noted, "the feature has much to offer; and, if its seamy-side ramifications—plus the Heflin name—are smartly exploited, the offering should attract profitable business."[46] This "combination of illicit love, murder and obvious premarital relationship," proclaimed *Variety*, is "a bawdy, daring story that must be restricted to the adult market. . . . The clandestine romance of the principals is unfolded with no punches pulled."[47]

Besides playing at the boundaries of what the Production Code would allow, the film also provides a critique of the broader social pressures that direct and constrain the choices of its central characters. This is especially well illustrated by the film's final maneuvers. Susan discovers she is pregnant soon after she marries Garwood. But rather than celebrating the prospect of a family, Garwood fears that the child will expose his adulterous affair with Susan, and cast suspicion on his supposedly accidental killing of Gilvray. Garwood drives her off to a ghost town in the Mojave Desert so they can have the baby in secret. The ghost town, Calico, becomes a particularly resonant metaphor for the film. Built on the get-rich dreams of gold digging, the deserted and obliterated community testifies to the ozymandian delusions of a society grounded in the pursuit of wealth. The town is a relic of an America of the past, the America celebrated in the optimistic expansionism of the western. With the frontier spirit replaced, and displaced, by a regulated consumer society, the devastated and depopulated town foregrounds the folly of such materialistic aspirations. As Garwood and Susan vainly seek to make a temporary home in this blighted landscape of sun, wind, and ruin, they are caught up in a parodic version of 1950s domesticity (husband outside washing the car, wife indoors doing the dishes).

For Garwood and Susan, the ghost town amounts to a hellish negation of their dreams of achievement, acceptance, and happiness. She becomes fully aware of Garwood's ruthlessness when he attempts to kill the doctor he brings in to save her and the baby. Susan thwarts his plan by tipping the doctor off, allowing him to escape to safety with the child. Garwood then confesses his crimes to the tormented Susan. Losey identified his speech as the film's "moment of truth" because it locates Garwood's perverse actions as part of a more a systemic corruption within U.S. society:[48]

> So what? So I'm no good. But I'm no worse than anybody else. You work in a store—you knock down on the cash register. You're a big boss—the income tax. Ward heeler—you sell votes. A lawyer—take bribes. I was a cop—I used a gun. But whatever I did, I did for you . . . How am I any different from those other guys? Some do it for a million, some for ten. I did it for 62,000.[49]

The final images of the film show an exposed and isolated Garwood scrabbling up a spoil heap from the old gold mines in a vain attempt to escape from the police. They shoot him in the back, and he collapses into the dirt. This may seem a fitting ending for a man who has manipulated others for his own advancement, and who has displayed such resentment for his lot in life, but at the same time there is also sufficient acknowledgment that Garwood is never fully an agent of his misplaced values and actions. As James Leahy puts it, "Garwood's commitment to a vision of the world as a place of ruthless competition is sufficiently one-sided or warped to be mildly pathological, yet it is intimately connected with many of the underlying assumptions of the world in which he lives."[50]

The Flower Carrier appears in the first half of the film, as an adornment within the living room of the luxurious suburban home Susan shares with her husband.

The script held in the BFI Joseph Losey Collection has no mention of *The Flower Carrier*. On page 2, Susan's living room is described as "comfortably and tastefully furnished in Barker Brothers' more expensive style of four years ago. There are overstuffed chairs and a couch; two bad landscapes on the wall."[51] In his interview with Michel Ciment, Losey recalled that he collaborated with visual consultant, John Hubley—an animator and co-founder of UPA studios who would soon face the blacklist—to invent "a style for *The Prowler* that I wanted to reflect the tawdriness of those Hollywood imitations of Spanish houses which were neither comfortable nor beautiful but status symbols."[52] As with the other films discussed here, it is difficult to specify just who was responsible for selecting *The Flower Carrier* for *The Prowler*. For example, included in the "Staff List" accompanying the script are art director Boris Leven, set decorator Jack Mapes, first prop man John Orlando and second prop man Al Hersh. Like Dalton Trumbo, Hubley, Orlando, and Hersh receive no official screen credit for their work on the film.[53] Any of these individuals, or someone else entirely, could feasibly have recommended the Rivera painting.

Rivera's image plays a strategic role in several scenes that outline the protagonists' failures and dissatisfactions. Susan meets Garwood, along with his partner Bud (John Maxwell), when she calls the police to report a prowler outside her home. Struck as much as by Susan's well-heeled lifestyle as by her looks ("that is quite a dish," Bud says approvingly), Garwood sees an opportunity for himself. He later returns on his own and begins to take advantage of the frightened, lonely woman. Left alone in the evenings while her elderly husband does his radio show, Susan is all too vulnerable to his aggressive seductions. Emotionally manipulated by the two men in her life, Susan, noted *Variety*, is "more a victim of circumstances than an out-and-out cheater."[54]

When Garwood visits the house with Bud, the action is restricted to the corridors and bathroom. When he returns, however, on the pretext of making an official follow-up call, Susan invites him into the living room for a coffee. While she is in the kitchen, Garwood scrutinizes a framed glamour photograph of Susan (Figure 6). "Looks like somebody round here's been in show business," he calls out. "That's right," she says off screen, and the film cuts to a long shot, roughly aligned with Garwood's perspective, that shows *The Flower Carrier* for the first time (Figure 7). Hanging on a wall of the living room, close by the doorway to the kitchen, Rivera's painting is immediately associated with Susan. In close succession, moreover, the film has presented three framed images that are inevitably in communication with one another: the photograph of Susan's past aspirations; the image of exploited labor in *The Flower Carrier*; and the framing of the domesticated Susan within the kitchen doorway.

The scene develops into a lengthy dialogue between Garwood and Susan. Discovering they come from the same small town in Indiana, they admit to one another that their lives have not measured up to youthful expectations. Garwood rails against the "lousy breaks" that have blighted his life and made him "just another dumb cop." He blames the poverty of his childhood on his father's lack of

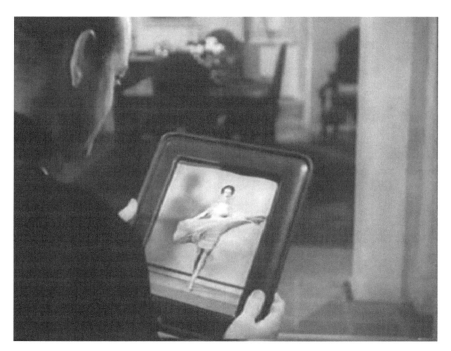

6. *The Prowler*.

7. *The Prowler*.

8.   *The Prowler.*

ambition, and sees a resentful coach as losing him a basketball scholarship that would have put him through college.[55] To enliven the flow of dialogue the film uses a range of camera set ups, including that shown in Figure 8, which once more connects Susan to *The Flower Carrier*. Here, the painting is out of focus in the background but it remains recognizable because its position within the shot has been carefully prepared for by the camera position shown in Figure 7. The shot in Figure 8 is organized along a 180-degree axis of alignment from Susan to Garwood to *The Flower Carrier*.

Garwood's next visit to the Gilvray house provides an opportunity for Susan to articulate her disappointments in life. Failing to make it as an actress in Hollywood, she married Gilvray for children and for security. But she is now the childless trophy wife of a rich, elderly, and possessive husband who keeps her a virtual prisoner in the home. Losey described Susan as

> the product of the thing that happens so often in America, and still happens everywhere that I know of in the west. In spite of all the pretensions which have grown up and have to some extent been realized, the wife is left alone, presumably with everything to see she's comfortable, but with no friends, with no values excepting those from her childhood, with no love, essentially, and in this case with no children.[56]

Gilvray is absent from home most of the time, but exerts control over Susan's life through a form of surveillance by radio. He insists that she listens to his evening

9. *The Prowler.*

broadcast and then quizzes her on it subsequently ("I have to listen because he always asks me how he was"). Gilvray's voice later comes back from the dead to haunt her, when, in the ghost town, Garwood accidentally plays one of his transcription discs on the phonograph.

When she tells him that Gilvray keeps the cigarettes locked in a drawer, Garwood taunts her that she too is under strict control: "Does he keep everything locked up? . . . Probably does. A mean, jealous guy like that wants his wife all to himself. I can't say I blame him—I'd do the same myself." Garwood liberates the cigarettes by opening the locked drawer with a hairpin, and he continues to extend the seductive metaphor:

GARWOOD: There! See how silly it is to keep things locked up.
SUSAN: Maybe. But it did delay you for a little while.
GARWOOD: Is that all he wants—to delay things?

At this point the film cuts to a reaction shot of Susan that once more juxtaposes her onscreen with *The Flower Carrier* (Figure 9). Framed again in the doorway of the kitchen as she fetches a beer for Garwood, Susan is identified as a domesticated proletariat who is destined to be exploited by the men in her life. Another remarkable feature of this shot is the way that a display of flowers has been arranged on the table right in front of Rivera's painting, which presents a kind of before-and-after sequence in association with Rivera's picture. As Susan is in the kitchen, the film cuts to Garwood rifling through Gilvray's drawer and finding a copy of his last will and testament. We realize retrospectively that this is the moment that inspires his murder

10.   *The Prowler.*

scheme. A close shot of the document is followed immediately by a cut back to the
wall with the Rivera painting: Susan walks out of the kitchen with a beer can in her
hand and walks left, in front of the painting, the camera panning to follow her movement (Figure 10). She rejoins Garwood, and he continues to probe her defenses.
"Why did you marry him, Susan?" he asks, and she stands up again and tells more of
her story. The camera holds tightly on her as she walks, panning around until she
pauses momentarily and speaks of the disappointment of her marriage. Figure 11
echoes Figure 8 in the way it places *The Flower Carrier* in the background, out of focus
but still visible, while Susan articulates her dissatisfactions. The scene closes with
Garwood making a sexual advance on Susan, which she rebuffs.

The painting appears for a final time in a scene that takes place after Garwood
and Susan have become lovers. During an assignation in the Gilvray home,
Garwood expresses his wish to escape his lowly position as a cop by buying a
motor court near Las Vegas. Susan does not warm to his plan, however, and Garwood shows his displeasure by putting on his jacket and leaving (Figure 12). This is
one of many occasions when Garwood psychologically brutalizes Susan when she
does not fall in line with his wishes and, as in Figures 8 and 11, *The Flower Carrier*
stamps its silent presence in the background of the image. This is the painting's
final appearance in the film. Garwood next meets Susan in the house after he has
killed her husband in a staged accident. She is packing up her effects, ready to move
out, and *The Flower Carrier* and the other paintings have been removed from the
walls. But Susan is prevented from starting a new life on her own when Garwood

11.   *The Prowler.*

12.   *The Prowler.*

convinces her that he did not intend to kill Gilvray, and asks her to marry him. She is about to leave the house forever, exchanging one problem marriage for one that is even worse. She may soon have the child she desired, but hardly under circumstances she would have wished for.

In a Lonely Place presents a resonant mood picture of Hollywood during an era of crisis and transition, when the movie industry was reeling from the pressures of HUAC, a downturn in cinema attendance, and the government-enforced breakup of vertical integration. The film was made by Santana Pictures, the independent production company set up by the film's star, Humphrey Bogart.[57] A well-known liberal, Bogart was one of the high-profile Hollywood celebrities who joined the Committee for the First Amendment protest against HUAC.[58] Along with such other luminaries as Lauren Bacall, Danny Kaye, Richard Conte, Gene Kelly, John Huston, William Wyler, Evelyn Keyes, Marsha Hunt, John Garfield, and Paul Henreid, Bogart flew to Washington during the Hollywood Ten hearings to oppose HUAC's assault on civil liberties.[59] Bogart himself had tangled with the anti-Communist crusade in 1940, when ex-Party informer John L. Leech named him as a political subversive—together with James Cagney, Philip Dunne, Melvyn Douglas, Franchot Tone, Fredric March, and other Hollywood figures. When these accusations made headlines, Bogart and company had to face the Dies Committee (HUAC) to deny they were members or supporters of the Communist Party.[60] This encounter with HUAC, suggests biographer Jeffrey Meyers, alerted Bogart "to the personal and political dangers of Communist witch hunts, which threatened the constitutional rights of all citizens, and made him sympathetic when colleagues had to face similar charges in 1947."[61]

Bogart's involvement in the Committee for the First Amendment turned sour when he came under fire for his political beliefs. With his career threatened by a barrage of hostile coverage from the right-wing press, Bogart was forced into a public act of recantation. Five months after the Washington jaunt, the March 1948 issue of *Photoplay* carried an article under Bogart's byline entitled "I'm No Communist," in which he distanced himself from both the Hollywood Ten and the Committee for the First Amendment.[62] While Bogart was clearly demoralized by the fallout from his HUAC experience, Nicholas Ray, the director of *In a Lonely Place*, also had reason to tread cautiously. Part of the generation that experienced a seismic political and cultural awakening during the Depression, Ray had worked in radical theater and in a range of left-oriented New Deal cultural projects.[63] Ray joined the Communist Party in the mid-1930s, and worked repeatedly with left radicals.[64] Despite his political background, Ray escaped blacklisting, reputedly because of the patronage of RKO head Howard Hughes.[65] Perry Bruskin, one of Ray's colleagues in the agitational Theatre of Action collective, characterized Ray as a sympathetic but not committed Marxist: "Nick, politically, was just a romantic. I don't think he was deeply political even when he was in this deeply political group. I think the combination of theatre and politics interested him, not politics itself."[66]

Bogart first worked with Nicholas Ray when the star chose him as the director of Santana's debut production, the earnest social problem film *Knock on Any Door* (1949). Bernard Eisenschitz suggests that Bogart admired Ray's first film, *They Live*

By Night (1948), because of "the intimist treatment beneath which a teeming social activity could be glimpsed."[67] While *Knock on Any Door* proved too leaden to deliver on such promise, this description does apply to *In a Lonely Place*. The film centers upon an unstable screenwriter, Dixon Steele (Bogart), who becomes the prime suspect in a murder case at the same time that he becomes romantically involved with his sophisticated neighbor, Laurel Grey (Gloria Grahame). As "a special figure moving through a vulgar world,"[68] Dix provokes suspicion because he is an enigmatic, undomesticated artist who deviates from consensual norms of behavior and sentiment. His relationship with Laurel disintegrates when she fears that Dix may indeed be a killer, her suspicions enflamed by his frequent outbursts of violence and by the skeptical judgments of others. The very exceptionalism that attracts her ultimately makes Laurel want to flee him ("Why can't he be like other people?" she laments).

In a Lonely Place is often read as a covert portrayal of blacklist-era Hollywood. Victor Perkins, for example, argues, "The relevance to the blacklist is clear, and we are invited, though not compelled, to see *In a Lonely Place* as reflecting on suspicion, deceit and hysteria in personal relations under a threat which, of course, it cannot name, that of the Hollywood witch hunt."[69] James W. Palmer similarly posits that the film "offers a critique of Hollywood itself for its bad faith in turning on its own artists, and for its complicity in promoting an atmosphere of paranoia."[70] Although the film focuses on the dynamics of paranoia internal to Steele's character, Palmer notes that it also sketches a broader culture of suspicion within the embattled Hollywood of the postwar years:

> In holding the mirror up to Hollywood, the film exposes that community's complicity in creating the conditions under which people betrayed their friends. . . . The film advocates a need for tolerance and trust by depicting a world where values collapse under the strain of mutual suspicions. . . . [It] focuses on a paranoia that extends beyond the psychological manifestations of a single man. The real crime that this film exposes is the undermining of human trust through a process of social exclusion.[71]

Although he is characterized as an elitist writer who disdains popular tastes, the film nonetheless aligns Dix with the screenwriters of the Hollywood Ten because of the way he is caught up within a persecutory culture. Dix's fears of exposure and betrayal are far from groundless because the film depicts a world in which "nearly all characters participate in conspiratorial patterns of behavior to exclude or isolate" him.[72] As artist, as celebrity, and as murder suspect, he comes under constant scrutiny from others. It is hardly surprising, then, that *In a Lonely Place* presents the most intricate, extended, and mysterious deployment of *The Flower Carrier*, situating the Rivera image both within an elaborate mise-en-scène of artistic references and also within a complex textual meditation on love, loyalty, art, and violence. The use of *The Flower Carrier* in this film is prepared for by a brief reference in the first chapter of Dorothy B. Hughes's source novel. The protagonist, a very differently conceptualized Dix Steele, visits the home of his wartime buddy Brub Nicolai (played by Frank Lovejoy in the film). Via free indirect discourse, filtered through Dix's subjectivity, the book describes the décor of the house Brub shares with his wife, Sylvia: "There was pale matting on the polished floor; there was a big green chair and heavy white drapes across the Venetian blinds. Good prints, O'Keeffe and Rivera."[73] While this particular reference locates Rivera's work as evidence of discriminating cultural tastes, the film itself situates *The Flower Carrier* within a more complex network of cultural associations.

Laurel and Dix are attracted to one another because of their shared aesthetic sensibilities, signaled in particular by the playful wit of their romantic interaction.[74] These bruised, tentative lovers find in one another an opportunity, no matter how brief, to establish a space apart from the vulgar machinations of Hollywood and the cultural universe it services. Decorously equipped with a wide variety of paintings, sculptures, and other art objects, their two apartments speak volumes about the enlightened cultural tastes they share. The art we see in their homes is not mere set dressing, but serves as a constant reminder that, amongst other things, this is a film about art. Dix is an artist who struggles to reconcile his aesthetic ideals with a popular, market-driven cultural institution that he has nothing but contempt for—he describes one producer as a "popcorn salesman." In its handling of the crime narrative, *In a Lonely Place* reveals a very different aesthetic agenda from the sensationalism of *The Prowler*. The multiple artistic references and the sustained discourse on the values of art reflect the film's own aspirations as an "enlightened" and distinctive Hollywood product.

While his relationship with Laurel develops, Dix is writing an adaptation of the lurid potboiler *Althea Bruce*. Laurel is the muse who inspires him to transform the tawdry melodrama, extravagant in emotion and incident, into a distinctively personal artwork that echoes his doomed relationship with Laurel.[75] Rejecting the novel's hackneyed formulas, Dix crafts a script that has the integrity of personal truth. The two versions of *Althea Bruce* find their counterpart in an opposition the film establishes between Laurel and the murder victim, Mildred Atkinson (Martha Stewart). When Dix takes the young hat-check girl back to his apartment, to read out the novel he doesn't want to look at it himself, Mildred is moved and thrilled by its cheap emotionalism. Vivaciously vulgar, Mildred is the ideal consumer of an aesthetically impoverished popular culture. Immediately out of place in Dix's high-cultural surroundings, she is an intrusive reminder of the marketplace his art must ultimately serve. By contrast, Laurel's refined tastes parallel those of Dix, distinguishing her from the crowds who flock to Hollywood's gaudy entertainments.

The film's self-reflexive discoursing on taste, culture, art, and cinema illustrates the cultural and aesthetic agenda of *In a Lonely Place* itself as a differentiated Hollywood product. This sophisticated exploration of human emotions effectively uses its murder mystery plot as a pretext, transfiguring Dorothy B. Hughes's original serial-killer novel into a Hollywood art film that reflects on its own operations. As most critics point out, the film retains very little from its source novel: besides introducing the Hollywood context, it also transforms Dix from a serial killer into a man who is brought to the brink of murder by pressures exerted from within and without. As Dana Polan puts it, *In a Lonely Place* "marks its difference from typical Hollywood plots and gropes towards another identity."[76] In demonstrating alternative possibilities for popular cinema, this is a non-Hollywood, anti-Hollywood Hollywood film.

The Flower Carrier is one of numerous well-known artworks displayed in Laurel's apartment. Besides emblematizing her enlightened tastes, they also distinguish her sensibility from the masculine accoutrements of Dix's taste. Laurel's home exhibits more feminine aesthetic preferences, favoring impressionist studies of women in particular. For example, Renoir paintings hang in the living room and hallway, while ballerina studies by Edgar Degas have a prominent position in her bedroom. Throughout the film, the mise-en-scène affiliates such artworks with individual characters and their emotional dilemmas. There are some intriguing choices here concerning when particular paintings are or are not included within shots, and which characters are associated with them. As the accompanying frame grabs make clear, *The Flower Carrier* remains a distinctive presence within a range of compositions because it is so readily identifiable from a distance. It is worth highlighting a few specific moments that illustrate the manner in which meanings tend to cluster around Rivera's painting.

The Flower Carrier is one of three art reproductions adorning the main wall of Laurel's living room, the setting for many key scenes that develop the relationship between the two characters. From left to right, these are Vincent Van Gogh's *La Mousmé* (1888), Pierre-Auguste Renoir's *La Loge* (1874), and *The Flower Carrier*. The juxtaposition of these paintings permits various interpretations, but one striking feature they share is the use of flowers. The young girl in *La Mousmé* holds a sprig of oleander as she sits in her chair, while in *La Loge* the fashionable woman in the opera box wears flowers in her hair and has a floral garland on her bodice.[77] As discussed earlier, within *The Flower Carrier* flowers are not decorative props but signifiers of exploited labor. The two canonical European paintings present sympathetic portraits of women by male artists, which nonetheless operate a gendered division of labor between the male artist-subject and the female model who is subordinated both to his gaze and to the gaze of the spectator.[78] A similar power differential is played out through the relationship of Dix and Laurel in the film, even though Dix himself is constantly subjected to the judgmental gaze of others.

Whereas the women in the two European paintings are displayed as objects of aesthetic pleasure, the woman who aids the peasant worker in *The Flower Carrier* has a more utilitarian role. The Rivera picture offers the flower not as ornamentation but as a crop gathered for the marketplace by peasant workers, who themselves are unable to benefit from the fruits of their labors. The painting thus intrinsically exposes the material conditions behind the production of the image, which the other paintings veil and take for granted. While Rivera's picture is in itself highly attractive as a work of art, its overt political subject renders it more than an exclusively aesthetic proposition.

Obviously enough, Laurel is the character most consistently associated with *The Flower Carrier*, as exemplified by Figure 13. Visually, the film connects her—in different ways, and at different points—with all three paintings on the wall. For example, in Figure 14 her stance mirrors in some ways the posture of the girl in

13.   *In a Lonely Place.*

14.   *In a Lonely Place.*

15.   *In a Lonely Place.*

La Mousmé: they face the same direction, and hold their arms and heads at roughly the same angles. Within the same shot, Bogart's posture echoes that of the *cargador* in *The Flower Carrier*, the comparison only underscored by the contrast between the peasant's white garb and Bogart's black jacket. Figures 15 and 16 illustrate another suggestive connection between the characters and other paintings. These frame grabs are taken from one of the final scenes, when the increasingly unbalanced Dix surprises Laurel at home as she is making plans to flee the city so she can avoid marrying him.

When Laurel leaves the room to hide the evidence of her imminent departure, Dix begins to realize that she is betraying him. As he picks up a cigarette from the table on the right in Figure 15, both *La Loge* and *The Flower Carrier* are held in the background of the shot. The camera then cuts to a closer view of Dix putting the cigarette to his mouth, the reframing juxtaposing him with the Renoir picture (Figure 16). He lights the match and raises it toward his face, and then pauses—a moment of illumination both literally and metaphorically. *La Loge* depicts a scene in which a man and a woman are together in the same space, a box at the opera, but have very different agendas—the woman looking out in the direction of the painter, while, behind her back, the man uses his opera glasses to spy on someone else in the auditorium. The man and woman within the film are also at this point looking, so to speak, in vastly different directions.

Laurel's affiliation with *The Flower Carrier* is merited because, as with Susan in *The Prowler*, she is involved in an abusive relationship with a psychologically

16.   *In a Lonely Place.*

unstable man. Volunteering herself into an increasingly subordinated role with Dix, Laurel allows him to consume her sense of self (and, almost, her life).[79] Once she has inspired Dix to work again, she takes on the role of handmaiden of his art—watching over him, tending house, and typing his manuscript. Dix also colonizes Laurel's subjectivity when she lets anxieties about his behavior erode both her sleep and her sense of self. But there is logic, too, in the way the film links Dix to *The Flower Carrier*. Dana Polan notes, "As a screenwriter, Dix is immediately caught up in a nexus of power that means he is never really able to be his own man."[80] As a writer within the Hollywood system, Dix must hand over the product of his labor to others, with no claim over what they do with it. His fragile status as a creative worker in the industrial battleground of Hollywood is illustrated by what happens to the Althea Bruce script. Even though the producer applauds its quality, Dix nonetheless fumes at the underhand appropriation of the script— which his agent passed on surreptitiously.

The most dramatic association between Dix and Rivera's painting occurs when it provides the backdrop to his first kiss with Laurel (Figures 17 and 18). This shot presents the closest view of *The Flower Carrier* in the film, but renders it a somewhat menacing accompaniment to the start of their relationship. The low angle camera sets the painting at an off-kilter diagonal, while the claustrophobic, out-of-focus kiss that it pans to, with Dix clutching Laurel's head in his hands (Figure 18), will itself later find a sinister echo in the scene where he strangles her.[81] The staging of the kiss against the backdrop of *The Flower Carrier* suggests how, in their

17. *In a Lonely Place.*

18. *In a Lonely Place.*

own distinctive ways, both Dix and Laurel carry extreme burdens that threaten to break them. They may survive, but the relationship will not.[82]

While the blacklist era is most often discussed in terms of the trials and tribulations facing radical screenwriters, the strange case of *The Flower Carrier* suggests an alternative way of thinking of responses to the repressive climate of postwar Hollywood. Several of these films seem to mobilize Rivera's painting as a coded signifier of left-wing political affiliation. A semiotic calling card for political voices that have been silenced during an era of repression and compromise, the painting's very muteness testifies to the legacy of such repression. While screenwriters were hampered in the words they were allowed to put into the mouths of their characters, *The Flower Carrier's* silent presence within the mise-en-scène can speak volumes by setting in play a suggestive network of intra-, extra-, and cross-textual associations. It is noteworthy, too, how often the painting is affiliated with unhappy and abused women as a gendered underclass.[83]

The painting would have been attractive to those filmmakers within or sympathetic to the Left for several reasons. Despite his uneasy relations with official party machines, Rivera remained a tireless advocate of leftist politics and the cause of proletarian revolution. His repudiation of Stalin may also have increased his appeal for leftist film practitioners who were disenchanted with the pro-Stalin orthodoxy of the CPUSA. Rivera's dedication to the cause of public art may have struck a chord with leftist creative practitioners working in the popular forum of Hollywood cinema, who similarly had to find ways of negotiating between their political convictions and the regulatory pressures exerted by commerce, by government, and by censorship. The controversy over the Rockefeller mural had established Rivera as a *cause célèbre* in the struggle for creative expression in the face of political repression, and this would have been an attractive reference point for left-wing filmmakers during the HUAC period. The dialectic between co-optation and subversion that characterizes Rivera's adventures in the United States may have had particular resonance for the Hollywood Left during this troubled period. Above all else, Diego Rivera and his work certainly embodied an alternative conceptualization of America and Americanism to that peddled so aggressively by HUAC and the FBI.[84]

4 A Monarch for the Millions

JEWISH FILMMAKERS, SOCIAL
COMMENTARY, AND THE POSTWAR
CYCLE OF BOXING FILMS

Peter Stanfield

> *Remember that Jewish boy in the Fannie Hurst era,*
> *that sensitive son of the unworldly Talmudist? He*
> *wanted to become a great violinist, a great surgeon, a*
> *great lawyer. His breed has vanished from today's fic-*
> *tion about the East Side. We are more "realistic" now*
> *and out typical Jewish lads become prizefighters, hood-*
> *lums, gangsters, and what not.*
>
> Meyer Levin, "The East Side Gangsters of the
> Paper-Backs: The Jewish Novels That Millions Buy,"
> *Commentary* (October 1953)

Champion (1949) opens and closes with a ringside radio commentator setting the scene for Midge Kelly's defense of his championship title: "Listen to the crowd. Actually, they're cheering more than a man tonight. They're cheering a story; a story that could only have been lived in the fight game: a story of a boy who rose from the depths of poverty to become champion of the world." After being bru-tally battered by his opponent, Kelly, played by Kirk Douglas, makes a dramatic comeback in the final round of the bout and holds on to his title. His victory comes at a high price, and he dies in his dressing room from a brain hemorrhage. The hero's rise from the gutter of ghetto life to the dizzying heights of a penthouse overlooking the city, followed by an equally dramatic fall, was already pure for-mula by the time Carl Foreman had turned Ring Lardner's short story into a screenplay. RKO, however, contested the idea of common ownership of this for-mula when they took Stanley Kramer, *Champion*'s producer, and production com-pany Screen Plays II to court on the grounds that they borrowed too freely from its own production of *The Set-Up*. Attorneys for Screen Plays II and United Artists, the film's distributor, countered that the two films were sufficiently different and that the Howard Hughes–run corporation was attempting a spoiling action against box office competition. Their cry of corporate bullying went unheeded and the judge ruled that *Champion* should be shorn of its offending scenes.[1] These scenes were relatively minor moments in a film that shared the same premise not only with *The Set-Up*, but also with many other boxing movies—that mobsters control boxing, and that corruption, inside and outside the ring, is endemic to the sport. The struggle against moral depravity is as much a part of the formula as the struggle against economic deprivation.[2]

Following the critical and box office success of *Body and Soul* (1947) and *Champion* (1949), the major studios and new independents produced a number of films that exploited the sport of boxing. These included *Killer McCoy* (1947), *Big Punch* (1948), *Whiplash* (1948), *In This Corner* (1948), *Leather Gloves* (1948), *Fighting Fools* (1949), *Duke of Chicago* (1949), *Ringside* (1949), *The Set-Up* (1949), *Right Cross* (1950), *The Golden Gloves Story* (1950), *Iron Man* (1951), *Roaring City* (1951), *Breakdown* (1952), *The Fighter* (1952), *Kid Monk Baroni* (1952), *The Ring* (1952), *Flesh and Fury* (1952), *Champ for a Day* (1953), *The Joe Louis Story* (1953), *Tennessee Champ* (1954), *The Square Jungle* (1955), *Killer's Kiss* (1955), *The Leather Saint* (1956), *Somebody Up There Likes Me* (1956), *The Harder They Fall* (1956), *World in My Corner* (1956), *The Crooked Circle* (1957), and *Monkey on My Back* (1957). The cycle continued sporadically into the latter part of the decade before ending with *Requiem for a Heavyweight* (1962). Boxing also featured prominently in a number of comedies of the period—*The Kid from Brooklyn* (1946), *Sailor Beware* (1952), and *Off Limits* (1953), for example—and in crime films and melodramas of the same period: *The Killers* (1946), *Till the End of Time* (1946), *Nobody Lives Forever* (1946), *Brute Force* (1947), *The Street with No Name* (1948), *Tension* (1950), *The Big Night* (1951), *Glory Alley* (1952), *Turning Point* (1952), *The Quiet Man* (1952), *From Here to Eternity* (1953), *On the Waterfront* (1954), *Kiss Me Deadly* (1955), and *The Big Combo* (1955).

A good number of these films had little or no input from Hollywood's left-leaning fraternity. Nevertheless, the boxing story attracted a disproportionately large number of left-wing Jewish filmmakers who played a significant role in the development of the cycle's key films. This chapter considers how the boxing story enabled some filmmakers to politicize and individualize a popular film cycle. These filmmakers understood that the boxing story offered a particularly viable vehicle for broad social commentary, a vehicle that could also be personalized by evoking a nostalgic vision of a ghetto community. In the same way that left-leaning writers and filmmakers made use of crime stories to offer a critique of contemporary society via a medium that appealed directly to the masses, they also made use of boxing stories. In this context, the boxing story, with its proletarian protagonist, his struggles with organized crime, and an unforgiving social and economic order, proved to be highly conducive to the articulation of a radical voice in American culture. Like a ventriloquist's act, the intellectual works through crime and boxing stories to speak in a common voice to the common man.[3]

The exemplary postwar boxing film is *Body and Soul*, the story of a poor New York Jewish boxer who throws aside friends, family, and lovers in his obsessive drive to succeed. The film has been described by Paul Buhle and Dave Wagner as embodying "the highest achievement of the American Left in cinema before the onset of repression."[4] According to Thom Andersen, along with *Force of Evil*, *Body and Soul* is one of the first American films to "implicate the entire system of capitalism in their criticisms."[5] With his producer Bob Roberts, John Garfield assembled a number of Hollywood's preeminent left-wing filmmakers, notably director Robert Rossen and scriptwriter Abraham Polonsky. The factors that led Garfield and Roberts to choose a boxing story for the star's first post–Warner Bros. film are complex and convoluted, but some are relatively clear.[6] Because boxing was extremely popular—after baseball it was America's favorite sport—mass interest in boxing would have been self-evident to these filmmakers. In *Golden Boy*, Clifford Odets's 1937 boxing drama, the screenwriters had a viable and compelling model on which to base their story. Like other liberal and left-wing Jewish filmmakers who worked on boxing movies—Carl Foreman (*Champion*), Budd Schulberg (*On the Waterfront*, *The Harder They Fall*), Irving Shulman (*The Ring*), Joseph Pevney (*Iron Man*, *Flesh and Fury*), Herbert Kline (*The Fighter*), Gordon Kahn (*Whiplash*), Aben Kandel (*City for Conquest*, *Kid Monk Baroni*, *The Fighter*), Robert Wise (*The Set-Up*), Art Cohn (*The Set-Up*, *Glory Alley*, *Tennessee Champ*), and Bernard Gordon (*Flesh and Fury*)—they were attracted to the history of Jewish involvement in boxing and, for a short while, Jewish domination of the sport both inside and outside the ring.

In the late 1920s and early 1930s, Jews were the dominant ethnic group in the ring; Benny Leonard, Barney Ross, and "Slapsie" Maxie Rosenbloom were joined by another twenty-seven world champions between 1910 and 1940. One should also include Max Baer in this list. He was a heavyweight champion and Hollywood actor who fought with a Star of David on his trunks but, according to some sources, was only passing as Jewish.[7] Throughout the 1920s and 1930s fully one-third of all professional boxers were Jewish, while by the late 1930s Italian boxers had superseded the Jewish champions, and by 1950 Jews had almost no presence in the ring at all. Greater social and cultural integration into the mainstream, economic advancement, and high postwar attendance in post-secondary school education meant that boxing was no longer viewed as a lucrative road out of the ghetto. As social historian of boxing Jeffrey T. Sammons has written: "The succession had gone from Irish to Jewish and would pass on to Italians, to blacks, and to Latins, a pattern that reflected the acculturation strategies of those ethnic groups located on the lowest rungs of the socioeconomic ladder. As each group moved up, it pulled its youth out of prizefighting and pushed them into more promising and meaningful pursuits."[8] Though Jewish presence in the ring declined rapidly, Jews maintained a significant presence outside the ring through management (Al Weill for Rocky Marciano, Irving Cohen for Rocky Graziano), promotion, matchmaking, journalism (*New Yorker*'s A. J. Liebling), and publishing (Nat Fleisher with *Ring* magazine), training (Mannie Seamon and Charlie Goldman, respectively Joe Louis's and Marciano's trainers), and sports wear manufacture (Everlast).[9] As Allen Bodner, the historian of Jews in boxing, notes, throughout the 1920s and 1930s neighborhood and championship boxing matches were significant "social and political events" in the life of east coast Jewish communities.[10] The left-oriented films in the boxing cycle draw covertly or overtly upon this heritage, building a formula that engages with the wider world of the sport in its various incarnations as live spectacle, as radio entertainment, and later as a key component in television's popularity, as well as linking with more romantically inclined ideas of the sport's role within working-class life and culture.

Numerous films featuring boxing had been made in the 1930s, but where they differed significantly from their counterparts in the 1940s and 1950s is that they downplayed or avoided the issue of moral and economic struggle. Little emphasis is given to the boxer's ethnicity, and the films tend to eschew a downbeat ending. Boxing movies from the 1930s such as *The Prizefighter and the Lady* (1933), *The Personality Kid* (1934), and *Cain and Mabel* (1936) highlight romantic intrigue, often across class boundaries, and the display of partially naked men provides ample opportunity for the expression of female sexual desire. None of these elements are absent from the postwar cycle, but they are contained within a narrative framework that valued social verisimilitude over romance.

Midway through Robert Aldrich's 1955 adaptation of Clifford Odets's *The Big Knife* (1949), friends of Hollywood movie star Charlie Castle (Jack Palance) gather in the early evening to watch one of his old movies, a fight film made eight or nine years previously, when Charlie still "had a lot of steam." The end of the picture shows Charlie's character recovering from a near knockout to win the fight. Charlie asks Hank, a scriptwriter who has grown disgusted with Hollywood and has plans to return to New York and write "the great American novel," what he thinks of the picture. "I keep wondering what would happen if you lost the big fight," replies Hank. "Not commercial," responds a cynical Charlie, adding, "he thinks he is still writing for Mercury or the Group. It would have turned out as Uncle Hoff describes as 'disaster.'" Hoff (Rod Steiger) is Charlie's domineering producer. Charlie once had dreams of making socially aware movies and great art, a dream he nurtured in the politically progressive theater of the 1930s (represented by his allusion to the socially committed Mercury and Group Theatres). But now that dream has soured and he is owned body and soul by Hoff.

Odets's play looks back to the 1930s, from the perspective of a once radical playwright who, at the height of the McCarthy witch hunts, must try to come to terms with the loss of his youthful ideals.[11] Charlie's estranged wife, Marion (Ida Lupino), challenges him to stand up to Hoff. "What do you believe in now?" she asks him. "What do you want?" he answers, and then continues: "The wide-eyed kid I was, nursing a cup of coffee in Walgreens, yelling about the sad state [waving his arms] . . . of whatever. . . . And, anyhow, what is all this arty bunk? You know this industry is capable of turning out good pictures, pictures with guts and meaning." Marion replies: "Sure, sure, we know some of the men who do it, Stevens, Mankiewicz, Kazan, Huston, Wyler, Wilder, Stanley Kramer, but never Stanley Hoff." These filmmakers were the cream of Hollywood's post-witch hunt liberals, including ex-Communist Kazan, but unlike Kazan, Charlie does not even have a home within Hollywood's liberal community. As Eric Mottram concludes in his analysis of the play, Charlie eventually "chooses right and is defeated by his own character, becoming the typical hero of the thirties rather than the postwar years—the American failure whose defeat exposes his fundamental decency in a bad time."[12]

Unique to the film adaptation is the use of the boxing movie that Charlie starred in, and an opening sequence that shows Charlie boxing with his trainer, as the voiceover narration informs the viewer that "Charlie Castle is a man who sold out his dreams, but he can't forget them." These images of boxing link back to Odets's earlier play *Golden Boy* (1937), a play formed in the hothouse of New Deal politics and first performed by the Group Theatre.[13] *Golden Boy* was made into a film in 1938, directed by Rouben Mamoulian and starring Barbara Stanwyck and William Holden. It is the story of a young man's tentative and short-lived claim on fame and glory as a boxer. Joe Bonaparte is the son of an Italian immigrant who has grown up in the polyglot world of New York's Lower East Side. His brother is a union organizer and his brother-in-law is a Jewish cab driver. His father's best friend is a Jewish storeowner, to whom he talks about his dream of Joe's becoming a concert violinist. There is no money in being a musician, and the modern, fast-moving world is no place for the sensitive male. Joe rejects his father's dream and becomes a boxer. "You could build a city with his ambition," a character says of Joe. Joe wants the high life: "Bury me in good times and silk shirts," he says. Joe is in a hurry to get somewhere, anywhere, but out of the ghetto: "That's what speed's for, an easy way to live," he says. To achieve his ambition to become "the monarch of the masses," Joe, like Charlie in *The Big Knife*, signs a contract with a manager who provides for his every whim, and in return Joe gives himself up body and soul.

Boxing provided Odets with an overdetermined masculine story form in which to consider the role of the artist within an exploitative capitalist society. The subject of prizefighting enabled him to couch these bourgeois concerns within a drama that he believed had the potential to reach out to the mass audience that was drawn in the hundreds and thousands to live boxing events in the 1930s. *The Big Knife*, on the other hand, was a chronicle of the failure to provide and sustain a socially engaged art for the masses.[14]

The vast majority of the boxing films in the 1940s and 1950s follow the line laid down by *Golden Boy* and represent an urban, proletarian, ethnic minority culture that portray the boxer's aspirations for success as deeply problematic. The films do not represent the boxer's story as a quick and glory-filled route out of the ghetto, the kind suggested by the climatic victory of Charlie Castle's character in the fight film he made for Hoff. Instead, these particular films are concerned with dramatizing defeat. As such they trail *Golden Boy*, which drama scholar Gabriel Miller has noted "follows the classic tragic formula of an individual's rise to power and subsequent fall, precipitated by the recognition of irreparable error committed in the use of that power; for this he suffers and dies, having exhausted all the possibilities of his life. Odets moves his hero toward an action that causes great suffering, and then by exposing the consequences of the deed reveals to him the true nature of his ambition."[15] Along with John Lahr's claim that Odets "pitted American optimism, which was grounded in the myth of abundance, against the demoralized resignation that came with the fact of scarcity,"[16] Miller's description of *Golden Boy* can also stand for the most important film in the cycle, *Body and Soul*. But it is also an apt description for a little-known King Bros. feature called *The Ring* (1951), directed by Kurt Neumann, with a script by Irving Shulman based on his novel *The Square Trap*. Shulman had achieved public recognition following the publication of *The Amboy Dukes*, an early postwar tale of juvenile delinquency that was adapted for film as *City Across the River* (1949). He later co-scripted *Rebel Without a Cause* (1955).

The social, racial, and ethnic dynamics of the boxing story are particularly explicit in Shulman's telling. *The Ring* replaces *Body and Soul*'s New York Jewish ghetto with Olvera Street, a little bit of Old Mexico forgotten by time and surrounded by modern Los Angeles. Residents make their living touting for tourist money and in unskilled trades. The young under-employed Latinos kill time in their clubhouse, listening to worn out phonograph records. Bullied by the local police force, excluded due to his race from a skating rink, and indignant that his father has been laid off work by his "Anglo" bosses, Tommy socks two Anglos who insult his girlfriend (Rita Moreno). Tommy is played by Lalo Rios, who had a featured part in Joseph Losey's *The Lawless* (1950). Pete Genusa (Gerald Mohr), a boxing manager, witnesses the fight and tells Tommy he has potential as a prizefighter. Genusa explains that a career in the ring is "the quickest way to get someplace, be

1. Publicity still for *The Ring* (1951). Tommy (center) and his friends get an unwelcome visit from the police. Courtesy of The British Film Institute.

somebody—better than any Anglo; better than any Anglo you can lick!" Tommy trains hard and wins his first few fights, becoming a hero to his younger brother and the local gang members. His father, however, is disgusted with his chosen profession, but with no other money coming into the home his position of authority is undermined. As his wife explains, boxing is "dangerous not dishonest . . . so we will pray for him." In the novel, Shulman explained that watching John Garfield in *Body and Soul* had fueled Tommy's dream. Tommy reasons that "stories and movies aren't made up, but come from real life; he had to become champion."[17] Shulman's ploy of bringing the conventions of the boxing story to the fore in *The Square Trap* directs the reader's attention toward the absurdity of Tommy's dream and the impossibility of succeeding in such a corrupt racket. But Shulman also recognizes the seductive power of the dream of becoming somebody like John Garfield's fictional fighter or Art Aragon, a popular Latino fighter who is given a cameo in *The Ring*. Hope for a better future is hard to come by in an environment where the racial and economic indignities Tommy, his family, and friends have to suffer determine their social reality; and boxing, despite all the evidence to the contrary, offers at least the possibility of making something of yourself.

Like Joe Bonaparte in *Golden Boy*, Tommy in film and novel wants it all and he wants it fast. Chasing after a bigger bankroll, Tommy forces his manager to get him fights for which he is ill prepared. He loses the bouts and his little star fizzles out. He never achieves the dream. Bruised and battered, but back with his family and friends, Tommy has learned a cruel but necessary lesson: that struggle to better one's self is important but not if it costs self-respect. Tommy never makes it out of the lower reaches on the fight card; he never gets star billing. In defeat, the more illustrious protagonists of *Golden Boy* and *Body and Soul* are compensated by their realization that their worth can be measured by one's relationship with the community in which they were first formed. On the other hand, at the end of the novel Tommy has nothing but a damaged face and a ripped spleen. He has no job, no prospects, no hope. Shulman reveals the dream to be utterly compromised, a horrible illusion:

> When he starts he has hope. Later he hopes for hope. In
> the end he prays for hope.
> But he doesn't have the things people think he has.
> Because he is caught in a square trap—the ring.[18]

The film version, however, ends on a relatively upbeat note, with Tommy burning his fight gear and protecting his little brother from following the same false dreams. Tommy is characterized as an exploited laborer, and his eventual recognition of his plight is perceived as the equivalent of a political awakening. He rejects the empty promise that Pete had held out to him, that boxing would make him somebody, better than any Anglo, and symbolically realigns himself with his father. When explaining to his family why he had lost his job, Tommy's father gave the excuse that when an "Anglo becomes old he is promoted to a boss, when a Mexican becomes old he is laid off." His father's sense of injustice and recognition of

Tommy's exploitation is further underscored in the novel: boxing, he says, is an "American sport . . . An Anglo sport. They love to see people beaten because they enjoy beating people."[19] The message of the film and of the novel is that whatever promises boxing offers, it cannot level social, economic, and racial inequality. But this was a message that clearly failed to make an impact on the reviewer for the *Hollywood Reporter* who panned the film, calling it "a depressing, rather pointless harangue on American discrimination against its Mexican minority group," and suggested the film would only be of interest to "East Los Angeles, the Mexican-American population and those who love films depicting minorities as abused in America."[20] When Tommy gives up boxing at the end of *The Ring*, it is not clear what new career path is open to him: only the vagaries of unskilled labor appear as an option. The strength of both novel and screenplay is that Shulman refuses to pretend it could be otherwise. Other films in the cycle, however, are concerned to show a world that exists outside of the ghetto, in particular a world of culture and education.

Odets's and Garfield's paths crossed repeatedly during the 1930s and 1940s, but they only once worked together on film, an adaptation of Fannie Hurst's *Humoresque* (1946).[21] In the screenplay, Odets returned to ground previously examined in *Golden Boy*, though this time refined culture prevails over the fistic arts. Garfield plays a musically talented Lower East End kid who, with the patronage of a wealthy woman (Joan Crawford), escapes from the New York ghetto. Early in the game of social advancement the young violin virtuoso is approached by a woman at a party held by his patron; looking him over she asks, "Are you a prizefighter? You look just like a prizefighter." The linking of violinist with the pugilist in *Humoresque* was not only a reflection upon Odets's play *Golden Boy*, and a comment on Garfield's persona; it was also yet another contraction between artist and boxer that was becoming common currency.

In the 1940 film adaptation of Aben Kandel's 1936 novel *City for Conquest*, New York's Jewish ghetto is refashioned as Irish, with James Cagney as a trucker who becomes a prizefighter to get enough money to support his brother's ambition to compose and conduct a symphony. The symphony is inspired by the city of New York in "all its proud passionate beauty and all its sordid ugliness." In *Kid Monk Baroni*, with a script by Kandel, the boxer sings and listens to choral music. In *Champion* the artist is a beautiful female sculptor who takes Midge Kelly on a tour of a museum filled with Greek statues, and then poses, objectifies, and seduces the prizefighter. The clay statuette she makes of Kelly underscores his manager's description of him as a Golem. (The idea of Midge Kelly, an Irish American, as a Golem, a clay monster brought to life but without a soul, a figure born of Jewish legend, complicates the question of ethnicity, suggesting, as with *City for Conquest*, an easy slippage across ethnicities in the boxing films of this period.)[22] In *Body and Soul*, Charley's girlfriend goes to art school, quotes William Blake, and lives with a "surrealist" sculptor who likes to use boxers and longshoremen as models.[23] The roommate of Charley's girl has some choice chat-up lines, which clearly evoke her sexual desire for strong proletarian men, and a way of running her fingers up, down, and around phallic sculpture. And in *Whiplash* the boxer *is* a painter. The contrivance that brings artist and fighter together is to the benefit of the artist. Joyce Carol Oates in her rumination on boxing noted "that the artist senses some kinship, however oblique and one-sided, with the professional boxer."[24]

Journalist A. J. Liebling takes the idea one step further: "A boxer, like a writer, must stand alone."[25] And he finishes his book on the "sweet science" by noting how one boxing commentator had compared Rocky Kansas's style to Gertrude Stein, *Les Six* and to nonrepresentational painting, all of them novelties that irritated him, while his opponent, Benny Leonard, reminded him of the classic verities. When Leonard floored Kansas with an "entirely orthodox blow to the conventional point of the jaw," it confirmed "the old masters did know something. There is still a kick in style, and tradition carries a nasty wallop." Boxing as a forum for debates on art and modernism probably did not carry much currency then or now, and Liebling preferred to fall back on the American classic *Moby-Dick*, linking Ahab and the white whale to Archie Moore and Rocky Marciano in his account of their bout that begot his ruminations on modernism and pugilism.[26]

In his journalism and his fiction, W. C. Heinz constantly made links between art and boxing; the idea that trainers mold their fighters like a master sculptor shapes his clay particularly appealed to him, though he gave too much agency to the boxer to think of him as a Golem. In his classic boxing novel, *The Professional* (1958), Heinz writes:

> When the bell rang I watched Doc's kid walk out slowly and then start to circle, his hands low, looking out the tops of his eyes, and there was no question about it. He was Doc's fighter. It is what a painter does in his paintings so that you would know them, even without his signature, and what a writer does in his writings, if he is enough of a writer, so you know that no one in the whole world but he could have been the writer.[27]

Elsewhere Heinz has written that "boxing divorced from danger is devoid of excitement and the emotion that is, of course, the quintessence of the art." This is an image that he linked to a quote from Rainer Maria Rilke, who wrote: "Works of art are indeed always products of having-been-in-danger, of having-gone-to-the-very-end in an experience, to where man can go no further."[28] In cases such as these, the imagined link between the artist and the boxer is not particularly oblique.

Screenwriters and playwrights like Odets, Polonsky, and Schulberg may have been responding to boxing as a particular social facet of ethnic minority urban life, but they were also drawing analogies between themselves as artists involved in "dangerous and adventurous" occupations and the world of the boxer. This analogy helped shore up their sense of self-worth in terms of class, ethnic, and masculine attributes that their actual position as intellectuals otherwise militated against. In his impressionistic history of Jewish gangsters, *Tough Jews*, Rich Cohen considers how and why his father's generation, which came of age during the Second World War, made folk heroes out of thugs and killers like Meyer Lansky, Louis "Lepke" Buchalter, Buggsy Goldstein, Abe "Kid Twist" Reles, Dutch Schultz, and Bugsy

Siegel: "They were always on the look out for someone other than their father, a destiny other than the domestic one they saw at home."[29] For Odets and his cohort, Jewish boxers offered a more legitimate figure with which to counter the stereotype of the effeminate, scholarly, artistically inclined Jew.

The cycle of boxing films ran parallel with Rocky Marciano's reign as heavyweight champion, and had begun at the end of Joe Louis's extraordinary dominance of the heavyweight class in the immediate pre- and postwar years. It also coincided with Sugar Ray Robinson's supremacy of the postwar welterweight and middleweight classes. Yet apart from black independent productions such as Oscar Micheaux's *Notorious Elinor Lee* (1940), two films starring Joe Louis, *Spirit of Youth* (1938), *The Fight Never Ends* (1948), and the biopic *The Joe Louis Story*, black boxers took a back seat to the travails of their white counterparts. Secondary roles such as those in *Golden Boy*, *Body and Soul*, and *The Set-Up*, or cameo roles for the likes of Joe Louis in *This Is the Army* (1943), *The Negro Soldier* (1944), *Joe Palooka, Champ* (1946), and *The Square Jungle*, are the sum of the cycle's engagement with African Americans. Apart from replicating the American film industry's general "disinterest" in representing African Americans, I suspect these acts of omission were also dictated by the filmmakers' concern to represent a relatively unproblematic view of urban, ethnic, class, and gender concerns.

In the bid to address issues of individual potency and social cohesion, the socially committed filmmaker marginalized race, with the exception of the Latino protagonists of *The Fighter* and *The Ring*. Nevertheless, the ability to create analogous relationships between art and boxing was widened to suggest a link between the sport and society at large. *Golden Boy*'s working title was the rather more all-embracing *American Allegory*. Writing about Ring Lardner's experiments with American vernacular, no less an authority on the centrality of sport in American life and letters than Virginia Woolf noted that "it is no coincidence that the best of Mr Lardner's stories are about games, for one may guess that Mr Lardner's interest in games has solved one of the most difficult problems of the American writer; it has given him a clue, a centre, a meeting place for the diverse activities of people whom a vast continent isolates, whom no tradition controls. Games give him what society gives his English brother."[30] During the Depression, prizefighting, alongside baseball, was one of the most important sports in forming this social cement. National radio networks NBC and CBS, which were founded in the late 1920s, in large part consolidated their dominance of the industry by broadcasting sporting events.[31] "Sports were among the first live events that radio brought into people's homes," writes radio historian Susan Douglas, noting that "boxing in the Depression assumed special metaphorical power when, out in the streets, real workers were often fighting with real cops or other agents of management over their livelihoods and 'hard times' indeed involved direct physical conflict. Approximately 8,000 professional boxers entered the ring in the 1930s in the hope that this sport would provide their financial deliverance, and nationally broadcast fights helped revitalize the sport."[32] Whether or not Douglas's claim that fights between boxers were linked in the public's mind to the struggles between labor and capital can be

2. Publicity still for *Champion* (1949). Riding the boxcars, Midge Kelly reveals his pugilistic potential. Courtesy of The British Film Institute.

sustained, world championship matches, such as that between Joe Louis and Max Schmeling in 1938, did work to link the nation together. And, according to Douglas, Louis "embodied America's conceits about its national strength, resolve, and ability to come back from defeat. Was America still the world's most vigorous, virile nation, despite the Depression, despite Hitler's conquests?"[33]

Many of the films in the cycle have a shared understanding that the boxing story has its roots in the Great Depression, an idea given visual expression in the opening scenes of *Champion*. While hoboing to California and the promise of a better life, Midge Kelly reveals his prowess as a fighter in railroad boxcars: "We've got our foot on a ladder. We're not hitchhiking anymore, we're riding. No fat guy in a big car is ever gonna make a monkey out of me." One review of *Body and Soul* saw the film as a Depression-era parable: "Here are the gin and tinsel, squalor and sables of the depression era, less daring than when first revealed in *Dead End* or *Golden Boy* but more valid and mature because shown without sentiment or blur."[34] Screenwriter Polonsky sold his story to the film's producers on the idea it was about the "Depression, Jews, and the fight game."[35] Though it is not discernible in the film, the shooting script locates, via an automobile's license plate, the film's setting at its conclusion as 1938.[36] Paul Buhle and Dave Wagner, historians of Hollywood's blacklist, argue that even though *Body and Soul* first appeared in 1947, it "could be described as the last film of the 1930s," the "culmination of the Depression

generation's struggle to emancipate American dramatic art from the film corporation's control."[37] This is also true of *Champion*, made two years later, symbolized
both in independent producer Kramer's behind-the-scenes battle with studio giant
RKO and in its initial Depression setting. On its release, however, *Body and Soul's*
reviewers did not emphasize the film's links to the 1930s; instead they highlighted
its opportune subject matter.

The *Hollywood Reporter* headlined its review: "Fight Yarn Gets Rugged Treatment," and followed up with "Enterprise steps out, with a walloping fight film,
exposing the vicious rackets still being worked behind the scenes of the boxing
game by unscrupulous promoters and greedy managers who allow their boys to
fight themselves to death. With newspapers splashing these stories all over their
pages, the subject is plenty timely and also box office."[38] *Variety* concurred with the
Reporter, calling the film as "timely as today's headlines."[39] *Daily Variety* filled in
some of the detail concerning its timeliness: "Topical yarn obviously designed to
take advantage of the recent New York inquiry into 'sports fixing,' with an emphasis on some of the crookedness manifested in professional boxing, *Body and Soul*
has a somewhat familiar title and a likewise familiar narrative. It's the telling, however, that's different and that's what will sell the film."[40] The trade press reviews that
linked the film's temporal location to a contemporary concern with corruption
in the fight game do not contradict the reviews and later critiques that stressed
continuity with the concerns of the 1930s. The subject of boxing allowed for both
versions, facilitating an allegorical reception of the film as an individual's and a
community's struggle with the vicissitudes of capitalism and more simply as a
melodramatic realization of the world of pugilism.

In supercharged symbolic events such as the 1938 Schmeling-Louis match, it is
easy to see boxing, as Sammons does, as "a microcosm of the larger society and, as
such, can isolate, magnify, and amplify conditions that are easily lost or difficult to
discern in the larger society."[41] On the other hand, boxing, as novelist Joyce Carol
Oates argues, "is not a metaphor for life but a unique, closed, self-referential
world."[42] It is the artist or social historian that gives boxing its larger meaning. The
films generally strived for social relevance on a local level, rather than on a national
scale. As such it is in terms of their delineation of an urban, proletarian, masculine,
and ethnically defined image of the neighborhood that the more politically
inspired films in the cycle find their most meaningful resonance.

In his book *Foreigners: The Making of American Literature: 1900–1940*, Marcus
Klein creates a rich account of how America in myth and idea was remade at the
turn of the century by Eastern European immigrants to the United States, when
first- and second-generation Jewish Americans rewrote American culture in their
own image. In Michael Gold's *Jews Without Money* (1930), Henry Roth's *Call It Sleep*
(1934), Daniel Fuchs's *Summer in Williamsburg* (1934), Klein traces the theme of conflict "between the old-country Jewish ideals and the powerful, disinheriting America."[43] He reads these novels alongside James T. Farrell's *Studs Lonigan* trilogy, and
other proletarian novels by Albert Halper and Meyer Levin. In each case, as he
noted specifically about *Studs Lonigan*, the "ghetto had served truly to be the basis

of a community—that ghetto community was better than the American and the time by which it was in the process of being dispossessed."[44] The ghetto, Klein argues, whether it was Irish, Italian, black, or Jewish, "could be presented for consideration as a kind of Home Town." He continues:

> It could be celebrated not only in spite of but also because of all of its deprivations and confusions and strangeness. The urban ghetto—chiefly in New York and Chicago—was not the only place in which the new American folk had been created, but it was in fact the usual place. Moreover, to tell the tale of one's youth in the ghetto was to secure several benefits at once. One could pay one's filial respects and thereby assuage guilt. By mythicizing the ghetto, one could further emigrate from it. In addition, one could make a statement and teach a lesson to all of those official Americans who persisted in thinking that they owned the country. And altogether one could say that here, too, was a genuine and informative typicality of the true America.[45]

The writers Klein discusses "were engaged in making cultural assertion from utterly dubious cultural materials. In all of their instances the underlying truth of the ghetto was the dissolution of the ghetto—which, because America, too, was a dubious material, was not the same thing as a process of Americanization."[46] The more socially conscious films in the cycle of boxing movies also drew upon a nostalgic evocation of the ghetto as a formative environment and as a superior moral space. The candy stores, diners, grocers, dance halls, tenement buildings, and milling street scenes all attested to a vital life experience, while the homosocial spaces of the barber shop, the pool room, the saloon, and the boxing gym underscored ghetto life as authentically masculine.

In films such as *Body and Soul* and *Golden Boy* the images of the ghetto society of the Lower East Side echo the street life represented in films of the early sound period, notably King Vidor's *Street Scene* (1931) with its rich portrayal of a polyglot New York. In this film, like many of the ghetto-centric boxing movies, the boundaries between public and private space are effaced by the social and romantic commingling that takes place on tenement steps. Where the boxing film differs from its earlier ghetto counterparts is in its masculinization of street life and emphasis on the homosocial spaces of the gym or pool hall. As such, the boxing movie shares something of the tough-boy vernacular displayed in a film like *Public Enemy* (1931), where the city streets are a school for tomorrow's hoodlums and racketeers. In films such as *The Set-Up* and *The Street with No Name*, films that otherwise have very little to say about the ethnic makeup of America's inner cities, the working or underclass environment and the masculine aspects of street life are nevertheless thoroughly highlighted.

The Set-Up's director was Robert Wise, who had learned his trade in the Val Lewton production unit at RKO. In *The Set-Up* Wise replays one of the unit's most famous tropes, as seen in *Cat People* (1942) and *Leopard Man* (1943), of the lonely, vulnerable walk of the heroine through the nightmarish nocturnal city. In *The Set-Up* aging boxer Stoker Thompson (Robert Ryan) is preparing for his bout against the newcomer Tiger Nelson. The film cuts backward and forward between Stoker and his wife, Julie, who walks the streets outside the boxing arena. The film's *mise-en-scène* and ambient sound track is extraordinarily effective in underscoring Julie's unhappy and uncertain state of mind as she contemplates her husband's choice to carry on boxing, searching vainly for the win that will get him a title shot and enough money to quit the game. Adjacent to Paradise City, the fight arena, are Dreamland, a dancehall located above a chop suey house, and the Hotel Cozy, where Stoker and Julie are staying. Cozy paradisiacal dreamlands are a million miles away from this tank town. Unseen except in silhouette, the Dreamland's dance orchestra provide the requisite swing, boogie woogie, and rumba backdrop to the depiction of an excessively defined masculine and proletarian space inside and outside Paradise City.

Julie's walk begins outside the arena as she listens to the sound of the crowd screaming for blood. Chilled, she turns away and walks past the Coral Ball Room. She is immediately accosted by a mash man—silk tie, wide lapels, thin moustache, and a flat line in seduction: "Lonesome?" "Like dancing?" "Want a cigarette?" "Betcha do a nice rumba." Though she dismisses him with a "get lost," his presence is threatening. At a cigar stand she listens to a live broadcast from the arena; thinking it is her husband that is being beaten she becomes weak and sick. "What's the matter lady," says the cigar man, "too rough for you?" She moves on down the street accompanied by Hawaiian music pouring out of a cocktail bar, and then walks past a gang of loitering punk motorcyclists and a tattoo parlor. A girl's scream cuts twice above the sounds of the street. Inside a penny arcade a girl's dress is blown above her head by a blast of air from an attraction. She is the screamer. Julie's worried look turns into a smile before reality intrudes once again as a boxing arcade game grabs her attention. Back on the street, hustlers glam suckers for small change and kissing couples pull themselves into the shadows and doorways. The roar of a motorbike engine is heard and then the sounds and the neon light of the arcade, dance hall, and bars give way to traffic noise and the sodium glare of headlights as Julie descends some steps before halting to look over the side of a bridge onto a busy road down below: the cars, buses, and trams howling and churning into the tunnels beneath her feet. The sequence finishes with Julie back in her room at the Cozy Hotel, looking through her window onto Paradise City and Dreamland. As she watches, from out of the alley, between the arena and the dance hall, her husband staggers into the street and falls into the gutter. The small-time racketeers who paid his manager in the expectation that Stoker would throw the fight, which he wins against all odds, have smashed his right hand.

With its representation of masculine exclusivity, *The Set-Up* revels in its portrayal of low-life losers, suckers and hucksters, dreamers and fools. Similarly, the story of FBI undercover operations in *The Street with No Name*, scripted by Harry Kleiner, seeks to represent a hyper-masculine image of America's inner-city underclass. To bring to justice the perpetrators of a crime wave that has hit Central City, FBI agent Gene Cordell (Mark Stevens) must infiltrate the city's underworld. Assuming a false identity, he travels to Central City by Greyhound bus. The bus terminal is the first view of the city; the next view is of Skid Row. To make his presence known, Cordell hangs out on the streets, in bars, and in pool rooms, finally making his play to gain the attention of the mob at the boxing gym where all the local faces gather. The physical contests between boxers, the machismo of the all-male habitués of the gym, all jostling for center stage, create a fitting climax to the sequence of scenes that began in the bus terminal ten minutes earlier. The film's offering of so much redundant detail in its catalogue of proletarian, homosocial spaces gives it the feel of a travelogue: a guided tour of the "other side" that authenticates this otherwise formulaic police procedural.

Joseph Losey's adaptation of Stanley Ellin's novel *Dreadful Summit*, which was filmed under the title *The Big Night*, with Ellin and Losey fronting for blacklisted screenwriters Hugo Butler and Ring Lardner Jr., prowls around similar nocturnal urban spaces as *The Street with No Name*. The pulp paperback edition of the novel tagged the story as "Eight savage hours of whiskey and women,"[47] but it is in fact a rather sensitive portrayal of a young man's rite of passage. It is an oedipal tale marked by the teenager's witnessing of his father's humiliation at the hands of a sports journalist. Taking his father's hat, jacket, and gun, the teenager sets out to seek revenge. Over the course of the night he visits bars and taverns, a nightclub, has his first sexual encounter, shoots a man, and, of course, watches a boxing match.

The film operates on the rhythm of first proffering the teenager the means to confirm his manhood, and then having him come up short when put to the test. He turns to the local druggist to borrow some money to get him to the fights, where he hopes to confront his father's tormentor, but ends up having to earn the money by babysitting. At the fights he is fleeced by a penny-ante chiseler, and, after turning down a drink offered by a fight fan (stoically played by Robert Aldrich), he notices that his father's hat has been stomped; pushing the hat back into shape he misses the fight, which lasts all of forty seconds. Failure follows upon failure. At the Florida Club he becomes inebriated and visualizes his father being beaten to the rhythm of a wild drum solo. The jump blues parleyed by a small black combo segues into a slow vocal and piano number performed by a black torch singer— "too young to be loved" is her lament. Much later, the teenager encounters the singer outside the club. He tells her he thinks she is "the most wonderful singer in the world." To his naive advance she responds with a smile, but then he follows up with "You're so beautiful, even if you're. . . ." His racism breaks the spell and his journey into the night continues—his encounters stalling rather than propelling him into manhood.[48]

Boxing, then, whether the film dealt with ethnicity or not, helped to authentic a view of the inner city as essentially masculine. At a point in time when this view of the ghetto was being embellished, rising standards of living, particularly among first- and second-generation Jews, and the geographic and economic distance of the authors of the films and novels that documented urban life, meant that ghetto representations were imbued with nostalgia. In his classic volume on boxing, Liebling wrote about what he considered would be the last great moment in boxing—the last few years of the 1940s and the first years of the 1950s: the end of Joe Louis's reign and the rise of Rocky Marciano and Sugar Ray Robinson. Nostalgic before the fact, Liebling noted that full employment and staying on at secondary school have militated against the "development of first rate professional boxers."[49] But the deleterious effect of good economic conditions was nothing compared to the calamitous effect of television on the sport. Utilized "in the sale of beer and razor blades," television networks by "putting on a free boxing show almost every night of the week, have knocked out of business the hundreds of small-city and neighborhood boxing clubs where youngsters had a chance to learn their trade and journeymen to mature their skills. . . . Neither advertising agencies nor brewers, and least of all the networks, give a hoot if they push the Sweet Science back into a period of genre painting. When it is in a coma they will find some other way to peddle their peanuts."[50] In his biographical portrait of former featherweight champion Willie Pep, sports writer W. C. Heinz noted how "in those days . . . boxing and Milton Berle sold TVs. Guys who didn't have sets gathered in bars or in homes of others who had sets to watch the fights."[51] Sammons concurs with these journalistic accounts: "When television merged with sport, America's games were changed forever."[52]

The first championship match broadcast was between Joe Louis and Billy Conn in 1946, a match watched in the main on television sets located in local bars. The match received over two-thirds of the listening figures for radio, which dwarfed the television rating. Despite low viewing figures, the bout acted as an important word-of-mouth advertisement for the new medium. The 1948 fight between Louis and Jersey Joe Walcott was equally effective in the promotion of television viewing; the Hotel New Yorker reported that its 150 rooms that were equipped with television sets were sold out to guests wishing to view the fight. One year later, a televised fight in New York City was seen in 16,500 bars and restaurants.[53] "By 1952 televised prizefights reached an average of 5 million homes; the figure rose to 8.5 million in 1955." As Sammons notes, the "new technology transformed prizefighting from a closed attraction to a mass spectator sport."[54]

The sport became increasingly commercialized and nationalized. By 1950 boxing was effectively under the monopoly control of the International Boxing Club, which in turn was controlled by Frankie Carbo and organized crime. In the late 1950s and the early 1960s *Sports Illustrated* campaigned relentlessly against mob control of the fight game, observing that in less than a generation it had gone from "an exciting sport to a perverted racket."[55] When Midge Kelly in *Champion* is wavering over whether to betray his manager and accept the mobster's conditions for a shot at the title, he is told he has a choice to either tear up his old contract or get a "liquor license and a television set." Boxing, organized crime, booze, and television were made for one another.

The popularity of boxing on television inevitably led to drama programs devoted to the sport. In March 1955 *Requiem for a Heavyweight* was broadcast—the first ninety-minute original television drama.[56] A critical and popular success, the Emmy award–winning show was written by Rod Serling and starred Jack Palance,

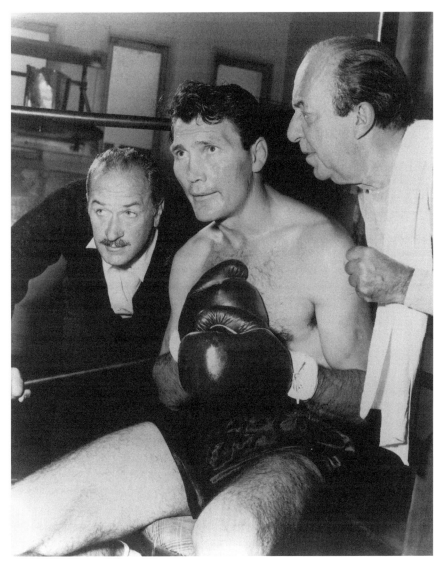

3. Publicity still for the television drama *Requiem for a Heavyweight* (1955), starring Jack Palance (center). Author's collection.

a role that links back to his parts in *The Big Knife* and as an ex-boxer in *Halls of Montezuma* (1951). *Requiem for a Heavyweight* was remade in 1962 as a feature film starring Anthony Quinn. In recognition of the film's precursor it begins with a slow tracking shot along the bar in a saloon, one close up of a pug ugly following after another, as they gawk up at an off-screen television set broadcasting a live boxing match. At the end of the tracking shot the scene abruptly cuts to the point of view of a fighter being pounded by the fists of Cassius Clay. Like the neighborhood boxing gyms and arenas in films like the *The Set-Up*, *The Big Night*, and *The Street with No Name*, this form of mediated, televisual, communal consumption of boxing was close to becoming a thing of the past by 1962, another mourned-for homosocial space. Moreover, boxing itself had been superseded in the television ratings game by the rival sports of basketball and football.[57]

Cassius Clay represented the new media savvy boxer, a fighter who personified the youthful vigor of the Kennedy years, and though he, more than any fighter before or after, was linked to a wider set of social concerns, boxing was a spent social force.[58] Quinn plays an aging boxer who has fought too many fights. After the bout his face looks like fresh chopped meat. A doctor revokes his boxing license and the old pugilist is forced to look for a new career. In the postwar cycle of boxing movies, Quinn's fighter represented the final appearance of the defeated yet noble prizefighter—the dispossessed son of the 1930s. *Requiem for a Heavyweight* was the last evocation of a nostalgic vision that the cycle of boxing movies had told over and over again: communal, ethnic, masculine values eroded by the strictures of a domesticated, feminized, private sphere of consumption. A monarch for the masses was nowhere to be found.

5   The Violent Poetry of the Times

THE POLITICS OF HISTORY IN DANIEL MAINWARING AND JOSEPH LOSEY'S *THE LAWLESS*

Doug Dibbern

In the decisive scene of the 1950 independent production *The Lawless*, small-town newspaperman Larry Wilder (Macdonald Carey) sits in a thin rectangle of light surrounded by darkness, contemplating a momentous decision. He can risk his safety and use his newspaper to save the life of a Mexican teenager railroaded by the system, or he can do nothing and save himself. From the dark, he hears a voice: "Remember, you like this town, you like your place in it. Don't let that heart of yours start bleeding." The faceless leading citizen exits, and Wilder paces the room, from the blackness of the far corner to the brilliant swath of sunlight that falls across his typewriter in the foreground. As he paces he reaches a decision and dictates to his junior reporter—"A kid named Paul Rodriguez went to a dance last night in Sleepy Hollow where the streets aren't paved and the people live in shacks"—then he sits down, now calm and completely illuminated, and types the conclusion of his missive to the people of Santa Marta, California: "As editor and publisher of *The Union*, I'm raising a fund to defend Paul Rodriguez. I'm putting my name on top of the list."

Wilder, a former progressive journalist who covered the war, faces the same choice that others in Hollywood faced at the time: he can keep silent or he can stand up for what he believes. In October 1947, the House Un-American Activities Committee (HUAC) began its investigation into Communist influence in Hollywood. Hollywood liberals then formed the Committee for the First Amendment (CFA) and flew to Washington to protest the hearings. Two years later, as *The Lawless* went into production, the House had found ten men in contempt of Congress, the studio producers declared they would no longer employ Communists, each of the major studio unions had instigated a loyalty oath, and the CFA had ceased to exist. Further hearings—with the fear of a blacklist for hundreds more—seemed imminent.

At first glance, *The Lawless* seems to be a simple—perhaps even simplistic—story about a white newspaperman who defends a Mexican teenager who has become the victim of sensationalized attacks in the press. But the film's politics work on multiple levels. Besides its ostensible subject matter, the movie also reflects the internal struggle of politically active liberals dealing with the Communist investigations of HUAC. And, in making comparisons between the subject of the film and the political events of the day, screenwriter Daniel Mainwaring (credited as Geoffrey Homes) and director Joseph Losey resuscitated the discourses surrounding events that had galvanized the left just seven years before. In 1943, seventeen Mexican American teenagers were convicted of murder and assault in a case that came to be known as the Sleepy Lagoon Murder; later that year, the city erupted in what were dubbed the zoot suit riots—a week in which bands of white servicemen roamed the city beating up Mexican teenagers who wore the flashy outfits known as zoot suits. Larry Wilder's choice between the darkness and the light, then, was much more than a decision about whether or not to help one Mexican American kid in some tiny rural California town; it was a decision about how the left might rouse history to fight the growing conservative consensus of the emerging Cold War.

Early in the morning of August 2, 1942, a young man named Jose Diaz died at Los Angeles General Hospital. The following January, seventeen young Mexican American men were convicted of murder and assault. Though some were sentenced to only one year in prison, three received life sentences. The Los Angeles press ran lurid headlines about the threat of juvenile delinquency and Mexican gangs. Communists and liberals in Hollywood saw a different picture. They saw a group of young men wrongly convicted, railroaded by a racist police department and court system, and they combined forces to combat the stories put forth by the mainstream press. Their efforts eventually helped get the Sleepy Lagoon defendants released on appeal in 1944; thus it should be no surprise that a liberal screenwriter in 1950 would look back to the World War II era as the perfect example of the success that leftists could achieve when they banded together.

The local coverage of the Sleepy Lagoon murder trial was one-sided and sensationalistic. Four daily newspapers dominated Los Angeles during the 1940s. William Randolph Hearst owned the conservative *Examiner* and *Herald-Express*. The *Times* and the *Daily News* were considered more moderate, though both were considered quite conservative by the Hollywood Left. Hearst's *Herald-Express* covered the trial more than any other paper, referring from the start to the "goons of Sleepy Lagoon," while a local tabloid, *Sensations*, ran a story in its December 1942 issue by Clem Peoples, chief of the Criminal Division of the Sheriff's Office, referring to "immoral gangsters" and "reckless madbrained young wolves" who prowled 38th Street, the neighborhood where the defendants lived.[1] The *Times'* coverage of the murder trial, though more even-handed than the coverage in the Hearst papers, still favored the prosecution. While defense lawyers argued that Diaz may have been hit by a car, not murdered, the *Times* frequently referred to his death matter-of-factly as "a murder," wrote about the "slayers," and asserted definitively that "Diaz was fatally stabbed."[2] Though seven testified in court about violent treatment at the hands of the police, their stories were not reported in the press.[3] When the convictions came in, the *Times* ran a series of articles defending the fairness of the trial, striving to quell the notion that the convictions were racially motivated, and criticizing leftist complaints of racism, saying that "the communists as usual are making trouble and confusing issues."[4]

The newspapers' handling of the zoot suit riots was similarly one-sided. Most historians now agree that the riots were instigated and almost entirely carried out by white servicemen against Mexican teenagers, but on the first day the riots made the papers, the *Times* headline blared, "Zoot Suiters Learn Lesson in Fights with Servicemen." The article's first paragraph read, "Those gamin dandies, the zoot suiters, having learned a great moral lesson from servicemen, mostly sailors, who took over their instruction three days ago, are staying home nights."[5] As the riots continued in the streets, the *Times* made conflicting statements about who was to blame, though the vast majority of stories told of zoot-suit assailants and their white victims. And after the riots had subsided, the paper opined in an editorial that the riots "have had nothing to do with race persecution, although some elements have loudly raised the cry of this very thing."[6]

The elements who raised the cry were, of course, the Communists and their liberal fellow travelers. Though neither Communists nor liberals published anything about the zoot suit riots, the Sleepy Lagoon Defense Committee published two pamphlets reacting against the mainstream press as it was raising funds to mount an appeal. The first, *The Sleepy Lagoon Case*, was credited to the Citizens' Committee for the Defense of Mexican-American Youth but was actually written by the committee's executive secretary, Alice Greenfield McGrath, a liberal non-Communist, with a brief introduction by Orson Welles. The second, *Sleepy Lagoon Mystery*, was written by Guy Endore, a Communist screenwriter who was later blacklisted. While both claim that the defendants had been railroaded by a racist system, they also reveal the differences between the liberal and Communist attitudes on the subject of racism in California. McGrath spends most of her essay attacking the racist declarations of one Los Angeles police officer. Endore, on the other hand, ties the convictions to a larger conspiratorial web that included the press, the police, and the court system, all manipulated by William Randolph Hearst at the bidding of every Communist's worst enemy, Adolf Hitler.

McGrath's pamphlet, representing the liberal non-Communist position, is straightforward, patriotic, and a little dull. She repeatedly evokes the declarations of friendship between American president Franklin D. Roosevelt and Mexican president Manuel Ávila Camacho. She criticizes the press, especially its use of the word "gang" in describing a loose group of friends from the neighborhood around 38th Street and for its incorrect accounts of an increase in juvenile delinquency among Mexican American youth, quoting a report by the Los Angeles Probation Department that claimed emphatically that "there is no wave of lawlessness among Mexican children" and that the increase in delinquency among Mexicans was less than it was for other ethnic groups.[7] McGrath devotes the majority of her pamphlet to attacking the testimony of one particular police lieutenant who spoke in court about the racially determining factors of violence among different ethnic groups. In doing so, McGrath implicitly argued that the troubles stemmed from the racist attitudes of a few individuals in power rather than from a systematic problem with American society or institutions as a whole.

Endore, on the other hand, spins a fascinating tale that begins with a mysterious teletype message that came from San Simeon, Hearst's Xanadu-esque mansion hideaway. Like McGrath, Endore criticizes the use of the word "gang," but other than that, Endore and McGrath are far apart. He claims that the case was concocted by a conspiracy. Hearst's reputed teletype read: "Chief suggests L.A. editors make survey of crime reports—all types—with particular emphasis on numbers of police bookings of Mexican and Negro citizens—and or aliens."[8] Hearst, Endore says, had been an agent of the Germans for almost fifty years, from the days of the Kaiser to Hitler, and refers to Hitler as Hearst's "old friend and employer."[9] Endore also writes more than six pages on the prejudices of the trial judge, Charles W. Fricke, whom McGrath doesn't bother to mention. Endore calls Fricke "the side of Hitleristic racial prejudice" and "biased to a degree that challenges comparison with the courts of Naziland."[10]

The liberal opposition, however, was just as biased as the prejudiced press it was contesting. Both the mainstream press and its liberal opponents used the events of 1943 as a political weapon. In his book *Murder at the Sleepy Lagoon: Zoot Suits, Race, and Riot in Wartime L.A.*, Eduardo Obregón Pagán pores through court transcripts to paint a different picture than either the mainstream Los Angeles press or its progressive opposition was willing to present. The press portrayed the defendants as dangerous "gangsters" and "wolves" who were "outlandishly garbed" in "comical clothing." Endore and McGrath portray the defendants as hard-working, patriotic Americans. They follow almost every mention of a defendant with a reference to his job history, his wife and children, or his military service. Pagán's account, on the other hand, is less rosy, far more complex, and far more interesting.

Both McGrath and Endore argued that there was no proof that Diaz had, in fact, been murdered. McGrath writes in her first paragraph, "It seems clear that Diaz was drinking heavily and fell into a roadway and was run over by a car."[11] Endore wrote that "he bore no knife wounds," and that "according to the doctor, these injuries could be explained as due to repeated falls on rocky ground or blows from a blunt instrument."[12] The doctor who performed the autopsy, however, testified in court that Diaz had two stab wounds, skinned and swollen knuckles, a three-inch long fracture at the top of his head, and a contusion across his swollen lip—all of which suggested that he had been stabbed and "forcibly struck on his head several times with a blunt instrument by a right-handed assailant/s."[13] Endore wrote that there were no "witnesses who could definitely link any one of the accused boys with the death of Diaz,"[14] but Pagán stresses that four people testified that they had seen a kid named Chepe Ruiz beating Diaz's body several times with a stick.[15] Pagán concludes that the boys were innocent of murder—he suggests that Diaz was killed by two friends before the defendants arrived at the party that night[16]—but his account paints the boys as violent and vengeful. Clearly, McGrath

and Endore eliminated these facts from their account to serve a larger political purpose—just as Losey and Mainwaring would do seven years later.

The HUAC hearings on Communism in Hollywood that took place in October
1947 didn't emerge from thin air. Rather, they were the culmination of more than a
decade of Hollywood battles between Communists, liberal anti-Communists, and
the right wing. The tension began in 1933 with the founding of the Screen Writers
Guild, and the next dozen years saw almost constant struggles between the liberals
and Communists within the union movement and the conservative forces opposed
to them.

Throughout this period, Communists and liberals repeatedly joined forces only
to inevitably rip themselves apart. Donald Ogden Stewart, a Communist who specialized in scripts about the milieu of the idle rich such as *Holiday* and *The Philadelphia Story*, formed the Hollywood Anti-Nazi League in 1936, which imploded
following the Molotov-Ribbentrop pact of 1939. Similarly, screenwriter Philip
Dunne, the archetypal Hollywood liberal anti-Communist, formed the Motion Picture Democratic Committee, which fell apart for the same reason. The Hollywood
Independent Citizens Committee of Artists, Scientists, and Professionals dissolved
in 1946 when liberals and Communist debated whether to favor Will Rogers Jr. or
Emmett Williams in the Democratic congressional primaries.

In 1947, when HUAC first issued subpoenas, a group of liberal anti-Communists—
headed by Philip Dunne, John Huston, and William Wyler—founded the Committee for the First Amendment. Their goal was not to defend the Communists themselves, but to defend the constitutional right to free speech. "For obvious reasons,"
Dunne wrote, "we consistently urged anyone who might have had damaging affiliations in the past to stay away from our organization."[17] They didn't know it then,
but this was to be the last time Hollywood's liberals and Communists would fight
on the same side, and it was, in part, the CFA's failure to effectively counter the
right wing that finally enabled HUAC to institute a blacklist.

The CFA's hopes were soon crushed, however. When the unfriendly witnesses
were called, they refused to answer any questions directly, instead launching dia-
tribes against the committee's authority. They were gaveled into silence, one after
another, and John Howard Lawson, the Communists' de facto leader in the movie
colony, was dragged screaming from the conference room. "It was a sorry performance," Huston wrote. "You felt your skin crawl and your stomach turn."[18] On
the flight back, Humphrey Bogart apparently lashed out at his CFA friends, yelling
at Danny Kaye, "You fuckers sold me out!"[19] After they returned to Hollywood, the
mood had changed dramatically. "The reporting in Washington, with us until that
moment," Huston wrote, "was now against us."[20] Abraham Polonsky, blacklisted
himself four years later, compared the atmosphere in Los Angeles to "a flu epidemic."[21] The next month, after the House voted to cite the Ten for contempt of
Congress on a vote of 346–17, Bogart had changed his tune. He told the press "that
the trip was ill-advised, even foolish, I am very ready to admit."[22] When the second
HUAC hearings came around in 1951, he—like everyone else in the CFA—didn't
bother to fight the investigations. In November 1947, studio executives issued what

came to be known as the Waldorf Statement, in which they announced they would no longer employ Communists. The three big unions voted to require their members to produce loyalty oaths, affidavits that declared they were not members of the Communist Party. Huston recalls that in the Screen Directors Guild, everyone—even his CFA co-founder William Wyler—voted in favor of the loyalty oath except himself and Billy Wilder.[23] Emmet Lavery at the Screen Writers Guild orchestrated the removal of any suspected remaining Communists from the board. And under Ronald Reagan's guidance, the Screen Actors Guild voted 1,307–157 in favor of their own loyalty oath.[24]

Years later, Philip Dunne wrote that in 1948, "the entire industry became demoralized as almost everyone scrambled for cover."[25] When he tried to organize a further protest, most writers "offered tirades against the behavior of [Ring] Lardner [one of the Ten] and his colleagues on the witness stand, thus, to my mind at least, shifting elsewhere the blame for what was troubling their own consciences."[26] Though Dunne flew to Washington to testify as a character witness for Dalton Trumbo and helped raise money to support the families of the Ten, he said that by 1948 he had become a "tired liberal. . . . 1948 marked a sort of watershed in my political career. I never again became heavily involved in organizational politics."[27]

Daniel Mainwaring brought his script for *The Lawless* to independent producers William Pine and William Thomas without many expectations. The two men were infamous for their crude products; one year they had contracted Mainwaring to write six scripts, including titles such as *Swamp Fire*, in which Johnny Weismuller fought alligators along the banks of the Mississippi to win the hand of his Cajun bride.[28] Mainwaring had recently made a dramatic change in his life as a writer. After producing a series of pulp mystery novels in the thirties and early forties, he dropped out of society for a while to work on a book he hoped would be different than anything he had ever done. This book was *Build My Gallows High*, which he later wrote for the screen as *Out of the Past*.[29] After this breakthrough, he was discouraged that he had to write more pulp for Pine and Thomas. He admits that when he brought his new script to them he wasn't "too sanguine" about its prospects.[30] He was surprised when they accepted it; perhaps their decision was based on the box office success of other recent socially conscious films about African American issues—films like *Home of the Brave, Lost Boundaries,* and *Pinky*.[31] The era was also witnessing a new interest in movies dealing with Mexican characters and themes—movies such as John Ford's *The Fugitive*, Anthony Mann's *Border Incident*, Budd Boetticher's *The Bullfighter and the Lady*, and Elia Kazan's *Viva Zapata!* Latino actors such as Gilbert Roland, Ricardo Montalbán, and Pedro Armendáriz were getting better roles than at any time since the craze for "Latin lovers" back in the 1920s.

Mainwaring had always been very liberal—though never so radical as to join the Communist Party—and the script crystallized themes he had been struggling with for the last seventeen years. He grew up in northern California, graduated from Fresno State, then worked as a reporter for newspapers in New York and

Los Angeles—including, ironically, Hearst's *Examiner*—throughout the twenties and early thirties.[32] It's not clear exactly what he did and didn't do during the crucial period of 1947 to 1951. Tom Flinn mentions that he had "a brush with Hollywood's witch hunters" but offers no further details.[33] Losey said that Mainwaring "was very badly hurt by the black list. Because he took a left wing position and because he remained loyal to his friends and put his name on some of the scripts of blacklisted people and took no money for it."[34] Mainwaring's widow, on the other hand, recalled differently. She claimed that Mainwaring fronted his name only once—for Paul Jarrico—and that the script was never produced.[35] The blacklist didn't damage his career, either; his name appeared on almost two dozen credits between 1951 and 1960.[36]

Mainwaring's concerns, however, definitely place him in the liberal camp. His work often focused on the prejudicial violence of small towns and the role newspapermen played in bettering the world. In a 1973 interview, he still bristled at the racism he saw in small towns: "Small towns are miserable places. Farmers I know up in the San Joachim Valley have been trying to put out a contract on [Cesar] Chavez to get him knocked off for organizing the migrant workers. They're sweet people."[37] His first novel—*One Against the Earth*, written in 1933—was about a hero lynched by an angry mob.[38] He was unhappy with every one of the six scripts he wrote for Pine and Thomas during that twelve-month span except for one, *Big Town*,[39] which *Variety* summarized as the story of "a crusading editor of Big Town's illustrated Daily Press after getting burned by yellow journalism."[40] In 1948, Mainwaring was serving as RKO's Screen Writers Guild representative when he was fired by Howard Hughes for his liberal inclinations. Several people tell the same story of Hughes offering them the chance to work on a film called *I Married a Communist*. If someone rejected the offer, Hughes knew he or she was politically suspect and fired the person on the spot. Mainwaring was one.[41] Losey recalls Hughes offering him the script as well.[42]

Losey himself had great respect for Mainwaring as a person and as a screenwriter: "He's a much underrated writer and he's a really quite noble man."[43] Mainwaring is the one who proposed Losey as director.[44] Losey claimed that he made virtually no changes to the script: "I worked with Mainwaring. We were very close friends and worked together, but the script was really Dan's."[45] Losey also maintained that the producers muddled the script, recalling that William Pine used to call story conferences while sitting on the toilet. The script "was corrupted by the producers," he said. "I mean all that business of the rape of the girl and the police car going up in flames were stuck in by them."[46] Mainwaring himself blamed the producers for muddling the ending as well, though the exact changes they made are unclear.[47] The script was also influenced by complaints from the Production Code Administration. In a letter to Paramount Pictures, Joseph Breen wrote that "this whole undertaking seems to us to be fraught with very great danger" since the film would be "a very definite disservice to this country of ours, and to its institutions and ideals." He admitted that the script had been unanimously approved by his office under the provisions of the Production Code, but he doggedly urged Paramount to reconsider going ahead with the picture anyway:

> The story itself is a shocking indictment of America and its people and, indeed, is a sad commentary on 'democracy at work,' which the enemies of our system of government like to point to. The shocking manner in which the several gross injustices are heaped upon the confused, but innocent, young American of Mexican extraction, and the willingness of so many of the people in your story to be a part of, and to endorse, these injustices, is, we think, a damning portrayal of our American social system.
>
> The manner in which certain of the newspapers are portrayed in this story, with their eagerness to dishonestly present the news, and thus inflame their readers, is also, we think, a part of a pattern which is not good.[48]

Mainwaring did revise the script after hearing from Breen, sending the PCA more than fifty pages containing revisions.[49] But Paramount went ahead with the picture and since the portrayal of certain newspapers and their reporters in the final film is still quite negative, it's not clear to what extent Mainwaring or his producers changed the script to assuage the PCA's concerns.

Losey had also long been involved in liberal causes, and politics had played an important role in his theater work for years. He graduated from Dartmouth and traveled extensively throughout Europe in the early 1930s—spending six months in Stalin's Soviet Union admiring the stage productions of Nikolai Okhlopkov, among others—before returning to New York in 1935. During that decade Losey matched his radical pro-Soviet politics with a radical Brechtian aesthetics, but after the war he drifted from both the politics of the Communist Party and the radical aesthetics of his youth. Though *The Lawless* was his second feature film, it has more in common with his theater work than it does with the films he directed in the sixties and seventies for which he is most famous. His theater work matched an overt political engagement with an avant-garde style influenced by figures such as Brecht and Meyerhold. "Certainly," Losey said, "*The Lawless* belongs to a very early period for me. . . . I was still trying to get out of my system, I suppose, some things which were very much a part of me in the thirties and early forties."[50] With his second film, Losey wanted—indeed, needed—to abandon his avant-garde theater style in order to produce a more commercially accessible work, while still maintaining a political commitment, particularly at a time when politics seemed more important than ever. His radical style would return again occasionally in his later work such as *The Servant*. A brief look at some of his most important theater work—his work on The Living Newspaper and on Brecht's 1947 production of *The Life of Galileo*— should show not only the important similarities with *The Lawless*, but also the important differences.

The government-funded Federal Theatre Project produced plays "for the people" from 1935 until 1939, when Republicans orchestrated its dissolution. The Project produced what was called The Living Newspaper as a way to employ out-of-work reporters and to educate the people through drama. Losey's first Living

Newspaper production, *Triple-A Plowed Under*, opened in March 1936. The play consisted of twenty disparate tableaux that touched on such topics as The Price of Milk, Farmers Organize, and The Supreme Court. The propagandistic subject matter, matched with Losey's radical staging, recalled Brecht's theories on the Epic Theater. The production presented each scene with masses of people instead of single characters; multicolored lights flashed here and there to illuminate different parts of the stage; the orchestra consisted only of percussion and trombones.[51] The critic Albert Goldman commented on the production's

> episodic treatment, mime and de-mystifying didacticism, and the thematic relationship of the involved groupings (farmers, consumers, middlemen, politicians) mediated by the stage company. . . . Patient, unembroidered explanations are required to show to farmers how the prices they receive for their produce are inflated by middlemen and passed on to consumers. . . . Government intervention, in the form of the New Deal Agricultural Administration Act (AAA or Triple-A) is soon exposed to vulnerable manipulation.[52]

Losey's second Living Newspaper production, *Injunction Granted*, which opened just a few months later, was a similarly episodic history of unionizing in the 1930s, in which he used—like Okhlopkov, whose radically decentered staging Losey admired—"a system of runways, platforms and hatches [which] provided the planes and areas which could be selected by complicated lights and which could overflow into the audience."[53] Like Brecht, Losey used projected headlines and cardboard signs to tell the story; a clown figure haunted the proceedings like a Greek Chorus; and the orchestra this time consisted of sixteen snare drums and sixteen bass drums. Losey's interest in Brechtian aesthetics began to wane, ironically, just as he was chosen to direct Charles Laughton in the American premiere of *The Life of Galileo*. Losey had little to do with the production, though, since Brecht himself maintained almost complete control.

Losey claimed that he joined the Communist Party in 1946 but quit soon after. He became good friends with many of the important Hollywood Communists, including Dalton Trumbo, Adrian Scott, Sidney Buchman, Francis Faragoh, and John Howard Lawson. It was around this time that the FBI began to monitor his activities, believing that he may have been serving as a contact for various Soviet agents. Losey's FBI file notes that he consorted with Communists and held party gatherings at his home. In October 1947, Losey helped stage a fundraiser for the Hollywood Nineteen, the leftists subpoenaed by HUAC. He soon became disillusioned, however, saying that Party activities in Hollywood were merely "a lot of meaningless so-called Marxist classes which were a bore and which never had any practical result."[54] By 1950 Losey was vacillating. He argued against the mandatory loyalty oaths in the Screen Directors Guild, but eventually joined almost everyone else in signing a voluntary declaration that he was not a Communist. That same year, Losey hired the lawyer Martin Gang, who was well known in leftist circles for helping people named before the committee get off the blacklist. Gang would present the committee's intermediaries with an affidavit his client had signed declaring that he or she was not a Communist and would be willing to provide names. Gang told Losey that he was to be named to the committee—by screenwriter Leo Townsend and his wife Pauline—and that he should prepare to testify himself. Losey instead flew to Italy to direct a picture with Paul Muni and never made another film in the United States.[55]

As Larry Wilder paces back and forth between the light and darkness in his small office, he might as well be Philip Dunne, liberal anti-Communist founder of the Committee for the First Amendment. Santa Marta might as well be Hollywood. In 1948, Dunne announced that he was "a tired man," gave up on political organizing, and gave up on the CFA. In the film Wilder tells Sunny Garcia, the local Mexican newspaperwoman, "you're looking at a tired man. . . . So I'm not taking sides or picking fights or telling them [the racist townsfolk] what to do. . . . Me? I'm for Mother's Day." But Wilder, like Dunne, was once a political firebrand. When he first starts wooing Sunny, he tells her, "I used to be like you—violent, impatient." Surprisingly, she says she's known him for years—she used to read his European dispatches over the teletype—and she urges him at every step to take up the cause of the Sleepy Hollow boys. She and Wilder are the living embodiment of the First Amendment, active and passive sides of the same coin.

The Lawless tells the story of Larry Wilder, Sunny Garcia, a young Mexican American teenager named Pablo Rodriguez, and the town of Santa Marta and its Mexican neighborhood across the tracks, Sleepy Hollow. At a dance in Sleepy Hollow, some white and Latino kids get into a fight and Pablo accidentally slugs a cop. Afraid and confused, he steals a car to escape. The local papers stir up a scandal with headlines warning about "fruit tramp riots" and a young hoodlum on the loose. After Larry Wilder decides to raise money for the boy's defense, the local white townsfolk rampage through the streets, first chasing some Mexican boys and eventually destroying Wilder's offices. Wilder tells the townsfolk that now he'll pack up and leave, but after Pablo thanks him for what he's done, Wilder joins forces with Sunny to continue publishing his paper any way that he can.

By calling upon the events of the past to construct his narrative, Daniel Mainwaring eschewed the conspiratorial ruminations of the Communist discourse on the events of 1943 and instead took up the liberal anti-Communist line. Because the film reflects the position of a progressive yearning for the idealism of the World War II era, the movie doesn't end with the white mob attacking the innocent Mexican kids; rather, they attack the newspaper office, the very symbol of the First Amendment. The angry white mob, like HUAC, was trampling on Americans' essential liberties, and the only path left, Mainwaring argued, was to regroup and fight as they had done years before. Mainwaring wasn't alone in conceptualizing HUAC as a lawless mob: Cy Endfield's *The Sound of Fury*, Joseph Mankiewicz's *No Way Out*, and Russell Rouse and Leo Popkins's *The Well*, all released in 1950 and 1951, also portray angry mobs as manifestations of the fascist tendency that liberals saw as dominating American political life at the time. In each film, a white mob takes the law into its own hands to attack blacks, Mexicans, the working class, or the freedom of the press.

The similarities between the events in *The Lawless* and the events of 1943 are overwhelming. Instead of Sleepy Lagoon, Mainwaring calls his Mexican neighborhood Sleepy Hollow. Instead of headlines about zoot suit riots, the local papers ran headlines about Fruit Tramp Riots. Both McGrath and Endore condemned the press's use of the word "gang" in describing the Mexican kids who hung around 38th Street. Outside the Sleepy Hollow dance hall, Sunny Garcia tells Wilder about the origins of the term: every boy "had a gang. Eight boys in a block. In Sleepy Hollow, that's a gang. Nothing much to do, so one gang fought another. Then the police would come and haul them off to jail. Pretty soon, people were saying we were all juvenile delinquents." Racial tensions simmered for months before the zoot suit riots because white servicemen and Mexican girls were trading sexual slurs on the streets of L.A. Many of the initial fights broke out when white servicemen picked fights at Mexican American dances.[56] The violence in Sleepy Hollow similarly begins when the white teenager Joe Ferguson and his buddies try to force some Mexican girls to dance with them at a "Good Fellowship Dance." Larry Wilder covers the dance for his paper precisely because he expects that violence might break out.

Pablo and his friend Lopo make their living picking tomatoes; the white characters refer to Mexicans as "fruit tramps." If Mainwaring wanted to write a script about anti-Mexican discrimination, he easily could have written about regular working folk in the barrio. More than 300,000 Mexicans lived in the Los Angeles area at that time; but in a segregated city, even a liberal like Mainwaring probably knew little about the lives of most Mexican Angelenos. Throughout the thirties and forties, though, the leftist discourse on Mexican Americans centered on migrant fruit and lettuce pickers and their struggles for better working conditions. No wonder, then, that Mainwaring's Mexicans are fruit pickers rather than the urban immigrants he might have encountered every day.

Throughout the riots of 1943, the L.A.P.D.'s unwritten policy on confrontations between Anglos and Mexicans was to arrest the Mexicans en masse and let the white people go. After the brawl at the Good Fellowship Dance, the Santa Marta police arrest eleven Mexican boys, but only one white boy. Both Endore and McGrath mention the inequalities the defendants faced because they couldn't afford quality legal representation. In *The Lawless*, one public defender represents all eleven boys, urging them to plead guilty to a lesser offense to save everyone the time and money of a trial. Both Endore and McGrath make every effort they can to mention that a defendant has served in the armed forces. Mainwaring, too, points out that Lopo and Pablo's older brother served in the army—Pablo's brother, in fact, died on the Normandy beachhead. The most important similarity, however, is on the discourse surrounding the press.

The liberals and Communists of 1943 knew full well that the fight over Sleepy Lagoon and the zoot suit riots was a fight over the power of words. Mainwaring does, too. Indeed, the film plays out like a step-by-step primer on precisely how yellow journalism comes into existence. As usual, Mainwaring takes the liberal rather than the Communist position, portraying the problems as stemming from individual failures rather than from structural problems with the culture as a whole. Mainwaring constructs two competing newspaper ideologies, with Wilder's *Morning Union* struggling to choose between them. On the liberal side, Mainwaring invents Sunny Garcia and her Spanish weekly, *La Luz* (The Light). Sunny repeatedly urges Wilder to use his paper as a weapon. "You can do a lot of good with it [the newspaper]," she tells him. "You can tell the people over there to—well, to look across the tracks." And later, after Pablo's arrest, she implores, "Can't you do anything? Tell the people he's a poor scared kid. Tell them to let him go." On the conservative side, Mainwaring creates Jan Dawson, a *Stockton Express* reporter who comes out to Santa Marta when she hears salacious tales of Mexican violence. Her paper's very name elicits comparisons with Hearst's *Examiner* and *Herald-Express* back in Los Angeles. The first sensationalized stories come not from Dawson, though, but from within the staff of the *Union* itself. Still uncommitted in the town's political landscape, Wilder's paper could eventually tip to either the right or the left, it seems. Wilder's assistant, Jonas Creel, freelances for the *Express*, and though he wasn't at the Good Fellowship Dance, he has no compunction about painting the evening's events as if he had, telling Dawson over the phone that "a gang of fruit tramps threw a dance for some other gangs over in Sleepy Hollow. . . . One of the kids—one of the ringleaders—a kid called Paul Rodriguez—slugged a cop."

When Jan Dawson arrives the next day she explains to Larry Wilder that she took Creel at his word and shows him the *Express*'s headline—the words "FRUIT TRAMP RIOTS" bearing a remarkable resemblance to the headlines of "ZOOT SUIT RIOTS" that Hearst's papers ran the previous decade. Dawson's disregard for the truth stems more from a politically naive desire to dramatize her story than it does from the right-wing agenda of her bosses. She and Wilder wax nostalgic about their newspaper days back in New York, but her fondness for the career doesn't include any desire to actually investigate the truth. She seems much happier inventing her own melodramatic vision of the world. A young girl named Mildred Jensen stumbled upon Pablo hiding in her barn and then hurt herself by walking into a post, but when Dawson visits the girl for an interview, she feeds Mildred her lines. "Now, dear, try and remember just what happened," she says. "You went down to the barn and he jumped out of the dark and grabbed you!" Sure enough, the next edition of the *Express* runs a headline that reads "Teen-Age Girl Charges Attack by Fugitive Youth." Later, Dawson describes the arrest of Rodriguez in purple prose, though she didn't witness the incident: "Rodriguez stood there, mud-covered, sullen, cruel, a trapped animal if ever I saw one. I moved closer to him, stared deep into his eyes, hoping to find some spark, some little ember of remorse, but all I could see was cruelty." Her biases are made clear when she says over the phone of the Mexican townspeople, "They all look the same to me." In 1943, the press depicted the zoot suit riots, for the most part, as Mexican attacks on white servicemen when, in fact, the opposite had been the case; in Mainwaring's script, a murderous band of white townspeople roam through the streets overturning cars and beating up innocent civilians, but the *Stockton Express* writes only of a "Fruit Tramp Riot" that never occurred.

Mainwaring and Losey paint the violence in Santa Marta as erupting from a complex interplay of racial, sexual, generational, and class conflicts. They take pains, though, to emphasize the strengths and weaknesses of each side in every conflict, thus emphasizing the culpability of individuals rather than of larger social forces. Like the liberals and Communists before him, Mainwaring depicts his Mexican characters, for the most part, as noble, patriotic Americans. Mainwaring's Mexicans are a touch more complex than the ones depicted in the left-wing pamphlets of 1943, though. Pablo is carefree and easy, dreaming of one day owning his own orchards. Lopo, on the other hand, who fought the Nazis in Europe, is more cynical. When two white kids confront them after a car accident, Lopo throws the first punch. Pablo, like the real Sleepy Lagoon defendants and unlike the defendants portrayed in the pamphlets, actually does commit some crimes. He does punch a policeman—though accidentally—and later he steals both an ice cream truck and a car on his run from the law. And during the race riot at the end, Lopo takes a wrench to the white crowd with relish. Mainwaring doesn't indict virtually every white person the way that Endore did, either. Some of the press—Larry Wilder, for instance—are good people. Most of the policemen are decent men who castigate the white teens for picking fights and who chide their more violent fellow policemen. The defense lawyer is harried, but a decent man. There is no racist judge, no discussions of the biologically determining factors of the races, and no references to fascism or Hitler. Indeed, one of the most sensitive and progressive characters in the entire film is Joe's father, the wealthy white Mr. Ferguson. Pablo's father had urged his son to stay away from Americans, but when Joe reacts angrily that he doesn't have any friends across the tracks in Sleepy Hollow, Mr. Ferguson tells him, "It would be good if you did have." When the boys from Sleepy Hollow are arrested after the dance, Mr. Ferguson pays their fines, and after the *Union* has been destroyed at the end of the film, Mr. Ferguson offers to put up the money to get the press running again. Had Mainwaring taken a position closer to that of Guy Endore, the result would perhaps have been a more twisted, more paranoid, and conspiratorial film along the lines of *Out of the Past*. Instead, his more mainstream liberal position has produced a story in which open-minded people from various racial and class backgrounds can work together to make the world a better place.

In drawing portraits of each group, Mainwaring and Losey continually highlight the commonalities between the Anglo and Latino communities. The very first shot of the film shows Pablo Rodriguez and a white man loading a truck together in the foreground and a multicultural group of workers picking tomatoes in the background. Later, when the workers gather to collect their pay, the foreman calls out two names—Jackson and Lopez. Pablo complains, "There must be an easier way to make a living," and Lopo says, "There is. For Anglos." But at that very moment a white couple walk by—presumably the Jacksons whose name we've just heard—and Pablo says, "Some of them don't do so good either. So quit your beefing." In one of the most effective sequences of the film, Losey shows Pablo and Joe primping themselves for Saturday night immediately after their initial altercation. Pablo runs into his backyard to take a shower, wearing nothing but a white towel.

He hangs his suit on an old wooden ladder and picks some clothes drying on the line just as a train passes in the background—an elegant visual reminder that Pablo's family lives on the wrong side of the tracks. The shower itself consists of a wooden cubicle behind the house; the shower head is a hose with an attached can filled with holes. Losey dissolves from Pablo in the shower to the shadow of Joe in his bathroom showering behind frosted glass. Joe steps out of his shower wearing nothing but a white towel—just like Pablo—but his bathroom is, not surprisingly, a bit more sophisticated. Still, while the trappings of wealth divide them, the visual parallels between the two teenagers confirm that their values and ambitions are the same. The boys also face similar intergenerational conflicts at home. Pablo's father rankles when his son calls him "Pops." "When my father spoke," he says, "I listened. But you—you tell me how to speak." Joe faces similar problems with his parents, ignoring his mother's yelled queries when he steps out of the shower. His relationship with his father is equally strained. When his father chides him for getting into a fight, Joe says, "Okay. Take their side like you always do." Later, at the Good Fellowship Dance, Losey and Mainwaring again stress the similarities that bind the various communities in Santa Marta. The dance floor is filled with white couples and Mexican couples, young and old; any class divisions seem invisible. The music itself consists of a variety of styles intended to appeal to a variety of backgrounds—some Mexican music, a big band number, and a waltz that Lopo plays especially so that Larry Wilder and Sunny Garcia might be able to dance together.

Throughout the movie, Joseph Losey reinforces Mainwaring's political views with his visual style. In his own life, he had formerly associated an avant-garde, Brechtian technique with a radical political commitment. In making a commercial picture for Pine and Thomas, though, he had no choice but to abandon his earlier radical style. Like most progressive filmmakers of the period, he shot on location and emphasized naturalistic acting and working-class themes. Indeed, most of his important movies made in the States—*The Prowler*, *M*, and *The Big Night*—focused on a working-class milieu and made extensive use of actual locations. They shot *The Lawless* in Marysville and Grass Valley, California, in just eighteen days,[57] and the local detail is one of the film's greatest strengths. At the Good Fellowship Dance, for instance, Losey shows a Mexican band shaking maracas in time with a 78 record. Mexican girls chew gum and look bored in skirts and sweaters leaning against a wall decorated with dried cornstalks. Much of the film is shot with natural light at night by cinematographer Roy Hunt. Almost everyone who has reviewed the film lauds its detail: "What gives it an edge of brilliance," Tom Milne wrote, "is Losey's eye for small-town locations: the shabby dance hall in the Mexican quarter, the sleepy high street, the one-horse newspaper office, the cosy front porches and the churchgoers, all swept away in sudden primitive starkness as the fugitive is relentlessly hunted over a fantastic wasteland of rocks and rubble."[58]

Losey's aesthetics are never completely naturalized, though. Even in the most quotidian details of the film, he delights in aesthetic flourishes for their own sake, a constant reminder that what we're watching is a work of art, not reality, an acknowledgment that the arguments put forth are political arguments, not representations of the world as it really is. He places almost all the action inside the frame, rarely using off-screen space: there are no unseen Communist-inspired conspiratorial machinations going on. The evils of the town—the angry mob, the right-wing ruminations of the press—are all on view just as the workings of HUAC were in the papers every day. Losey also does great work with tracking shots and camera pans to continually emphasize that Santa Marta is an actual place, not a studio set. As the camera follows Wilder and Garcia walking through town at dusk, for instance, they happen upon a man burning leaves in the street. In Wilder's newspaper office, Losey sets the camera in the hall and tracks or pans from one room to another to follow Wilder's agitated pacing, giving the audience a sense of the office's layout, the desks covered with typewriters and stacks of papers, and the strange, hulking printing press in the back room. Again, the moving camera provides the audience with an excellent sense of the physicality of the space, but it also shows that wherever Wilder goes, he can't escape the presence of the enormous printing press in the back room, the very embodiment of the First Amendment that's been plaguing his mind. And at two moments when Wilder's actions have helped Pablo reunite with his family, Losey sets up two rhyming deep-focus shots that show Wilder in the immediate foreground and Pablo embracing his mother and father in the extreme background, stressing—on a purely visual level—the profound effect that Wilder's decisions about how to use his press will have on other people's lives.

Losey also uses texts to make political points that the characters themselves seem unable to articulate. Foremost among these texts is the name of Wilder's newspaper—*The Union*—stenciled on the paper's front window. The name itself hints at Mainwaring's yearning for a merging of the factions of the Left, so it's only appropriate that for most of the film the newspaper's name is reflected backward across the wall behind Larry Wilder. Throughout the movie, Losey shows us this word again and again; it flares up against the back wall of the newspaper office as a reminder. Finally, in the film's climactic scene, the angry mob turns away from its Mexican victims and turns instead toward Wilder's *Union* offices, to attack, like HUAC, the First Amendment itself. The mob hangs outside the offices below, still too nervous to actually run up the stairs to the second floor and demolish the paper. As Lopo Chavez stands at the top of steps, holding the mob at bay—"in the army, they paid me to kill people like you," he yells as he wards them off with a wrench—Losey cuts back to the offices where Sunny Garcia stands with the words "The Union" splayed dramatically across the blank wall behind her, larger than ever before. Suddenly, someone in the crowd throws a rock and the words shatter with the broken glass. As Sunny cowers among the shards of letters, the crowd rushes up the steps and breaks open the door.

With most of their artistic decisions, Losey and Mainwaring took the liberal rather than the Communist line on the events of 1943. Clearly, the commercial dictates of Hollywood wouldn't allow a more radical political or aesthetic stance. At the same time, their liberal position was clearly a deliberate choice, since the movie was a kind of apostrophe to the liberal anti-Communists themselves. A movie influenced more by the Communist discourse would have centered on a vast conspiracy—it would have been more paranoid, more avant-garde, more ethically obtuse, but would have failed in its primary political objective: to galvanize the liberals of the day to return to the fight against the hardening Cold War consensus.

When the film was completed, producers Pine and Thomas knew they had made a picture unlike anything they had done before. *The Lawless* became the first film distributed by Paramount to open at "a small, so-called 'art' house" rather than at a big commercial theater. The *New York Herald Tribune* argued that the film was a "radical departure" for Pine and Thomas and that the film "may revolutionize distribution methods at Paramount and perhaps other studios and may even effect story production in Hollywood." Pine agreed, saying that "the story wasn't made for the mass appeal that our other pictures have quite frankly been aimed at" and that before the premiere he was awaiting the reaction "with quiet concern."[59]

His worries were soon dispelled. The reviews were uniformly glowing. Bosley Crowther began his *New York Times* review by saying, "Let's have a real salute this morning to . . . an exciting picture on a good, solid social theme . . . , a forthright little picture with which everyone may be pleased and humbly proud."[60] The *Variety* reviewer wrote that "the footage [is] constantly on the march and alive with excitement, particularly in the mob scenes and the mass running to earth of the frightened young Mexican."[61] Howard Barnes of the *New York Herald-Tribune* said that "mob violence has rarely been more vividly portrayed on the screen than it is in 'The Lawless.' "[62] Both the *Daily Worker* and the *Daily People's World* gave the film positive reviews as well.[63] The French—not surprisingly—were even more glowing. In *Cahiers du Cinéma*, Marc Bernard wrote, "It is the most beautiful of films. I breathe easier after each viewing. . . . It has a youthful tone, it is irresistible, like a morning swim." And in the same issue, Pierre Rissient, with a certain genre-bending flare, called it "the greatest western and even the only western ever made."[64] No reviewer, though, made any mention of the Sleepy Lagoon murder trial, the zoot suit riots, the House Un-American Activities Committee, or the Committee for the First Amendment.

Since then, the film has been largely overlooked. No one has yet published an essay on the film in the English language. The movie has never been available on video, and no one, as far as I can tell, distributes the film commercially. The 16 mm print I was able to track down at the George Eastman House had sprocket hole damage, proof that the film hadn't been projected in years. Losey scholars, it seems, are the people who most often bother to see the film today. But it's not too late for film scholars, like Larry Wilder, to redeem the past in the struggles of the present day.

6   Dark Passages

JAZZ AND CIVIL LIBERTY IN THE
POSTWAR CRIME FILM

Sean McCann

> *Music in pictures should say something without being
> obviously music.*
>
> Duke Ellington

In the moments leading up to the climactic scene of Otto Preminger's 1959 *Anatomy of a Murder*, Jimmy Stewart sits down at the piano and plays the music of Duke Ellington.[1] The setting is the home of defense attorney Paul Biegler, played by Stewart, who waits with his co-workers and closest friends—fellow lawyer Parnell McCarthy and secretary Maida Rutledge—for a verdict in the controversial murder trial that provides the subject and dramatic architecture of Preminger's film. Now, as all three await the jury's decision and muse on the uncertainties and mysteries of the law, Stewart's Biegler improvises a meditative jazz ballad and thereby establishes both an important feature of his character and a central symbolic element in Preminger's design.

To be more accurate, the music Stewart's Paul ("Polly") Biegler softly plucks out before launching into a rollicking boogie-woogie version of "Danny Boy" was written and performed by Ellington's collaborator Billy Strayhorn. But Ellington, who together with Strayhorn composed the legendary score for Preminger's film, also appears briefly as a character in the movie. Leading a small combo and graced with the name Pie Eye, Ellington shows up in a road-house scene where Biegler joins him for a short four-handed jam session. (His only line comes when he importunes the departing attorney: "Hey, you ain't splitting the scene, man!") Stewart's later solo exercise thus reinforces a connection between the two characters and underlines a point also made by Stewart's skill at the keyboard and his comic ability to meld genres and musical traditions. In the friendship between the white lawyer and the black musician, as in Biegler's jazz chops, we are asked to recognize the qualities also on display in the attorney's courtroom appearance—liberality, skill, wit, and a canny ability to conceal urbane worldliness beneath the appearance of down-home good humor.

But this use of jazz not only works to deepen and clarify the characterization that is one of Preminger's central concerns. Along with Ellington's score, it also serves the film's overarching artistic and ideological project. Preminger's eagerness to hire Ellington, giving the composer his first film score and associating the project with the current fad for jazz-scored movies, cast *Anatomy of a Murder* in the vein staked out by Preminger's recent productions. Like his other independent films of the fifties—*The Moon Is Blue* (1953), *Carmen Jones* (1954), and *The Man with the Golden Arm* (1955), each of which capitalized on Preminger's readiness to abandon the studio system and challenge the Production Code—*Anatomy of a Murder* offered itself as a social drama that highlighted a liberal challenge to conventional mores. In this respect, Preminger's use of jazz, and his foregrounding of Ellington's contribution to the movie, complements the film's sensational subject matter (the murder trial of army lieutenant Frederick Mannion, who is accused of killing the rapist of his wife) and still more of the dangerous sexual provocation the film casts as the central element of that story. Fifteen years earlier, Preminger had wanted to use Ellington and Strayhorn's "Sophisticated Lady" as the theme song for the title character in *Laura*, but had bowed to composer David Raksin's objection that the intimation of sexual experience would be too direct. The result was Raksin's composition of the film's celebrated but anodyne theme song. *Anatomy* has a different Laura at the center of its story—not Gene Tierney's coolly elegant career girl, but the southern working-class housewife Laura Mannion, played by Lee Remick as a barely restrained sexual dynamo. Now, in full control of his own production, Preminger brought Remick's considerable libidinal power to the fore and used Ellington's jazz to play up the later film's more direct emphasis on the subversive force of erotic desire and the moral ambiguity that accompanied it.

Such boldness with middle-class manners made the Preminger of the fifties seem, in David Hadju's nicely turned phrase, "a radical by Hollywood standards."[2] In no small part, however, that image came not only from Preminger's daring, or from the ironic detachment encouraged by his celebrated neutral style, but from the way Preminger made use of those qualities to reshape and integrate the cultural materials of the forties into the new ideological framework that flourished during the Cold War. *The Man with the Golden Arm*, whose treatment of Frankie Machine's morphine dependency introduced the subject of addiction to Hollywood film, both drew on and significantly departed from Nelson Algren's 1949 novel—remaking a social drama of urban decline into a story of individual dependency and self-reliance. In the process, it played a signal role in resuscitating Frank Sinatra's career. *Carmen Jones* had been a long-running Broadway production during the mid-forties, whose book and lyrics were penned by the presiding genius of the American musical and leading Popular Front figure, Oscar Hammerstein II. Only a year after *Anatomy*, Preminger would famously break the blacklist by crediting Dalton Trumbo as the screenwriter for *Exodus*. With each film, Preminger thus established his daring not only by challenging industry censorship, but by his willingness to use thematic materials and artists associated with the social democratic politics of the forties, while at the same time recasting those materials so that they seemed both resonant and acceptable in the era's new context. *Anatomy* itself offered one particularly striking example of the strategy in the star turn it gave to

Joseph N. Welch, the attorney made famous by the fatal blow he delivered to Joseph McCarthy in 1954's Army-McCarthy hearings. Cast here as the folksy but clever judge who presides over the film's country courthouse, Welch appears simultaneously as a figure of enlightened liberal tolerance and a reminder that the ideological conflict dramatized in McCarthyism seemed now a thing of the past.

Preminger's films of the fifties were in fact definitive expressions of Cold War liberalism, and especially so in their greatest strengths: the long takes that emphasized the complex interactions among small groups; the resistance to point-of-view shots that encouraged the audience to withhold its judgment; the deep feel for the complex workings of social institutions; and the moral ambiguity that all these features combined to produce and that Preminger emphasized as the core feature of every dramatic conflict. By the terms of the "new liberalism" that blossomed in the fifties, the world was, as Lionel Trilling wrote, "a complex and unexpected and terrible place" whose multifarious ramifications undermined all political dogmas and demanded a demeanor of subtlety and irony.[3] Like Trilling, *Anatomy* points to the transformative effects of Cold War mobilization as the context for its dramatic conflicts. The seductive Laura Mannion and her explosive husband arrive to upset Michigan's upper peninsula en route between stations in Korea and Germany, and they dispatch in the process the rapist and murder victim Barney Quill—the representative of a fading cultural order built on the declining logging and mining industries. Like Trilling, too, Preminger's film echoes the predominant language of Cold War liberalism, proffering itself as a challenge to sentimentalism and intolerance, but also providing an implicit defense of the virtues of liberal democracy. The law on display in its courtroom theatrics is an imperfect and morally dubious institution nevertheless admirable for its flexibility and for the presumed wide berth it gives to what Preminger praised as "individual autonomy." Preminger himself noted the implication. Remarking that "in spite of all the beefs you hear, this is really the only free country," he boasted of the fact that, when he screened the movie for the Russian Academy of Film, his viewers simply failed to understand it.[4]

Music in *Anatomy* underscores that perspective and illuminates the full range of the ideological transition Preminger effected. As an element of his characterization, Polly Biegler's love of jazz establishes him—as Laura Mannion notes when she comes across his record collection—as a "funny kind of lawyer." Marking him as a sophisticate and a covert cosmopolitan in the seemingly isolated world of the upper peninsula, it also establishes his affinity, not only with Pie Eye, but with the sexually dangerous Laura. They share taste in music, a neutral and dangerous meeting ground at the road house where Pie Eye plays, and, as Wynton Marsalis notes in his appreciation of Ellington's score, theme songs that echo each other closely. Ellington himself remarked that he wanted Biegler's theme to reflect a "smoldering and sophistication—a thing that is in the interior of this man."[5] That intimation of hidden depths, which echoed Cold War liberalism's fascination with psychological interiority, likewise underscored the portrait of Biegler offered by Preminger's film. For, as he would in John Ford's *The Man Who Shot Liberty Valance*, Stewart both drew on the image of naive virtue he had established in the great populist movies of the thirties and forties and, by showing it to be a consciously maintained public performance, cast that persona in a newly ironic light.[6]

As the movie's prime symbol of the pleasures and dangers of urbanity, though, jazz also becomes more subtly the movie's principal explanation for the social negotiation that it suggests enables democracy to work. In the critical scene with which we began, Biegler improvises implicitly to manage the dramatic tension while waiting for the verdict. As he plays, his colleague Parnell McCarthy expands meditatively on the significance of that tension, giving voice to a classic pluralist defense of the conflict and resolution inherent to liberal society.

> Twelve people go off into a room. Twelve different minds, twelve different hearts, twelve different walks of life. Twelve sets of eyes, ears, shapes, and sizes. And these twelve people are asked to judge a human being as different from them as they are from each other. And in their judgment they must become of one mind, unanimous. It's one of the miracles of man's disorganized soul that they can do it, in most instances do it right well.

That the movie gives us reason to doubt the conclusion to this encomium—the jury comes to a verdict, but it's not obvious that the outcome is just—doesn't undermine Preminger's appreciation for the effective working of democratic institutions. As in his *Advise and Consent* (1962), and as in the contemporaneous language of pluralist political theory, the process of negotiation becomes itself the central value. Since it is played underneath Parnell's meditation, Biegler's piano solo becomes almost explicitly the objective correlative for the law's office as social mediator. More generally, in an echo of what might be called the Ellison/Murray theory of American culture, jazz becomes—by virtue of its syncretic ability to bring together black and white, the energy of erotic passion and the discipline of musicianship—the emblem of American liberalism's capacity for flexibility and innovation.

That intimation is all the more resonant in that Ellington, like Sinatra—and to a lesser degree Ralph Ellison—found himself during the fifties retooling a career that had been shaped strongly by the political environment of the thirties and forties. Ellison himself had begun developing his theory of African American culture as the proof case for American freedom only after being disappointed by the aesthetic rigidity of the Communist Party. Though neither Sinatra nor Ellington had ever been as far to the left, both were prominently associated with the public face of the Popular Front, and Ellington's music was sometimes taken as an expression of the artistic virtues of populist democracy.[7] In Sidney Finkelstein's definitive Popular Front history *Jazz: A People's Music*, for instance, Ellington's orchestral compositions in particular appear as the heroic fulfillment of art's ability to transcend the class and racial divisions that marred American society. In their scope and ambition, and in their ability to overcome the distinction between elite and vernacular music, large-scale productions like "Black, Brown, and Beige" and the Popular Front revue "Jump for Joy" were taken to demonstrate what Finkelstein saw everywhere intimated in jazz—that "national freedom is inseparable from the democratic struggle, and the future of one people is wrapped up with the future of all." Predictably, as a critic who saw orchestral jazz as the analog to populist mass democracy, Finkelstein had little taste for the newly emerging musicians of the later forties. Bebop, he remarked perceptively if unsympathetically, amounted to a "bundle of contradictions." Rather than an artistic synthesis that anticipated the realization of popular democracy, it was "directly the product of the contradictions in our social life."[8]

But Ellington, who, like many American artists at the time, moved away from his earlier social democratic politics during the fifties, also began during the decade to assimilate some of the bebop styles that had sidelined the big bands, and Preminger's film would itself emphasize the transition. The score that Ellington and Strayhorn created for the film built on the large-scale compositions that had been Ellington's métier—displaying, according to Marsalis, Ellington's tonal and harmonic sophistication and his use of his full-scale band at its most accomplished. Tom Piazza seconds the judgment, calling the score, in terms Finkelstein might have approved, "a vernacular American symphony."[9] But Preminger's movie notoriously fails to make full use of Ellington's composition. What we hear accompanying the filmic narrative is not the complete Ellington band, but usually isolated soloists—an impression that is underscored not only by Biegler's piano solo, but by Ellington's appearance in the film, where he leads a small group whose format, if not musical style, is closer to the bebop combos than to the big bands with which Ellington was traditionally associated.[10] In all these ways, as in its thematic implications, Preminger's use of Ellington's music points away from the Popular Front language of democratic fraternalism and toward the emphasis on individual virtuosity and personal freedom that bop had placed at the center of jazz.

In this respect, *Anatomy of a Murder* can be seen as the culmination of a political and cultural transformation that was worked out among other places in the conventions of the thriller movie and in particular in the use of jazz within it. Like Orson Welles's contemporaneous *Touch of Evil*, Preminger's film can perhaps be best understood as a film that uses the dramatic architecture of the crime story as a means to dramatize what it casts as a fundamental change in a political and cultural order. Like Welles's Hank Quinlan, the absent Barney Quill of *Anatomy* represents the declining authority of a masculinist culture that appears backward and corrupt especially before the rise of a newly international, and implicitly interracial, order—one whose ostensible, dawning freedoms are defined by its erotic as well as by its military and diplomatic connections. Welles's film alluded to that transition in part through the use of jazz styles that hinted at cosmopolitan and interracial liberties.[11] So too with Preminger. Still more directly than *Touch of Evil*, the music of *Anatomy* artfully registers the rise of Cold War liberalism, by both drawing on and reshaping the roles that jazz had played throughout the major styles of the postwar cycle of crime films.

Jazz features prominently in the mid-century crime film, of course—almost always, as David Butler notes, in association with "sex, crime, and anxiety."[12] But its distinctive meanings in that context can be further clarified by noting that the symbolic uses of noir jazz so dramatically invert the Popular Front celebration offered by the likes of Finkelstein that the two might be thought in their antagonism to share an imaginative universe. That was certainly the case, for example, in the paradigmatic Popular Front film *Body and Soul* (1947). Establishing a stark contrast between the vampish torch singer Alice, who exemplifies the seduction that lures boxer Charley Davis (John Garfield) into corruption, and the painter Peg, whose ability to depict Charley's ideal character represents the benevolent claim that she and his working-class community possess on him, *Body and Soul* casts jazz as the background music of a parasitic society. But, at the same time, in its subtle use of its title theme, the film imagines a version of jazz, along with boxing, redeemed from corruption and reunited with the life of the people.[13] Just as in Finkelstein, and as in the film's depiction of Charley Davis's strength, the effect was to decry the commercial degradation of popular expression and to envision it as a barely restrained force of democratic union.

The vast majority of postwar crime films—particularly, the fatalistic thrillers retrospectively associated under the loose rubric of film noir—emphasizes only the former part of that dialectical image.[14] For jazz as it appears in the postwar crime thriller resembles what Finkelstein unhappily saw in bebop and in an older history of the music that he hoped Ellington's artistry would transcend. The sonic analog to the metropolitan labyrinth, jazz symbolizes not only, as critics have noted, the potent combination of eros and mortality, but the perils of urban freedom in a socioeconomic context ruled by competition and desire.[15] As the theme music for a dark demimonde of nightclubs, cocktail parties, and diners, jazz is frequently used to align erotic power and racial transgression with a market freedom implicitly, and sometimes explicitly, opposed to the promise of homosocial fraternity.

That picture is evident throughout some of the major films of the noir canon. It undergirds *Blue Dahlia* (1946), for example, where the "monkey music" that torments William Bendix is aligned with the devious complications of civil society and opposed to the fraternity of his war buddies; or *Phantom Lady* (1944), where Elisha Cook Jr.'s famed orgasmic drum solo dramatizes the movie's fascination with the covert pleasures and destructive appetites of the city—to which the alliance between the film's otherwise sexually neutral protagonist, the aptly named Kansas (Ella Raines), and police inspector Burgess is nominally contrasted.[16] (As always in Robert Siodmak's films, there are subtle reminders of the fragility of such distinctions.) But the locus classicus, of course, is *DOA* (1950), where the poison that will kill Edmond O'Brien's Frank Bigelow is none too subtly equated with the febrility of a saxophone solo played by a black musician and the intensely erotic, interracial context of "The Fisherman's Club" where the music is played.[17]

As Kathryn Kallinak and others point out, such depictions of jazz inevitably associate the music with the contagion of racial and sexual "otherness."[18] But it's worth adding a clarification to that point. What's being depicted in the postwar crime film's anxious or sensational depictions of jazz is not just the peril of sexual and racial mediation, but, by the same token, a nightmarishly exaggerated version of a form of urban sociability underwritten by the unpredictable force of commercial exchange.

The significance of that point can be clarified by noting how closely in certain respects the story told by *DOA* resembles the more subtle narrative of Jacques Tourneur's *Out of the Past* (1947) (written by soon-to-be blacklisted screenwriter Daniel Mainwaring). The latter film, too, features a brief, though highly resonant nightclub scene, where both jazz and interracial sociability are emphasized. Beginning his pursuit of the lethal siren Kathie, Robert Mitchum's Jeff finds an entry to the world she inhabits by traveling to the Harlem nightclub frequented by her maid Eunice. As James Naremore remarks, the respectful conversation that ensues avoids the pandering and exoticism evident in a film like *DOA*. But the nightclub is still an ambivalent portal into what seems at first glance a dangerous other world, and one that is contrasted to the narrow community of the small California town where, in the narrative frame that precedes the movie's central flashback, the film begins. The transition is marked by a trumpet fanfare and the conventional close-up on the bell of the horn, and its significance will be alluded to subtly as Jeff's pursuit of Kathie continues. When the two meet in Acapulco, Kathie arranges a rendezvous by recalling the "American music" of the nightclubs on Fifty-sixth Street. (The music they hear is not jazz, but surely the allusion is to the famed Fifty-second Street institutions of the bop renaissance.) Later, as Jeff tracks her in San Francisco, where she is at her most lethal, Kathie is associated with a solo piano that, in its labile shift from barrelhouse to ballad, anticipates *Anatomy of a Murder* and implicitly reminds us of Kathie's connections with pleasure and vice, along with her dangerous mutability.

That Jeff is drawn to Kathie and likewise effective on the interracial terrain of the Harlem nightclub both marks his allure—already Mitchum is a hipster—and explains his fatality. The point is a more subtle variation on the suggestion made melodramatically in *DOA*, where the film's soundtrack consistently aligns the poison working in Bigelow's system with a blues and represents the small-town sweetheart he has lost by sweet strings. There, just as in *It's a Wonderful Life*, for example, the contrast between corrupt city and virtuous town is highlighted by the difference between African American music and conventional popular song. In all these cases, moreover, that contrast is joined to an intense anxiety about the vast extension and unpredictability of a capitalist economy. *Out of the Past* underlines that concern when Jeff briefly lectures Kirk Douglas's gambler Whit on the economics of small-town commerce. "It's very simple," Jeff explains. "I sell gasoline. I make a small profit. With that I buy groceries, the grocer makes a profit. They call it earning a living." Though his tone is sardonic, Jeff's effort to distinguish a localized world of face-to-face relations from the torturously complicated, cosmopolitan transactions dramatized by the remainder of the movie is both sincere and, importantly, hopeless. If the lecture casts Whit as an emblem of parasitic luxury and Kathie as a figure of *fortuna*, in the reference to globally traded commodities (groceries, gasoline), it also reminds us of a point made by the film's heavy reliance on coincidence and chance meeting. When his former partner accidentally runs across Jeff and Kathie hiding in San Francisco, or when Whit's accomplice, the ethnically marked Joe Stephanos (who also stands out for his black clothing in the high key shots of the California landscape), finds Jeff living under a new identity in an isolated small town, Tourneur's film reminds us that it's impossible to insulate any corner of market society from the instability and competition that characterizes the economy at large.

As the eagerness of Jeff's neighbors to betray him suggests, then, small-town life in *Out of the Past* is no less predatory and unpredictable than its apparent metropolitan alternative. Likewise, the fair Ann, with whom Jeff hopes to forget the dark allure of Kathie, in her inquisitiveness and her own dawning impatience with the narrowness of small-town life, is hinted to be less different from her opposite number than she initially seems.[19] So fatalistically does *Out of the Past* view such matters that it casts Jeff as a man who aspires, much as in the classic literature of American modernism, for a kind of sheerly wordless, and entirely homosocial, escape from ordinary communication. His only reliable relations are fittingly with the taxi driver, who reminds him, "You don't have to tell me nothing," and with the deaf-mute "kid"—who so thoroughly represents the natural isolation to which Jeff aspires that he kills Stephanos with a fishing line. Jazz, then, is one alluring expression of the fatal communicativeness of modern life. As the introduction to an intensely eroticized and deadly world, it functions as the musical counterpart to a society where, in their compulsive talk, people calculate, deceive, and wittingly and unwittingly betray one another. Against it, only soundless isolation will seem like a secure alternative.

With its more sentimental contrast between the open world of the city and the neighborly realm of the small town, *DOA* stakes out a less extreme view of such matters. Indeed, the film's frame narrative, in which Bigelow recounts to a room full of sympathetic police the events leading toward his ensuing death, establishes a contrast between the reconstructive effort of his narration and the bewildering events surrounding his murder.[20] If jazz, in its association with sex and racial transgression, becomes a kind of poison, the homosocial dialogue that takes place within the civic confines of the police station stands as an alternative discovered, tragically, too late. But despite this important difference *DOA*, like *Out of the Past*, aligns the lethal pleasures of jazz with the terrifying extensiveness of the market. The explanation for Bigelow's poisoning—that in his work as an accountant he notarized an invoice revealing an illegal international transaction in iridium—can seem so arbitrary and, in its intimations of foreign contagion from the orient, so melodramatic, that few viewers give it much thought, preferring to focus on the compelling possibilities raised by a story featuring a man narrating his own death. But, for all the creakiness of the movie's plot, the disappointingly unmotivated conclusion fits well with the air of fatality that the film evokes. What Bigelow discovers in unraveling the cause of his death might be called the antiformalism of the market, where the incalculable extension of commercial transaction challenges both personal autonomy and narrative coherence as well as national and ethnic boundaries. His mortal vulnerability is thus revealed to be the direct counterpart to the swaggering machismo with which he first declares himself to be "all alone in the big city," just as his victimization by the contingent circumstances that lead to his death turns out to be indistinguishable from the exuberant openness to chance with which he arrived in San Francisco.[21]

In many of the classic films of the postwar crime cycle, in short, the ambivalent fascination with jazz corresponds with a deep anxiety about the unregulated energies of the capitalist market and with an associated awareness of the mercurial tendency of personal freedom to become lethal entrapment. In both aspects, moreover, jazz is resonant not only because it speaks to conventional ideas about the allure and danger of desire, but because, in its implicit and sometimes explicit association with African Americans, it lends powerful cultural resonance to the images of both unregulated passion and degrading constraint. Paula Rabinowitz plausibly suggests that we are meant to view Eunice in *Out of the Past* as Kathie's "aura"—a figure who in her association with pleasure and deception anticipates the fatal qualities of Kathie herself (and who thereby fulfills in her person something like the function that Preminger wanted "Sophisticated Lady" to serve in *Laura*).[22] Much the same point might be made about the role played in *Body and Soul*, for example, by Ben Chaplin (Canada Lee), whose corruption and death closely shadow Charley Davis's story. If at one level, his presence signals the film's and Charley's progressive contempt for racism, at another and more resonant level it provides, in the symbol of the abused and doomed black man, a warning to Charley of the dangers he faces.

A more direct example of the way complex intimations of both liberal enlightenment and degrading constraint could be intensified by the association with jazz can be seen in the signal role it plays in *To Have and Have Not* (1944). The film features two musical numbers that combine to effectively highlight the story's main dramatic tensions. In the first, Lauren Bacall (as Marie Browning) underscores her growing romance with Humphrey Bogart (Harry Morgan) when, accompanied by Hoagy Carmichael (Cricket), she performs the Carmichael/Johnny Mercer ballad "How Little We Know." The song, suitably intimate and romantic, highlights the tension of a romance bordering on serious commitment. ("Maybe it happens this way,/ Maybe we really belong together,/ But, after all, how little we know.") With the second number, Carmichael himself assumes the central role, performing his "Hong Kong Blues," whose narrative recounts the story of a Memphis man trapped by opium addiction in Hong Kong. Now fronting a full and integrated band and performing in an integrated Caribbean café, Carmichael sings of "a very unfortunate colored man" whose fate—imprisoned by colonial authorities and longing for return to the United States—provides an ostensibly humorous counterpoint to the situation facing Harry and Marie. Threatened with the possibility of perpetual imprisonment in Martinique, they avoid the confinement of Carmichael's colored man only by committing to a war effort that will remove them from both petty commerce and a racially integrated and pleasure dominated colonial entrepôt.[23] Harry will implicitly leave behind his business as a charter boat captain to serve the French resistance. Marie likewise abandons her incipient singing career to become his helpmeet, a transition she marks in the film's final scene: as she walks away from the café's dance floor, she first vampishly switches her hips toward Harry and then breaks into a conciliatory smile. The erotic, interracial, and commercialized terrain marked by jazz thus acts both to identify the liberality of the film's natural anti-fascists while also standing for the personal freedoms they will have to leave behind in their struggle against Nazism.

The major films associated with the noir canon frequently tell a similar story. Against the tacit peril of racialization, they often offer an alternative frame emphasizing populist allegories of class predation—as if, in perceiving their worlds correctly, the protagonists of noir might elude the threat of racial transgression and displace it with an awareness of popular solidarity. In *Out of the Past* or *The Killers* (1946), as in *Body and Soul*, jazz is one defining element of a ruthless world where the strong prey on the weak and the working man hero is as vulnerable to a parasitic and feminized elite as he is to the fatal women with whom they are aligned. Quite frequently, too, as in *DOA*, that image is countered, even if ineffectively, by the intimation of a civic order built on the democratic bonds created among mutually protective men. Thus, in Siodmak's *Killers*, for example, the alliance established between Edmond O'Brien's insurance agent Jim Reardon and Sam Levene's police detective Sam Lubinsky provides the frame by which the tragic fall of Swede (Burt Lancaster) and the ruthlessness of Kitty (Ava Gardner) and her entrepreneurial husband Big Jim Colfax can be measured and, if only retrospectively or imperfectly, understood.[24] It is not incidental that Kitty first lures Swede by singing a blues-tinged ballad, or that in the movie's climactic scene she, too, will be associated with a labile piano solo that in its transition from ballad to boogie woogie echoes the motif in *Out of the Past*.[25] But, if Kitty like Kathie is a fatal embodiment of treacherous fortuna, her influence will ultimately be countered by the solidarity of Reardon and Lubinsky. In the alliance they forge between insurance and the law, and in their opposition to an implicit connection between crime and rapacious industry, those two populist figures can be seen to figure the lingering elements of the ideology of civic fraternalism that had been a prominent part of American filmmaking during the war.[26]

In a number of the movies often associated with the noir canon—*This Gun for Hire* (1942), for example (screenplay by W. R. Burnett and the soon-to-be-blacklisted Albert Maltz), *To Have and Have Not* (1944), or *Key Largo* (1948)—that ideology provides the explicit normative vantage from which criminality and heroism are judged. And, as in *The Killers*, whose screenwriter Anthony Veilleman had came to the project from having only recently worked on Frank Capra's wartime propaganda series *Why We Fight*, many of the most celebrated films noirs preserve a kind of watered down version of that language of public commitment and populist allegiance. Over the course of the latter forties, however, as anti-fascist rhetoric faded before the concerns raised by demobilization and the emerging conflict of the Cold War, that ideology would come to seem increasingly feeble and disconnected from any larger public aims. These were years, of course, when the stylistic traits now associated under the noir rubric came to their greatest prominence, and the context may help explain something of the oft-noted political ambiguity of the noir canon, which has struck critics as manifesting, among others, both an "incarnation of . . . [the] critical power" of the Popular Front and a nihilist "demonization of the metropolis."[27] If neither of these views, or any of the other efforts to fix the critical meaning of film noir, seem either entirely correct or completely misguided, that may be due not only to the great diversity of the films associated under the label and of the political convictions of their creators, but because the postwar crime thriller, rather than encapsulating a particular ideological perspective, dramatized some of the uncertainty that arose as the United States was in the midst of effecting a major political, economic, and ideological transition.

That transition would be evident among other places in Siodmak's subsequent noir classic *Criss Cross* (1949), which again features Burt Lancaster (Steve Thompson) as a fatally passive working man driven by his erotic obsession with an inconstant woman and which once more contrasts that destructive relation to an alternative homosocial connection with a representative of the law—here, Steve's childhood friend, detective lieutenant Pete Ramirez. That the face of civic responsibility is now a fully anglicized Mexican American is particularly appropriate; for, in that gesture, *Criss Cross* alludes to the prominent intimation of wartime filmmaking that American civic institutions would forge a new national compact out of America's multiethnic working population.[28] In Los Angeles, that hope had been overshadowed by the reality of American racism and by the violence of the zoot suit riots. So, it is fitting that Siodmak's film makes its own version of civic interracialism seem both impuissant and emotionally empty. Though Ramirez seeks to deter Steve's passion for Anna (Yvonne DeCarlo) by threatening to jail her, his methods are cruel and arbitrary. ("I should have been a better friend. I shoulda stopped you. I shoulda grabbed you by the neck. I shoulda kicked your teeth in," Ramirez laments in words that both capture his brutality and his ineffectuality.) Quickly abandoning his role as Steve's protector to become his prime accuser, Ramirez abandons his friend in the moment of his greatest vulnerability, as Steve waits in a hospital bed for a visit from the gangster who is sure to kill him. Ironically, then, the judgmental Ramirez closely resembles the femme fatale who leads Steve to his doom—both characters rebuke and abandon Steve after promising to save him—while actually playing a more direct role in bringing about his friend's death.[29]

But if the law appears censorious and effete, in Anna's sexual allure *Criss Cross* hints at the prospect of a different mode of assimilation. Before taking the part, Yvonne DeCarlo had established her reputation by playing exotic roles that combined the suggestion of sexual license and racial ambiguity. Here once more she embodies a dark Venus who introduces the protagonist to a racially liminal world, and Siodmak's film is itself strikingly ambivalent in its depiction of that peril. Though Anna is venal and selfish and will destroy the two men who love her, Siodmak's film treats her with far more sympathy than was allowed Kitty in *The Killers*, showing her as a fearful woman who is abused by her husband and the police and who shares fully in the sexual desire that joins her fatally to Steve. More significantly, *Criss Cross* indulges Steve's longing gaze and luxuriates in the erotic freedom Anna embodies—particularly in the magnificent, extended dance number featuring Esy Morales y sus Rumberos. Widely acknowledged to be perhaps the most effective depiction of live jazz in the films of the era, the extended sequence is, as Alain Silver notes, the "key" scene in the movie, since far more directly than in *The Killers*, and without any of the perspective shots that in the former film cast Swede's love for Kitty in a doubtful light, the moment both establishes and legitimizes the depth of Steve's passion.[30] Almost directly countering the narrowly confined spaces of the homosocial barroom, where Steve meets Ramirez, with the vibrant space of the dance floor (and shifting likewise from deep focus shots that foster a sense of entrapment to close ups that highlight the vitality of the actors' movement), the dance number dramatizes the force of erotic obsession and implicitly defends it as a kind of doomed but glorious rival to the restraints of civic responsibility.

In this manner, *Criss Cross* points ambivalently toward an alternative use of jazz. In its most obvious features, Siodmak's depiction of Esy Morales and his music resembles the paranoid vision on offer in a film like *DOA*. In the heightened tempo established by quick cutting among the dancers, the musicians, and the yearning Steve, Siodmak creates an impression of erotic intensity and febrile communication similar to the one fostered in *DOA*. In the implicit interaction among all its participants, too, *Criss Cross* anticipates the later film's intimation that jazz functions as a vehicle of interracial sexual transaction—a suggestion that Siodmak, justly renowned for his striking imagery, underlines with a subtle visual cue. The musicians who play the Latin jazz in the extended dance sequence are shot in profile, prominently displaying the white blouson sleeves of the traditional rumbero costume. Toward the climax of the film, after he has been drawn by his love for Anna into the failed heist that will lead to his death, Steve is shown in a full arm cast that resembles a rigidly confining version of the musicians' dress. (As if to draw attention to the connection, a nurse asks him if he's dressed to go dancing.) Much as in *DOA*, the implication is that, as Steve has been sucked into the erotic web surrounding Anna, he begins to resemble the musicians who have earlier paid her tribute, undergoing a racialization that provides a negative counterpart to the seemingly idealized assimilation represented by Detective Ramirez.

But just as its treatment of Ramirez is less sympathetic than we're first led to expect, *Criss Cross* offers a far less hysterical vision of jazz communication than this description may suggest. In Siodmak's film, the musicians and dancers are not the frenzied celebrants of *DOA*'s nightclub, but virtuosi transfigured by the power of music and their own artistry. Indeed, since the entire, several-minute-long sequence manages solely through its combination of visual narration and musical rapport to establish the intense connection among the movie's main players, it strangely ends up fulfilling a role similar to that played by mute male friendship in *Out of the Past*. In a movie that, like all the major examples of film noir, emphasizes the impenetrable complexity of devious calculation, the dance scene, as Silver notes, "defies misconstrual."[31] For Siodmak, only the inarticulate force of heterosexual passion itself seems free of the deception, and betrayal that characterizes the world of talk.

Similar uses of jazz were a minor but illuminating feature of some of the movies now known as classic noirs, and though they usually appear only, and fittingly, as fleeting digressions in a film's larger narrative structure, often, as in Siodmak's case, they express more fundamental assumptions that point toward entirely different implications than those evident in the more notorious passages of noir jazz. Among the wartime films often described as early entries in the cycle—*This Gun for Hire*, for example, or *To Have and Have Not*, as more directly in *Casablanca*—the affiliations mediated by nightclub music occasionally appear, as they do in *To Have and Have Not*, as precursors to a wartime solidarity that will surpass and displace them. But, interestingly, in the years after the war a handful of films would continue to offer defenses of a jazz sociability, and the erotic freedom with which it was associated, without viewing it as a mere stepping stone to an implicitly grander civic purpose.

Edward Dymytrk's *Crossfire* (1947) might be seen to point the way here. Like so many of the anti-fascist films of the era, Dymytrk and Adrian Scott's celebrated indictment of anti-Semitism contrasts bigotry to the fraternal care apparent among a band of soldiers (represented in heroic guise here by Robert Mitchum's Sergeant Keeley) and the concerned public officials (Robert Young's Captain Finlay) who represent the state. But, set as it is after the conclusion of the war, and making the movie's villain, Montgomery (Robert Ryan), himself a career soldier, the movie still more forcefully raises doubts about the militarization of American society. The articulate voice of those doubts is the film's murder victim, Joseph Samuels (Sam Levene), who prophetically warns that the war has encouraged a dangerous brutalization of America's fighting men—a complaint born out when he is viciously beaten to death by the bigoted Monty.

Though Samuels was famously transformed from gay man in the source novel to Jew in the film because of Production Code pressure, the character remains both in his words and his actions a defender against abusive public authority of private liberties. Samuels will himself be revealed after his death to have been a veteran, but Monty is not wrong to perceive, as he does with disgust, that Samuels stands for the personal freedoms and pleasures of civilian life. Meeting the vulnerable Corporal Mitchell in a bar, Samuels quickly separates the soldier from his buddies and entices Mitchell (who will therefore become the prime suspect in Samuels's murder and the film's central object of sympathy) to his apartment, where he plays classical and big band records as they talk.

More than a few hints of a subversive eroticism survive in this depiction, not least in the shared tastes in music, both classical and big band jazz, that help bring together Samuels and Mitchell.[32] If, as Peter Stanfield points out, *Crossfire* signals its radical political affiliations in part through its subtle use of jazz, by the same token it casts both political commitment and sexual freedom as a form of *sub rosa* association whose covert nature is demanded by the bigotry and omnipresent surveillance that characterizes the film's image of public life. That Samuels is implicitly compared to the B-girl Ginny Tremaine (Gloria Grahame)—who like Samuels is drawn to Mitchell's vulnerability when she meets the corporal in a bar and who like Samuels will be made to suffer for her sympathy—only heightens the implication. In its dominant narrative, *Crossfire* echoes the Popular Front invocation of an inclusive fraternal democracy forged especially in the war against fascism.[33] But in its evident doubtfulness about the underside of wartime fraternity, and in its allusion to fleeting erotic alliances, impromptu meetings in bars, and the dark niches of the city (like the theater balcony where Mitchell hides, or the enclosed patio where he talks with Ginny), the film points toward a more individualistic and erotic image of urban freedom.

A less ambivalent rendition of that image appears in *Dark Passage* (1947), whose nightmarish impression of a world of total and yet invisible discipline is unrivaled by any film in the noir canon. No movie of the period offers a more pervasive sense of loneliness and vulnerability (created especially by its use of subjective point of view for the first third of the film) or renders the atmosphere of constant surveillance more omnipresent or more mysterious. Against that sense of unyielding public oppression, *Dark Passage*, too, elevates a vision of concealed private encounters. As J. P. Telotte notes, the only refuge Vincent Parry (Humphrey Bogart) discovers in his flight from constant persecution is a "network of similarly lonely and isolated types,"[34] and their briefly established yet intense connections—as evocatively under-explained as is the film's general air of inescapable surveillance—are, as in *Crossfire*, substantiated mainly by simultaneous erotic and musical affiliation. Thus, Parry first relaxes his suspicion of Irene Jansen (Lauren Bacall) when he discovers that she is a fan, as she says, of "legitimate swing." Similarly, the main defining characteristic of Parry's "only friend," bohemian George Fellsinger, is his dedication to the trumpet. In the film's oft-noted "magical" conclusion, where having escaped the oppression of San Francisco Parry and Irene are reunited in a wondrous otherworldly vision of Peru, those and similar intimations are redeemed and apotheosized. In *Criss Cross*, the dance floor of the film's central nightclub setting appears to burst open suddenly at the interior of an otherwise confined warren of narrow spaces. In *Dark Passage* a similarly expansive but far more vast and luxurious nightclub suddenly appears in the film's final scene to replace the many earlier images of entrapment. In this fantasy image of a seaside nightclub where soft Latin jazz plays, we see a vision of a worldly paradise that simply inverts the terms of the preceding narrative. Through the greater part of the film, Parry is a vulnerable private individual, trapped in his own frightened perspective. Now in this wordless scene, secure in the affections of Irene and in his freedom from surveillance, he appears to be, as Telotte notes, "just another patron, quietly enjoying himself" (131).

What is especially striking about *Dark Passage*, in short, is that it lacks any suggestion of the kind of civic or fraternal vantage proposed, even if fatalistically, by many of the most prominent postwar crime films. We encounter no voice of authority, no representative of justice or public commitment, no substantial image of homosocial bonding. In both the film's paranoid central narrative and in its concluding utopian vision, Parry appears as a private man in pursuit of individual freedom and personal satisfaction. It is a vantage that, far more radically than *Crossfire* or indeed perhaps of any film in the noir canon, appears to presume not just the discrediting of public authority but its complete irrelevance to a form of happiness that seems otherwise so insubstantial and fleeting that it is best represented by brief snatches of music. What the film also lacks, therefore, is a figure likewise missing from *Crossfire*–a lethal femme fatale or even a B-girl of the sort whose sexual vulnerability, in films like *The Big Heat* and the urban exposé movies of the fifties, represented the decadence of the postwar metropolis.[35] Failing to discover much value in the ethos of public fraternity, these films have little need for the mythic figure who most threatened it.

A still more resonant variation on that attitude can be seen in the subsequent Bogart vehicle *In a Lonely Place*. Nicholas Ray's film offers in effect a far richer and less abstract version of the social anxiety evident throughout *Dark Passage*. Like Parry, Bogart's Dixon Steele finds himself a man under relentless surveillance—the object of mistaken but unyielding police suspicion and, equally, of the constant disapproving scrutiny of his film industry peers. Like Parry he is a man who has fallen from worldly stature to public ignominy—in this case, less from unjust prosecution than because of his declining fortunes in the crisis-beset movie business—and he, too, remains stranded in painful isolation by his aggressive sensibility and elevated tastes. Unlike *Dark Passage*, the movie makes it clear that the brief happiness Dix discovers with his lover, Laurel (Gloria Grahame), is doomed by the combination of his violent temper and her inability to withstand her doubts about it. But here again we are given no alternative in the fellowship of public spirited men to the instability of sexual desire. In fact, Dix's wartime buddy Brub resembles *Criss Cross*'s Ramirez; in his role as homicide detective, he is as much Dix's persecutor as the rescuer he would prefer to be. So, too, the movie lacks a femme fatale or B-Girl. The film's most dangerous and most vulnerable women are not the erotic free agents who terrify in most films noirs, but aspiring wives and mothers—whether in the murdered hat-check girl Mildred (whose death significantly both leads to and dooms Dix and Laurel's happiness), or in Brub's censorious wife, Sylvia, or in Laurel herself, who becomes both more doubtful and, like Mildred, more endangered by her lover's jealous possession, as she comes closest to becoming Dix's spouse.

It's fitting in light of the profound distrust of domesticity that *In a Lonely Place* shares with *Dark Passage* and *Criss Cross* that the film offers us but one brief and unshadowed image of happiness. Sitting at a piano bar as the singer Hadda Brooks croons a soft ballad, Laurel and Dix are shown in a moment of fleeting erotic intimacy. Both the setting and context differ importantly from the film's comparable reprieves from anger and suspicion—the domestic scenes in the secluded world of Dix and Laurel's garden apartments, for example, where despite their announced happiness, the two are constantly interrupted and overseen by intruders, or the beach picnic scene where Sylvia deftly sabotages a brief suggestion of connubial satisfaction. In this moment, by comparison, the evident source of happiness is not domestic compatibility but sexual desire, a suggestion of public intimacy indicated by a tight close-up of Laurel whispering languorously in Dix's ear. Not surprisingly, that scene—wordless, like the comparable moments in *Criss Cross* and *Dark Passage*—is soon interrupted when Laurel points out that even here Dix remains under the surveillance of the police and, perhaps more significantly still, when we see that the detective tailing the couple has arrived with his wife. Responding furiously to the reminder of domestic authority, Dix stubs his cigarette out on the piano, occasioning a striking reaction shot of Brooks. The pianist is shown wincing at the keyboard as if in actual physical pain.

That reaction shot, a signature Ray visual fillip, adds little to the narrative development of *In a Lonely Place*, but it goes a long way toward establishing the film's political sensibility. For, if in her hurt reaction to Dix's violence, the jazz singer seems at first glance but one of the many women who react doubtfully to the writer's aggression, the fact that she responds not with the horror or fear shown by Sylvia and Laurel, but with wounded sensitivity, aligns her rather with Dix himself, who throughout the film wears a look of pained suspicion. In the moment of her reaction, Brooks turns dramatically from a background figure into a fully dimensional person whose subjectivity is displayed in her hurt realization of her insignificance to the people who surround her. Like Dix, an artist ignored by her world, and like him therefore a "nobody," Brooks is also significantly perhaps the only character in the film who is shown to respond to Dix without engaging in the kind of probing surveillance practiced by every other person he encounters.[36] In the implication of the two figures' shared vulnerability, Ray thus echoes a prominent theme of much of the critical discourse of the fifties—that, in his alienation, the artist surrounded by mass society shares in the status of the racial minority. Likewise, in their shared perceptiveness (only Dix immediately understands who must have killed Mildred, and only Brooks fails to misperceive him), Ray suggests that the minorities victimized by a repressive democracy are the sole figures to see it clearly. Dana Polan claims that the film's pointed if brief notice of Brooks reflects "the frequent concern in Ray's films to give attention to excluded groups and their forms of cultural expression."[37] But, true though that undoubtedly is, it doesn't go far enough. In the cultural expression of the excluded group, Ray implies the promise of a kind of sociability alternative to the conformity and oppressive surveillance that characterizes ordinary society.

Much as in the musical allusions in *Dark Passage* or in the dance sequence in *Criss Cross*, in other words, the brief image of the piano bar offered by *In a Lonely Place* functions as a nearly utopian promise of what recent critical theorists have referred to as a counterpublic.[38] In its most prominent face, the major films of the postwar crime cycle preserved an ideological vision, indebted both to the Popular Front and, more significantly, to the rhetoric of wartime mobilization. It was a vision that emphasized the conflict between individual desire and social responsibility, between the enticements of the market and the resources of civic commitment, and that fittingly aligned those contrasts with a populist concern about the vulnerability of the common man to parasitic elites. *In a Lonely Place*, by contrast, can be seen to mark a pivotal moment in the realization of an alternative perspective that dispatches the language of class and popular democracy and emphasizes instead the conflict between a hegemonic public authority and the subversive forms of personal freedom and ad hoc alliance that resist it. The implication is similar to the suggestion that would soon be made in *The Sweet Smell of Success* (1957) (screenplay by the blacklisted Clifford Odets), whose prominent use of the Chico Hamilton Quintet calls on jazz to function far more directly as a model of a hip interracial affinity at odds with a demagogic, and masculinist, popular culture.[39] But it is also comparable to the vision that was being developed contemporaneously in the work of a poet like Frank O'Hara, whose rhapsodic poems about the pleasures of the city, including bop, celebrated the fleeting beauties of private satisfaction, covert pleasure, and personal liberty.

That in the world of Hollywood film such a vision was fostered in part by left-wing artists (Dmytryk, Ray, Odets) who had good reason to fear political intolerance should come as little surprise. But the contribution those artists made to the transformation in the cinematic meaning of jazz points more significantly to a far broader shift in popular attitudes about the qualities of public freedom. In the years following the late forties, the social democratic politics prominent in the thirties and forties plummeted rapidly in influence. As they came under concerted political attack from the right and as the industrial and urban economic order on which they had been premised began to cede ground to the growing signs of a new postindustrial economy, the political and cultural languages of social democracy were gradually displaced by the rights-based liberalism that blossomed especially during the sixties and seventies. It was a context in which both the rising demands for African American civil rights, and the productive resources of African American culture, would increasingly appear not as the marginal or problematic forces they had been made to seem during earlier decades, but the definitive face of the possibilities and limits of American liberalism.

Recognizing the ways in which the crime film's use of jazz participated in and anticipated that transformation, we are now in a position to appreciate the full resonance of the transition marked by *Anatomy of a Murder*. In his distinctive and artful use of Ellington's music, Preminger managed to draw on and combine the two images of jazz that had been prominent in the crime films of the forties and fifties. On the one hand, in its association with Laura Mannion, jazz could be called on as a representative face of a dangerous erotic freedom associated with the uncontrollable liberties of the Cold War economy. On the other, in the artistry of Polly Biegler, it stood for the ability of the culturally savvy individual to recognize and negotiate the powerful energies that coursed through his world. Casting Jimmy Stewart as an ironist and a covert hipster, Preminger's film declared definitively that the legacy of the Old Left was over and that a new politics of cultural freedom was being born.

7 Documentary Realism and the Postwar Left

Will Straw

> *The documentary film, regarded as one of our chief warborn boons, need not be an end-of-the-war casualty, like female welders.*
>
> Noel Meadow, *Screen Writer* (1946)

In 1943, Noel Meadow, a New York publicist and one-time tabloid journalist, bought the Stanley Theatre in Manhattan for the purpose of exhibiting wartime documentary films.[1] Meadow had been the press agent for the Stanley in 1942, when it broke U.S. attendance records for a Soviet film with *Guerrilla Brigade*, the American release of the 1938 fiction film *Vsadniki*. Set during the First World War, *Vsadniki* was produced to glorify the Soviet Army on the eve of World War II, and its U.S. release in the midst of that war was part of the broader nurturing (and exploitation) of U.S.-Soviet solidarity. Over the next two years, and in collaboration with producers like Maurice Lev or Joseph Plunkett, Meadow assembled war-related documentary feature films out of newsreels and other available footage, showing them at the Stanley and distributing them throughout the United States. These features included compilation titles such as *One Inch from Victory* (which used enemy footage provided by the Soviets) and *What Price Italy?*[2]

At the end of the war, Meadow formed Noel Meadow Associates, to undertake the American distribution of films imported from Europe. The first film handled by the new company was the French fiction film *Resistance* (*Peleton d'Execution*, André Berthomieu, 1945). *Resistance* catered to an American interest in topical, war-related films but signaled as well the shift by Meadow and other independent distributors away from an exclusive interest in documentaries. The U.S. release of *Resistance* was one step in Meadow's effort to develop a broader, postwar market for European feature films in the United States, building outward from specialized cinema houses in Manhattan. Over the next decade, Meadow imported, promoted, and occasionally wrote the subtitles for such films as *Dedée* (Yves Allegret, 1948), *L'Aigle à deux têtes* (Jean Cocteau, 1948), and *El* (Luis Buñuel, 1952). His various companies, such as Omnifilms and Uniworld, distributed foreign features alongside domestically produced educational films and documentaries.[3]

Noel Meadow (who died in 1968) was a minor but emblematic figure in the wartime and postwar culture of the American Left. His name is absent from the available lists of those blacklisted or witch hunted, and his personal political commitments are not clear. Nevertheless, Meadow's creative and entrepreneurial activities in the 1930s and 1940s followed the key pathways of progressive American culture. In the 1930s, Meadow had co-produced a stage comedy dealing with matrimony in the new Soviet Union, and reported for American magazines on developments in Soviet dance. His writing output in the 1940s included liner notes for 78rpm albums released by the fellow-traveling Stinson record label, among them "Fighting Songs of the U.S.S.R.: Songs That Glorified the Unconquerable Red Army" and "Memphis Favorites," by the New Orleans jazz band the Memphis Five. In their combination, these albums occupy significant portions of that terrain of progressive affinities which Michael Denning has called the "cultural front."[4] While serving as managing editor of the New York–based trade paper *Writers' Journal*, Meadow wrote regularly for the *Screen Writer*, the journal of the Screen Writer's Guild, during the period of its most intense radicalism.[5]

Over several articles published in the *Screen Writer*, in 1946 and 1947, Meadow urged film exhibitors and distributors to help build theatrical markets for documentary and international films within the United States. As a film exhibitor, publicist, and commentator, Meadow expressed one of two competing visions concerning the documentary film and its place within a progressive postwar cinema. The better-known of such visions, to which I turn shortly, imagined a Hollywood commercial cinema transformed from within by the forms and ideals of the wartime documentary. For Meadow, in contrast, the postwar flourishing of the documentary was to occur outside Hollywood, within a broader pluralizing of American film culture that would serve, over time, to diminish Hollywood's centrality. Meadow's call for a new pluralism expressed both his entrepreneurial commitment to the theatrical distribution of non-Hollywood films and his faith in the newly internationalist viewing habits instilled in Americans by the experience of the war. The institutions on which a plural postwar film culture might rest, in Meadow's view, included theaters specializing in documentary films and cinema clubs for children that combined entertainment and progressive instruction. Meadow had written enthusiastically about one such organization, the New York Matinee Club, in 1946, recounting its success in screening the anti-racism film *The House I Live In* for groups of children during National Brotherhood Week.[6] To the regret of Meadow and others, the withering of public interest in the documentary was diagnosed soon after the war's end. In 1947, Wesley F. Pratzner, a minor producer of wartime documentary films, wrote an article for the *Public Opinion Quarterly* entitled "What Has Happened to the Documentary Film?" Pratzner quoted, at length, Noel Meadow's acknowledgment that "the documentary film, which gave such bright promise of permanence, went into comparative eclipse on V-J day."[7]

The other vision of a postwar role for documentary has become more deeply inscribed within our understanding of wartime and postwar progressive film culture.

This vision was expressed in the call to filmmakers to take the lessons of wartime documentary production back to Hollywood, and to make documentary the core of a moral and aesthetic transformation of mainstream, commercial filmmaking. If, in the United States, the postwar project of building audiences for documentary films quickly receded, to a cultural space occupied by specialized professionals (such as educators), the debate over how Hollywood films might incorporate documentary elements attracted high-profile public figures writing across a range of venues. Within a broad corpus of liberal and left-wing publications, from *Harper's* through the *Daily Worker*, one finds the same films serving as points of reference in an ongoing reflection upon possible new roles for the Hollywood film. The early references in this discussion were often to isolated moments of non-studio filming in mid-1940s films: to the scenes of Third Avenue bars in *The Lost Weekend* (1945), for example, or those of the abandoned aircraft field in *The Best Years of Our Lives* (1946). As the category of the "semi-documentary" film solidified, attention came to focus more exclusively on the cycle of such films produced by Twentieth Century Fox (*House on 92nd Street*, *13 Rue Madeleine*, *Boomerang!*, *Call Northside 777*, and *Iron Curtain*). Progressive responses to the Fox cycle, from the welcome promise of *House on 92nd Street* (1945) through the cold disappointment of *Iron Curtain* (1948), allow us to trace the left's growing disenchantment with the semi-documentary project.

The postwar semi-documentary is not a lost object within film studies,[8] but it has almost always been one of uncertain status and limited interest. Our understanding of the progressive response to postwar cinema has long been clouded by film scholarship's later enshrining of the film noir as the most vital expression of a postwar sensibility. Film noir came to be understood, conveniently, as both a conscious, programmatic intervention by politically engaged filmmakers (such as Orson Welles or Nicholas Ray) and a cluster of symptoms through which collective or individual psyches betrayed themselves. This flexibility has made film noir a key example in virtually every significant wave of theoretical development marking film studies' history as a discipline. The semi-documentary, in contrast, has been easily dismissed as merely programmatic, a set of filmmaking protocols so self-conscious as to be formulaic and gimmicky.

Likewise, film noir scholarship, from its beginnings, has grappled with the abundance of competing claims about noir's precursors or constitutive features. This has made the film noir a richer focus of polemic and ongoing research than the semi-documentary, which still inspires only the loosest of explanatory gestures. In the late 1940s, observers saw the semi-documentary in the vaguest of relationships to Italian Neo-Realism, the newsreel, the 1930s social documentary, and the wartime government instruction film. Later, more academic commentary has done little to clarify these relationships. In what follows, I examine a selection of progressive assessments of the postwar semi-documentary, by writers whose political affinities range from left-liberal through Stalinist-Communist. In these assessments, we see the promise of the semi-documentary flourish in the immediate postwar period, then wither amid the hardening of Cold War divisions.

Over three days in March 1948, the American Communist Party's *Daily Worker* ran a series of articles on Hollywood's turn to documentary—on what it called the American cinema's semi-documentary "new look."[9] This lengthy appraisal of the form was published two months prior to the May 1948 release of *The Iron Curtain*, Twentieth Century Fox's semi-documentary treatment of the Igor Gouzenko case. The Gouzenko affair had erupted in late 1945, when the Canadian government announced its discovery of a Soviet spy ring engaged in stealing atomic secrets. Since 1946, the American Communist Party had been active in countering what it saw as war-mongering hysteria in the responses of the U.S. government and mainstream media to the Gouzenko case. The *Daily Worker's* campaign against *The Iron Curtain* began before the film's release. It involved appeals to readers to boycott the film and reports on efforts to block its exhibition. The paper's ultimate condemnation of the semi-documentary cycle seems inseparable from its attempts to discredit *The Iron Curtain*.

The *Worker's* earlier judgments of films within the semi-documentary cycle had been largely positive. Since the Popular Front period of the mid-to-late 1930s, and most fervently since U.S. entry into World War II, the *Daily Worker* had sought to fulfill most of the functions of the mainstream daily newspaper, expanding its sports coverage and reviewing cultural events using criteria that were not always explicitly political.[10] Despite the Communist Party's return to orthodoxy after 1945, the *Worker* continued to comment matter-of-factly on the entertainment value of newly released films. The tone of its movie reviews, in the years 1946–1948, was one of a genial populism that relished brisk, effective filmmaking and a lack of pretension. This sensibility allowed the paper to respond positively to *House on 92nd Street* (1945), the first film in Fox's semi-documentary cycle. The *Worker* was slightly more reserved about *13 Rue Madeleine* (1946), drawing attention, in its review, to the film's lapses into generic formula: "Despite its use of the documentary technique *13 rue Madeleine* remains only another melodramatic thriller, with a story tailored to fit James Cagney." *Boomerang!* (1947) and *Call Northside 777* (1948) were praised for dealing with miscarriages of justice, and for their reliance on "factual material." *T-Men* and *Kiss of Death* (both 1947), films at the margins of the postwar semi-documentary cycle, were both embraced for their refusal to render the gangster life glamorous— the former, in particular, for its avoidance of the "fancy-pants night club life" of films noirs like *I Walk Alone*. One week before it reviewed *The Iron Curtain*, *The Daily Worker* praised *The Naked City* (1948) for its lack of glamour and concern with the downtrodden, noting, in its only reservation, that "the film's reality is limited by a concern for surface effects, never probing causes."[11]

What stands out most strikingly in the *Daily Worker* film reviews during this period is their slightly puritanical suspicion of glamour and melodrama. This suspicion led the newspaper to favor semi-documentaries over thrillers like Douglas Sirk's *Sleep My Love* (1948), whose studio-bound production seemed to go hand in hand with their glamorous, upper-class settings. (The *Daily Worker* reviewed the Sirk film alongside *Call Northside 777*, calling the former a "slick little chiller-diller.")[12] The "toughness" of a film like *T-Men* stood, for the *Daily Worker* reviewer, as the mark of a welcome honesty.[13] The highly touted capacity of these films to narrow the gap between Hollywood fiction and the documentary rendering of location, character, and event was only a secondary reason for enthusiasm. As the campaign against *The Iron Curtain* got under way, however, the *Daily Worker* came to focus more pointedly on the aesthetic and ideological premises at the heart of the semi-documentary project.

On April 10, 1947, Darryl F. Zanuck had announced production of *The Iron Curtain* as a semi-documentary film, claiming it was based on a report by J. Edgar Hoover to the House Un-American Activities Committee.[14] The fuller source for *The Iron Curtain* was the report of a Canadian Royal Commission, though the Canadian government refused to support production of the film. Three weeks before its release, the *Daily Worker* reported at length on the efforts of the New York Arts, Sciences and Professions Council of the Progressive Citizens of America (PCA) to stop Twentieth Century Fox's distribution *The Iron Curtain*.[15] The PCA, formed by Henry Wallace progressives disenchanted with Harry Truman's apparent betrayal of Rooseveltian ideals, condemned *Iron Curtain* as a simple capitulation by Fox to the House Un-American Activities Committee and to its call for more films critical of the Soviet Union. By March 16, 1948, the *Daily Worker*'s David Platt was referring to an imminent "cycle of war-mongering films," which was to include *Portrait of an American Communist, I Married a Communist,* and *Vespers in Vienna*.[16] (The first of these was never made; the second and third were released in 1949, with *Vespers in Vienna* retitled as *Red Danube*.)

Platt's warning of this new cycle came on the same day as the first of the *Daily Worker*'s three feature articles reevaluating the semi-documentary film. The author of these pieces was Herb Tank, a merchant seaman turned playwright and journalist who served for a time as the *Daily Worker*'s regular film critic. The 1948 series expressed the *Worker*'s growing ambivalence about the postwar semi-documentary, a form that it had initially welcomed with minor reservations. Noel Meadow, in the sentence serving as epigraph to this article, had compared the fate of the wartime documentary to that of the wartime female welder. In a highly suggestive passage, Herb Tank began his three-part assault on the semi-documentary by drawing parallels between the semi-documentary film and the lengthened skirts of postwar women's fashion: "The old Hollywood film has a new look. Unlike the new look in skirts which tend to cover up more and expose less the new screen look appears to show more and cover up less. At least it seems that way on the surface."[17]

Tank devoted much of this first article to a genealogy of the semi-documentary, which departed from most contemporary understandings of its history. Conventional wisdom of the time saw the semi-documentary as inspired by wartime collaboration between Hollywood and the institutions of wartime public education. Most progressive observers of the wartime documentary cherished its roots in an enlightened state apparatus that mobilized new sorts of professional expertise (such as clinical psychology) to produce carefully structured works of civic instruction. The very form of the wartime documentary, therefore, took shape in the interweaving of official, institutional voices and emerging systems of expert knowledge (like those of psychiatry or sociology). From the beginning, Tank and the *Daily Worker* set out to revise this history, situating the documentary impulse within a longer history which was properly that of left-wing activism. In this revised account, the officially sponsored wartime documentary cycle became a mere interval within that history:

> The documentary became a worldwide film movement [in the 1930s]. In America, it developed independently of Hollywood, resulting in the making of such fine films as the three Pierre Lorentz [sic] films *The Plow That Broke the Plains, The River,* and *The Fight for Life;* van Dyke and Steiner's *The City;* Paul Strand's *The Wave;* Frontier Films' *People of the Cumberlands* and *Native Land. . . .*
>
> War-time film makers pressed by war-time needs quite naturally took over the form and the film techniques developed by the socially minded film makers of the thirties.[18]

Tank's assertion of a fundamental continuity between the social documentary of the 1930s and the official wartime instruction films of Allied governments was hardly outlandish. The career and ideas of John Grierson bridged the two, as did many of the principles underlying practices such as Pare Lorentz's filmmaking work for the Federal Resettlement Administration in the late 1930s. Nevertheless, the *Daily Worker*'s enshrining of the 1930s social documentary as definitive in the history of the form was part of a broader pulling back from the experience of the war to reassert more longstanding political continuities. Within this longer view, the wartime documentary became a temporary, imperfect expression of the progressive search for truth, rather than its most perfect achievement. Having "lent" the documentary form to the institutions of wartime instruction, the left now witnessed the betrayal and distortion of that form within Cold War propaganda films like *The Iron Curtain.* It was therefore important for the Communist left to reclaim the documentary impulse as its own.

In "More on Hollywood Documentary Style," the second article in the *Daily Worker* series, Herb Tank returned briefly to the 1930s, describing the marginalization of the social documentary by the "vast big business network of film distribution," which saw no commercial potential in the form. In the years that followed, Tank suggested, a lingering, collective hunger for "real people, real problems, real places on the screen" found at least partial satisfaction in isolated films like *The Grapes of Wrath,* or in the documentary moments of wartime films such as *Sahara, A Walk in the Sun,* and *The Pride of the Marines.* (These latter films, however, were compromised by their recourse to "hokum and contrived situations.") This hunger for truth survived into the postwar period, and Hollywood studios scrambled to invent the means for satisfying it. In Tank's account, the postwar semi-documentary film responded to no social necessity—nothing comparable to the wartime desperation for useful information—but to the transformed tastes of moviegoers, who now looked to films for enlightened instruction. *The House on 92nd Street* appealed to postwar audiences, Tank suggested, through "the power of scenes that did little more than describe the methods used by the FBI to combat Nazi spies."[19]

Tank singled out *Boomerang!*, which told the story of a small-town miscarriage of justice, as the last of the redeemable semi-documentaries. Following its release, he argued, the form was corrupted, in part by its decline into gimmickry but, more important, by its mobilization in the service of "unrealistic themes and social distortion": "But *Boomerang!* was the last of the 'semi-documentaries' to deal with a social theme. The documentary method of going to the actual in order to photograph it is now being transformed in Hollywood into a new look for the same old studio contrived hokum. It is becoming a new package for old goods."[20]

The last of Herb Tank's pieces, on March 19, 1948, was entitled "Today's Films: Holly'd On-the-Spot films conceal truth." Here, we find a significant shift in the substance of the *Daily Worker*'s critique of the semi-documentary film. It is no longer the descent of the semi-documentary style into gimmickry that is condemned, nor the inevitable contamination of the documentary impulse by melodrama or "hokum." (Both of these developments could leave the semi-documentary ideal itself as a positive model.) Rather, the constitutive features of the semi-documentary had rendered it a dangerous tool of deception. The various stylistic innovations that distinguished postwar Hollywood filmmaking were now in the service of an insidious propaganda:

> Contact with the documentary film movement has improved the Hollywood product. On the spot shooting has made for an appearance of greater reality. So has the sharper more realistic documentary style photography so much less glossy and high-lighted than the usual Hollywood output. . . . But the real rub in the Hollywood look of realism will be the outright war-mongering films. Almost every one of the promised anti-Soviet films is being made with the new look. Exteriors for *The Iron Curtain* were filmed in Canada. Whenever possible actors not well known to movie audiences are being used so they will more likely be identified as real people. The photography is harsh and contrasty. Some parts of *The Iron Curtain* were filmed to simulate newsreels. The new look is aimed at wrapping up the biggest lies in the most realistic packages.[21]

This passage introduces one of the eccentric sidelines in the polemics over *The Iron Curtain*: the debate over the film's use of unfamiliar actors in small parts. This controversy deserves extended attention, for it condenses several of the semi-documentary's paradoxes and incoherences. The casting of non-actors in small background roles had been a widely touted feature of the semi-documentary since *The House on 92nd Street*, though its intended effect was never coherently expressed. Intended to heighten a film's verisimilitude, the semi-documentary's use of "real" people in small roles served, in fact, to reinforce the distinction between the films' recognizable stars, rich in connotative resonances, and the faceless performers who peopled their backgrounds. This was already, within the studio system, one effect of the division of labor between stars, character actors, and extras, and of the long-standing recourse to typecasting in the filling in of backgrounds. In films like

Call Northside 777 and *Boomerang*, the recognizability of performers declined with the size of their parts—as we moved into the texture of crowds or community, and sometimes saw "real" non-actors in these contexts—but this was true of most Hollywood films anyways.

Herb Tank, who elsewhere heralded *Naked City* and *House on 92nd Street* for their use of real-looking performers in small parts,[22] condemned *The Iron Curtain* for employing actors outside the pool of recognizable character actors and bit players. (In fact, filmographies confirm that most of those playing small parts in *The Iron Curtain* were prolific, hard-working bit players.) This, he suggested, made it more difficult for audiences to recognize the contrived, fictional character of the film. Bowsley Crowther's two *New York Times* pieces on *The Iron Curtain*, which sharply criticized the film for being propagandistic, singled out its casting of unattractive character actors to play the roles of minor Soviets in the film.[23] Darryl F. Zanuck's lengthy response to Crowther noted that "we could hardly see fit to use our handsomest character actors, but rest assured that the players we selected flattered their prototypes."[24] In his separate review of *Iron Curtain*, Tank argued once again that the use of unfamiliar faces made performers "more acceptable as Soviet agents," presumably because audiences had no prior sympathy with them. At the same time, the weaknesses of *Iron Curtain*, for Tank, had just as much to do with its typecasting of its leading performers, which exploited their familiarity and the resonances of their previous roles: "June Havoc, for example, had to make little change in her characterization of the Dragon Lady type in Intrigue to that of Karanova, the slinky blond spy, in *Curtain*."[25]

At the end of the day, the *Daily Worker's* condemnation of the semi-documentary project could not successfully resolve its own incoherences. If stylistic features like sharper location photography and the use of unfamiliar actors, once hailed as ways of seeking after truth, were now condemned as tools of deception, this hardly led to calls for a highly theatricalized, self-reflexive filmmaking laying bare its own devices. Ultimately, it was *The Iron Curtain's* message which condemned the film in the newspaper's eyes, and the campaign against it moved away from questions of style and form to the coordination of public protest against the film's war-mongering character. On May 21, 1948, the *Daily Worker* again turned to an ostensibly independent organization—the National Council of American-Soviet Friendship—for reports on the nationwide campaign to picket screenings of *Iron Curtain*. Alongside the coalitions of "clergymen, civic leaders, YWCA officials and labor leaders" who joined in these protests, local Wallace for President Committees were prominent in the demonstrations, according to the *Worker*. David Platt's report on these campaigns offered an unexpected comparison: "Not since the opening of the anti-Negro film *Birth of a Nation* in 1915 has an American movie encountered such widespread opposition from the decent people of the country. *The Iron Curtain* is even more vicious than D. W. Griffith's notorious lynch film because it propagandizes for a war that can lead to the total destruction of human life."[26]

The release of *The Iron Curtain* constituted a milestone in the postwar unraveling of the progressive coalition that had nourished the wartime documentary and embraced, however reservedly, the postwar semi-documentary. *The Iron Curtain* was inseparable from the broader conjuncture into which it was released, but this in no way diminishes its own, important role in forcing and revealing political fault-lines in and out of Hollywood. Milton Krims's self-justificatory account of writing *The Iron Curtain*'s screenplay, in the pages of the *Screen Writer*, signaled both the change of political line at that magazine and the new sorts of political retrench-ment that had settled in by late 1948:

> I will close where I started—with reference to my conscience. It is not every writer who makes Pravda and a by-line article by Ilya Ehrenberg. Nor is it every picture that brings mass picketing and riots to otherwise peaceful American streets. I'm rather pleased I wrote *The Iron Curtain*. Once and for all it was proven to me that the Communist who demands for himself all the rights of free speech is unwilling to grant them to anyone else, especially his opposition. Up where I come from, everybody has a chance to say his own piece the way he sees it. And if it makes for confusion—it also makes for free men.[27]

Outside the *Daily Worker*—in film periodicals like *Hollywood Quarterly* or the *Screen Writer*, national magazines such as *Harper's*, *Commentary*, and *Life*, and aca-demic journals including *American Quarterly* and *Public Opinion Quarterly*—a rich debate over the direction of postwar cinema transpired between 1945 and 1950. Within this debate, the semi-documentary was a privileged point of reference, but a set of broader themes brought unity to a diverse corpus of analyses and polemi-cal interventions. In order of declining generality and popularity, these themes included the following: 1) the role of Hollywood films in the adaptation of the American people to life under postwar conditions; 2) the trend in certain American films of the time toward on-location filming and documentary realism; 3) the wide-spread use within films of psychological themes, and of psychiatrists or psychoana-lysts as major narrative figures; and 4) the popularity, in postwar films, of first-person narration and the use of the "subjective" camera.

Seemingly disparate, these issues all came to turn around the cinema's status and potential as an instrument of socially useful knowledge, as what Tony Bennett and others might call a "civic technology."[28] In our time, on-location shooting and first-person point-of-view shooting may divide the semi-documentary procedural from the film noir. In the immediate postwar period, both were viewed as technologically mediated tools for scientific investigation (of social environments or psychological realities, respectively).[29] It was an article of faith among progressive postwar thinkers that the wartime collaboration between Hollywood and the institutions of wartime public education had produced a model of civic-minded filmmaking appropriate to postwar life.[30] In 1945 and 1946, the liberal left still believed that enlightened expertise, mobilized and mediated by the institutions of government, might be employed within the production of fiction films. The formal dilemma posed here was that of how the films themselves might be "institutional"—that is, how they might both embody and represent the workings of enlightened postwar institutions.

Near the end of his final assault on the Hollywood postwar semi-documentary, Herb Tank noted in *The Daily Worker* that "of the three most recent Hollywood 'documentaries,' two of them had as their purpose the glorifying of government agencies."[31] No feature of the Hollywood semi-documentary film has clouded its reputation more than its celebration of the state apparatus, from the FBI of *House on 92nd Street* through less conventionally heroic bodies like the Treasury Department (*T-Men*, 1947) and the U.S. Post Office (*Appointment with Danger*, 1951). It is easy to diagnose, in the semi-documentary film's institutional voices and upholding of government authority, both a reterritorialization of film noir's oneiric disorder and an ideological foundation for the militarized Cold War state.

Nevertheless, the use of institutional procedures to frame the semi-documentary had loose grounding in the faith of wartime progressives in forms of scientific knowledge. The commitment to rationalism had been one basis of the left's antipathy to fascism; it persisted in postwar progressive suspicion of the emotionalism which marked thrillers like *The Big Sleep*, a tendency denounced by Communist cultural critic V. J. Jerome as typical of the "Brute-Cult" of mid-1940s cinema.[32] A rationalist project for postwar cinema imagined fiction films engaged in an ongoing transfer of knowledge between the most innovative of mid-century intellectual disciplines (like psychiatry or sociology) and the moviegoing public.[33] Set against this vision, however, the scope and accomplishment of the postwar semi-documentary film could well appear limited. Virtually all the semi-documentaries of the postwar period revolved around public institutions, but these were almost never the innovative institutions of wartime or postwar social science. *House on 92nd Street* and *13 Rue Madeleine* focused on the FBI and Office of Strategic Services, glorifying relatively old-fashioned sorts of undercover work. *Boomerang!*, *Call Northside 777*, and *Naked City* likewise located "expertise" at the lowest, most local levels of institutionalized authority and in longstanding forms of dogged professionalism. By the late 1940s, when stories featuring contemporary federal institutions were more clearly predominant, the semi-documentary offered little more than low-budget variations on the police procedural (such as *State Department: File 649*, or *Port of New York*, both 1949).

If the institutional focus of the semi-documentary sprang in part from the faith in professionalized knowledge, it came, as well, from the earnest efforts of (mostly) progressive filmmakers to produce films that exalted collective over individual action. Writer-producer Lester Koenig (later blacklisted) was among many progressives who hailed the wartime battle film's submersion of individual characterization within visions of group solidarity.[34] This dimension of the Popular Front war film is well enshrined within histories of the period, but the effort to pursue the battle film's collectivist vision within the institutional thriller is less obvious. In the police procedural semi-documentary of the late 1940s, as Frank Krutnik has noted, "the individual serves as a necessary, but necessarily regulated, part of the system."[35] The emotionally flat heroes or male couples of institutional procedurals like *Appointment with Danger* or *Union Station* (1950) may seem weak inheritors of the battle film's dryly determined collectives, but both betrayed the mid-1940s suspicion of sentimental individualism.

In 1947, Jay Richard Kennedy wrote, in the pages of the *Screen Writer* of his work with the United States Treasury on a semi-documentary film chronicling the struggle against worldwide narcotics smuggling. *Assigned to Treasury* (released in 1948 as *To the Ends of the Earth*) was directed by Robert Stevenson, who later accepted the much-proffered assignment to direct *I Married a Communist* for RKO. Sidney Buchman, the producer of *To the Ends of the Earth*, was blacklisted in 1951, and Kennedy himself pursued a varied career which took him from the Republican Brigades in Spain to a position, in 1966, as vice-president of Frank Sinatra's business concerns. Over almost six densely argued (and pedantic) pages of "An Approach to Pictures," Kennedy described his attempts to write this film in a manner that balanced the individual-centered story of heroism with those lessons about environment and collectivity put forward by the best wartime documentaries. Remarkably, Kennedy described having undertaken a study of eighty feature films in preparation for the assignment, discovering in the process that "the prewar film technique seemed to concern itself most actively with the Great Man, the individual who bends all situation to his fabulous will."[36] Kennedy opposed this "technique" to that which he discovered in the documentary films made during the war:

> The other technique, the wartime "documentary" like the prewar Hollywood technique referred to above, likewise taught me many important things. How to find people and events in their native habitat (among other things, by actually bringing a camera there!), the power of understatement, of matter-of-factness, the attention to small, but exciting detail which creates the illusion of reality, faith in the dramatic values implicit in the environment (dramatic situation), which prevents gilding the lily or distorting it. All of this proved invaluable.[37]

In his script for *Assigned to Treasury*, Kennedy claimed to have developed an approach to character that synthesized the lessons of prewar fiction and the wartime documentary. His "documentary characterization" was a "technique of unfolding character which is as dominant as the authentic factual revelation of dramatic situation and strikes the same tone and matter-of-fact spirit."[38] "Documentary characterization" was intended as a means of producing knowledge about character, but its realization followed the stylistic paths of understatement and diminished tone. Revealingly, Kennedy acknowledged that a key requirement of the "fact-drama" method of storytelling was its desexualization: "Among other solutions, in the middle section of *Assigned to Treasury*, the girl is totally absent. She is kept alive in the story only by her bearing upon it."[39] In *Assigned to Treasury*, as in the semi-documentary more generally, the puritanical resistance to melodramatic intensities seemed to reduce main characters to the institutional settings in which they worked. This flattening of character to setting could be embraced, then, as a way of producing knowledge about character, as one more technique in the postwar project of progressive instruction.[40]

This flatness was never total, however. At the heart of the semi-documentary was the tension between its restricted institutional frame and the rich possibilities offered by narrative worlds outside the studio backlot. This tension does not map easily onto that between right and left, as if the semi-documentary film enacted the struggle between an ascendant security state and a populist, neorealist opening onto social life. The incoherence of the semi-documentary resides in the ways in which, at least initially, it set two sorts of progressive inquiry against each other. One form of inquiry was invested in the rational procedures of the liberal state, the other in the populist exploration of urban lifeworlds. The most perceptive postwar writing on the semi-documentary worked to delineate this tension. In 1948, Siegfried Kracauer devoted one long paragraph of "Those Movies with a Message" to *Boomerang!*, the most widely discussed of all the postwar semi-documentaries. *Boomerang!* was, perhaps, the least institutionally centered of films within the semi-documentary cycle, but it cast the relationship of hero-individual to broader social environment in a manner typical of the others. However much *Boomerang!* opening framed its story as that of the hero's movement within an institutional context, the broader social world of the film opened up to swallow both. "Along with the case itself," Kracauer wrote, "the whole social texture from which it emerges is brought to the fore."[41] The following year, Parker Tyler noted how so many American films of the period, from *Citizen Kane* through *Boomerang!*, had become documentary through their employment of investigative narratives that followed the deductive pathways of scientific discovery, in a movement Tyler labeled a "journalism of science."[42] In *Call Northside 777*, *T-Men*, the *Naked City* and most of the semi-documentaries that followed, the institutional frame was one from which characters departed. As narratives got under way and characters followed their investigative paths into Kracauer's "social textures," the richness and diversity of those textures were always at odds with the solemn flatness of the institutional point of departure.

One of the last public statements by film publicist and distributor Noel Meadow took the form of a press release published by the *New York Times* in 1961:

> Noel Meadow has formed Survival Pictures, a new company that will offer silent and sound films in 16 mm and 8 mm for use in fall-out shelters. The films will be approved by an advisory group of leaders in all walks of life and will be suited for the morale of underground inhabitants—when and if. Claustrophobia being the principal consideration, the pictures will be composed of outdoor subjects and travelogues, in addition to messages by world figures.[43]

Clearly satirical, Meadow's announcement simultaneously targeted the absurdities of Cold War survivalist preparation and elite-driven civic instruction. Like all of Meadow's public interventions, this one was coy about his precise political allegiances. In its mockery of enlightened advisory groups, however, and in its vision of pacifying travelogues, it revealed how cynically the project of quasi-official documentaries (and, indeed, of novel exhibition venues) had come to be viewed, two decades after Meadow had embraced the form in the early years of World War II.

8 Cloaked in Compromise

JULES DASSIN'S "NAKED" CITY

Rebecca Prime

Is it the director's fault if the title lies, if the city hasn't been unveiled to us but on the contrary, its reality modestly hidden? After all, we can still find in it, in filigree, the traces of another sort of reality.

Jean Paul Marquet, *Positif* (1955)

The Naked City (Universal, 1948) was Jules Dassin's heartbreaking big break. The film was a commercial and critical success, its vivid depiction of New York recognized with Academy Awards for best cinematography and editing. Yet Dassin walked out of the film's premiere in tears. Gone were his shots of bums on the Bowery, his satirical jabs at Upper East Side socialites; what remained was a portrait of a city that James Agee described as "bursting with energy, grandeur, sunlight, and human variety" but stripped of the stark contrast between wealth and poverty that the director considered its most defining aspect.[1] Utterly disillusioned, he swore he would never make another film.

More than just the familiar tale of Hollywood taking a hatchet to a director's vision, *The Naked City*'s transformation from the social document Dassin imagined to a rather innocuous Hollywood genre film has political dimensions that become evident when examining the film's production. *The Naked City* finished shooting on October 21, 1947, just one day after the first congressional hearings of the House Un-American Activities Committee commenced.[2] During the hearings, one of the film's writers, Albert Maltz, was called to testify. Considering the committee's obsession with the presence of Communist propaganda in Hollywood films and the film industry's rapid capitulation to the committee's concerns, it stands to reason that a film with a blacklisted screenwriter would receive particularly close scrutiny from the studios. *The Naked City* was further compromised by a personal tragedy: the untimely death of producer Mark Hellinger in December 1947. Without Hellinger around to protect his project, the executives at Universal had free rein to edit the film as they saw fit, which—as Dassin put it—meant excising any scene that "smelled of politics."[3]

Considering the impact of these events on the final form of *The Naked City*, it is curious that accounts of the film deemphasize the political drama of its production in favor of the stylistic and thematic contributions it made to postwar realism and to the film noir subgenre of the police semi-documentary.[4] A more historical emphasis, however, reveals the degree to which *The Naked City*'s troubled production history mirrors and reflects the tensions dividing Hollywood during a period of intense political, economic, and cultural upheaval. With America rapidly embracing the new conservative, capitalist ethos of the Cold War, Hollywood progressives like Dassin and Maltz suddenly found themselves at odds with the nascent political climate. The conflicting artistic and political visions that contributed to *The Naked City*'s final form serve to illustrate the complex interplay between liberal and conservative impulses that characterized Hollywood during the late 1940s.

The Naked City belongs to the small cycle of semi-documentary police dramas that enjoyed a brief heyday in the years immediately following World War II. As its name suggests, the semi-documentary was a hybrid form, combining techniques associated with documentary filmmaking with plots derived from Hollywood genre formulas. The enthusiasm for documentary aesthetics within the film industry is usually ascribed to the war, during which time many film personnel were recruited or conscripted to work on government documentaries.[5] The war had also accelerated the development of technological advances such as faster film stocks and lighter 16 mm cameras that facilitated location shooting.[6] From an industry perspective, this yen for realism was to be encouraged, at least with regard to film style. By 1948 Hollywood had entered its postwar economic slump, and the inflation of labor and production costs encouraged the studios—even conservative MGM—to welcome the cheaper production values of the semi-documentary.[7] However, the film industry's embrace of the documentary was half-hearted, encompassing aesthetic but not ethical considerations. This conception of the genre reflects the influence of the two men most closely associated with its development: Louis de Rochemont and Darryl Zanuck.

In 1943 Zanuck hired de Rochemont to produce a new series of "living journalism" films for Fox, the first of which was the surprise hit *The House on 92nd Street* (1945, dir. Hathaway).[8] With its voice-of-God narration, story line drawn from police case work, location shooting, use of authentic documentary footage (actual FBI footage of photographed surveillance), and casting of non-actors (in this case, FBI agents playing themselves), *The House on 92nd Street* established the basic parameters for the semi-documentary cycle, which de Rochemont described as aiming to "strike the right proportion between actuality and entertainment."[9] De Rochemont's liberal attitude toward the intermingling of fact and fiction reflects his experience as the creator of *The March of Time* newsreel, an acclaimed series that transformed news into narrative.[10] De Rochemont's priorities were well matched by Zanuck's, whose interest in stories pulled from the headlines, and in unexpected plot twists, was matched by his disdain for the documentary. In an early script conference for *The House on 92nd Street*, Zanuck warned: "We have to do what we do dramatically or it will fall into the category of documentary features and there is just no market for them. . . . We have to make up our minds to make an entertaining picture or we should just turn the material over to *The March of Time* and forget about making a picture out of it."[11]

After the success of *The House of 92nd Street*, de Rochemont produced three other semi-documentaries for Fox: *13 Rue Madeleine* (1947, dir. Hathaway), *Boomerang!* (1947, dir. Kazan), and *Call Northside 777* (1948, dir. Hathaway). By 1948, the semi-documentary cycle had peaked with the release of *He Walked by Night* (Eagle-Lion, 1948, dir. Werker/Mann), *T-Men* (Eagle-Lion, 1948, dir. Mann), and of course *The Naked City* (1948).[12] Unlike films noirs, with their isolated and alienated antiheroes, the protagonists of the semi-documentary crime film were usually law enforcement officials and were depicted in such a favorable light as to prompt the French critics Raymond Borde and Etienne Chaumeton's blunt summation that "the American police procedural documentary is in fact a documentary in praise of the police."[13] By reassuring the viewer of the efficiency and integrity of American social institutions, especially its legal organizations, the semi-documentary can be seen to serve an affirmative, conservative function. Reviews of *The House on 92nd Street* support this perspective, indicating how the film tapped into fears of domestic insecurity. The *New York Times* wrote that "had the FBI failed in its protection of top military secrets there is no telling what the consequences might have been on the battle field," while the *Los Angeles Times* suggested that "you will sleep all the easier of nights after viewing the feature and knowing more of this amazing system of protection for the USA."[14] Other semi-documentaries such as *Call Northside 777* and *Boomerang!* do, however, reveal a more nuanced depiction of government institutions by dramatizing real-life instances in which the American justice system proved fallible. As Will Straw notes, this concern with the factual depiction of miscarriages of justice, along with the use of documentary technique and the rejection of glamour and melodrama, endeared the semi-documentary to sections of the progressive press, at least initially.[15]

As the semi-documentary cycle took off, so did concerns about the implications of its casual use of realist aesthetics. In a feature article, the *New York Times* admonished Hollywood for twisting the truth to "suit dramatic convenience," calling the practice "an evil of mass communication."[16] The *New Republic* noted the need to distinguish between "reality" and the "verisimilitude" offered by the semi-documentary, which—while completely false—persuades through "the ancient fallacy that you cannot deny the evidence of your own eyes."[17] By 1948, the "semi-documentary" label had more to do with marketing than with the film's treatment of reality; as the *New York Times* observed, "The current habit publicists for producers have of claiming that every low-budget picture of crime of violence is a semi-documentary epic establishes the importance of the genre beyond a doubt."[18]

The semi-documentary's evolution within Hollywood is of political and cultural significance. While the industry was happy to adopt selective documentary techniques for commercial and economic reasons, it wasn't about to embrace other aspects of non-fiction filmmaking, most particularly its emphasis on education, if they came at the expense of entertainment. The path of the semi-documentary's development resonates with the "paradigm shift" that Lary May argues occurred in Hollywood in the aftermath of World War II. During the immediate postwar years, the liberal New Deal culture that had flourished in Hollywood before the war was rapidly replaced by conservatism, as Hollywood realigned itself with corporate interests and "the new 'American' ideology of corporate consensus, class harmony, and abundance."[19] Haden Guest likewise interprets the semi-documentary's fascination with the processes of law-enforcement as a "collective expression of Hollywood's gradual conservative turn," calling attention to the parallels between the popularity of on-screen policing and "the studios' controversial 'policing' of their own backlots" as a result of the blacklist.[20] Rather than evolving in the direction of the documentary, the semi-documentary took after its Hollywood side, lending support to the emerging "culture of consensus" through its positive depiction of law enforcement and existing social institutions.

Yet the postwar public was clearly yearning for something more than escapism, judging by the enthusiasm with which the semi-documentary was greeted.[21] A contemporary analysis of the popularity of "movie realism" attributes this change in public taste to the war, which "swept aside sham . . . and taught us to respect direct action and plain speaking. . . . Finally, in a long-brewing reaction against phony studio sets and 'actors,' we found a new, newsreel, newspaper reality in the semi-documentary technique—actual locations, peopled by men and women whose glamour came from within, not without."[22] However, the semi-documentary was not the only type of film feeding the public's craving for realism. Reviews of Roberto Rossellini's *Rome: Open City* (1945) likewise highlight the film's refreshing difference from Hollywood productions, with critics praising the film's "hard simplicity and genuine passion" as opposed to "the slickly manufactured sentiments of Hollywood's studio-made pictures." Another reviewer compares the film's effect to that of "a great violinist playing great music on a cheap fiddle, whereas too many Hollywood productions remind me of somebody's tomboy sister playing 'Hearts and Flowers' badly on a Stradivarius."[23] The success of *Rome: Open City* had an invigorating effect on foreign film exhibition, creating an unprecedented demand for other Italian films in the "documentary" style.[24]

While the appeal of Italian Neo-Realism strikes some similar notes to the semi-documentary, namely its use of location shooting and casting of nonprofessional actors, aesthetics alone do not explain the excitement created by *Rome: Open City*. American critics responded to the directness of the film's relationship to the recent reality of German occupation, evidenced both in its aesthetics (which were dictated by circumstances as opposed to box office considerations) and in its engagement with ideas. The *New York Times* suggested that the "feeling that pulses through [the film] gives evidence that it was inspired by artists whose own emotions had been deeply and recently stirred" and referred to the film's "deep, genuine moral tone."[25] The *Philadelphia Sunday Record* likewise explained the film's "moral fervor" in light of the history of the Italian Resistance: "People under the oppressor's heel aren't apt to say, 'I want to be entertained. I don't want anything serious. No ideas, now.' They begin to think straight about basic values. And so does their art."[26]

While Italian Neo-Realism is often cited as an important influence on the semi-documentary police procedural, the fact that *The House on 92nd Street* was released in

1945 while *Rome: Open City* was not shown in America until 1946 clearly indicates that these were independent developments, at least initially.[27] In direct contrast to the semi-documentary's emphasis on aesthetics over ethics, Italian Neo-Realism was an "ethics of aesthetics."[28] Its technical components were an extension of its moral position, its investigation of reality driven by a "fundamental humanism" that Bazin saw as its greatest strength.[29] As should be clear even from this very cursory discussion, Italian Neo-Realism could not differ more starkly from the American semi-documentary in terms of its ideological underpinnings. In their concern with the situation of the individual in modern society, the Italian Neo-Realists were fundamentally opposed to the focus on abstract institutions, technology, and consensus that runs through the semi-documentary police procedural. In its humanist vision and concern with social issues, Italian Neo-Realism appealed to America's prewar political and cultural paradigm and to the Hollywood that had risen up in support of labor and anti-fascist causes during the later 1930s and early 1940s.

How did these divergent conceptions of cinematic realism affect the development of *The Naked City?* Jules Dassin and Albert Maltz approached the film from the perspective of men who had received their political education courtesy of the Depression and the New York radical theater scene of the 1930s. Malvin Wald brought to the film his background making government documentaries during World War II. Mark Hellinger contributed his fascination with New York and with New Yorkers, along with his unabashed admiration for the NYPD. What ties these somewhat disparate visions together is their concern with "authenticity"; although drawing inspiration from different sources, Dassin, Maltz, Hellinger, and Wald—all native New Yorkers themselves—were concerned with bringing an authentic vision of the city to the screen.

Like most successful experiments, *The Naked City* has a contested genesis, with Wald, Dassin, and Hellinger taking credit for the film's innovations, most notably its extensive use of location shooting, casting of unknown actors, and detailed focus on the workings of a homicide department.[30] As a member of the First Motion Picture Unit of the Army Air Forces during World War II, Wald was introduced to the work of documentary filmmakers such as Robert Flaherty and Joris Ivens and became convinced of the potential for a new sort of film, one that combined "the artistic documentary technique of Flaherty with the commercial product of Hollywood."[31] He persuaded Hellinger to finance a one-month research trip to New York Police Headquarters, where he did his best to penetrate the insular culture of the NYPD, spending his days watching the police perform routine tasks such as questioning suspects in a criminal line-up. In the name of research, he even "spent several uncomfortable hours at the city morgue watching the medical examiner and his assistants perform autopsies." His embrace of the documentary form extended to the screenplay, for which he formatted the introductory sequences using "the documentary-style of presentation of a divided page with one half for the visuals, the other half for the narration."[32]

Whereas Wald was excited by documentaries, Hellinger was excited by New York.[33] For many years the highest-paid columnist for the nation's largest paper, the

New York Daily News, Hellinger *was* New York to many people, and perhaps also to himself. His columns specialized in the tabloid staples of celebrity gossip and reports from the underworld, the latter of which were facilitated by his strong ties with the New York Police Department.[34] Despite this stock-in-trade in society's extremes, his writing nonetheless maintained a populist touch that led to his reputation as a modern O. Henry. Christopher Wilson suggests that "Hellinger's art . . . was one of exposé only in the sense that it revealed the private stories of people making real or potential headlines, celebrities transformed into commoners or the reverse. In Hellinger's fictional world the well known and the half known merge with the millions of little people inhabiting the city."[35] This interest in "the little people" that Wilson detects in Hellinger's columns was also apparent among the latter's concerns as a film producer. Shortly after starting as an independent producer with Universal in 1945, Hellinger articulated his filmmaking philosophy to a group of friends. Among his ideas was the notion that more attention should be paid to casting bit parts; "an automobile mechanic . . . who looks like a mechanic and talks like one can add a touch of documentary authenticity to a picture."[36] What Wilson's analysis and Bishop's observations suggest is that Hellinger had an interest in extending his position as the Bard of New York to the big screen, telling the stories not only of the rich and (in)famous but also of the "bit players."

Dassin's motivation meshed neatly with both Wald's and Hellinger's. Like Hellinger, Dassin deeply loved New York and was excited by the prospect of bringing it to the screen, but he also hoped to further another agenda: "to push movies towards documentary aesthetics—that was one of my secret projects."[37] He had come to Hollywood in 1941, accompanied by the mixed feelings common to many theater people who joined the mass migration from New York in the late thirties and early forties.[38] During his first unhappy years as a contract director at MGM, he was so miserable that he "wanted to go back to New York forever."[39] Things began to look up for him once he began working with Hellinger, whom he credits with giving him the freedom and protection he needed to grow professionally.[40] Hellinger's respect for Dassin is likewise evident in his decision to grant Dassin the right to approve the final screenplay for *The Naked City*, a rare privilege for a director.[41]

Although Dassin claims to have despised Wald's original screenplay, he nonetheless saw an opportunity to make the film he had "always dreamed of" on the streets of New York.[42] His dream drew inspiration from a number of sources: his interest in applying documentary approaches to Hollywood films, *Rome: Open City*, and *The House on 92nd Street*. Dassin had grown interested in the documentary form in part as a reaction to the restrictions of the Hollywood studio system: "[My interest] began with our sitting around the table [at MGM] and grumbling about the poor material they made us use. . . . I used to talk about [the need to take into consideration documentary approaches] all the time to friends, to directors at lunch tables at MGM. They all used to say, 'Oh, stop boring us!'"[43] Dassin was also highly impressed by *Rome: Open City*, acknowledging the film's influence on *The Naked City* on numerous occasions.[44] "When I saw *Rome: Open City*, I said 'that's the way we have to go.' To use the documentary form to bring a city to life, to bring a thought to life, using what existed or what could exist."[45] Finally, he situated *The Naked City* in relation to the semi-documentary, giving Henry Hathaway credit for pioneering the use of location shooting with *The House on 92nd Street*: "Hathaway forged the path and I must confess that *The Naked City* also played a decisive role. We were free from the studio."[46] Dassin's desire to get out of the studio was motivated not only by artistic ambitions; filming in New York also offered the advantage of putting 2,500 miles between him and the studio's watchful eyes.[47] After his dispiriting experiences in Hollywood, he now had the opportunity to channel his admiration for the aesthetic and social concerns of Italian Neo-Realism into a film he would shoot on location in his home town of New York City. No wonder he felt "relieved."[48]

While Albert Maltz's contributions to the film may be relatively slight, they are nonetheless significant with regard to the film's political orientation.[49] A friend of Dassin's from New York and an active member of the Hollywood Communist Party, Maltz could be counted on to share Dassin's politically informed perspective. However, unlike other writers on the Left, he also understood the need to balance politics with artistic effect, a view that no doubt contributed to his successful Hollywood career.[50] In his story notes to Mark Hellinger, he expresses a vision for the film that bears an uncanny resemblance to the views of the Soviet documentarian Dziga Vertov. He suggests "that the CAMERA EYE, whenever possible, reflect the rich and infinite detail of the daily life of New York: the small boy hitching on the back of a truck; the alley cat digging for its food in an open garbage pail . . . the architectural beauty and squalor that exist side by side."[51] Maltz also urges Hellinger to make the natural sounds of the city part of the film's sound track and calls attention to the importance of "casting, wherever possible . . . utterly real faces–of working women who look like working women, of men awakening in the morning who look as men do." These comments suggest the degree to which Maltz supported Dassin's vision for the film. His reference to "the architectural beauty and squalor that exist side by side" recalls Dassin's conception of New York as a city of contrasts, while his interest in on-location sound and in casting non-actors echoes Dassin's desire to bring the tenets of Italian Neo-Realism to bear upon the film.

This overview of *The Naked City*'s pre-production highlights the diverse influences underlying the film's conception. However, any conflict between these agendas and priorities only emerged after the film had finished shooting and the HUAC hearings had begun. Dassin remembers the production as "a very, very pleasant experience."[52] Along with cinematographer Bill Daniels and unit production manager Gil Kurland, Dassin flew out to New York in mid-May 1947 to scout locations and shoot exteriors. Production began on June 16 and continued over the next three hot and hazy summer months. Whether due to the shortage of available soundstages, as Kurland indicates, or as a deliberate choice, the film's interiors were shot in real apartments, a decision Dassin would later come to regret.[53] "I had a romantic notion that I had to shoot real interiors in order to get a sense of reality. . . . All that did was to limit the movements of the camera and consequently, the staging of the scene."[54] He remembers improvising many of the film's street scenes, enlisting passers-by as extras and adding elements that weren't in the script but that elaborated his vision of the city.[55]

1. Jules Dassin ignores the crowds while directing Ted de Corsia on the Lower East Side of Manhattan. Courtesy of the Academy of Motion Picture Arts and Sciences.

In addition to frequent delays on account of the weather, the greatest problem the production faced was crowd control. Dassin used a variety of tactics to try to deal with the swarms of onlookers, who could number over five hundred for any given scene. To shoot surreptitiously on the street, he borrowed a trick from the police, using the sort of panel truck equipped with two-way transparent mirrors used by the police for surveillance.[56] On other occasions, he hired a juggler as a distraction ("It's the best ruse I know to move a mob from one spot to another").[57] The NYPD were also involved in crowd control, in addition to being on hand as technical advisers for the film.[58]

Principal photography finished on September 12, but Dassin remained in New York another month to supervise the film's final bridge sequence before returning to Los Angeles on October 16.[59] Whether or not he was actually involved in the film's editing is unclear, but it does seem that he was content with the shape of film when he returned to New York in early November.[60] However, "because of all the blacklist talk in the air," he was concerned with how political events might affect the film and made Hellinger swear not to change the final cut.[61] Dassin already knew that Universal was not happy with the film. At a screening of an early cut, Universal executives ("I remember their names because we made fun of them—one was Spitz and the other was Getz") dismissed the film as a "travelogue" and threatened to use the exteriors for stock footage and throw away the rest. Reporting their reaction to Dassin afterward, Hellinger told him, "That's what they think!"[62]

Dassin doubted that Hellinger betrayed him; all he knew is that Hellinger died in late December and that the film he saw at its New York premiere bore little resemblance to the film he had seen in Los Angeles in November. Cut from the film was "anything connected with poor people or poverty or struggle."[63] One scene that was excised began with a close shot of a fancy jewelry store, and then pulled out to reveal two homeless men exchanging a hat for a pair of shoes; another scene, shot on New York's then-notorious Bowery, panned from a sign for the Hotel Progress down to the derelict sleeping on the street beneath it.[64] Another scene, in which Lieutenant Muldoon (Barry Fitzgerald) tries to console the parents of a murder victim, was drastically shortened in order to remove its commentary on social conditions.[65] At the film's New York premiere, Mayor William O'Dwyer called Dassin to the stage to take a bow. Instead, Dassin walked out.

The question that remains concerns the degree to which *The Naked City*'s censored presentation of New York was accepted as authentic. Universal's public relations department certainly did their best to focus attention on the film's authenticity, coming up with press release after press release that emphasized the 107 locations used in the film, even going so far as to claim that certain scenes were shot in the tenement apartment where Dassin grew up.[66] Much attention was also paid to the fact that the majority of the cast were unknown New York theater and radio actors who had been selected so that the realism of the story would not be ruptured by familiar faces. More disconcerting is the emphasis placed on surveillance. One press release begins: "There are over a thousand New Yorkers who don't know that they will shortly be seen in a motion picture" and closes with an anecdote of a young woman checking her appearance in front of the concealed camera and thus ruining the shot, much to the chagrin of the technicians hidden inside the truck.[67]

Much of the press generated by the film appears to be dictated straight from these press releases. One article after another describes *The Naked City* as the story of New York itself, while as many call attention to the "thousands" of New Yorkers who may have been caught on film unawares. *Cue* proclaimed: "New York is the star of 'Naked City.' . . . Two-hundred thousand New Yorkers watched them shooting 107 location sequences, but most of them won't know they participated in the making of a movie until they see themselves on the screen."[68] Indeed, numerous articles focused not on the actors appearing *in* the film, nor on what the film is about, but rather on the process of production itself. Instead of including images from the film as illustration, they used production stills depicting the rapt faces of real New Yorkers observing the production.[69] Another theme common to many reviews is the vivid feeling with which New York is depicted. *Variety* praised the "breathtaking photography by William Daniels, who will make payees think they are really seeing the metropolis for the first time," while the *Los Angeles Times* called attention to the film's "documentary feel which strengthens the suggestion that [the action] is really happening before you." Summing up the consensus opinion, the *Morning Telegraph* wrote that *The Naked City* "lays New York open, bare and quivering to the touch, as no other picture has ever done. . . . Since the story was photographed in New York, since it shows what the city is like . . . the picture has been given substance and weight and reality that is seldom achieved in any film."[70]

Bosley Crowther of the *New York Times* was one of the few critics to see this emphasis on the "spectacle of production"—on the supposed authenticity that the film derives from being shot on location in New York—as a diversionary tactic. In his opinion, by capitalizing on New York's (and Mark Hellinger's) mythic appeal, *The Naked City* was able to detract attention from its rather run-of-the-mill plot.[71] While a number of American reviews referred to *The Naked City*'s documentary elements or described the film as a semi-documentary, comparisons to Dassin's other source of inspiration—Italian Neo-Realism—were notably absent.[72] Nor did reviews call direct attention to the presence of social commentary or a moral perspective in the film. The *Daily News* praised Dassin's "sharp feeling for people" and the *Motion Picture Herald* mentioned the "broad canvas of the city's steel and slums, as well as its less shabby side," but these comments are only a faint echo of Dassin's hope for a film that would reveal the stark contrasts between rich and poor that defined *his* New York. All claims aside, *The Naked City* wasn't naked, but rather cloaked in the compromises built into the semi-documentary form.

Institutions of government were involved in all stages of *The Naked City*'s production, from Malvin Wald's research with the NYPD to Mayor O'Dwyer's speech at the film's premiere. This aspect of the film's pedigree suggests that its conservative orientation was perhaps not only the result of Universal's savagery in the editing room, but was rather more deeply embedded in the film's genesis and generic structure than Dassin had realized. America's ideological shift toward the right that the HUAC hearings made all too clear had already begun prior to October 1947, as the semi-documentary's fascination with law enforcement suggests. Rather than the moral realism associated with the films of Rossellini and De Sica, the realism put forward in the semi-documentary was limited to the surface of things, to the image of a city and its inhabitants but not to a more profound investigation of the human condition.

Considered in this light, the novel emphasis on *The Naked City*'s circumstances of production evident in its marketing campaign and press coverage seems all the more insidious. Not only is illusion presented in the guise of reality in the film, but the "reality" of the film's production is likewise fetishized and packaged for public consumption. While the glossy photo spreads juxtaposed images of the production filming on Park Avenue with shots from the tenements of the Lower East Side, their aim was not to call attention to contrasting social conditions but rather to illustrate the scope (and therefore authenticity) of *The Naked City*'s portrait of New York. The film's success also furthered the commoditization of New York by prompting the Mayor's Office to establish a film commission to facilitate the process of location filming.[73] A film that Dassin had thought would be an opportunity for Communist-influenced social critique turned out to be an opportunity for capitalist development. Instead of the harsher aspects of reality, the public got the distractions of popular culture, the "spectacle of production" providing a sign of the changing times that would find their fullest expression in the "production of spectacle" of the HUAC hearings.

The Progressive Producer in the Studio System

ADRIAN SCOTT AT RKO, 1943–1947

Jennifer Langdon-Teclaw

I liked the old studio world. I miss it sometimes. It was comfortable. You knew who your friends and enemies were. Your enemies were up there in the front office, making inter-studio deals, playing gin-rummy in Palm Springs, or off somewhere consorting with exhibitors. Your friends were all the other writers, the salaried underpaid producers, directors, editors and analysts you had coffee with in the commissary. The Communists, that's who they were to be perfectly honest. The Reds.

John Paxton

A key figure in the circle of young progressive filmmakers working at RKO during the 1940s, Adrian Scott was both one of the "salaried underpaid producers" and one of the Reds. A member of the Screen Writer's Guild, the Hollywood Anti-Nazi League, and other progressive groups, Scott was in many ways the quintessential Popular Front Communist: committed to the tripartite agenda of anti-fascism, anti-racism, and progressive unionism, but inspired less by Marxism than by the American tradition of radical democracy.[1] Screenwriter John Paxton, his friend and longtime collaborator, saw the wellspring of Scott's radicalism as his "compassion and great intolerance for any injustice or evil that transcended any kind of ideology."[2] Scott's creative work and commitment to the Popular Front agenda were inextricably intertwined, and like many in this younger generation of filmmakers, Scott believed movies were both an art form and a powerful ideological tool.[3] With his muckraking faith in the power of film to raise public consciousness, Scott understood filmmaking not only as his job, but as his primary mode of political activism.[4]

However, as numerous film historians have noted, the studio system, with its hierarchical power structure and tendency to prioritize profits and "entertainment" over art or social content, presented significant challenges for Hollywood radicals like Scott. While they recognized the political and creative limitations of Hollywood's mass production system, the film radicals still struggled to shift the balance of power, however slightly. From the campaign to unionize the film industry to the daily "shop floor" attempts to shape the aesthetic and political content of mainstream Hollywood films, they resisted the strictures and indignities of the studio system. Thus, as film historian Thomas Schatz notes, "Studio filmmaking was less a process of collaboration than of negotiation and struggle—occasionally approaching armed conflict."[5]

This essay explores this process of negotiation and struggle through the brief but illuminating career of Adrian Scott. As a "salaried underpaid producer," Scott occupied a rather different niche in the Hollywood hierarchy from independent producers like David O. Selznick and Walter Wanger or a powerful studio production head like Twentieth Century Fox's Darryl F. Zanuck.[6] However, I argue that Scott's status in the studio system is less significant than the ways in which his progressive political commitments informed his work as a producer and shaped his approach to challenges ranging from studio censorship of radical film content to troubled labor relations. Focusing on two of Scott's lesser-known films—*Cornered* (1945) and *So Well Remembered* (1946)—this essay examines the interplay between Scott's political vision and his responsibilities as a producer, particularly in the context of the shift from the anti-fascism of the war years to the anti-Communism of the Cold War era.

Adrian Scott arrived in Hollywood in the late 1930s, following a stint in New York, where he had worked as film editor for *Stage* magazine and pursued his dream of becoming a playwright. Between 1938 and 1941, he worked as a freelance screenwriter, shuttling between MGM and Paramount, racking up co-writing credits on largely forgettable films like *The Parson of Panamint* and *We Go Fast*. In 1942, he signed a screenwriting contract at RKO and, following the box office success of *Mr. Lucky*, a wartime conversion narrative starring Cary Grant, Scott became known as one of the studio's rising young talents. Nonetheless, he chafed at the relative powerlessness of writers within the studio system and realized that in order to translate his political and artistic vision onto film he would need greater autonomy and control over the filmmaking process. Though many of his left-wing friends turned to directing in search of creative control, Scott believed that the producer, who had a foot in both the business and creative sides of the film industry, held the real power in the studio system.[7] As a producer, he would make the key decisions that shaped the final film, choosing the source materials, working closely with the screenwriters and directors, overseeing casting and locations, and so on. As a producer, Scott would also be in a far better position to protect the political integrity of his projects against incursions by the powerful studio gatekeepers who monitored markets, profits, and the business of filmmaking.[8]

Though the move from writing to producing was somewhat unorthodox within the studio system, the fact that Scott was under contract at RKO worked in his favor in several ways. First, the wartime labor shortage forced smaller studios like RKO to scramble to recruit new talent, creating more opportunities for quick promotion and enabling Scott to make an end run around the traditional hierarchies within the studio system. Second, RKO was one of the only major studios without an entrenched and supremely powerful production head like Darryl F. Zanuck or Louis B. Mayer. Frequent turnover in high-level personnel and constant tinkering with management structures and strategies kept the production system at RKO unusually fluid, preventing the emergence of a clear "house style" and giving studio workers somewhat more autonomy. In the early 1940s, Charles Koerner replaced the notorious micro-manager George Schaefer as head of production. Recognizing that his background in exhibition gave him little expertise in the nuts and bolts of film production, Koerner took a hands-off approach to running the studio, relying on small production units that worked fairly independently.[9] Koerner also returned the studio to its earlier policy of renting space to independent producers and directors like David O. Selznick and Orson Welles, providing an example of more autonomous filmmaking.[10] Thus, RKO was the ideal studio for someone like Scott who hoped to translate his political vision to film with minimum interference from the studio executives.

Promoted in 1943, Scott put together his own production unit, which soon established a reputation for low-budget melodramas that combined social justice themes, noir stylistics, and box office appeal.[11] Screenwriter John Paxton and director Edward Dmytryk formed the backbone of Scott's unit, working with him on four extremely successful films—*Murder, My Sweet, Cornered, So Well Remembered,* and *Crossfire*—between 1944 and 1947.

Murder, My Sweet was a labor of love for Scott. In combing through the RKO vault in search of a project that would launch his producing career with a bang, he found Raymond Chandler's pulp novel *Farewell, My Lovely,* which RKO had purchased in 1940. For Scott and his progressive cohort who wanted to "tell it like it is," pulp fiction held enormous appeal: the frank sexuality, lust, and passion; the colliding worlds of the mean streets and the mansions of Los Angeles, a collision that exposed a gritty underbelly of greed, corruption, and class politics. Chandler's hardboiled hero Philip Marlowe grappled with his desire to be a knight-protector for the innocent and downtrodden, while cynically recognizing the violence and sordid realities of both human nature and capitalist power relations. Neatly combining the realism of wartime noir and the idealism of the Popular Front progressives, *Murder, My Sweet* received stellar reviews and earned a tidy profit for RKO. The film was a turning point for the three men, and they quickly became seen as something of a team at RKO, though they continued to work independently on other projects.[12] The breakaway success of *Murder, My Sweet* made Scott the hottest producer on the RKO lot, and one friend remembered that, by the war's end, he was hailed as "the new boy wonder, 'the new Thalberg.'"[13]

This comparison with MGM wunderkind Irving Thalberg is intriguing. At first glance, Scott, a middle-class Irish Catholic who followed his literary aspirations from Amherst College to Broadway to Hollywood, seems to have little in common with Thalberg, a German Jew who chose business over college, climbing the ranks from secretary to general manager at Universal to vice president at MGM by his early twenties. Nonetheless, though Scott never achieved the power or mystique of

Thalberg, he too was seen as something of a young genius during his tenure at RKO, a man of great talent and taste, with a knack for selecting just the right literary property, cast, and crew to produce films that appealed to both critics and audiences. And, though Scott was certainly ambitious, he, like Thalberg, stood out for his quiet integrity and lack of affectation in an industry notorious for overblown egos, self-aggrandizement, and pretension.[14] "Everyone loved Adrian," recalled Norma Barzman. He was an "extraordinarily lovely person. Very few people who are as good and sweet as Adrian are forceful and make an impression. Usually 'good' and 'sweet' mean 'weak.' But that wasn't so for Adrian." Many agreed with her, from old friends like actress Betsy Blair, who remembered Scott fondly as "such a well-spoken, polite, sweet man . . . the most charming man," to relative strangers like film historian Bruce Cook, who described Scott as "one of the most decent men I have ever met."[15] Film critic David Hanna, contrasting the "gentle, soft spoken and apparently unexcitable" Scott with the "cigar chewing, loud voiced movie impresario" of the old days, argued that Scott epitomized a new breed of Hollywood producer: thoughtful men "with a more objective attitude toward the screen's function—and consequently a more detached view of their own importance."[16]

Indeed, Scott saw himself as a different kind of Hollywood producer, particularly in his relationship with screenwriters. For most writers, the producer was a nemesis, one of Paxton's "front office men." As Ceplair and Englund describe the relationship, "It seemed that no matter where the writer wandered in the studio maze, the producer appeared to thwart his progress. He had to be dealt with and satisfied. So the writer had to learn early that it was the producer's idea of a good screenplay which mattered, not his own."[17] Scott, despite having crossed the line into management, was determined to remain one of the "friends" rather than one of the "enemies," and he sought above all to create collaborative working relationships, especially with his writers. Paxton thought Scott was a brilliant producer, with an unerring gift for "concepts and constructions," and credited him with many of the key plot points and stylistic innovations in his screenplays, from the flashback sequence in *Murder, My Sweet* to the "right-house-but-the-wrong-address" ploy in the denouement of *Crossfire*.[18] Though he did not take screen credit for his script contributions, Scott worked closely with his screenwriters and saw his role as inspiring, rather than harassing, frustrating, or intimidating them. Screenwriter Alfred Lewis Levitt, recalling his experience working with Scott on *The Boy with Green Hair*, gushed: "Adrian Scott was the greatest producer who ever lived. He spoiled me for anyone else. Adrian would challenge every scene, challenge every line in every speech, every word in every line, and he managed to do it in such a way that you couldn't wait to get back to the typewriter to try it again. He was absolutely marvelous, a lovely person, a gentle man who was also capable of being very tough if he had to be, but never for very long. I thought all producers were going to be like him! I found out that I was wrong."[19]

As a writer-friendly producer, Scott brought screenwriters into the production process in ways that were not common within the studio system. He consistently invited Paxton onto the set, not only for possible rewrites, but simply to watch the filming. He also invited Paxton to watch the rushes and introduced him to the actors. Paxton recalled a minor stir when Scott introduced him to Dick Powell during the filming of *Murder, My Sweet*: "I will never forget the look of alarm and confusion on the face of the star when Adrian presented me as the Writer. He was a talented and friendly enough man, this actor, but I don't believe he had ever met a writer before." Paxton also fondly recalled being invited along on trips to scout locations. "This was exhilarating, to be out with the fellows, crowded into the back seat of a stretch-out [limousine], suffocated by cigar smoke." Paxton makes clear that Scott's inclusion of him was unusual: "We [writers] had our place and we were expected to keep it. I might never have met a motion picture star if my friend, sponsor, and producer had not been Adrian Scott—a quite remarkable, and in his quiet way, a very radical man."[20]

Scott's quiet radicalism and personal integrity served him well, and in producing, Scott found his métier. However, he also quickly learned that producing in some ways simply raised the stakes of filmmaking, as evidenced by his work on the productions of *Cornered* and *So Well Remembered*. Both films challenged his skills as a negotiator, though in very different ways. On *Cornered*, a thriller dramatizing the fascist threat in postwar Argentina, Scott battled with RKO executives over the film's political content, a perennial issue for radicals working within the studios system. On *So Well Remembered*, an adaptation of James Hilton's novel about political corruption and class relations in a British mill town, Scott brokered a pioneering labor exchange program for British film workers after a conflict with Hollywood craft unions threatened to halt production in London. Scott's work on these two films illuminates the ways in which his political commitments shaped his approach to both the creative and business challenges faced by the progressive producer in the studio system.

Unlike *Murder My Sweet*, a project Scott had chosen for himself, *Cornered* was assigned to him by William Dozier, the head of RKO's story department, who hoped to capitalize on the success of *Murder My Sweet* with another gritty low-budget thriller. Saddled with a flimsy, overpriced treatment for a manhunt story by Ben Hecht and Herman Mankiewicz,[21] Scott hired John Wexley, a Communist screenwriter with impeccable anti-fascist credits for his work both on- and off-screen.[22] Wexley first proposed the key politicizing change—shifting the site of the manhunt from the Caribbean to South America—after reading a State Department White Paper by Cordell Hull that exposed Juan Peron's Nazi sympathies and his establishment of a proto-fascist police state in Argentina. Wexley's suggestion that the hero should chase his prey to South America in order to "reveal the guilt of Argentina—the criminal acts, the anti-U.S. acts," must have appealed enormously to Scott, who believed that, despite the impending military defeat of the Nazis, fascism continued to pose a significant danger both at home and abroad. Scott gave Wexley the go-ahead, and in late 1944 he began researching the political situation in Argentina and outlining the story's new trajectory.[23]

From the very beginning, the studio executives had qualms about the decision to set the story in Argentina. Since the mid-1930s, the U.S. government, via the

1.   Publicity still of Dick Powell in *Cornered* (1945). Courtesy of The British Film Institute.

Good Neighbor policy, had worked feverishly both to protect American political and financial interests in South America and to expose German attempts to establish a fascist beachhead in the western hemisphere. Despite diplomatic and economic incursions by the Nazis, most South American countries remained technically neutral throughout the war, though fears of fifth column agitation to the south continued to haunt the American psyche. Even as the war drew to a close, the Hollywood studios, still fearful of jeopardizing their foreign markets, tried mightily to avoid antagonizing those nations that were neutral or even sympathetic to the Nazis.[24]

This sensitivity to relations with South America had a significant impact on the development of *Cornered*. On February 8, 1945, RKO executive William Gordon forwarded a telegram to Dozier, along with a memo outlining the studio's position on using Argentina as the film's setting. The telegram reiterated the studio's concern for its financial interests in Argentina and suggested altering the film's locale to Spain, which had remained neutral during the war. Explaining to Dozier that the United States might soon "come to some understanding" with Argentina, Gordon suggested that it would be "impractical and highly risky" to move forward with the project. However, Gordon felt that it would be premature to share these concerns with Scott, and Wexley continued to work on *Cornered* as an exposé of pro-Nazi designs in Argentina.[25]

The first full draft of Wexley's screenplay, completed on March 26, 1945, opens with a chorus singing "La Marseillaise," punctuated by machine gun fire, as the French Resistance liberates a POW camp in the final days of the war. One of the prisoners is Gerard, a Canadian RAF lieutenant who searches for his wife, Celeste (a member of the French Resistance), only to learn that she had been executed months earlier after enduring unspeakable torture. Gerard becomes obsessed with finding Vaudrec, the collaborationist who turned Celeste over to the Gestapo. Though Gerard's French contacts insist that Vaudrec is dead, Gerard refuses to believe it. Tracking Vaudrec through bank transfers to his widow, Gerard follows the trail to Buenos Aires, where he infiltrates a nest of collaborationists and escaped Nazis who have established themselves in the "best" circles of Argentine society, from wealthy bankers and industrialists to corrupt government officials and police informants. Convinced that one of these villains is really Vaudrec, Gerard plays a dangerous game of cat and mouse, eventually uncovering a vast fascist conspiracy to take over Argentine industry as a springboard to eventual world domination.

However, he also stumbles across the Argentine Resistance. Though they know of Gerard's work with the French Resistance, they fear that his deranged desire for revenge will undermine their own careful work. Their leader, Santayana, is a lawyer who uses his social position to gather information on the fascist network in order to publish it in the underground press. Santayana and his lieutenants explain that they cannot turn to the authorities for help; they will only get "excuses and lies" because the government and the secret police are part of the conspiracy. However, they must convince Gerard that killing Vaudrec in revenge will not bring justice; the justice they seek will come when they reveal the fascist conspiracy to the people of Argentina.

Wexley did an enormous amount of research on Argentina and created an elaborate and constantly evolving backstory, though little of it found its way into the final script in the form he originally imagined. Wexley's notes for the project, for example, reveal his attempts to dramatize the vast scope of Nazi ideology and tactics, from fascist control of all radio and newspapers to the indoctrination of soldiers by former Junker officers teaching in Argentine schools.[26] Though Scott no doubt applauded the anti-fascism in Wexley's script, his handwritten notes reveal his frustration with the repetition and lack of clarity in the earliest versions of the screenplay. In his personal copy of the first draft continuity, dated January 16, 1945,

Scott crossed out huge sections—sometimes entire pages—of dialogue. Despite Scott's attempts to tighten the script, however, Wexley's final version remained overly complicated and repetitive. Part of the problem was that Wexley knew and perhaps cared too much about the threat of fascism, and he tried to put everything he knew into his screenplay.

Not surprisingly, Wexley's screenplay caused great consternation among the studio executives as it made the rounds at RKO. On April 3, 1945, Dozier fired off a memo to Scott with a critique that cut to the heart of Wexley's indictment of the fascist Argentine government. The requested changes included deleting all references to the network of secret police, official wiretapping, and the existence of an anti-fascist resistance movement or an underground newspaper. Several weeks later, in a lengthy memo to Dozier, RKO executive James Francis Crow echoed his critique: "Now of course all this is all right with me personally. I believe Argentina really has been guilty of such things as these. . . . But does the company wish to do battle with Argentina—just now, when Argentina has made a technical declaration of war against Germany, and has become, or is trying to become, a technical member of the United Nations? What will the OWI think of this? And the State Department—at a time when the State Department is trying to foster world unity?"[27] To forestall an imbroglio with either the Argentine or U.S. government, Crow emphasized that the script should show that the underground operates secretly so as not to tip their hand to the Nazis, not because the local authorities are themselves part of the fascist conspiracy.[28]

Significantly, director Edward Dmytryk shared the studio executives' concerns with Wexley's screenplay, arguing that it was "too much of an attack against fascism" and advocating significant changes, which Wexley feared would "whitewash" the Peronists.[29] His fears were confirmed when Dmytryk flew to Buenos Aires on April 11, ostensibly on a creative reconnaissance mission, though Wexley believed that Dmytryk had gone to Argentina to "get the government's approval of the script." Whatever Dmytryk's original motives, he returned from Buenos Aires convinced that RKO might face a full boycott in Argentina if *Cornered* was filmed from Wexley's screenplay. This assessment hit a nerve with the studio executives, and Wexley was removed from the project. Wexley believed that Scott was "very embarrassed about the whole affair. He was working under great pressure and ashamed of what was going on, with Dmytryk trying to take the content out before shooting his picture."[30]

By mid-April, it must have been clear to Scott that he could not overcome the objections to Wexley's script. Though he was committed to making political films, Scott understood the importance of box office success and recognized that even if a film's radical content survived the scrutiny of the studio executives and the censors in the Production Code office, the film still had to appeal to the taste and expectations of the moviegoing public. Acquiescing to Wexley's removal from the project and the studio's demands for substantial revisions, Scott turned next to his friend John Paxton. By May 3, 1945, Paxton had completed his first revision of the screenplay, addressing not only the political objections raised by Dozier and the other RKO executives, but also the creative problems that had concerned Scott. Though Paxton retained Wexley's general plot and managed to keep the key political elements of Gerard's character (his impressive war record, work with the French Resistance, and imprisonment by the Germans), he excised Wexley's painstaking delineation of the fascist infiltration of Argentine industry, as well as all references to wire tapping and other illegal secret police tactics and any implications of direct collaboration between the Nazis and the Argentine government.

Given these compromises, Paxton's version of *Cornered* is a more conventional manhunt thriller than originally envisioned by Wexley. Nonetheless, *Cornered* remains an anti-fascist film at heart. "Today there is only the right side and the wrong side," says one of the film's minor characters, and this principle guides Paxton's dramatization of anti-fascism throughout the film. The right side, obviously, is the Resistance, depicted as an international movement of "ordinary" people driven by a hatred of fascism and a desire for justice. In contrast, the wrong side is depicted as a viper's nest of Europeanized decadence and corruption. Constrained by the studio executives from depicting the fascist infiltration of Argentine industry, Paxton and Scott drew instead upon images of the moral bankruptcy of upper-class society to suggest capitalism's collaboration with fascism. Though *Cornered* is rife with melodramatic intrigue, the film makes clear that the high stakes are explicitly political. Raising the specter of escaped Nazis infiltrating circles of power throughout the postwar world, Santayana insists to Gerard that their enemies are "more than war criminals fleeing a defeated nation. They do not consider themselves defeated. We must destroy not only the individuals but their friends, their very means of existence, wherever they start to entrench themselves. Not only here but everywhere. In the United States, in England, in France, in Alaska or East Africa."[31]

During the production of *Cornered*, Scott walked a political and creative tightrope, compromising where he had to and carefully picking the battles he felt were necessary to preserve the anti-fascist message in *Cornered*. Though he could not protect Wexley or the critique of the Peron government in his original screenplay from the depredations of the studio heads, Scott did not take the easy way out and change the film's setting to assuage their political concerns. Instead, he continued to fight for *Cornered* as an exposé of the postwar menace of fascism *in Argentina*. In his role as producer, Scott employed a number of strategies that enabled him to maneuver the project through the production process without completely sacrificing its political message. One of the most important was hiring John Paxton, a writer Scott knew he could count on both creatively and politically.[32] Though Paxton later claimed that "he had no feeling for the script" and that his work on *Cornered* was "a hack job,"[33] his revisions significantly improved Wexley's original screenplay. The strategies of indirection employed by Paxton and Scott may have blunted the critique—as the studio executives had intended—but also enabled them to preserve the film's anti-fascist vision. Certainly by 1945 American audiences were well acquainted with films dramatizing the "right side" and the "wrong side," and Scott relied on the ability of astute filmgoers to read between the lines and understand *Cornered* as an anti-fascist film. Similarly, casting can also be seen as an extratextual strategy for politicizing the film. Dick Powell, of course, had signed on early, starring as Gerard in a reprise of the tough guy persona he had established in *Murder My Sweet*, but for the supporting roles, Scott assembled a cast of international and left-wing actors, including Walter Slezak and former Group Theatre members Morris Carnovsky and Luther Adler.[34] Scott may have hoped that at least a segment of the moviegoing audience was familiar with these actors from earlier anti-fascist films and would read *Cornered* within the framework of this larger body of political film work.

Scott's political commitments also shaped his approach to challenges presented by the business rather than the creative side of filmmaking. In the summer of 1946 Scott and key members of his production unit, including Dmytryk and Paxton as well as assistant director Ruby Rosenberg, dialogue director Bill Watts, and sketch artist Maurice Zuberano, traveled to England to film *So Well Remembered*. Among the first American production companies to go abroad after the war, Scott and his crew were pioneers in a real sense, an example of international cooperation in filmmaking.[35] This film was to be the first of a planned series of joint productions between RKO and the Rank studio, the leading production company in Britain. RKO president Peter Rathvon was particularly committed to rebuilding the overseas audience, arguing that "we can and should do everything possible to make our films more suitable to the Foreign market, while losing none of their value in the Domestic market."[36] RKO's decision to send Scott to oversee this joint production attests to the confidence the studio executives had in his abilities, despite his youth and relative inexperience as a producer. From his correspondence with Rathvon throughout his stay in England, however, it is clear that Scott felt a keen pressure to meet the expectations of both RKO and the Rank organization for a successful and profitable joint venture.

These external pressures did not, however, blunt Scott's desire to meld his creative and political work, as is clear from *So Well Remembered*. A melodrama set in an English mill town between the wars, the film follows George Boswell (John Mills), a crusading councilman and newspaper editor, whose liberal reform efforts focus not only on winning better working and living conditions for the millworkers, but also on "saving" the beautiful but troubled Olivia Channing (Martha Scott), whose is shunned by the townspeople as the daughter of the exploitative, disgraced mill owner. Juxtaposing George's visionary reform impulse against Olivia's scheming ambitions—which result in the death of their infant son in a diphtheria epidemic, a scandal during George's run for Parliament, the end of their marriage, and the near destruction of the romance between George's foster daughter and Olivia's son by a second marriage—provides ample grist for a sustained critique of capitalist greed and its human costs. Though not filmed in an overtly noir style, the political themes place *So Well Remembered* clearly within the emerging Scott-Paxton-Dmytryk oeuvre.

Filming in postwar England sorely tested Scott's skills as a producer, however. One of the key challenges he faced was the slow pace of work and disregard for budget at the Rank studio at Denham. As historian Robert Murphy explains, "Britain did create excellent films, but in terms of production values their standards were generally lower than those made by Hollywood. Poor labour relations and poor production planning drove up costs, and an 'art for art's sake' ethos among British producers hardly helped."[37] Accustomed to greater professionalism from the factory system in Hollywood, as well as the breakneck shooting pace of his own low-budget productions, Scott reported with horror the case of a British film that had languished in the editing department for twenty-one weeks.[38] Financial concerns particularly loomed large for Scott. Based on figures given him during his scouting expedition to London the previous April, Scott estimated a final cost of about 275,000 pounds ($1,100,000). However, after their arrival in England, Scott learned that the stages he had been promised would not be ready on schedule and would cost another million dollars to reproduce, forcing him to scramble to make arrangements to shoot on location.[39] Scott's frustration with the British system was compounded by the fact that he and his crew were on a particularly tight schedule: As American workers in England, they were subject to staggeringly high income taxes if they remained in the country longer than six months—a budget constraint about which Rathvon sternly warned Scott.[40]

The pressure on Scott to complete filming on time and on budget was exacerbated by a conflict with the Association of Cine-Technicians (ACT) that threatened to abort the production before filming had begun. Though Scott and RKO had arranged for the necessary labor permits with the Rank organization, upon arrival they "ran smack into the Association of Cine-Technicians, which represents practically the whole field here: producers, writers, directors, and all technicians as we know the word."[41] At issue was labor reciprocity—or the lack of it. The British workers were outraged that the American film crew expected to be able to work freely in England, while Hollywood unions—particularly the International Alliance of Theatrical Stage Employees (IATSE)—routinely denied British film workers access to studio work in America. This grievance paralleled a long-standing frustration among British filmmakers that "American films seemed to enjoy untrammeled access to British screens, [while] British films only rarely reached an American mass audience." Indeed, it was this frustration that had fueled J. Arthur Rank's pursuit of joint production agreements with Hollywood studios like the one with RKO that brought Scott and his crew to England.[42] The ACT's previous attempts to institute a reciprocity agreement with IATSE had been rebuffed, and letters from ACT to IATSE leaders were ignored. With an American film crew now on their home turf, they saw an opportunity to leverage an agreement and passed a resolution refusing to work on *So Well Remembered*—in effect excluding Scott and his crew from the Denham studio—unless one British representative for each member of the American crew was sent to work on a Hollywood film.[43]

Part of the problem lay with the British film workers misunderstanding of the union structure and history of labor conflict in Hollywood. In Britain, the ACT represented the vast majority of film workers, and they assumed that most American film workers were similarly represented by IATSE. In Hollywood, however, union representation was far more diffuse, with separate talent guilds for screenwriters, directors, and actors, while the unions representing the wide array of film technicians and laborers, such as painters, carpenters, electricians, and grips, were affiliated largely with IATSE, an organization notorious for its mob connections, red-baiting, and strong-arm tactics, as well as its long history of direct collusion with the studio executives in the Motion Picture Producers Association (MPPA). IATSE's corrupt stranglehold on Hollywood labor was challenged in the 1940s by the Conference of Studio Unions (CSU), founded in the wake of the volatile cartoonists' strike against Disney Studio in 1941. Led by left-leaning Herbert Sorrell, by 1945 the militant CSU claimed nearly 10,000 members (compared to IATSE's 16,000) and was seen as a shining example of "progressive unionism" in Hollywood. In March 1945, a jurisdictional dispute led to an industry-wide CSU strike that lasted eight months and resulted in violent confrontations between strikers and police and IATSE thugs outside Warner Bros. studio.[44]

Once Scott recounted this tortured history of Hollywood labor relations and assured the ACT representatives that none of the American film crew was affiliated with IATSE, the British film workers were somewhat mollified.[45] After a week of negotiations, they agreed to resume work on *So Well Remembered*, as long as Scott and his crew arranged for statements from their own unions "agreeing in principle to some sort of reciprocity and expressing a willingness to negotiate on it." Paxton immediately wrote to the Screen Writers Guild, while Dmytryk and Ruby Rosenberg wrote to the Screen Directors Guild, Bill Watts to the Dialogue Directors, and Maurice Zuberano to the CSU.[46] Ironically, only the Screen Writers Guild, which already allowed British writers to work freely in the industry, responded promptly to the request for a statement. Eventually, Scott was forced to ask Rathvon to intervene: "From the studio at this point my top, urgent need is a cable (to me) under your signature assuring the union that whatever agreement Mr. Rank makes with the union, in regard to sending these technicians, will be agreeable to you." Rathvon promptly sent the cable, but cautioned Scott, "We cannot promise to overcome Union objections in Hollywood, but we can certainly make a try." Nonetheless, Scott reported back that Rathvon's cable "had the desired effect. That part of the agreement is under control."[47]

Scott's diplomatic handling of Rank and the British film technicians during the production of *So Well Remembered* was lauded by the top men at RKO and enhanced his reputation as a rising star at the studio. His friend Bob Sparks wrote to him, "Depinet and Reisman have written Mr. Rathvon of the splendid job you and Eddie and your company are doing, both as to what you are getting on film as well as a fine public relations deal in your English associations. This comes as no surprise to me. I felt from the beginning, unless Eddie punched somebody in the nose, you two were a cinch to supplant the State Department."[48] Jack Votion of RKO London later concurred: "You may not know it but both you and Eddie did a lot for us in the competent, efficient and modest way you handled yourselves over here."[49]

Significantly, even after the conflict with the ACT had been resolved, Scott continued to work actively to develop the Anglo-American worker exchange program.

Another producer might well have let the matter quietly drop once production had resumed on his film, but the labor reciprocity project clearly appealed to Scott. It resonated with his political commitment to the internationalism and progressive unionism of the Popular Front and reflected his personal desire to challenge institutional hierarchies in the film industry and create more collaborative working relationships. By the time filming on *So Well Remembered* wrapped in the fall of 1946, Scott had secured Rathvon's approval for his plan to bring four British film technicians to RKO to observe the inner workings of the studio. He was particularly anxious that the British film workers be assigned to one of his own productions: "I'm afraid that if they are just haphazardly assigned to any old picture and not given the treatment that has been accorded to us here, the whole project is likely to blow up in our face."[50] Though Scott wanted to reciprocate the generous treatment his unit had eventually received from the British film workers, he also envisioned the worker exchange program as part of a larger agenda for international labor solidarity: "It is a most healthy and progressive approach to international labor relations, and bound to result in mutual benefits. . . . I think one very minute contribution to One World was made in England."[51]

After his return from England, however, Scott's attempts to finalize the worker exchange program ran smack into the escalating labor crisis in Hollywood. In September 1946, the CSU went on strike yet again over a jurisdictional conflict; the resulting lockout of CSU workers dragged on for three years and replicated the 1945 strike in its red-baiting, picket-line violence, and mass arrests. By 1947, however, anti-Communist sentiment had gained considerable ground and red-baiting had a far greater impact than in earlier strikes. None of the major talent guilds dared openly support the strike, while the public backing of the CPUSA and a handful of leftist unions and front groups only exacerbated the situation. The CSU strike proved disastrous for the Hollywood Left, leading to the dissolution of the CSU by 1949 and foreshadowing the left-liberal split over support for the Hollywood Ten and the demise of the Popular Front in the film industry.[52]

Not surprisingly, this labor conflict complicated Scott's plans for the Anglo-American exchange program. The key sticking point was the proposal to bring British special effects technicians to Hollywood. This was an area that both Scott and the ACT agreed would be of particular benefit to the British film industry. As Scott explained to RKO studio manager Leon Goldberg, "These departments in England are woefully weak. As a consequence, pictures are held up for days or the work is pretty shoddy for want of skilled men in this field."[53] However, special effects fell under the jurisdiction of IATSE, and in January 1947 Goldberg met with IATSE boss Roy Brewer to get his approval to bring the special effects men to RKO. Though Brewer did not foresee any objection from the IATSE International as long as the men were present only as observers and their union had jurisdiction over this particular type of work in the British film industry, Goldberg reported to Scott a week later that Brewer and IATSE president Dick Walsh had vetoed the program because the ACT "had just come out publicly in favor of the Conference of Studio Unions."[54] Scott wrote to ACT general manager George Elvin, "I am personally miserable about the outcome of this. I can only conclude that the IATSE is maintaining a consistently high rate of undemocratic unionism." He assured Elvin that RKO was still moving forward with plans to bring an associate producer and two assistant directors to Hollywood. Over the next six months, Scott continued to work on a list of alternative recommendations, but his progress on the project was hampered by the fact that IATSE controlled the job categories that would have been of real benefit to the British film industry.[55] Finally, in early August 1947, two British film workers—assistant directors, rather than technicians in IATSE-controlled fields—arrived in Hollywood to observe the filmmaking process at RKO.[56]

In the midst of these negotiations, however, Scott's own commitment to progressive unionism was called into question by John Gossage, an associate producer who had worked on *So Well Remembered* and was slated to participate in the exchange program. After Scott worried that visiting British technicians crossing the CSU picket line might be "a bad thing," Gossage challenged him: "How do you account for the fact that people like Eddie, yourself and Ruby are still working?"[57] "Clearly, there is no answer to this," Scott replied with great embarrassment. "Clearly, we shouldn't be working if we profess to be progressive unionists. Clearly, if I try to answer this, I will make a huge fool of myself . . . which I will now proceed to do." Explaining that the talent guilds had voted not to recognize the CSU strike, he elaborated, "The Screen Writers Guild, of which I am a member, voted nothing at all, and suggested to their members that it was up to them individually whether or not to pass through picket lines. The Guild board guaranteed to support any member who did *not* go through the lines providing he could prove that he was in physical danger! In much the same manner all the guilds and unions responded. This was how progressive unionism in Hollywood rallied to the support of the CSU. Only one small body of trade unionists took action in favor of the CSU and there were very few individuals, therefore, who could act. It is a regrettable and shameful history, and I personally am very ashamed."[58]

Significantly, however, Scott believed the political value of his work as a filmmaker justified his actions: "During the strike I produced a necessary and progressive picture in *Crossfire*, which boldly attacks anti-Semitism."[59] Despite his desire to further progressive unionism through the worker exchange program, his top priority remained his creative work, which for him was inseparable from his political commitments. Indeed, his description of *Crossfire* as a "necessary" film reflected both his faith in the consciousness-raising power of film and his growing concerns about the postwar political situation. The sweeping Republican victory in the 1946 elections emboldened conservatives and intensified the emerging Cold War with the Soviet Union, and by the summer of 1947, Scott saw ominous portents everywhere. Fears of rising inflation and a return of the Depression, concerns about the reintegration of war veterans, rhetorical and legislative challenges to the New Deal order, a flurry of anti-labor legislation, and particularly a surge in anti-Semitic and racist incidents seemed to mirror the dislocations that had fueled European fascism after World War I and suggested to him that America was "on the road" to fascism.[60] In this context, *Crossfire*'s depiction of the murder of a Jew by a bigoted G.I. was a cry of alarm, Scott's warning to the American people that it *could* happen here.[61]

Crossfire, Scott's final film at RKO, was perhaps his greatest achievement as a producer, a film that dramatized the anti-fascist, anti-racist politics of the Popular Front and in many ways set the bar for postwar social problem filmmaking in Hollywood. Scott's previous experiences as a producer shaped the film in important ways. While his work on both *Cornered* and *So Well Remembered* undoubtedly boosted his confidence in his ability to shepherd progressive films through the studio system, Scott's earlier struggles with studio executives over the anti-fascist message in *Cornered* heightened his own anxieties about tackling the issue of domestic anti-Semitism. His perception that this was a potentially explosive topic was reinforced by the initial response of the Breen office to *The Brick Foxhole*, the literary source for *Crossfire*: "The story is thoroughly and completely unacceptable, on a dozen or more counts. It, also, goes without saying that any motion picture following, even remotely, along the lines in the novel, could not be approved."[62] Breen's rejection of the novel was influenced, no doubt, by the fact that the murder victim in *The Brick Foxhole* was homosexual, a taboo topic under the Production Code. Most critics have assumed that was the reason the filmmakers changed the victim to a Jew in the film. Certainly, Scott was concerned about getting this project past the industry censors, but it is clear that his political concerns—his belief that rising anti-Semitism was a harbinger of fascism in America—were more important than censorship issues in this case. From the beginning, he intended to make a film exposing the dangers of anti-Semitism, rather than homophobia, and he chose *The Brick Foxhole* for its explication of the irrational hatred that fueled a wide range of prejudices. However, changing the focus from homophobia to anti-Semitism did not necessarily eradicate the political objections to the film. The announcement of Scott's plans to produce an anti-anti-Semitism film provoked a flurry of controversy within the film community, and he received a number of telephone calls from colleagues who felt "genuine anxiety about the project and thought it would be better left alone."[63]

Against this backdrop of anxiety and nay-saying, the production of *Crossfire* became an agonizing experience: "For two years, we feared not that we would not make a good picture, but that we would not make a picture at all. Through all the long months before we started work, fear consumed us." The early story conferences, held in England amid the intense pressures of work on *So Well Remembered*, produced not a script but a laundry list of reasons why the film couldn't be done. Paxton recalled that he was ready to give up, but Scott "explained, exhorted, cajoled, bullied, persuaded, helped" until he came around.[64] Hoping to avoid a repeat of his experience on *Cornered*, Scott worked closely with Paxton to craft a "clean" screenplay, one that anticipated the myriad possible objections from both RKO and the Breen office but remained uncompromising in its dramatization of the potentially violent consequences of domestic anti-Semitism. Though Scott later castigated himself for "self-censorship" in the writing of *Crossfire*,[65] his strategy worked. According to Paxton, "Except for very minor editing and some clumsy meddling by the censors, the script was shot almost exactly as prepared by Scott.[66]

Crossfire's critical and box office success confirmed Scott's faith that American moviegoers wanted to see hard-hitting, progressive films: "That tired, dreary ghost who has been haunting our halls, clanking his chains and moaning, 'The people want only entertainment,' can be laid to rest once and for all. The American people have always wanted and more than ever want pictures which touch their lives, illuminate them, bring understanding."[67] The audience response to *Crossfire* also reassured the RKO front office and inspired production head Dore Schary to implement a new B-unit devoted to "experimental" films. Scott was to have a key role in the new production unit, and in the fall of 1947 he was at work on two projects for this unit: *The Boy with Green Hair*, a full-color antiwar fantasy film co-written with leftists Ben Barzman and Al Levitt, and *Mr. Lincoln's Whiskers*, a fanciful comedy based on a one-act play Scott had written in the early 1940s. Expanded into a full-length screenplay by Paxton, *Mr. Lincoln's Whiskers* was to be Scott's first opportunity to direct his own film. In addition to these feature film projects, Scott also was developing a series of documentary shorts "for use in combating minority prejudice," and had convinced a number of leading Hollywood talents to donate their services to this educational project.[68]

The success of *Crossfire*, however, also brought Scott, along with director Edward Dmytryk, to the attention of the House Un-American Activities Committee. For the rabidly conservative—and openly anti-Semitic—members of HUAC, *Crossfire* provided incontrovertible evidence of Red influence on film content. Both men, along with eight others, were called as "unfriendly" witnesses and charged with contempt of Congress for their refusal to cooperate with HUAC's investigation. After his return from the Washington hearings in early November 1947, Scott met with Peter Rathvon, once one of his staunchest supporters, who now pressed Scott to make a public statement disavowing any Red connections. Believing that a statement would be a tacit acknowledgment of HUAC's right to inquire into political affiliations, Scott attempted to find a middle ground that would satisfy Rathvon without compromising his own conscience: "I was willing to express my loyalty to the constitution and to our democratic institutions and was prepared at all times against their violent overthrow." More importantly, perhaps, Scott believed that he had already made a public declaration of his political commitments—in his creative work: "I was against intolerance and prejudice (I had said so by originating and participating in *Crossfire*). I was opposed to slums and diphtheria and political crookedness (I had said so by participating in *So Well Remembered*). I was opposed to fascism (I had said so by participating in *Cornered*)."[69]

Over the course of three meetings with Rathvon, Scott found that the negotiating skills so critical to his success as a producer were inadequate in this new political context. Presented with Scott's proposed statement, Rathvon "turned it down flat" and insisted that public opinion was the overriding issue: "It was generally held by the public that communists were agents of a foreign power—whether this was true he was not in a position to say—but public opinion must be satisfied. . . . The only way to resolve his dilemma was for me to make a public statement which with the principles involved I refused to do."[70] Thus, on November 26, 1947, Rathvon handed him a dismissal notice, and Scott's career as a Hollywood producer came to an abrupt end.

Publicly, Scott stirringly defended both his Americanism and his record as a filmmaker, while denouncing the studio heads' capitulation to HUAC. Privately, however, he seemed rather stunned by his dismissal: "It is quite clear that something . . . extraordinary has happened when a studio will forgo the services of employees who engineered an enormous gross from a small investment. The ideological patterns of studio owners have now taken precedence over profits."[71] As a radical producer, Scott had banked on the overriding power of the profit motive in Hollywood, believing that progressive films were indeed possible within the studio system so long as they were successful at the box office. This was the essence of his strategy as a producer: to make films that entertained while raising public consciousness about critical political issues. And, as his work at RKO demonstrates, his strategy paid off. The 1947 HUAC investigation, however, definitively brought the Cold War to Hollywood and marked the beginning of the end of the Popular Front and the possibilities for progressive filmmaking within the studio system. As Rathvon later explained to journalist Lillian Ross: "I sure hated to lose those boys. . . . Brilliant craftsmen, both of them. It's just that their usefulness to the studio is at an end."[72]

Scott, like many blacklisted Hollywood radicals, continued to work in the film industry, writing for both movies and television behind a front. Though he was a talented enough writer and continued to inject a Popular Front ethos, even in work he despised as "hackery," in producing Scott had found his métier. Thus, the blacklist, which effectively excluded him from work as a producer, was particularly devastating for him. In the late 1960s, as the blacklist began to crumble, he was hired, under his own name, as a producer for MGM-London and Universal Studios, but his greatest creative successes were behind him. In 1971, Scott reunited with John Paxton to work on a television version of *Mr. Lincoln's Whiskers*, but the following year, just a few weeks before the program aired, he died without ever seeing another screen credit that read "Produced by Adrian Scott."

10   *The House I Live In*

ALBERT MALTZ AND THE FIGHT
AGAINST ANTI-SEMITISM

Art Simon

My dear Albert,

This is probably the first letter I've written anyone in quite a few moons. However, in every instance there's an exception to the rule and in this instance, you're it!

I have just seen "Pride of the Marines" and throughout my entire chaotic existence, I have never been so emotionally moved by anything—whether it be a film, a book or a story. Honestly, Albert, I was genuinely awed.

You see, you must first understand—excuse me, I know you do understand—that my anxiety and interest in our social and discrimination (or what have you) problems have been hungrily awaiting such valuable assistance. When I think of the tremendous amount of Americans who will see and hear and be made aware of this deplorable problem, I tell you Albert, it's wonderful. A thousand guys like me could talk to kids in schools and people in auditoriums for a year and we'd still only reach a small amount in comparison.

Please don't think I'm going overboard on this thing; it's just that I'm completely convinced that the greatest, most effective weapon has suddenly come to life for the millions of bigoted, stupid, anti-everything people. I'm sure that they have read it in books and newspapers and I'm sure they've heard it on their radios, and I'm also sure that they have been talked to—but I tell you Albert, this is it—just plain movies. You've got to hit 'em right in the kisser with it, and, baby, you really did.

So there—I've said my piece and unlike the Arab and his tent and his silence, I will very loudly fold up my soapbox and make a helluva lot of noise on my way out.

Fondly,

Frank

P.S. If you haven't already guessed how I feel—just for the record, I know you are the best goddam writer around. And believe me, it's a big "around."

Frank Sinatra wrote this letter to Albert Maltz in August 1945.[1] *Pride of the Marines*, with a screenplay by Maltz that told the story of returning veteran Al Schmid, had just been released. But this was not simply a fan letter from one of America's most popular entertainers to a notable screenwriter. In fact, Maltz and Sinatra had collaborated only three months earlier on the production of the RKO short *The House I Live In*. It would become an important text of the Popular Front, that coalition of left and liberal forces devoted to anti-fascism, the fight against lynching and anti-Semitism and the campaign on behalf of a socially democratic electoral politics.

The work of the cultural left in the United States continues to be the subject of considerable scholarship. Dating back over a decade now, the most significant contribution has probably come from literary studies where Alan Wald and Barbara Foley, to name only two whose work has been particularly groundbreaking, challenged longstanding Cold War critical attitudes toward the work of left-wing novelists and poets. Since the publication of the first important books on the subject, the focus on the cultural left has widened to include several fronts, from the Federal Theatre to the role of the left within jazz and café society to the films of Hollywood radicals.[2]

I want to use this essay to focus on the work of one such radical whose contribution to left culture cut across literary forms and who, in 1945, had two films in release that expressed Popular Front concerns about anti-Semitism. That figure is Albert Maltz, a writer whose career is interwoven with almost a half-century of cultural production and debate on the left, but whose work, it seems to me, deserves far more attention than it has been granted.[3] This seems particularly the case given the amazing arc of his career, a trip through which moves from the worker's theater and such plays as *Peace on Earth* (1934) and *Private Hicks* (1935) to the proletarian novel and short story in *The Way Things Are* (1938) and *The Underground Stream* (1944) to Hollywood and screenplays for *Pride of the Marines* (1945) and *The Naked City* (1948), to the inquisition by HUAC and Maltz's role as one of the Hollywood Ten. While Maltz tried to resume his screenwriting career after the blacklist, his efforts during the 1960s met with little success. Still a talented writer, as evidenced by his novel *A Tale of One January*, he was displeased with what Don Siegel did with the screenplays for *Two Mules for Sister Sara* and *The Beguiled*.[4]

When not writing for the screen or working on a novel, Maltz was, to borrow the title of his 1950 pamphlet, a "citizen writer," penning editorials and essays in conjunction with his life as an activist. For many, his name would be forever linked to a debate that broke out within left literary circles around an article he contributed to *New Masses* in 1946. In "What Shall We Ask of Writers?" Maltz identified a confusion on the part of the left-wing literary community, the source of which, he wrote, "is the vulgarization of the theory of art which lies behind much left-wing thinking, namely, 'art is a weapon.' "[5] Maltz expressed concern that the slogan now acted as a "straitjacket" on the creative mind, that it insisted that "unless art is a weapon like a leaflet, serving immediate political ends, necessities and programs, it is worthless or escapist or vicious."[6] For Maltz, the crucial distinction to be drawn was between the social novelist, who imbues his or her work with a philosophical or political point of view, and the propagandist who uses the novel for narrow tactical purposes. Maltz's article set off a firestorm within the cultural left and he was mercilessly attacked in subsequent issues by, among others, novelist Howard Fast and *New Masses* editors Mike Gold and Joseph North. Maltz's essay, his critics argued, insisted on a false separation between art and politics and pointed inevitably toward the liquidation of radical literature. North contended that the straitjacket about which Maltz had warned was illusory, however rhetorically useful, and that no one on the left had prescribed for Maltz, or any other writer, what to include in their writing or how to present it. The battle waged on in print and in private. Many came to Maltz's defense. In a private letter to Joe North, Louis Harap referred to Howard Fast's article as "slanderous, obtuse, insensitive, smug—just the kind of thing our enemies love to see."[7]

At first, Maltz stood his ground, telling Mike Gold in a letter dated February 12, 1946, "The beliefs I held—I hold . . . and will continue to hold despite your unfriendly haste in asserting that a man who supports a family and his serious writing by part-time work in the film industry is thereby suspect. Ten more such slanderous columns on your part will not affect my principles, my loyalties, my writing or my public acts."[8] But after several months of criticism, some of it legitimate, some unfair and inaccurate, Maltz reconsidered his argument and, in a second *New Masses* piece, admitted to making serious mistakes in his original article. He was welcomed rather quickly back into the fold but would never again shed the identity of poster boy for how the Party punished those who dare deviate from its line. The mainstream press had a field day for what they insisted was his coerced recantation.[9]

Only after some three decades had passed could Maltz address in detail his response to the criticism. In the oral memoir he recorded for UCLA he summarized it as follows: "In the final analysis, however, despite my intentions, it was not primarily with my intellect that I wrote my second article. It was largely written by my emotions. . . . I didn't perceive then what I realized subsequently: that I was incapable of calm, analytic thought as a shell shocked soldier under artillery bombardment in the front line."[10] Faced with either accepting the criticism leveled at his first article or leaving the Party, Maltz's choice was clear. The Party was for him, as he put it, "the movement that represented in my eyes at the time the hope of mankind for a decent future."[11]

It would be wrong to let Maltz's work as citizen-writer rest in the shadow of the *New Masses* affair. In the same year as his incarceration at a federal prison in Virginia, the result of his being held in contempt by Congress, International Publishers issued a collection of seven papers delivered by Maltz at various public events. Together they make a spirited defense of the tradition of literary dissent, giving an account of how figures such as Tolstoy, Zola, and Stendhal endured attacks from the powerful and the popular. Maltz insisted that America was no less implicated in this tradition and cited Emerson, Thoreau, and Bryant as authors whose "names stank in good society once."[12] The pamphlet is, of course, Maltz's own plea to take the lessons of history seriously in his own time, to recognize the threat posed by those who found him guilty of un-Americanism and who sought to purge the honorable tradition to which he also subscribed. Prior to entering prison, Maltz had maintained a remarkably active political schedule, participating in conferences, steering organizations, and writing and delivering lectures. Typical were the kind of speeches he gave in 1945, the same year as *The House I Live In*. Maltz spoke at the behest of the *California Eagle*, a black-owned newspaper, on the role of black troops during the Civil War. Later that year he kicked off an effort to raise a million dollars for Jews around the world at an event at the Embassy Auditorium sponsored by the Jewish People's Fraternal Order.

Undoubtedly, Maltz recognized in his Cold War persecutors an anti-Semitism he had written about and warned against a decade earlier. Unlike John Howard Lawson and Samuel Ornitz, two of his fellow members of the Hollywood Ten, Maltz had not written ghetto pastorals about Jewish life in his literature of the 1930s. His writing during the Great Depression tended to follow the contours of proletarian literature in its focus on the disinherited, the working class, and, occasionally, its relationship to Communist Party politics. But by the end of the 1930s, Maltz took a more public stand with regard to issues around race and religious tolerance. His awareness of anti-Semitism dated back to childhood and an incident in which a gang of boys shouted anti-Semitic slurs and threw rocks through the back window of the Maltz family home in Flatbush, Brooklyn.[13] As an adult he joined a small seminar to study the subject further.

In 1939, The League of American Writers responded to the growing threat of domestic anti-Semitism by issuing *"We Hold These Truths . . . ,"* a pamphlet containing statements by fifty-four leading American writers, statesmen, educators, clergymen, and trade-unionists.[14] The League's National Council asked Maltz to write the pamphlet's introduction. He took the occasion to put forth an argument that would also be at the foundation of *Equality*, a magazine he would help found later that year. Anti-Semitism was an attack on the nation's founding principles, Maltz told his readers, and over the course of the short introduction he invoked Lincoln, Washington, and Jefferson, the battle at Valley Forge, the Declaration of Independence, and the Constitution. "The destroyer of the Jew," he wrote, "is inevitably the destroyer of the Bill of Rights."[15] Maltz also noted how "anti-minority movements" had been used against trade unionism and its efforts "to establish unity amongst workers of different nationalities, language groups, colors in opposition to the conscious manipulation of race feeling by employers."[16]

On a trip to Philadelphia with friend and one-time coauthor George Sklar, Maltz was shocked to hear that the day before their arrival anti-Semitic leaflets had been dropped by plane over the city. Upon returning from Philadelphia, he moved quickly in the spring of 1939 to help found *Equality*, a magazine devoted to combating the anti-Semitism issuing from Father Charles Coughlin's *Social Justice*. Out-of-work longshoremen were hired to stand on street corners and sell *Equality* right next to the men hawking Coughlin's magazine. Maltz wrote the prospectus to raise the initial money and then composed three editorials for the first issue, all published anonymously. In "To All People of Good Will," *Equality*'s first editorial, Maltz laid out the magazine's philosophy: the fight against anti-Semitism is organically linked with the fight for democracy. Challenging the Coughlinites meant not simply defending the Jews but defending the core values at the heart of the nation. "Minority hatred," Maltz wrote, "is a social cancer alien to democracy, and silence in the face of it is either stupid, foolhardy, or purposely vicious."[17] While the magazine devoted considerable space to Jewish culture (the first issue carried a story by Sholem Aleichem) and the plight of the Jew in a hostile world, it specifically targeted Catholics with its anti-fascist message. In "Equality Is Not Divisible," Maltz alerted readers to two anti-lynching bills pending in Congress and insisted that "white supremacy is brother to the anti-Semite, the anti-Semite to the anti-Catholic."[18] The magazine also took to the airwaves, broadcasting "The March of Equality" in New York and Jersey City over WHOM on Sunday nights.

Maltz's emerging attention to the problem of anti-Semitism did not spring solely from personal experience. He must surely have been aware of more systematic efforts within the left to confront the issue, not only as it addressed the plight of Jews suffering under the Nazis but its effects within U.S. borders as well. In a speech at the National Conference of the Jewish Communists, later published as the pamphlet *Anti-Semitism and the Struggle for Democracy*, James Ford, one time CP candidate for vice president, made an argument also familiar to readers of *Equality*, that anti-Semitism was akin to racism and anti-Catholicism. In a speech delivered in front of the Harlem Division of the Communist Party, Ford declared, "The struggle against anti-Semitism is an integral part of our fight for a progressive America. . . . The defeat of anti-Semitism requires the unification of all the progressive forces among the Jewish people, and their alliance with all the forces within the camp of progress, particularly the Negro people."[19] Whereas Ford was more likely to quote Marx and Lenin, Maltz was, in a more assimilationist voice, apt to frame the matter with reference to Jefferson and Lincoln.

In *Equality* as in "*We Hold These Truths . . . ,*" the perils of inaction were repeatedly underscored. Silence assisted the enemy; only a direct confrontation with anti-Semitism could prevent the scourge in Europe from spreading across the Atlantic. Even as the war drew to a close, combating anti-Semitism remained central to Maltz's politics and he insisted in various texts both private and public that, for him, anti-Semitism was inseparable from fascism. He even spoke through others, as when he served as ghostwriter for a speech delivered by Edward G. Robinson at Soldier Field in Chicago. Even though the enemy has been defeated, Robinson warned the crowd, "the juices of hatred still flow."

With the war in Europe ending, Maltz had the opportunity to reach a much wider audience with essentially the same message. In 1945, as Maltz was working on the screenplay for *The Robe*, producer Frank Ross invited him to dinner at the home of Mervyn LeRoy. Also at LeRoy's house that night was Frank Sinatra. At some point during the evening, Sinatra spoke about his efforts to take a public stand against race prejudice. As Gerald Meyer has demonstrated, Sinatra was closely identified with Popular Front anti-racism.[20] That year he made appearances across the country to speak about racial tolerance, many of them at high schools.

Maltz recalled that at LeRoy's house either Sinatra or Ross remarked what a good idea it would be if Sinatra's concerns could be put on film. The next day Ross spoke to Maltz about the project, and in less than a week Maltz had written the script for a short film and decided that Earl Robinson's Popular Front anthem "The House I Live In" perfectly fitted the concept.[21] However, in Maltz's hands that concept underwent some modification. The anti-racist message would now have to be inferred from a film short devoted principally to the subject with which Maltz had been concerned since the late thirties, anti-Semitism.[22]

The song's lyrics had been written by Abel Meeropol. Earl Robinson had set them to music in 1942.[23] As Robinson noted in his autobiography, the song had enjoyed considerable notoriety before Sinatra would turn it into an even more popular, as well as personal, anthem. Robinson had performed it at a May Day rally in Union Square in 1943, and in 1944 Universal Pictures had used it in *Follow the Boys*, its celebration of USO shows.[24] But the song's meaning would be forever tied to its use in the RKO short and to Sinatra's incorporation of it in his fight against racism.

The House I Live In took three days to shoot at a total cost of a little over $16,000. Sinatra, Maltz, and LeRoy donated their labor and RCA waived royalty fees for the song. At every opportunity, the studio's promotion materials for the film trumpeted the nonprofit aspect of the production. According to RKO files and its distribution literature, net proceeds were to be turned over to "some agency working in the field of juvenile delinquency." Studio-written captions to accompany publicity photos claimed that "all profits for the film will go to agencies active in training juveniles to be good Americans." In its request that RCA waive fees, RKO characterized the film as dealing with the juvenile delinquency problem, and referred to it as being made under the auspices of the U.S. Fair Employment Practices Committee. In his autobiography, Earl Robinson claimed that proceeds were to be given to the California Labor School in San Francisco and that it raised over $100,000 in roughly the first two years of its exhibition.[25] Maltz claimed that the film was distributed to 20,000 schools across the country and that it played in the RKO, Warner Bros., and Paramount theater chains.

Maltz's name does not appear anywhere in the production file, despite his name rather prominently placed in the credits. Nor does his name appear on the posters and lobby cards produced for theatrical display or in the ads run in local newspapers. Rather, all these materials present the film as a collaboration between Ross, LeRoy, and Sinatra. Thus, while Sinatra was certainly identified at this time with the fight for racial tolerance, a point stressed in studio materials for local theaters, the man whose career had been most devoted to social activism was largely absent from the film's promotional literature. As might be expected, *The Daily Worker* framed the film somewhat differently. While it consistently ran photographs of Sinatra whenever the film was mentioned, it referred to it as "the stirring Albert Maltz short."[26] In the RKO letter to theaters announcing the soon-to-be-released featurette and in the program for the press screening, Maltz is identified as the author of *The Cross and the Arrow*.[27] Perhaps as a result of studio competition, there was no mention of him as the author of *This Gun for Hire* or *Destination*

Tokyo. Studio publicity for *The House I Live In* gave equal attention to the film as entertainment and social message, reminding theater owners of Sinatra's commitment to working with youth and preaching tolerance.

Most of *The House I Live In* is set in an alley just outside a studio where Sinatra is recording some new songs. After he finishes a rendition of "If You Are But a Dream," a rather conventional love song, Sinatra takes a cigarette break in the alley. He steps outside just as a gang of boys chases one of their classmates into the alley and up against a wall. Before the first punch can be thrown, Sinatra steps in and demands an explanation. "We don't like him. We don't want him in our neighborhood or going to our school." Sinatra asks why. "We don't like his religion," shouts one boy. Another adds, "Look Mister, he's a dirty . . ." before Sinatra cuts him off. "You must be a bunch of those Nazi werewolves I've been reading about," Sinatra tells them.[28] The boys resent the charge. The ringleader tells Sinatra his father was wounded in the war and needed blood transfusions. After the victimized boy, evidently Jewish, confirms that his parents have donated at the blood bank, and Sinatra suggests that maybe some of that blood helped save the life of the other boy's father, the crooner tells them, "Look fellas, religion makes no difference, except to maybe a Nazi or someone that's stupid. God created everybody. He didn't create one people better than another. Your blood's the same as mine; mine's the same as his." Throughout the scene, the Jewish boy remains pressed up against the wall with Sinatra sitting between him and the gang. After his remarks about religious tolerance and our common humanity, Sinatra moves seamlessly to a lesson about shared national identity. Articulating what Michael Denning has identified as the Popular Front's "anti-racist ethnic pluralism," Sinatra tells the boys, "Do you know what this wonderful country is made of? It's made up of a hundred different kinds of people and a hundred different ways of talking and a hundred different ways of going to church. But they're all American ways."[29]

Sinatra illustrates this point with a story drawn from recent history. He tells the boys about the sinking of a Japanese battleship, the *Haruna,* shortly after the attack on Pearl Harbor. At Sinatra's request, the boys close their eyes to imagine the events and as they do, LeRoy cuts to archival and reenactment footage depicting the successful aerial attack.[30] The pilot of the plane was Colin Kelly; the bombardier was Meyer Levin. Sinatra is explicit about the religious background of both fliers and then asks the boys, "Do you think they should have called the bombing off because they had different religions?" At this point LeRoy pulls his camera back slowly so that the boys join Sinatra in the frame, a subtle figuring of the inclusiveness at the heart of this little story. For the boys, the tale of the *Haruna* is something they can only imagine with their eyes closed. But for their parents sitting in the theater, Sinatra's recollection may well have reminded them of an incident that was front-page news four years earlier. Indeed, on December 12, 1941, the *New York Times* featured the heroics of Captain Colin Kelly, describing how after his plane was hit by Japanese gunfire, Kelly kept his plane aloft while he told his crew to bail out. Once they had jumped safely away, the pilot went down with the ship. Kelly's picture ran on page six that day next to a second story about the commendations announced by General Douglas MacArthur. The following day, the paper ran a picture of Kelly's widow and son.

The *Times* account does not mention Levin, although he was in fact the bombardier. But in Maltz's confection, the sinking of the *Haruna* is not the tale of Kelly's bravery, but rather a lesson in cooperation between a Presbyterian and a Jew, the power and necessity of transcending religious differences. Maltz does not even have Sinatra mention Kelly dying after the successful bombing of the ship. The implication is clear: wartime teamwork cannot be abandoned after the war has ended, and there can be no posthumous victory for the "Nazi werewolves."

Just one year earlier, Kelly's name had been used in an anti-Semitic bumper sticker:

First man killed—Mike Murphy
First man to sink a Jap warship—Collin [*sic*] Kelly
First man to down five Jap planes—Eddie O'Hara
First man to get four new tires—Abie Cohen[31]

Sinatra's story to the kids challenges the anti-Semitic assumption that Jews sat out the war only to profit from its economy. Maltz has not only tailored the past to fit the needs of the Popular Front, he has inserted Jews into the wartime consciousness of America's children.

In fact, in that same year, Maltz would make the point even more explicit in his screenplay for *Pride of the Marines*. Here Maltz drives home a point articulated subsequently by historians, that World War II had a transforming effect on Jewish American claims to citizenship.[32] In *Pride of the Marines* the point is made by Lee Diamond, Al Schmid's Jewish Marine buddy and partner in the foxhole from which Schmid successfully held off waves of attacking Japanese soldiers and in which he lost his sight to a blast from a Japanese grenade. Back in a Red Cross Naval Hospital where Diamond is recovering from wounds and Schmid is trying to cope with his blindness, a group of soldiers discuss the American society to which they are returning. After a couple of the men express fears about the postwar economy, Diamond's response makes it clear that his wartime contribution has earned him the right to criticize the society on whose behalf he fought. "I know what I fought for," he tells his fellow marines. "I fought for me, for the right to live in the U.S.A. and when I get back into civilian life, if I don't like the way things are going, okay, it's my country, I'll stand on my own two legs and I'll holler and if there's enough of us hollerin' we'll go places. Check?"

Maltz ties a postwar image of America explicitly to concerns about anti-Semitism several scenes later when Schmid and Diamond are en route to Schmid's home in Philadelphia. After Al states resentfully that employers will not hire a blind war hero, Lee replies, "There's guys who won't hire me because my name is Diamond instead of Jones, because I celebrate Passover instead of Easter. . . . You see what I mean? You and me, we need the same kind of a world, we need a country to live in where nobody gets booted around for any reason." No longer a guest in America, the Jewish war veteran returns as a full participant in civic affairs, one with "a right to speak my mind out," as Abe Meeropol's lyrics put it.

In *Pride of the Marines*, as in the story of the sinking of the *Haruna,* the Jew emerges as an equal partner in the fight against Japanese imperialism.[33] By fighting heroically in the Pacific, Lee Diamond demonstrates that the Jewish contribution to the war was not limited to the fight against Nazi fascism and thus confined to a fight on behalf of its European brethren. American Jews fought for their country, not simply their people. Maltz's scenario thereby imagines the best possible outcome of assimilation, a postwar society in which ethnic Americans need not abandon either side of the term. Thus Sinatra, the child of immigrants who has made it big in America, tells the nation's postwar story with the Jew cast not as newly arrived foreigner, but as full citizen. In fact, in both films, it is the child of immigrants who now articulates what a postwar America should mean. When Sinatra sings that America is "the little town or city where my people lived and died," he imagines himself and his family as long tenured citizens of the nation, an assertion more fantasy than fact.

The story of the *Haruna* may start the boys thinking, but in the few minutes they spend with Sinatra they are ultimately transformed by his greatest gift, his voice. With a pat on the head for the youngest boy, Sinatra tells them it is time he go back to work. "What do you work?" asks the boy. "I sing." "Ah, you're kiddin," is one boy's skeptical response. To prove it, Sinatra gathers the gang around him and sings the title song. LeRoy's camera, pitched at a low angle, now pans the boy's adoring faces as Sinatra sings his answer to the song's opening question: What is America to me?

The first refrain of Abe Meeropol's song, and the answer to this question, offers a list of common sites and everyday events. America is "the house I live in, a plot of earth, a street, the grocer and the butcher and the people that I meet." The song's second refrain invokes names such as Lincoln, Jefferson, and Paine and cites Gettysburg and Bataan, but Sinatra does not sing this part to the children. With these conventional references to patriotism omitted, what the boys hear is an integration of people and places: "The place I work in, the worker at my side. The little town or city where my people lived and died." They also hear again about a pan-ethnic nation: "The children in the playground, the faces that I see; all races and religions, that's America to me."

Punctuated by Meeropol's song, the film's warning against anti-Semitism comes dressed very much in the language Maltz had used years earlier in *Equality* and *"We Hold These Truths . . ."* Maltz's script defines anti-Semitism as anti-Americanism. The script and the song combat religious discrimination by imagining an America that celebrates difference under the unifying banner of the people. When Sinatra defends the Jewish boy he defends all immigrants. "My dad came from Italy," he tells the boys, "but I'm an American. But should I hate your father because he came from Ireland or France or Russia? Wouldn't I be a first-class fathead?" Attacks on Jews are therefore defined as attacks on that most precious of Popular Front emblems, a point Sinatra makes in his performance when he winks at the boys just as he sings "the people" in the last line of the song.

Whereas during the late thirties radicals like Maltz and his comrades had insisted on linking the fight against anti-Semitism with the more general struggle against race prejudice, by 1945 this approach was quickly becoming fixed as the central strategy for a variety of faith-based community agencies.[34] As Stuart Svonkin has demonstrated, the notion of the "unitary character of prejudice," a term coined by historian John Higham, would become the guiding principle for mainstream Jewish and many Christian organizations combating domestic anti-Semitism after the end of World War II. "The unitary concept of prejudice" Svonkin writes, "identified anti-Semitism, white racism, and all other forms of bigotry as inseparable parts of the same phenomenon. Jewish leaders embraced this idea and concluded that the security of American Jews was dependent upon the realization of full equality for all Americans."[35]

Thus, when *The House I Live In* hit movie screens, it spoke in terms widely accepted and soon to be deployed throughout the intergroup relations movement, an ongoing effort on the part of religious-identified agencies and secular organizations to deal with the problems of race prejudice and religious intolerance.[36] These groups would be among the film's most enthusiastic supporters and play an important role in its nontheatrical as well as theatrical distribution. Maltz's script was particularly well timed. Historians have subsequently identified 1945 to 1947 as the years during which domestic anti-Semitism reached its high point.[37] News that a Hollywood studio had prepared a short on the subject of anti-Semitism was of immediate interest to the American Jewish community, and its various self-defense agencies were anxious to see the film get maximum distribution. In October 1945, the community services department of the American Jewish Committee (AJC) sent a memorandum to various local branches. "It is the consensus of opinion of many who have seen the picture prior to its release that it does an excellent job and should receive as wide a booking as possible. Anything that you can do to make sure that it is shown in your commercial theatres will be valuable although chances are that the picture will be popular and will need little promotion."[38] But the AJC also sought access to the film for its own exhibition contexts and preferred not to wait two months for it to be issued in a 16 mm format. In association with the National Conference of Christians and Jews, it sought to persuade RKO to release 16 mm prints immediately. In a memo to the AJC, Jules Cohen, executive director of the Brooklyn Jewish Community Council, stressed his organization's immediate need for the film and noted that the New York City Board of Education was "extremely anxious to get this film as quickly as possible."[39] Still, the strategy of muting the anti-Semitism issue with a call to fight prejudice generally can be seen in distribution materials produced by the AJC. In a booklet devoted to "selected films on human relations" issued by the agency's film division, *The House I Live In* is described somewhat benignly as "An appeal for brotherhood by Frank Sinatra who persuades a group of youngsters to stop discriminating against other children in the neighborhood."[40]

Maltz's film succeeded, therefore, at projecting parallel concerns, simultaneously articulating a warning against anti-Semitism and an image of Popular Front tolerance. Some film scholars have misread it on this point by suggesting that the attack on anti-Semitism displaces a focus on questions of race. In their book *Blacklisted*, Paul Buhle and Dave Wagner refer to the "blandness of the message" and claim "no minorities are present, not even Jews, and the boy picked on could be either Catholic or Protestant."[41] No one in the film refers to the young victim as a Jew but there is absolutely no doubt that he is being chased because he is Jewish. Sinatra interrupts the one boy who is about to yell "dirty Jew." Furthermore, his accusation that the boys are talking like Nazis and his explicit reference to Meyer Levin as a Jew make the boy's religious identity clear to anyone who is paying attention.[42] David Platt, film critic for *The Daily Worker*, had no trouble identifying the boy as Jewish when he reviewed the film in 1945.[43] In fact, the argument of the film pivots precisely around this duality, that the boy is unmistakably a Jew and yet not explicitly spoken of as one. Sinatra can thereby fold one form of discrimination into a brief talk about the un-American character of discrimination in general. Buhle and Wagner claim the film's blandness "needs to be seen in the context of the times." But I would argue that one properly reads the film in its context, not by dismissing both as bland, but by seeing how it deploys strategies first enlisted by Maltz several years earlier and then by intergroup relations organizations at the end of the war.[44]

In an essay on the representation of race in American wartime film, Thomas Cripps briefly discusses *The House I Live In*. Apparently reluctant to allow the film to be about anti-Semitism alone, he criticizes it for "preferring the relatively safe ground of religious bigotry rather than the emerging national issue of racism, and recycling the metaphor of the poly-ethnic platoon into a juvenile gang."[45] Given that domestic anti-Semitism was at its height in 1945, it is not clear how taking on religious bigotry was relatively safe ground. While, as I suggest below, the film was widely incorporated into the struggle for racial tolerance, its content is primarily concerned with religious prejudice. Asking the film to be about something else hardly justifies the vague complaint that the film, to use Cripps's phrase, "missed its mark." Furthermore, the poly-ethnic platoon common to the Hollywood war film is not recycled in the rather homogenous gang of white kids. The Jewish boy is hardly "swarthy," as Cripps refers to him, and only his dark hair separates him from his classmates.

Thus, like Buhle and Wagner, Cripps reads the film through the lens of the past half-century, a period during which race, far more than anti-Semitism, remained at the center of political struggle and the most persistently divisive domestic issue. From this perspective, *The House I Live In* looks like a retreat from controversy. But a properly historicized reading of the film must recognize the urgency of its agenda, one that addressed the shadow cast by anti-Semitism over an America just coming out of the war.

The House I Live In may be unique among studio products, but documents in the archives of the American Jewish Committee suggest that the idea of star-centered tolerance films was in circulation at least one year earlier. An anonymously authored report for the AJC titled "Movies Have a Job to Do" insists on the importance of factual films in spreading the message. "Include talks by Frank Sinatra and Humphrey Bogart," the report suggests, "and other actors interested in promoting tolerance. Find appropriate settings to shoot brief 'talks with the people' like Bogart's recent denunciation of racism."[46] I have not been able to locate where or when Bogart made this denunciation, but the idea of a "talk with the people" certainly characterizes *The House I Live In*. Furthermore, the transcript of Bogart's talk contains some striking similarities to the script Maltz would write for Sinatra. Bogart's talk, titled "How to Get in Good with Hitler," tells its audience to ignore "the race-bunk." There are no superior races, Bogart says. "Examine a man's brain. It tells you nothing about his 'race.' Test his blood. It tells you nothing about his 'race.'" And in a remark later echoed by Sinatra's alley speech to the boys, Bogart tells his listeners, "Healthy blood plasma can save the life of any wounded soldier of any color."[47]

There is no doubt that Sinatra and Bogart pursued such projects out of genuine conviction, but their public personas also played a strategic role. Both were capable of combining the tough guy stance with an appealing sincerity. Both implied there was nothing weak about taking a stand against prejudice. Although Sinatra was a romantic crooner, bow-tied and boyish, as *Time* referred to him in October 1945, the kid from Hoboken often struck a much tougher pose when visiting schools and preaching tolerance.[48] In November 1945, when he visited Gary, Indiana, in an effort to end a white boycott of an integrated high school, Sinatra reportedly told the crowd, "I can lick any son of a bitch in this joint."[49] There is just a trace of this persona at the beginning of *The House I Live In* but Maltz has decided tough kids need something other than tough talk. Furthermore, the film makes it clear that the boys in the alley do not know Sinatra is a famous singer. They are won over by the force of his argument and the message of his song, not the power of his celebrity.

In its review of the film, *Time* told readers, "To keep the bobby-sox trade in their seats, Sinatra tosses in two songs."[50] But in fact, the film's two songs are much more than a gesture toward Sinatra's fans. The juxtaposition of "If You Are But a Dream" and "The House I Live In" is a significant rhetorical feature of the film. The first song presents Sinatra as professional singer. The film's initial long shot situates him within the technology of the recording studio. Sheet music in hand, his head angled up toward the microphone, Sinatra gazes rather dreamily as he sings to future, as yet unknown listeners. This is the professional Sinatra accompanied by technicians and musicians who supply the full diegetic music. On the other hand, Sinatra's performance in the alley suggests that "The House I Live In" expresses his authentic beliefs, who he is and what he thinks when he is outside the studio and off the job. Born of conviction, not of commerce, this song is not for sale but for the boys.

However, a slight detail in the film encourages yet another reading of this scene. Headed back to work, Sinatra opens the door leading back into the recording studio. He then decides to prove to the boys he really is a singer and as he gathers them around, Earl Robinson's melody comes on the sound track. One could argue, therefore, that the swelling music is coming from inside the studio, that "The House I Live In" is the next song Sinatra will record. The rendition in the alley becomes a rehearsal appropriately addressed to the people before it goes to the microphone. This reading would suggest that like so many Popular Front artists, Sinatra was able, on occasion, to combine his politics with his profession.[51] "If You Are But a Dream" may be a love song, but it is "The House I Live In" that comes from Sinatra's heart.

In Joel Katz's documentary *Strange Fruit* (2002), a history of the well-known anti-lynching song made famous by Billie Holiday and written by Abe Meeropol, Michael Meeropol tells of going with his father to see a screening of *The House I Live In*. When he saw that the film contained only the first refrain of his song, Meeropol stood up and shouted, "Shit, they've ruined my song" and made such a scene the family was asked to leave the theater. It was the second refrain that contained the lines "The house I live in, my neighbors white and black." While Sinatra does sing "All races and religions, that's America to me" (during which LeRoy cuts to the Jewish boy still up against the wall but inching closer to the boys), the omission of this more specific reference to race coincides with the all-white makeup of the kids in the alley. As I have noted, the content of the film addresses issues of religious and ethnic heritage while racial difference remains absent. Yet despite this absence, the film still came to signify a statement on racial understanding. That is, its various exhibition contexts fashioned it as a film about race. In part this was due to Sinatra's identification with the cause and the frequency with which he had enlisted the song as part of his activism. Indeed, he had, by this time, become so associated with race relations through public appearances and statements on radio that his presence in the film allowed it to be read along racial lines.

The film's varied exhibition also suggests the extent to which audiences were willing to read problems of religious and racial understanding in nearly equivalent terms. In fact, what may have been the first public screening for *The House I Live In* took place as part of a community meeting to deal with a racially charged encounter between Los Angeles youth. In November 1945, Mexican American and black students at Hollenback and Roosevelt high schools in L.A. squared off, giving rise to fears of a race riot comparable to the zoot suit incident of 1943. However, adults and youth from the opposing neighborhoods joined forces to avert violence and held a meeting at the Soto-Michigan community center. With five hundred people in attendance, the meeting consisted of a round table discussion that included various community leaders, a talk from boxing champion Henry Armstrong, and songs by Earl Robinson. The event was topped off by a screening of *The House I Live In. The Daily Worker* reported that when Sinatra's image came on screen, "the kids hailed him joyfully."[52] The details of the film could not, therefore, limit its social application. As it made its way into circulation in November 1945, *The House I Live In* found neighborhoods, if not a nation, in need of its message, a message that could be configured to address not just religious but also race conscious interventions.

By the end of *The House I Live In*, Sinatra has changed the boys from a violent gang into a tolerant, perhaps even appreciative group of chums. Whereas earlier in the film Sinatra had referred to the boys as "fellas," his closing line to them is "so long, men." They have come of age in the course of these ten minutes. The utopian image of America conjured by Sinatra's song has, as in so many Hollywood musicals, resolved the momentary conflict. As the boys leave the alley, the most outspoken of them bends down to pick up the Jewish boy's books. He hands them over and together they walk shoulder to shoulder out of the frame.

A month after Sinatra wrote to Maltz congratulating him on *Pride of the Marines*, Maltz wrote back. He thanked Sinatra for a gift he had just sent. But in addition he thanked him for contributing an article to *Modern Screen* in which Sinatra had warned his fans against race prejudice. "It's my feeling that America is by no means safe from itself," wrote Maltz. "I don't know what the future will bring but I am convinced that if it is a good future, as I hope, it will only come after really sharp struggle against the fascist elements. And the one crucial weakness of the democratic forces is race prejudice."[53] At this point, Maltz may well have understood anti-Semitism and race prejudice as equivalent terms. Either way, his optimism about the people seems diminished here. It seems further diminished when he addresses artists and writers in New York in March 1948 and suggests it is time the people reacquaint themselves with the Bill of Rights.[54]

By 1948, of course, Maltz had seen first hand how anti-Semitism and anti-Communism had joined forces. Ten of the original Hollywood Nineteen and six of the Hollywood Ten were Jewish. He had traveled in two years from *The House I Live In* to the House Un-American Activities Committee, where his future would be decided by men whose contempt for Jews was part of the public record.

While some of Maltz's statements might suggest an emerging pessimism about the political health of the people, he remained committed, after the war and the demise of the Popular Front, to the language of democracy and its historical ideals. Indeed, as the far right bathed itself in the rhetoric of patriotism, Maltz continued to mobilize a language that had informed the left throughout the period of his political maturation, a stance that embraced the Bill of Rights and the founding fathers. "I will take my philosophy from Thomas Paine, Thomas Jefferson, Abraham Lincoln," he said in his statement before HUAC on October 28, 1947, "and I will not be dictated to or intimidated by men to whom the Ku Klux Klan, as a matter of Committee record, is an acceptable American institution."[55] But seeking to repossess the language and iconography of Americanism was not enough. Maltz's attack on the committee also invoked the specter of fascism and anti-Semitism. After declaring, "I challenge the right of this Committee to inquire into my political and religious beliefs," he continued, "I would rather die than be a shabby American, groveling before men whose names are Thomas and Rankin, but who now carry out activities in America like those carried out in Germany by Goebbels and Himmler."[56]

At the beginning of *The House I Live In*, Sinatra charges the gang with sounding like Nazi werewolves. Just two years later, Maltz was attacked by men to whom he attached a similar label. But unlike the film's gang of boys, Maltz's congressional opponents had the power to destroy, or nearly destroy, the creative productivity at the heart of his career and the aesthetic compliment to his activism. In the thirty years that passed between his encounter with HUAC and the recording of his oral memoir at UCLA, Maltz continued to understand his experience in terms of an encounter with "an American fascism." He recognized that compared to what the Europeans had experienced, blacklisting was, in his words, "a minor price which we in America had had to pay for joining in that struggle. It is the philosophy I still lean on today I find." Leaning on that philosophy may have served to dilute Maltz's post-blacklist bitterness, but he remained under no illusion about what taking part in the struggle had cost in artistic terms. "While I don't regret the stand I took," he said, "and would do the same thing over, I do regret that I was not permitted to do the work that I feel was in me to do."[57]

11 Red Hollywood in Transition

THE CASE OF ROBERT ROSSEN

Brian Neve

In his important essay on the work of the Hollywood Left, Thom Andersen asks whether there is anything either politically or aesthetically distinctive about the oeuvre of the writers and directors associated with the Communist Party in the thirties and forties. Andersen partly answers his question by proposing the notion of film gris as a hybrid form of film noir and as a distinctive creation of left-wing filmmakers in the period from 1947 to 1951.[1] Although more recent research has greatly increased knowledge of the film production of the Hollywood Left, there is still work to be done in exploring Andersen's original question.[2] Robert Rossen is interesting as a case, in part because of his long association with Warner Bros., from 1936 to 1944, and his membership in the Communist Party from 1937 to approximately 1947. Rossen is also one of the directors associated with the notion of film gris, although his role in *Body and Soul* (1947) has often been seen as secondary to that of writer Abraham Polonsky. As a contracted screenwriter Rossen's particular interest in social themes had a synergy with the broad and generic concerns of the Warners studio in the Popular Front period of the late thirties and then in the war years. This essay relates the recurring themes and motifs of Rossen's work at Warners to the period at the end of the war and in the late forties, when he took advantage of a rise in independent production and began directing.

Rossen's New York work from the early thirties exhibits an early concern with anti-fascism, and with the economic context of life. His unsuccessful 1935 Broadway comedy *The Body Beautiful* dealt humorously with a "burlesque dancer" so "innocent of mind"—in critic Brooks Atkinson's words—that she saw her nude dancing as spiritual rather than commercial or pornographic. Realist and idealistic strands recur in Rossen's work, deriving in part from his Jewish immigrant family background and hard childhood on the streets of New York's East Side. He worked his way through NYU but also passed time in poolrooms and did some prize fighting. *Corner Pocket*, an unfinished 1936 play, dealt with the frustrations and hopes of young men frequenting a New York pool hall. It was in that year that Mervyn LeRoy's admiration for *The Body Beautiful* led directly to Rossen, newly married, signing a contract with Warner Bros.[3]

Three themes recur in the ten film credits that Rossen attained before leaving the studio in 1944: class and the experiences of proletarian lives; social and other constructions of the "gangster" and racketeer; and anti-fascism. Rossen's first assignment and credit at Warners, *Marked Woman* (1937), had its origins in the campaigns against organized crime and racketeering of New York prosecutor Thomas E. Dewey. Charley Lucania (Lucky Luciano) was notorious for his narcotics and gambling interests, but he had been convicted and sentenced by the New York State Supreme Court on June 7, 1936, for "compulsory prostitution." Given the time pressures on the studio line, producer Lou Edelman had to reassure head of production Hal Wallis that "the boy knows what it's about." Working with transcripts of the trial and interviews with key witnesses, Rossen and Abem Finkel contributed two distinctively left-wing motifs: first, the class and gender solidarity of the women who were used and abused as part of the rackets; second, and related to the first motif, the economic context of life and work in Depression America. We learn from the outline treatment that the women are "all living in the same apartment for economic reasons," while at work the women are shown early on as part of the "goods and chattels" on display, as Luciano (Vanning in the film) takes over a gambling and drinking joint.[4]

The first treatment was called "Five Women," and the "solidarity" of the women "victims" remained as a key motif in the film even after Bette Davis returned to the studio after suspension to be assigned to the leading role. At the film's conclusion the Dewey character (Humphrey Bogart), having secured the conviction by persuading the women to testify, is tipped for higher office, while the women link arms and walk off into the mist—their future uncertain. Wallis saw a version in January 1937, while the previews were in February and the film was released in April. To Jack Warner, "anyone having anything to do with this picture deserves tremendous commendation." The Communist *Daily Worker* also praised the film: their reviewer felt that there was no happy ending, and that "as far as the girls are concerned theirs is a hopeless future."[5]

Later in 1937 Rossen worked on another Dewey case in which the prosecutor had secured a conviction of racketeers exploiting the New York produce market. Again, court transcripts were used as the key source, and Rossen worked on this occasion with fellow leftist Leonardo Bercovici, whom he had known in New York. Rossen and Bercovici had been writing a play in New York, and it was Rossen who urged him to come to Hollywood and helped him secure work at Warners. Before *Racket Busters* (1938) they worked on an unmade script called *Who Asked to Be Born*, for the Dead End Kids.[6] The B-picture *Racket Busters* recounts the efforts of racketeers to take over a truckers' association, and of the Dewey figure to convince the truckers to testify. Instead of hostesses/prostitutes, here the working-class figures are members of the association. Throughout the film the issue of cooperating with the prosecutor in the public interest is related to a parallel story of the struggle to maintain solidarity in the truckers' association. Pop, the longtime leader of the association, is a revered figure, while the "common man" character, Denny (George Brent), is finally persuaded to testify by his wife. (Indeed, he only joins the mob because of

concerns for the welfare of his pregnant wife.) The principle of testifying is throughout associated with that of sticking up for labor solidarity, against the self-interest
linked with involvement with the racketeers. The last line of the film, at the trial, is
from Denny, and it contains some verbal echo of the ending of *Marked Woman*.
Denny remarks: "You know, Nora, I've learned one thing from Pop and all this business: people like us, we've only got one out, and that is to stick together." The *New
York Times* review noted that "the Warners have contributed a realistic invocation
to solidarity and a popular front," while the *Daily Worker*'s David Platt, writing during the war years about Warners as the "100% pro-New Deal studio," remembered
Racket Busters as "strongly pro-union."[7]

Rossen's treatment for *Dust Be My Destiny* (1939) addresses a national issue in a
way that was not the case in the source material, an unpublished novel by Jerome
Odlum. This was the first of four films on which Rossen worked that starred John
Garfield, an iconic figure in the blacklist story and in Andersen's discussion of film
gris. Joe Bell (played by Garfield) is a fugitive from justice, convinced that people
like him will never get a fair trial or a break. Tempted into crime by circumstances,
he is finally found innocent at a trial that the treatment makes, as in *They Won't Forget* (1937), a national event. A top attorney takes on the case and a supportive newspaperman argues that it was not one "boy" on trial but "a million boys all over the
country." Yet Hal Wallis took advice from Mark Hellinger, who wanted it turned
into a "heart warming story," and, following Wallis's instructions, line producer
Lou Edelman ordered that the filmmakers "take out all of the migratory scenes
and sociological references. This is the story of two people—not a group. It is an
individual problem—not a national one. Consequently, we do not give the trial
national significance." Edelman wanted instead a flavor of Thornton Wilder's *Our
Town*, and the finished film softens and sentimentalizes the story.[8] The *Daily Worker*
recommended the latest of the Warners crime films "for its acting, its production
and, with reservations, for its social point of view," but saw the conclusion as a
"melodramatic escape from reality." In the *New York Times* future John Ford screenwriter Frank S. Nugent was cynical about what he saw as the formula of an "inter-
minable line of melodramas about the fate-dogged boys from the wrong side of
the railroad tracks." The conclusion here is less that Rossen's social intentions were
marginalized but that the writer provided a vital social element to an entertainment that may have been "harmless," in Richard Maltby's term, but that attracted
audiences in part because it engaged with elements of their Depression lives.[9]

Rossen's other two credits from the thirties at Warners were *They Won't Forget*
(1937) and *The Roaring Twenties* (1939). The first was broadly faithful to a Ward
Greene novel, *Death in the Deep South*, which itself loosely followed the 1915 Leo
Frank case, in which a Jew was accused of murdering a fourteen-year-old girl and
then lynched. In the film the victim is a gentile northerner rather than a Jew,
although in both novel and film the first suspect, a black janitor, is brutally treated.
The film opened in July 1937 during a period of liberal concern at a renewed wave
of lynching in the South, and with contemporary reviewers commenting on its relevance to the Scottsboro case. Rossen's precise role, working with Aben Kandel, is

not easy to determine, although he was likely to have worked closely with director Mervyn LeRoy, who brought him to Warners and originally had him on personal contract. Several characteristic Rossen motifs—an ambitious and cynical D.A., and a group of town notables who stir up the local mob—do not appear in the novel. Rossen also worked during the latter part of the protracted production process of *The Roaring Twenties* (Raoul Walsh, 1939), a film developed from Mark Hellinger's crude and rambling treatment of Prohibition life and times, "The World Moves On." It is again difficult to separate out individual contributions, and the final script was credited to Rossen together with the writing team of Jerry Wald and Richard Macauley. But Rossen's political sense fitted perfectly with the pro–New Deal element of the gangster film and the sense that the Eddie Bartlett character (James Cagney), the doomed would-be "big shot," was primarily a victim of circumstance and environment.

Three of Rossen's remaining four films under his Warners contract were directly or indirectly related to the rise of fascism in Europe. His best-known script in this period is an adaptation of Jack London's *The Sea Wolf*, a relatively high-budget, "quality" production, directed by Michael Curtiz and released in 1941. An early Rossen version began with the voice of the Van Weyden character (Alexander Knox), looking back forty years to the events to be recounted, and seeing the "struggle for human dignity" as the link between those events and "this whole modern scene." Edward G. Robinson said of his role as the despotic captain Wolf Larsen that he was "a Nazi in everything but name."[10] A woman character is introduced into the story (to be played by Ida Lupino) and extra scenes were written, in part at Lupino's urging, for two social fugitives aboard the "Ghost," played by her and John Garfield. Their struggle is presented as one for the dignity and survival of Depression "nobodies": Leach (Garfield) is on the run from the police in San Francisco, and the struggle of Leach and Ruth displaces the novel's emphasis on a Hobbesian war of all against all. After the revolt against Larsen has failed, Leach tells his fellow shipmates that the captain "needs you to break your backs for him; maybe someday you'll get wise to that." The production brought together figures who would later suffer during the blacklist era: Rossen, Garfield, Knox, and Howard da Silva were blacklisted and Edward G. Robinson and cinematographer James Wong Howe were graylisted in the late forties or fifties.

Out of the Fog (Anatole Litvak, 1941), for which Rossen was again teamed with Jerry Wald and Richard Macauley, was an adaptation of Irwin Shaw's 1939 Group Theatre fable. Like *The Sea Wolf* it also features working-class "nobodies," Depression figures who strive for a better life and who stand up to symbols of fascist power. John Garfield plays Goff, a "tinpot Dillinger" who terrorizes a Brooklyn pier where two aging men, played by Thomas Mitchell and John Qualen, struggle to fulfill their dream in life, to buy a new fishing boat. The men devise a plan to fight back by murdering the gangster figure, and when the time comes, although neither can go through with their plan, the Goff character overbalances into the sea and drowns. The Production Code would not have allowed the two men to go unpunished, had they actually taken the law into their own hands.[11] It is a happy ending, of sorts, as long as you don't believe that the evils associated with the Garfield character are systematic and don't disappear with his death. Rossen struggles to give this petty tyrant a social background. To Goff, a "bum off the break rods," "the superior people make the inferior people work for them, that's the law of nature. If there is any trouble you beat them up a couple of times and then there is no more trouble. Then you have peace."

The same year Rossen authored the screenplay of *Blues in the Night* (Anatole Litvak, 1941), a film that failed to fulfill the studio's considerable commercial expectations. It deals with an itinerant group of jazz musicians who travel Depression America, and whose free-form music becomes a symbol of authentic working-class culture and the music of the people, in contrast to the industrialized and commercialized music of the big bands. There seems to be a kind of wish fulfillment from Rossen about the future prospect of more collaborative, independent filmmaking, more insulated from the Hollywood culture industries. There are striking montages (by Don Siegel), but the bulk of the film provides a melodrama based on sexual jealousies at a roadhouse run by an ex-criminal. The women are simply coded: the character played by Warners standby Pricilla Lane remains part of the jazz group, while the Kay Grant figure (Betty Field) is a prototype femme fatale, upsetting the unity of the group by luring its brightest, most sensitive, and vulnerable (and foolish) member temporarily away. When he returns to resume playing the blues, Kay Grant provokes a melodramatic conclusion in which she is killed in a car crash amid thunder and lightning. The film ends with a highly romantic and sentimental view of both jazz and the Depression, as the reunited group, free of racketeers, big bands, and preying women, jam happily into the night while riding a freight-train box car.

Pearl Harbor changed the Hollywood agenda, and Communists worked in particular on pictures dealing with the war experience and European resistance movements. Rossen became chairman (until 1944) of the Hollywood Writers Mobilization, a quasi-governmental body set up on December 8, 1941, by the Screen Writers Guild to coordinate the contribution of writers to the war effort. Most wartime scripts were vetted by the Office of War Information, a process that broadened the New Deal influence over film.[12] Rossen's final Warners project was to adapt a novel dealing with defiant Norwegian resistance to Nazi occupation; to director Lewis Milestone the moral of *Edge of Darkness* (1943) was "united we stand, divided we fall." David Platt in the *Daily Worker* found the film to be "powerful propaganda for a second front," a policy that Rossen had urged the Hollywood Writers Mobilization to support in 1942. To writer Paul Trivers, writing in 1944 in the Communist Party's cultural periodical *New Masses*, Rossen's changes to the novel's story helped "audiences recognize there is no escaping the struggle today, that there is no personal life apart from the struggle."[13]

The radical screenwriter entered the patriotic mainstream, and Rossen was now a $1,500 a week writer, relative to his $200 a week status on joining the studio.[14] Yet memos record a number of discontinued projects, including *The Treasure of the Sierra Madre*, from the novel by progressive writer B. Traven, which Rossen began writing but which John Huston finished as writer-director after the war. Rossen was spending much time on his role at the Mobilization, and he later complained of being pushed by the Party into being a "functionary." He also invested considerable time researching and writing an original treatment of what was intended as a home front story. Rossen spoke at the 1943 Writers Congress of the hopes for the postwar world, and the shift from stories of disillusionment—*Out of the Fog* was referred to specifically—to stories in which ordinary people stand up for themselves. Rossen's treatment, called *Marked Children*, or *Blood of the Lamb*, is interesting in terms of its mix of motifs from thirties crime drama with a sociological interest in the lives of working people in a war plant adjoining a naval base. Rossen's story deals with a fourteen-year-old girl who runs away from her grandparents to look for her mother in the war plant.[15] She falls into "bad company" and joins a "new family" with a sailor and a war widow. There are links with the social concerns of *Dust Be My Destiny* as well as the more hardboiled elements that were characteristic of his work on *Blues in the Night*. The idea drew on the contemporary attention given to youth crime and the zoot suit riots, and Rossen consulted the Youth Corrective Authority in California on the youth delinquency problem. Yet the prospects for such a project seeing the light of day were limited, given Hollywood's virtual abandonment of the social problem picture in 1942. The OWI and the Office of Censorship were likely to oppose such projects, with the latter being particularly hostile to the distribution abroad of any film showing internal American weaknesses and divisions that the enemy might exploit as propaganda.[16]

In 1943 the leftist writer John Bright, then at Warners, was introduced to President Franklin D. Roosevelt, who told him of the great contribution that the studio had made to the Democratic Party. Yet by 1947 Roosevelt was no more and the political culture had shifted with the beginnings of the Cold War and the Republican sweep in the 1946 congressional elections. At two sets of hearings in 1947 Jack Warner blamed a host of leftist writers whom he claimed to have fired, including Rossen, for attempting to inject Communist propaganda into scripts. At the time when *The Strange Love of Martha Ivers* (directed by Lewis Milestone) was being shot at Paramount (in October 1945) Rossen joined pickets at Warners, protesting at the "outrageous violence perpetrated by hired thugs and police at your studio today."[17] In 1947 Rossen and Milestone were both named among the nineteen "unfriendly" witnesses called to the Washington hearings, although neither was required to testify.

Rossen made only two more films purely as a writer, both under a contract with his old Warner Bros. head of production Hal Wallis, who had set up an independent production company in partnership with Joseph Hazen at Paramount. Rossen's relationship with Wallis was quickly to break down when the writer left first for Enterprise and then Columbia Pictures. But, after a brief "polish job" on *The Searching Wind* (1946), he did write one significant film as part of the Wallis contract, *The Strange Love of Martha Ivers* (1946), from a short story by John Patrick. This was Rossen's third film as writer with Milestone: after *Edge of Darkness* he had worked closely with the director in adapting Harry Brown's novel for *A Walk in the Sun* (1946). Much later, after Rossen had named names in desperation in 1953,

Milestone, who was himself graylisted in the early fifties, was one of the few members of the "old gang," in his own words, to stay friends with him.[18]

To Milestone it was Rossen's "bright idea" to use the Patrick notion as a prologue and then to write a new script based on events that followed some fifteen years later.[19] In Rossen's script, although not in the completed film, the gap in time is given political significance by the use of posters for Hoover in 1928, after the prologue, and for Roosevelt in 1944, when the boy, now a man, returns to his home town. Rossen's work on the film reveals something of the way he used and transformed the old Warners motifs into the evolving visual and verbal rhetoric that the French would term film noir. Script and film contain familiar Rossen elements, including pool halls, bus stations, and freight yards. The prologue reveals the social and psychological origins of the political and economic power of postwar Iverstown, where the bulk of the film is set. The three main characters are introduced as children: Martha Ivers, unhappily living with her aunt; the local boy Sam Masterton, with whom Martha tries to escape; and Walter O'Neill, whose interests his father is trying to advance with Mrs. Ivers. Immediately there are issues of class, and also melodrama, as—amid thunder and lightning—the young Martha strikes her aunt with a cane, and the old woman falls to her death. Sam Masterton, apparently a witness to the murder, leaves town.

The rest of the film is set in 1944, when the adult Sam Masterton (Van Heflin), a sometime gambler and war veteran, finds himself back in Iverstown when, accidentally, he drives off the road. "The road curved—but I didn't," he says, suggesting Rossen's mix, and noir's mix, of social determinism and individual agency. There he discovers the "strange love," the human relations corrupted by greed and ownership, of the title. (Rossen's script was originally called "Love Lies Bleeding.")[20] Martha Ivers (Barbara Stanwyck), now a wealthy industrialist employing 30,000 workers, is married to Walter O'Neill (Kirk Douglas), who is running for reelection as the town's district attorney. The truth of the aunt's death has been covered up, and indeed an innocent man has been prosecuted by Walter and executed for the crime. The extent of Sam's knowledge of the circumstances of the sixteen-year-old crime remains unclear, creating doubt over his role and motives. He is nonetheless the investigator of the film, unraveling—for whatever reason— the personal and social corruption in the town in a way that relates to his previous involvement in the fight against fascism in Europe. He is no idealist, like the Frank McCloud character in the later *Key Largo* (1948), but he does have a war record "few can equal," and the corruption that he discovers also has wider social implications. Iverstown is presented as a company town where everyone is a party to the deceit and false values on which power rests. The garage owner whom Sam meets tells him that Walter is a "sure bet" ("No odds—no takers") for reelection as DA, and will also some day run for president. (Walter's secretary answers Sam's polite enquiry about how the campaign is going that morning with the remark that the "election is going good every morning.") Sam's motives are at first ambiguous, but his class position is underscored by his relationship while in the town with a young woman on parole, Toni Maracek (Lizabeth Scott), someone who is, like Sam, from the wrong side of the tracks. There are echoes here of Rossen's wartime interest in dislocated families. Milestone remembers Wallis interfering, for example by insisting on additional close-ups of Lizabeth Scott, and there were also adjustments to take care of the objections of the Breen office, which was concerned with the indication of "elements of illicit sex" that were "treated without proper compensating moral values." Breen also insisted that it be made clear that Toni Maracek was not a prostitute and that Sam definitely intended to marry her at the end.[21] Yet in the film Sam and Toni have adjoining hotel rooms, indicating a postwar pushing at Production Code rules.

Later work described by Andersen as film gris, such as director Joseph Losey and writer Dalton Trumbo's *The Prowler* (1951), represents a critique of the false values of postwar America, and while Rossen's script is dated September 1945, there is something of the same feeling. Showing off her wealth and power Martha tells Sam how she has had a tree replanted outside her window. Sam's response, and Rossen's, is, "What nature could do if she had money." In lines cut from the film Walter tells his wife and partner in crime, "You are my father's estate. His gift to me. He brought me up to believe that it's a son's duty to protect his inheritance." He refers later (and in the film) to the "power and the riches that you'd learned to love so much, and that I'd learned to love too." The film presents public life as a front, thinly disguising the determining material forces. The distortion of personality, the "strange love," is matched by an equal distortion of social organization. To Manny Farber the film was a "jolting, sour, engrossing work," showing modern life as a jungle. The Motion Picture Alliance for the Preservation of American Ideals, without analyzing the film, was quick to pave the way for the HUAC "investigations" by referring to it as containing "sizeable doses of Communist propaganda."[22]

The dialogue at the climax of the film also recalls the contemporary discussion by future Hollywood Ten member Adrian Scott of a film project—what would become *Crossfire* (1947)—on "personal fascism."[23] Sam confronts Martha with the facts of her two murders, of her aunt and of the man falsely convicted of killing her. The exchange recalls both Wolf Larson's "fascist" perspective in *The Sea Wolf*, and also the reference, even more explicit in *All the King's Men*, to public benefits gained at the expense of corruption:

MARTHA: What were their lives compared to mine? What was she?
SAM: A human being.
MARTHA: A mean vicious, hateful old woman who did nothing for anyone. Look what I've done with what she left me—I've given to charity, built schools, hospitals—I've given thousands of people work—What was he?
SAM: Another human being.

Of course the lines also hint at another issue of the costs and benefits of totalitarian power that might have been on Rossen's mind as he pondered—as he said he did at this time (the time of the Duclos letter) —the implications of his Communist Party membership.[24] Sam has exposed light and air to the "contract" between

Martha and Walter, and after he leaves them they play out their last moments, with Walter giving us a final analysis from Rossen that runs counter to classical Hollywood's, and Joe Breen's, focus on individual villains:

> WALTER: Don't cry. It's not your fault.
>
> MARTHA: (Sobbing) It isn't, is it, Walter?
>
> WALTER: No, nor mine, nor my father's, nor your Aunt's. It's not anyone's fault—it's just the way things are—it's what people want and how hard they want it and how hard it is for them to get it.

Rossen worked on one further script for Hall Wallis, *Desert Fury* (Lewis Allen, 1947). There is plenty of deviant sexual behavior for its time, and another contractual relationship, this time between two men, one of them threatened by the attentions his (ostensibly business) partner is paying to a woman. (There is also a scene of scalding coffee being poured down someone's neck, six years before the similar scene in Fritz Lang's *The Big Heat*.)

The same year—which saw an unprecedented upsurge in independent production—Rossen wrote a script for Columbia Pictures and its star, Dick Powell. Powell was an interesting figure in this period; he was at one point strongly interested in appearing in *Crossfire*, in his efforts to rebrand himself from crooner to serious actor, and he successfully lobbied for Rossen to be allowed to direct his script of *Johnny O'Clock* (1947). Rossen's first directing credit is a modest studio-based crime melodrama that exhibits, in the phase used by Bertrand Tavernier, "directorial grace."[25] As with *Desert Fury* there is a contractual relationship between brain and muscle, but Rossen's work here plays on the broader social resonance of gambling, rather as Abraham Polonsky did in *Body and Soul* (which Rossen directed from Polonsky's script) and most of all in *Force of Evil*. A casino is central to *Desert Fury* and *Johnny O'Clock*, while an exchange between Walter and Sam in *The Strange Love of Martha Ivers* also plays on the connection between gambling and American life in the postwar, and post-Roosevelt, era:

> WALTER: Well, perhaps this is where I should remark that all life is a gamble.
>
> SAM: You don't need to bother. I know it. Some win, some don't.

In *Johnny O'Clock* the relationship is between the casino owner, Johnny O'Clock, (Powell) and a powerful "business associate," Guido Marchettis (Thomas Gomez), who heads a shadowy outfit also based around gambling. When a further partner, a corrupt cop, murders a gambler, Marchettis's corrupt business empire comes under investigation by a wry, world-weary detective (not unlike the Finlay character in *Crossfire*), Kotch (Lee J. Cobb). The clock conceit recurs in plot, dialogue, musical score, and in the studio sets: a large clock looms over the pavement outside the hotel where O'Clock lives. O'Clock is a cold, calculating man, a cog in the Marchettis machine, although he thinks himself independent and invulnerable, a man in on a "sure bet" compared to the "suckers" who frequent his casino. (One is reminded of Orson Welles as Harry Lime in *The Third Man*, as he looks down from the Ferris wheel at the expendable "dots," the "suckers," below.) For Rossen there

1. Dick Powell in *Johnny O'Clock* (Columbia Pictures, 1947).

is perhaps some element of self-disgust here, in terms of his own role in Holly-wood's mass entertainment mission, its own "sure bet"; Marxist screenwriters had to admit, in Polonsky's iconic phrase, that everything was "addition and subtrac-tion" and that the rest, including much of their dialogue, was just "conversation." O'Clock's lack of apparent feeling for the world may or may not be related to the fact that he is crucially (like Sam Masterton in *The Strange Love of Martha Ivers*) a war veteran. To Marchettis, talking of his relationship with O'Clock—near to its end—there was "nothing between us but cash." With Kotch closing in, O'Clock's first impulse is to run and hide, but finally, pressured by a good woman, he drops

2. "The Last Hurrah." During production of *Body and Soul* (Enterprise Studios, 1947), clockwise from top left: Robert Rossen, Lilli Palmer, Gottfried Reinhardt, Abraham Polonsky, Anne Revere, Joseph Pevney, and John Garfield. Courtesy of The British Film Institute.

the pose and reenters society, joining up with Kotch's implicit social ideals. With O'Clock injured by a shot from the detective, he needs physical support, so that the three characters, in the last shot of the film, are linked arm in arm, a reluctant if affirmative alliance, facing an uncertain postwar future.

The modest success of *Johnny O'Clock* led to an approach by Roberts Productions, including John Garfield, to direct Abraham Polonsky's script of *Body and Soul* (1947) for the new Enterprise Studios. A few years earlier Rossen had expressed an interest in making a boxing film with Budd Schulberg, who was writing the exposé that would be published in 1947 as *The Harder They Fall*.[26] To Polonsky, Rossen was chosen in part because he was in the Party, and those involved with the Roberts company made sure that he made no changes to the script during filming. The film's editor, Robert Parrish, has provided an account of the filming of the climactic fight, which shifts the film stylistically from a treatment that recalls the Warner Bros. tradition (including montages), albeit with several distinctive crane shots.[27] James Wong Howe's wild shots from inside the ring, sometimes out of focus, give the fight a much more visceral, brutal feel. Furthermore, much has been made of Polonsky's and Rossen's disagreement over the ending. According to Parrish, Rossen had suggested the use of Ernest Hemingway's story "Fifty Grand" at the end. But the director later favored a final scene, following the defiant victory of

Davis (Garfield) in the ring, in which the boxer dies a squalid death at the hands of Roberts's minions. Polonsky wanted the film to end with the Davis victory, and with the couple being "swallowed up" by the neighborhood; he later recalled that Rossen was "more driven to a kind of tragic melodrama than I am."[28] Both versions were shot, but Rossen accepted that Polonsky's affirmative ending was more in keeping with the tone of the story as a Depression fable of the streets. Yet in terms of the importance of "happy endings" to conventional Hollywood practice one could make a case for Rossen's initial ending and relate it to the downbeat conclusions of several of his earlier films at Warners. The film's assistant director, Robert Aldrich, always supported what he felt was the "proper" ending, of the death of a hero who is aware that "the probabilities are that he'll lose."[29]

Rossen elicits fine performances, in particular from Garfield and from Canada Lee as the dignified black boxer; the staccato playing between Davis and his mother (Anne Revere) in the scene with the charity worker has particular impact. The success of the film opened doors for Polonsky (who immediately directed *Force of Evil*) and for Rossen, who soon after formed his own company and signed a contract with Columbia Pictures that gave him considerable artistic autonomy.[30] Rossen's powerful contract at Columbia was perhaps one of the factors that scared industry conservatives such as William Wilkerson, founder and publisher of the *Hollywood Reporter*, into believing that New York "intellectuals," with their notions of "life as a struggle," were threatening the "pure entertainment" tradition in Hollywood.[31] Rossen talked to Arthur Miller about a film version of his play *All My Sons*, but finally agreed to write, direct, and produce a film of Robert Penn Warren's Pulitzer Prize-winning 1946 novel, *All the King's Men*, the rights of which had been purchased by Columbia's New York office.[32] Yet before he could go ahead he was required, in the light of events in Washington, to write a letter to Harry Cohn, stating that he was no longer in the Party. Just as *All the King's Men* attempted to visualize the rise of an American version of European fascism, so Rossen was able to translate a number of elements from the much admired low-budget Italian films seen in America just after the war. The bulk of the filming took place in Stockton, California, with interiors as well as exteriors being shot on real locations. Nonprofessionals were used extensively, and much of the shooting took place in available light.

In terms of the theme of the film, it is interesting that the year before Rossen had worked in a supervisory capacity with writer and Hollywood Ten member Alvah Bessie on the scripting of *Ruthless* (Edgar G. Ulmer, 1948), although neither was credited. Ulmer's film uses a biopic structure to recount the central character's lifelong pursuit of wealth and corporate success, at the expense of human relationships. On his death a character remarks, in the last line of the film, "He wasn't a man, he was a way of life." Ulmer's film shares something of the structure and even the politics of Orson Welles's *Citizen Kane* (1941), and Rossen's film was also to nod toward Welles with the giant portraits of Willie Stark at rallies and the director's addition of a "March of Time" sequence.

Rossen, who consulted Warren throughout, filmed scenes that covered the bulk of the novel, and then cut around a full hour of the material, in particular scenes dealing with the personal relationships, following unsuccessful previews. Rossen even makes a personal appearance as a newspaperman, speaking the first line of the film. Rossen used *The Roaring Twenties* as a model in preparing the final edit, and Stark's death recalls the final scene in that film, and also the fate of another over-reaching figure of 1949 film, Cody Jarrett (James Cagney) in *White Heat*. Jarrett's last line is "Made it, Ma, Top of the World," while Stark's is "Could have been the whole world, Willie Stark."[33] It is also interesting that the French writers Raymond Borde and Etienne Chaumeton cited the film in their seminal 1955 work on film noir, noting its debt to films on crime. Certainly Anne Stanton becomes something of a femme fatale in Rossen's version, suggesting the way that Stark is corrupted by the old aristocratic order at Burden's Landing.[34]

The detachment from the political events provided by the character of Jack Burden (John Ireland) was arguably attractive to Rossen. Burden, a character "too rich to work," is a fellow traveler who is dissatisfied by the remoteness of the upper class world of Burden's Landing to the lives of ordinary people. The Stark campaigns connect this scion of the defeated southern aristocracy to history and to change.

Stark becomes a hero to the people from whom he came, just as Charley Davis is a hero to the people of his Lower East Side community. He makes deals with oil companies and buys off the upper class community. Burden's speech to Anne Stanton at the end of the film, after Stark's death, in which he suddenly calls on her to help him make people see Willie Stark as Adam Stanton saw him, seems uncharacteristic of Burden and an effort to give the film a neat concluding message. It also suggests Burden's final surrender to the old order, an element that was not likely to appeal to Rossen's old Party colleagues. Edward Dmytryk and Ring Lardner Jr. later reported a Los Angeles meeting of the Hollywood Ten at which various Party luminaries, including John Howard Lawson—who had apparently advised Rossen against making *All the King's Men*—heavily criticized the film. Both remembered this meeting—presumably late in 1949—as the moment when Rossen finally cut all connections with the Party.[35]

With its jack-boots and searchlights, Rossen's film makes reference to fascism while also raising the dilemma of Rousseaueque democracy that political scientists at this time were beginning to see as at the heart of totalitarianism. Stark tells the crowd: "Remember, it's not I who have won, but you. Your will is my strength, and your need is my justice." Yet this "general will" leads not only to progressive change but also to dictatorship and corruption. To documentary filmmaker and critic Paul Rotha at the time the "basic weakness—and danger—of the film is that little attempt is made to show how the real machinery of democratic action in the hands of people educated in democratic ways of action could have worked." The "hicks" support Stark, just as the "suckers" kept Johnny O'Clock in business. There seems to be no alternative to Willie Stark. Yet the seductiveness of political power is rarely better demonstrated, particularly in the performance of Mercedes McCambridge as Sadie Burke, a role that was enlarged following the popularity of the character at previews.

The *Hollywood Reporter* saw the film as "an arresting celluloid study of the effect of a demagogue on the mass mind."[36] Yet—one is reminded of the line about Martha Ivers's public contribution in *The Strange Love in Martha Ivers*—the real benefits to the previously ignored working people, in terms of new hospitals and roads, are manifest in the film as part of this American dictator's contract with his electorate. Rossen's film associates Warren's notion of original sin mainly with the Stark character, so that the novelist's sense of the partial complicity of the people in the corruption is undermined. Instead the director emphasizes Stark's control over the popular media in order to maintain something of the affirmative, Popular Front notion of "the people." Rossen's crowds do not constitute a mob, and when ordinary people can see behind the media image, and see Stark up close—as Robert Hale, the father of the girl killed in Stark's son's drunken car accident, does in an extended scene invented for the film—they reject him.[37]

Rossen directed *The Brave Bulls* (1951) in Mexico in the spring of 1950, but was then blacklisted; his next film was *Mambo* in 1955. He was to appear twice before HUAC during its second wave of hearings, beginning in 1951. In that year he testified that he was no longer a Communist. Unable to get his passport renewed he appeared the second time as a cooperative witness, providing—or more precisely confirming—the names of fifty-three Communists.[38] Only with his pool-room drama *The Hustler* (1961) did Rossen return to critical and commercial success, and to a variation on his earlier themes. It is in the transitional period of the late forties that Rossen's work indicates some of the ways in which the Hollywood Left took advantage of postwar conditions to articulate a tougher and meaner perspective on the distortions of American business and political structures than had previously been possible, or would be possible in the fifties. On his premature death in 1966 he was preparing a film that would have again dealt with the relationship between notions of American reality and myth; "Cocoa Beach" was to relate the hopes and struggles of transients in a local community to the nearby Cape Canaveral, symbol of America's imperial reach.

12　Swashbuckling, Sapphire, and Salt

UN-AMERICAN CONTRIBUTIONS TO TV COSTUME ADVENTURE SERIES IN THE 1950S

Steve Neale

The mid-to-late 1950s witnessed the appearance of a number of costume adventure series on Britain's then-new commercial television channel, ITV, on national and local TV in the United States, and, indeed, on TV stations in many other parts of the world.[1] These series, which were an increasingly important component of what Brian Taves has identified as the third of four major cycles of costume adventure in the period prior to the 1990s,[2] included "The Adventures of Robin Hood" (initially broadcast in the United Kingdom from 1955 to 1959 and on CBS in the United States from 1955 to 1958), "The Adventures of Sir Lancelot" (initially broadcast in the United Kingdom and on NBC in the United States in 1956 and 1957), "The Buccaneers" (initially broadcast in the United Kingdom and on CBS in the United States in 1956 and 1957), "Sword of Freedom" (initially syndicated to local TV stations in the United States in 1957 and 1958 and broadcast in the United Kingdom between 1958 and the early 1960s),[3] and "Ivanhoe" (initially broadcast in 1958 and 1959 in the United Kingdom and initially syndicated in the United States in 1958). These programs are of historical interest not only because of their international success,[4] but also because they were often scripted by blacklisted writers.

Since the publication in 1980 of Ceplair and Englund's *The Inquisition in Holly-wood*, it has been known that Ring Lardner Jr. and Ian McLellan Hunter wrote scripts for "Robin Hood."[5] It has also been known that a key role was played by producer Hannah Weinstein and by her company, Sapphire Films. Since then, a number of publications have added to the list of blacklisted writers, the TV series to which they contributed, and our knowledge of the part played by Sapphire and Weinstein.[6] It is now known, for instance, that Norma Barzman, Robert Lees, Adrian Scott, Maurice Rapf, and others wrote scripts for "Robin Hood" too, that Lardner and Hunter wrote scripts for "The Adventures of Sir Lancelot" and "The Buccaneers" in addition to those they wrote for "Robin Hood," and that Waldo Salt wrote scripts for "Robin Hood" and "Ivanhoe" as well. It is also known that these scripts were either written pseudonymously or were allocated a pseudonymous credit at some point during production. However, the contributions made by Lardner, Hunter, and Salt to "Sword of Freedom," and by Salt and others to "The Buccaneers," have rarely been noted. Precise details as to which writers wrote which scripts under which names are in short supply. Given the secrecy that surrounded their work, the fading memories of those who worked on the series, and the partial nature of available archival evidence, it is now probably impossible to provide these details in full. However, a number of largely untapped archival sources, notably the letters, papers, and scripts of Ian McLellan Hunter, Ring Lardner Jr., Robert Lees and Fred Rinaldo, Waldo Salt, and Adrian Scott,[7] do exist. Using these sources in conjunction with some of the published accounts listed above, I aim to add more flesh to the bones of existing records. I also aim to add new names, such as Hy Craft, Howard Dimsdale, Arnaud D'Usseau, Anne Green, Millard Lampell, Arnold Manoff, Sam Moore, Arnold Perl, Fred Rinaldo, and Janet Stevenson, to the list of blacklisted contributors. First, however, I want to underline the importance of the role played by Weinstein and Sapphire.

Hannah Weinstein was born Hannah Dorner in New York in 1911. Throughout the 1930s and 1940s she worked as a journalist, publicist, and campaigner for radical causes. She was a supporter of Roosevelt's New Deal and campaigned for third-party presidential candidate Henry Wallace in 1948. After Wallace's defeat and her failed marriage to Peter Weinstein (and just prior to HUAC's second series of Hollywood hearings), she left the United States with her children in 1950 and went to France. There she produced her first film, *Fait divers à Paris* (1952), and renewed contact with a number of Hollywood exiles, among them Ben and Norma Barzman, Lee and Tammy Gold, John Berry, Jules Dassin, and Abraham Polonsky, all of whom had gone to France in the late 1940s and early 1950s. With Polonsky and Boris Karloff, in whose house in France she initially lived, she began planning a TV series, "Colonel March of Scotland Yard." She then went to London in 1952 and in an uncredited capacity produced three pilot episodes that were reedited and released in 1953 as a feature film entitled *Colonel March Investigates*. On the basis of these pilots, a series was commissioned and distributed in the United States by Official Films. Blacklisted writers, among them Walter Bernstein and Abraham Polonsky, wrote scripts for "Colonel March," which Weinstein again produced in an uncredited capacity. Cy Endfield, who had been blacklisted in the early 1950s, directed the three pilot episodes.[8]

"Colonel March" was a moderate success. With the advent of ITV in Britain now imminent, Weinstein set up a new company, Sapphire Films, in 1954, planning further TV productions and planning, too, to provide further paid employment for blacklisted writers. She began negotiations with Official Films in the United States and with Associated Television (ATV) and its subsidiary, the Incorporated Television Programme Company (ITP), in Britain for production funding and for regional, national, and international distribution for a new series, "The Adventures of Robin Hood." Once the project was agreed, initial outlines and scripts were written in New York by Ring Lardner Jr. and Ian McLellan Hunter and edited (in an uncredited capacity) by Howard Koch, a blacklisted writer living in London.[9] Filming began at Nettlefold Studios in Surrey early in 1955, and on location in the country-side nearby. "Robin Hood" was an instant success. It was followed in rapid succession by "The Adventures of Sir Lancelot," "The Buccaneers," and "Sword of Freedom," all produced by Weinstein and Sapphire, all funded and distributed by ATV, ITP, and Official Films, and all frequently scripted by blacklisted writers.

Unlike like "Robin Hood," "Sir Lancelot," and "The Buccaneers," "Sword of Freedom" failed to secure network distribution in the United States and received notably lukewarm reviews.[10] The swashbuckling trend was continued by "Ivanhoe," "The Adventures of William Tell" (which was initially transmitted in the United Kingdom between 1957 and 1959 and syndicated to local TV stations in the United States in 1958), "The Adventures of Sir Francis Drake" (initially transmitted in the United Kingdom in 1961–62 and on NBC in the United States in 1962), and "Richard the Lionheart" (initially transmitted in the United Kingdom in 1961–62).[11] But Weinsten and Sapphire turned away from swashbucklers and went on to produce "The Four Just Men" (1959–60), an adventure series based loosely on the novel by Edgar Wallace.[12] Episodes of "The Four Just Men" were scripted by Ring Lardner Jr., Ian McLellan Hunter, and other blacklisted writers.[13] However, the escalating costs associated with extensive location shooting and a cast of four rotating stars (Richard Conte, Dan Dailey, Jack Hawkins, and Vittorio De Sica) led to the demise of Sapphire and "The Four Just Men" and helped prompt Weinstein's return to the United States.[14] When she left the United Kingdom in 1962, reruns of "Robin Hood" were still being broadcast. When she arrived in the United States, it was still in syndication and was to remain so for many years to come.

"The Adventures of Robin Hood"

More is known about the contribution made by blacklisted writers to "Robin Hood" than to all of Sapphire's other series put together. However, very little was known until recently about the specific contributions made by individual writers either to the series as a whole or to its constituent episodes, and very little is known about its origins. Hal Hackett, president of Official Films, claimed that "Robin Hood" was Official's idea; Ring Lardner Jr. claimed it was Weinstein's idea.[15] One of the few things that can be said with any confidence is that Lardner and Ian McLellan Hunter played a major part in its early development. They helped establish its emphasis not just on social justice, humor, and wit, but on the constant threat of informing and betrayal. Lardner had been one of the Hollywood Ten. He had worked as a screenwriter on *Woman of the Year* (1942), *The Cross of Lorraine* (1943), *Cloak and Dagger* (1946), and *Forever Amber* (1947) prior to being blacklisted. Like Ian McLellan Hunter, who fronted for Dalton Trumbo on *Roman Holiday* (1953), he had also written scripts for the *Dr. Christian* films in the late 1930s and early 1940s, many of which were directed by future blacklistee Bernard Vorhaus. Lardner and Hunter were based in New York. Because they found it difficult to secure passports, they were initially unable to travel to London. (According to Lardner, Hunter eventually secured a passport and made occasional visits to London before moving his family to England in 1958.)[16] Whether Weinstein traveled to the United States to propose that they write scripts for the series or whether she contacted them by post or via an intermediary remains unknown. However, once the process of production of scripts was under way, communication was nearly always by letter, as script editor Albert Ruben later explained:

> The way it worked was that Hannah and Sid Cole, who was her producer, and I would meet in London when we'd get an outline, let's say, for an episode. My job was primarily to take copious notes as Hannah and Sid discussed the problems. It was a regular story conference, except that the writers weren't there. Then, immediately after the conclusion of the meeting, I would go to my office and sit down at my typewriter and write a letter to the writers with all the material that had come out of the story conference.[17]

According to Bernard Dick, Hunter alone wrote the opening episode, "The Coming of Robin Hood," under the pseudonym Lawrence McLellan.[18] Letters to and from Lardner and Hunter and Ruben written on April 4 and 9, 1955, respectively, indicate that it was Weinstein who "came up with 'Lawrence McLellan' as a pseudonym" with "'Ian Larkin' in reserve," and that Lardner and Hunter themselves proposed the name Eric Heath.[19] Along with John Dyson and Paul Symonds, these were the false names predominant on the credits of "Robin Hood" throughout the first season (1955–56) and for much of the second (1956–57). Most of these scripts were written in tandem by Lardner and Hunter. A letter to Albert Ruben indicates that the names Oliver Skene and Samuel B. West, both prominent in the credits of the third season (1957–58) as well as in those of subsequent Sapphire series, were chosen as additional pseudonyms by Lardner and Hunter in April 1957.[20] As the success of "Robin Hood" prompted more seasons, more series, and more scripts, and as Lardner and Hunter themselves became involved in the planning and scripting of other series, these and other names, notably Neil R. Collins, were increasingly used by other writers as well.[21] In addition, script editor Peggy Phillips and director Ralph Smart were used as fronts.[22]

The attribution of specific scripts to specific writers is thus not a straightforward matter. However, in addition to the types of sources mentioned above, an invaluable resource exists in the form of documents in the Ring Lardner Junior Collection, which list episodes of "Robin Hood," "The Adventures of Sir Lancelot," and "The Buccaneers" with the initials or names of their authors, and the names, addresses, and pseudonyms of the "Writers Involved In Rerun Settlement with Official Films."[23] Using these sources in combination, it is possible to correlate the names of writers with pseudonyms and episodes and to draw up a reasonably complete picture of who wrote which episodes under which names. What follows is a listing of episodes by season and title, with the names on the credits in quotation marks and the names of the writers in parentheses. On occasion the titles of episodes in the annotated listings referred to above differ from the titles on the credits themselves. Where there are substantial differences, I have specified the former in parentheses.

Season One

"The Coming of Robin Hood," Lawrence McLellan (Ian McLellan Hunter)

"The Moneylender," Ian Larkin and Eric Heath (Ring Lardner Jr. and Ian McLellan Hunter)

"Dead or Alive," Eric Heath (Ring Lardner Jr. and Ian McLellan Hunter)

"Friar Tuck," Eric Heath (Ring Lardner Jr. and Ian McLellan Hunter)

"Maid Marion," Anne Rodney (Anne Green)[24]

"A Guest for the Gallows," Eric Heath (Ring Lardner Jr. and Ian McLellan Hunter)

"The Challenge" ("The Archery Contest"), Eric Heath (Ring Lardner Jr. and Ian McLellan Hunter)

"Queen Eleanor," Eric Heath (Norma Barzman and Mischa Altman? Ring Lardner Jr. and Ian McLellan Hunter?)[25]

"The Ordeal" ("Murder Story"), Eric Heath (Ring Lardner Jr. and Ian McLellan Hunter)

"A Husband for Marion," John Dyson (Ring Lardner Jr. and Ian McLellan Hunter)

"The Highlander," Eric Heath (Ring Lardner Jr. and Ian McLellan Hunter)

"The Youngest Outlaw," John Dyson (Ring Lardner Jr. and Ian McLellan Hunter)

"The Betrothal" ("The Betrothal Party"), Paul Symonds (Ring Lardner Jr. and Ian McLellan Hunter)

"The Alchemist," Eric Heath (Ring Lardner Jr. and Ian McLellan Hunter? Adrian Scott and Fred Rinaldo?)[26]

"The Jongleur," John Dyson (Ring Lardner Jr. and Ian McLellan Hunter)

"The Brothers," Eric Heath (Ring Lardner Jr. and Ian McLellan Hunter)

"The Intruders," Paul Symonds (Ring Lardner Jr. and Ian McLellan Hunter)

"Errand of Mercy," John Dyson (Ring Lardner Jr. and Ian McLellan Hunter)

"The Vandals," C. Douglas Phipps (Robert Lees?)[27]

"Richard the Lionheart," Paul Symonds (Ring Lardner Jr. and Ian McLellan Hunter)

"Will Scarlet," John Dyson (Ring Lardner Jr. and Ian McLellan Hunter)

"The Deserted Castle," Eric Heath (Ring Lardner Jr. and Ian McLellan Hunter)

"Trial by Battle," Arthur Behr (Waldo Salt)[28]

"The Byzantine Treasure," Paul Symonds (Ring Lardner Jr. and Ian McLellan Hunter)

"Secret Mission," Ralph Smart (Ring Lardner Jr. and Ian McLellan Hunter)[29]

"The Inquisitor," Anne Rodney (Anne Green)

"Tables Turned," Anne Rodney (Anne Green)

"The Traitor," Norma Shannon (Norma Barzman?) and Ralph Smart (Mischa Altman?)[30]

"The Thorkil Ghost," Arthur Behr (Waldo Salt)

"The Knight Who Came to Dinner," Eric Heath (Ring Lardner Jr. and Ian McLellan Hunter)

"The Prisoner," Anne Rodney (Anne Green)

Season Two

"A Village Wooing," Neil R. Collins (Waldo Salt)

"The Scientist," Neil R. Collins (Ring Lardner Jr. and Ian McLellan Hunter)

"Blackmail," Paul Symons (Ring Lardner Jr. and Ian McLellan Hunter)

"A Year and a Day," Neil R. Collins (Waldo Salt)

"The Goldmaker," Paul Symonds (Ring Lardner Jr. and Ian McLellan Hunter)

"The Imposters," Norman Best (Gordon Kahn)[31]

"Ransom," John Dyson (Ring Lardner Jr. and Ian McLellan Hunter)

"Isabella," Neil R. Collins (Waldo Salt)

"The Hero," John Dyson (Ring Lardner Jr. and Ian McLellan Hunter)

"The Haunted Mill," Paul Symonds (Ring Lardner Jr. and Ian McLellan Hunter)

"The Black Patch," John Dyson (Waldo Salt)

"Outlaw Money," John Dyson (Ring Lardner Jr. and Ian McLellan Hunter)

"Hubert," Ralph Smart and Anne Rodney (Anne Green)

"The Dream," Anne Rodney (Anne Green)

"The Shell Game," Anne Rodney (Anne Green)

"The Final Tax" ("Death Tax"), Paul Symonds (Ring Lardner Jr. and Ian McLellan Hunter)

"The Bandit of Brittany," Milton S. Schlesinger (Maurice Rapf and Sam Moore)[32]

"Flight from France," Milton S. Schlesinger (Maurice Rapf and Sam Moore)

"The Secret Pool" ("The Secret Pond"), John Dyson (Ring Lardner Jr. and Ian McLellan Hunter)

"Fair Play," Sidney Wells (Arnaud D'Usseau)[33]

"The Dowry," Neil R. Collins (Robert Lees)

"The York Treasure," Clare Thorne (Janet Stevenson)[34]

"Food for Thought," Sidney B. Wells (Arnaud D'Usseau)

"Too Many Earls," Milton S. Schlesinger (Maurice Rapf and Sam Moore)

"Highland Fling," Leighton Reynolds (Ring Lardner Jr. and Ian McLellan Hunter)

"The Infidel," John Dyson (Robert Lees) and Basil Dawson

Season Three

"The Charter," John Dyson (Robert Lees)

"Brother Battle," Leslie Poynton (Adrian Scott and Fred Rinaldo)[35]

"My Brother's Keeper," Neil R. Collins (Waldo Salt)

"The Mark," Robert Newman (Arnold Manoff)[36]

"The Bride of Robin Hood," Oliver Skene (Ring Lardner Jr. and Ian McLellan Hunter)

"To Be a Student," Sidney B. Wells (Arnaud D'Usseau)

"The Christmas Goose," Oliver Skene (Ring Lardner Jr. and Ian McLellan Hunter)

"The Rivals," Leslie Poynton (Adrian Scott and Fred Rinaldo?)[37]

"The Profiteer," Samuel B. West (Ring Lardner Jr. and Ian McLellan Hunter)

"Too Many Robins" ("The Imposter"), John Dyson (Robert Lees)[38]

"The Crusaders," Samuel B. West (Ring Lardner Jr. and Ian McLellan Hunter)

"Castle in the Air," Oliver Skene (Ring Lardner Jr. and Ian McLellan Hunter)

"At the Sign of the Blue Boar," Sidney B. Wells (Arnaud D'Usseau)

"The Elixir of Youth," Samuel B. West (Ring Lardner Jr. and Ian McLellan Hunter)

"The Genius," Oliver Skene (Ring Lardner Jr. and Ian McLellan Hunter)

"The Youthful Menace," Arthur Dales (Howard Dimsdale)[39]

"The Minstrel," Leslie Poynton (Adrian Scott and Fred Rinaldo)

"The Doctor," Leslie Poynton (Adrian Scott and Fred Rinaldo)

"Lincoln Green," Neil R. Collins (Waldo Salt)

"Farewell to Tuck," Arthur Dales (Howard Dimsdale)

Season Four[40]

"The Oath," Arthur Dales (Howard Dimsdale)

"Hostage for a Hangman," Arthur Dales (Howard Dimsdale)

"A Race Against Time," Arthur Dales (Howard Dimsdale)

"The Adventures of Sir Lancelot"

The success of "Robin Hood" led Weinstein, Ruben, Lardner, and Hunter to discuss ideas for additional series as early as winter 1955. According to a letter from Ruben to Lardner and Hunter written on November 18, a series about King Arthur and the Knights of the Round Table had been discussed prior to deciding on "Robin Hood," and it was Hal Hackett and Official Films who revived this idea.[41] Plans and outlines not only for "The Adventures of Sir Lancelot" but for "The Buccaneers" as well were well underway by early 1956; production on "Sir Lancelot" began in March; by May, Adrian Scott in Los Angeles was writing a detailed response to a preview of the opening episode of "Sir Lancelot."[42] Scott's involvement in "Sir Lancelot" was far more substantial than his involvement in "Robin Hood." Either alone or in tandem with Fred Rinaldo, he wrote over a dozen episodes.[43] Along with Lardner and Hunter and Weinstein and Ruben, he and Rinaldo were largely responsible for its tone and its other characteristics.[44] This was partly a matter of policy, partly a matter of necessity. There was some concern when it was realized that in the United States, "Robin Hood" and "Sir Lancelot" "will follow each other on Monday nights. On different networks, to be sure, but still contiguous enough to spotlight their similarities—especially since the creators are the same two guys. . . . We have to do something to make it ['Sir Lancelot'] look like a different animal than 'Robin Hood.'"[45] One way of doing this was "to dress Sir L. up more, give it more pageantry, more horses, more, in other words, of the full panoply of knights in armor."[46] Another was to assign the scripts for "Sir Lancelot" to a different team of writers. While Lardner and Hunter produced the bulk of the "Sir Lancelot" scripts, and Ruben and Weinstein worked with them to achieve a distinctive formula, the contributions of Scott and Rinaldo, who had not yet written anything for "Robin Hood," helped to differentiate the scripts of the new series. The formula that emerged, with Lancelot as the principal defender of the values of the Round Table, proved relatively successful. But the series lacked the distinctiveness of "Robin Hood" and there were no further seasons.

"The Knight with the Red Plume," Leighton Reynolds (Ring Lardner Jr. and Ian McLellan Hunter)

"The Ferocious Fathers," Leighton Reynolds (Ring Lardner Jr. and Ian McLellan Hunter)

"The Queen's Knight," Leighton Reynolds (Ring Lardner Jr. and Ian McLellan Hunter)

"The Outcast," Leslie Poynton (Adrian Scott and Fred Rinaldo)

"Winged Victory," John Ridgely (Adrian Scott)

"Sir Bliant," John Ridgely (Adrian Scott)

"The Pirates," Leighton Reynolds (Ring Lardner Jr. and Ian McLellan Hunter)

"The Magic Sword," Leighton Reynolds (Ring Lardner Jr. and Ian McLellan Hunter)

"Lancelot's Banishment," Peggy Phillips (Adrian Scott and Fred Rinaldo)

"Roman Wall," Harold Kent (Hy Kraft? Ring Lardner Jr. and Ian McLellan Hunter?)[47]

"Caledon," Leighton Reynolds (Ring Lardner Jr. and Ian McLellan Hunter)

"Theft of Excalibur," Hamish Hamilton Burns (Adrian Scott and Fred Rinaldo)

"The Black Castle," Peggy Phillips (Sam Moore)

"Shepherd's War," Leslie Poynton (Adrian Scott and Fred Rinaldo)

"The Magic Book," Leslie Poynton (Adrian Scott and Fred Rinaldo)

"The Ruby of Radnor," Hamish Hamilton Burns (Maurice Rapf and Sam Moore)

"The Lesser Breed," Peggy Phillips (Adrian Scott and Fred Rinaldo)

"Witches' Brew," Peggy Phillips (Adrian Scott and Fred Rinaldo)

"Sir Crustabread," Leslie Poynton (Adrian Scott and Fred Rinaldo)

"Double Identity," Harold Kent (Hy Kraft)

"Lady Lilith," Leslie Poynton (Adrian Scott and Fred Rinaldo)

"The Ugly Duckling," Leslie Poynton (Adrian Scott and Fred Rinaldo)

"The Missing Princess," Leslie Poynton (Adrian Scott and Fred Rinaldo)

"The Mortaise Fair," Leslie Poynton (Adrian Scott and Fred Rinaldo)

"The Thieves," Hamish Hamilton Burns (Adrian Scott and Fred Rinaldo)

"The Princess of Limerick," Leslie Poyton (Adrian Scott and Fred Rinaldo)

"The Buccaneers"

Following research into the possibility of a series on the pirate Henry Morgan,[48] "The Buccaneers," like "Robin Hood" and "Sir Lancelot," was initially devised and scripted by Lardner and Hunter. However, coupled with the pressing demand for scripts for Sapphire's other series, dissatisfaction with the initial format led Lardner and Hunter to hand the series over to Waldo Salt, Arnold Perl, and Millard Lampell.[49]

The focus was shifted away from Woodes Rogers (Alec Clunes), who was prominent in the first two episodes, and toward Dan Tempest (Robert Shaw), who made his initial appearance in the third episode. As a reformed pirate, Tempest acted as an unofficial ally of the British in the Caribbean, fighting other pirates as well as the tyrannical (and slave-trading) Spanish. Later on, the setting was changed to the seas around the South Carolina coast and the American mainland as Tempest and his crew set about "righting wrongs, fighting oppressors, avenging cruelty," as Salt himself put it.[50] As is clear from Salt's papers and from the listings in Lardner's papers, Salt, Perl, and Lampell wrote most of these episodes.[51] Michael Wilson acted as a script editor, and wrote the episode entitled "Dan Tempest and the Amazons."[52]

"Blackbeard," Thomas A. Stockwell (Ring Lardner Jr and Ian McLellan Hunter)

"The Raider," Terence Moore (Ring Lardner Jr. and Ian McLellan Hunter)

1. Title credit for "Dangerous Cargo," an episode of "The Buccaneers."

"Captain Dan Tempest," Terence Moore (Ring Lardner Jr. and Ian McLellan Hunter)

"Dan Tempest's War with Spain," Zachary Weiss (Waldo Salt)

"The Wasp," Peter C. Hodgkins (Millard Lampell)

"Whale Gold," Zachary Weiss (Millard Lampell)

"The Slave Ship," John Cousins (Waldo Salt)[53]

"Gunpowder Plot," Terence Moore (Waldo Salt)

"The Surgeon of Sangre Rojo," Thomas A. Stockwell (Waldo Salt)

"Dan Tempest and the Amazons," Zachary Weiss (Michael Wilson)

"The Hand of the Hawk," Peter C. Hodgkins (Millard Lampell)

"Marooned," Peter C. Hodgkins (Arnold Perl)

"Gentleman Jack and the Lady," Zachary Weiss (Waldo Salt)

"Mr Beamish and the Hangman's Noose," Terence Moore[54]

"Dead Man's Rock," Peter C. Hodgkins (Millard Lampell)

"Blood Will Tell," Zachary Weiss (Waldo Salt)

"Dangerous Cargo," Zachary Weiss (Waldo Salt)

"The Return of Calico Jack," Zachary Weiss (Waldo Salt)

"Ghost Ship," Peter C. Hodgkins (Millard Lampell)

"Conquistador," Terence Moore (Arnold Perl) and Basil Dawson

"Mother Doughty's Crew," Zachary Weiss (Waldo Salt)

"Conquest of New Providence," Terence Moore (Arnold Perl)

"Hurricane," Terence Moore (Arnold Perl) and Peggy Phillips

"Cutlass Wedding," Thomas A. Stockwell (Millard Lampell?)[55]

FOR

SAPPHIRE FILMS LIMITED

Produced by
PENNINGTON RICHARDS

Directed by
LESLIE ARLISS

Screenplay by
ZACHARY WEISS

2. End credit for "Dangerous Cargo." Zachary Weiss was a pseudonym for Waldo Salt.

"The Aztec Treasure," Terence Moore (Arnold Perl)

"Prize of Andalusia" Basil Dawson and Zachary Weiss (Waldo Salt)

"The Spy Aboard," Neil R. Collins (Waldo Salt)

"Flip and Jenny," Neil R. Collins (Arnold Manoff)[56]

"Indian Fighters," Neil R. Collins (Waldo Salt)

"Mistress Higgins' Treasure," Thomas A. Stockwell (Millard Lampell?
    Arnold Perl?)[57]

"The Decoy," Albert G. Ruben (Arnold Manoff)

"Printer's Devil," Terence Moore (Waldo Salt)

"Sword of Freedom"

Less attention has been paid to "Sword of Freedom" than to any of the other
Sapphire series. Along with "The Four Just Men," it is the only such series currently
unavailable on DVD. It focuses on the rebellious Marco del Monte (Edmund Pur-
dom), a fifteenth-century Florentine painter who finds himself constantly at odds
with the tyrannical Medici family and its ruling regime. The series emerged as a possibility in the autumn of 1956.[58] Hunter undertook background research in Venice the
following year. He and Lardner again wrote the opening episodes and the episode
entitled "Choice of Weapons."[59] Waldo Salt wrote at least four scripts.[60] Adrian Scott
may have written some or all of the scripts attributed to Robert Westerby.[61]

"Francesca," Lewis Hart (Ring Lardner Jr. and Ian McLellan Hunter)

"The Sicilian," Samuel B. West (Ring Lardner Jr. and Ian McLellan Hunter)

"Portrait in Emerald Green," Leighton Reynolds (Waldo Salt)

"Forgery in Red Chalk," Leighton Reynolds (Waldo Salt)

"Caterina," Robert Westerby (Adrian Scott?)

"The Duke," Robert Westerby (Adrian Scott?)

"The Bracelet," Robert Westerby (Adrian Scott?)

"The Hero," Robert Westerby (Adrian Scott?)

"Choice of Weapons," Samuel B. West (Ring Lardner Jr. and Ian McLellan
    Hunter)

"Marriage of Convenience," Robert Westerby (Adrian Scott?)

"Serenade in Red," Leighton Reynolds (Waldo Salt)

"The Pagan Venus," Robert Westerby (Adrian Scott?)

"Chart of Gold," Leighton Reynolds (Waldo Salt)

"Ivanhoe"

"Ivanhoe" is probably best known now as an early TV vehicle for Roger Moore in
the title role. Like Robin of Locksley in "Robin Hood," Ivanhoe returns home
from the Crusades to find that the corrupt and tyrannical Prince John has usurped
the throne of King Richard. With the help of Gurth and Bart, two freed serfs, he
sets about righting wrongs and restoring social justice. Quite how Waldo Salt
became involved in "Ivanhoe" is not yet known.[62] The series was produced, as noted
above, by Columbia Screen Gems. Its associate producer was Ben Berenberg.

Berenberg's name appears on the series outline in Salt's papers.[63] He is also credited as the author of the opening episode, "Freeing the Serfs," and of a series of tie-in "Ivanhoe" novels published in Germany in the early 1960s.[64] He was married to singer and actress Janice Mars. He himself wrote music and songs, and had been active in radical theater in the 1930s. (He worked on a show called "Red Vaude-ville.") He was thus sympathetic to the blacklistees and may have known Salt for some time. He and Salt (as M. L. Davenport) wrote the theme song and other inci-dental songs for the "Ivanhoe" series.[65] Other than that, very little is known about him.[66] Salt himself wrote the episodes entitled "The Black Boar," The Prisoner in the Tower," The Masons," and "The Princess," scripts for which can be found in his papers.[67] Among the pseudonyms he used was Felix van Lieu, a name that appears on the credits of "The Circus." However, there is no evidence in Salt's papers that he himself wrote this episode. There are two other scripts in Salt's papers. One is for "Murder at the Inn," which is attributed in pencil to Ben Berenberg and which was credited to Felix van Lieu, so it may have been written by Berenberg, by Salt, or by someone else.[68] The other is for "The Weavers."[69] Both the script and the credits attribute authorship of this episode to Robert Soderberg, a screenwriter best known for scripting "The Reckless Moment" (1949) and "Born to Be Bad" (1950). It should be noted, finally, that the credits for "The Ransom" in the London edition of the *TV Times* state that it was "written by Sheldon Star" from a "tele-play" by "Joel Carpenter" and Geoffrey Orme. Joel Carpenter, as noted above, was a pseudonym used by Arnold Manoff.

> "The Black Boar," Richard Fielder (Waldo Salt)
> "The Prisoner in the Tower," M. L. Davenport (Waldo Salt)
> "Murder at the Inn," Felix van Lieu (Waldo Salt?)
> "Counterfeit," S. B. Wells (Arnaud D'Usseau)[70]
> "The Princess," Felix van Lieu (Waldo Salt)
> "The Masons," Felix van Lieu (Waldo Salt)
> "The Circus," Felix van Lieu (?)

As we have seen, "Ivanhoe" was by no means the last major swashbuckling series. However, along with "Sword of Freedom," it was the last such series scripted in whole or in part by blacklisted writers. While details of their involvement in some of these series remains either partial or sketchy, it is clear that Ring Lardner Jr., Ian McLellan Hunter, Waldo Salt, Millard Lampell, Arnold Perl, Adrian Scott, Fred Rinaldo, Anne Green, Hy Kraft, Robert Lees, Maurice Rapf, Sam Moore, Norma Barzman, Arnaud D'Usseau, Howard Dimsdale, Arnold Manoff, and others wrote scripts for these series and in some cases played a major part in shaping their char-acters. Some of these writers wrote scripts for other TV series as well. The 1950s and 1960s witnessed a major expansion in TV production on both sides of the Atlantic. However clandestine the circumstances, that expansion enabled blacklisted writers to find paid employment and an outlet for their talents at a time when they were unable to write openly under their own names. The history of their contribution to TV in this period is only now beginning to be detailed.[71]

13 Hollywood, the New Left, and *FTA*

Mark Shiel

The effects of the anti-Communist witch hunts of the late 1940s and 1950s were profound. As Larry Ceplair and Steven Englund have explained, politically engaged directors, writers, and actors on the left of the political spectrum found that "opportunities for political activism virtually ceased to exist in the 'new era.'"[1] Leftist organizations in Hollywood such as the Independent Citizens Committee of the Arts, Sciences, and Professions and the local chapters of the U.S. Communist Party disintegrated. Many leftists were jailed or forced into exile or into lives of quiet compliance guaranteed by the continuing watchful eyes of the FBI. After 1956, with Nikita Khrushchev's revelations of endemic political persecution in the regime of Joseph Stalin and the Soviet repression of the Hungarian uprising, "Communists and ex-Communists passed through what seems to have been a Gethsemane of doubt and self-questioning."[2] Only a few of the Hollywood Ten (notably Lester Cole) remained committed to Communism, while those few others who took open political stands on any issue did so in a low-key way (for example, the participation by Ring Lardner Jr. and Herbert Biberman in demonstrations in support of Julius and Ethel Rosenberg, who were sentenced to death for spying). With rumors periodically circulating that the U.S. government had the capacity to instigate a program of mass internment of Communists akin to that of Japanese Americans in World War II, a climate of fear kept a lid on the resurrection of coordinated leftist activism in Hollywood. That climate persisted in the 1960s, despite the tremendous social and political upheavals into which Hollywood and the United States were then thrown.

Early in the decade, with a gradual softening of the hard geopolitical lines of the Cold War under Khrushchev and John F. Kennedy, the courageous personal interventions of filmmakers Otto Preminger, Norman Jewison, and Kirk Douglas had the effect of ending the blacklist as a tool of political repression, though perhaps only 10 percent of those blacklisted returned to successful careers in the film industry.[3] Defensive legal actions by blacklistees were still being fought in the courts in 1966, the Screen Actors' Guild anti-Communist "loyalty oath" established in 1953 was finally made optional in 1967, and the House Un-American Activities Committee (HUAC), forced into decline by progressive political pressure, changed its name to the House Committee on Internal Security in 1969 and disbanded six years later. As late as July 12, 1972, however, *Variety* reported that Steve D'Inzillo, then challenging incumbent Richard F. Walsh for the presidency of the International Alliance of Theatrical Stage Employees, was being forced to defend himself from allegations that he had been a Communist sympathizer and had participated in Communist Party meetings advertised in 1946 editions of the *Daily Worker*.[4] Skeletons in the cupboard of the Old Left continued to rattle, although the cultural and political landscape had radically altered since the last gasp of Communist and socialist organization in Hollywood during the bitter labor unrest of 1947.

In the 1960s, the so-called New Left emerged gradually and in a different ideological environment after the McCarthy era. Progressive political activism was dominated by the civil rights struggles and radical pacifism of SANE (the Committee for a SANE Nuclear Policy), CORE (the Congress on Racial Equality), and SNCC (the Student Nonviolent Coordinating Committee), and by the highly influential anti-Communist liberalism of Daniel Bell, Arthur Schlesinger Jr., Sidney Hook, and David Riesman, many of them former leftists from the Popular Front of the 1930s. Dominated by the self-consciously young baby-boomer demographic of late teens and twenty-somethings, the largest new political grouping on the American left, Students for a Democratic Society (SDS), announced its presence in 1962 with the Port Huron Statement, which questioned the materialism and militarism of the postwar *pax Americana* in terms that were idealistic but lacking in the hard political economic analysis of the Old Left. In an era of relative détente in the Cold War, SDS refused simplistic moral denunciations of the Soviet Union, voting in 1965 to permit Communists as members, a position that led it to break with its parent organization, the League for Industrial Democracy, which had been founded by Jack London and Upton Sinclair in 1905. Prioritizing a personal formulation of ethical responsibility and the self-consciously spontaneous principle of "participatory democracy," the New Left contrasted with the Old Left in its relative emphasis on consciousness-raising over the provision of basic material needs and its decentered and widespread organization on college campuses rather than factory shop floors.[5] These tendencies earned the New Left the criticism of Old Leftists such as Irving Howe in the journal *Dissent* and Leo Huberman in *Monthly Review*.[6]

By the late 1960s the greatest mobilizing issue for the New Left was the Vietnam War, its outright opposition to which meant that its position in national political life was significantly different from that of the Old Left in World War II. For the New Left, the Vietnam War became a core issue that accelerated a broad set of interlocking radical agendas defined around race, class, and gender, and a plethora of leftist organizations, from the Black Power activism of SNCC and the Black Panther Party to the revolutionary politics of the Progressive Labor Party, the Revolutionary Youth Movement, Weathermen, and the Third World Liberation Front, and the emerging radical feminism of groups such as Redstockings.

In contrast to the various Communist and socialist organizations of the 1930s and 1940s, these New Left groups had essentially no official membership in the Hollywood filmmaking community. While alienation from the mainstream of American politics and culture was powerfully expressed by filmmakers of a new generation, such as Dennis Hopper in the road movie *Easy Rider* (1969) and Gordon Parks in the blaxploitation thriller *Shaft* (1971), many of the most insightful and celebrated films of the day drew on the talents of former blacklistees: the social realist study of New York City poverty *Midnight Cowboy* (1969) was scripted by Waldo Salt; the satirical antiwar comedy *M*A*S*H* (1970) was scripted by Ring Lardner Jr.; and the revisionist western *Tell Them Willie Boy Is Here* (1970) was scripted and directed by Abraham Polonsky. The critical perspectives of former victims of the anti-Communist witch hunts reemerged with vigor in a time of renewed political dissent.[7] However, direct representations of the New Left were absent with only occasional exceptions, many of which performed poorly at the box office. These included *Zabriskie Point* (1969), *Medium Cool* (1969), *The Strawberry Statement* (1969), and *Getting Straight* (1970). The politicization of Hollywood cinema that these films exemplified was a minority tendency. But it was an important one that emerged with the social and political turmoil of 1968 and came to a head four years later when a significant number of high-profile progressive figures in Hollywood mobilized to support the Democratic Party's presidential candidate, George McGovern. McGovern ran on a platform aimed to appeal directly to elements of the New Left at the expense of traditional constituencies such as southern Democrats, labor unions, and blue-collar workers. Long a vocal opponent of the war in Vietnam and a critic of the South Vietnamese government, McGovern proposed a total cut-off of funds to Southeast Asian military operations, an amnesty for draft dodgers and antiwar protesters, and taxes on the wealthy to reduce inner-city poverty, and he came out in favor of a woman's right to choose, gun control, affirmative action, and busing to combat the segregation of schools.[8] In a year in which John Mitchell, attorney general in the Nixon administration, declared that "this country is going so far to the right you won't recognize it," McGovern retorted that "my one unique position, with reference to the competition, is to be to the left of them all."[9]

The McGovern platform, attempting to reach out to radicals from the mainstream, found favor in the entertainment industry, numbering among its supporters Warren Beatty, Robert Redford, Barbra Streisand, Peter Boyle, and Elliott Gould, all of whom participated in rallies, contributors' dinners, and other events to promote the Democratic candidate. Prominent among these was the "Four for McGovern" fund-raising gala concert at the LA Forum on April 15, 1972, featuring performances by Streisand, James Taylor, Carole King, and Quincy Jones and with a long list of Hollywood celebrities in attendance, including Beatty, Gould, Sally Kellerman, Jack Nicholson, Julie Christie, James Earl Jones, Shirley MacLaine, Mike Nichols, Goldie Hawn, Gene Hackman, Burt Lancaster, Jon Voight, Cass Elliot, Carly Simon, Robert Vaughn, Rob Reiner, and Britt Eklund.[10]

However, the political commitment of few Hollywood celebrities at the time brought them closer to the kind of personal price paid by the victims of the Hollywood blacklist than Jane Fonda, who was described by Gary Crowdus in an editorial in *Cineaste* in July 1975 as "the most popular and critically acclaimed Hollywood actress to have ever devoted herself to radical causes."[11] For Crowdus, Fonda's engagement with Black Power, feminism, and the war in Vietnam showed up the myth of "radical chic" popularized by right-wing voices and pointed to "the necessity for the left, especially those of us working in the cultural area, to break out of the leftist ghetto to which we have been confined so long and begin to intervene politically in the mainstream, to seek ways of relating to people out there in the real world."[12] In September 1972, Fonda initiated the Indochina Peace Campaign with her then-partner, and former president of SDS, Tom Hayden, in order to press the U.S. government to allow the implementation of the Geneva Accords originally formulated as an international solution to the conflict in Vietnam in 1954.

Fonda's early career as an actress from *Tall Story* (1960) to *Barbarella* (1968) had not been noted for its political significance, but the events of 1968, both in the United States and in Paris (where she was living with husband Roger Vadim), had kick-started a period of personal political radicalization to the left, beyond the New Deal politics of her upbringing.[13] Fonda's return to live in the United States near the end of 1969 coincided with the massive Moratorium against the War demonstrations and the siege of Alcatraz Island in San Francisco Bay by the emerging American Indian Movement. These events prompted Fonda toward a practical engagement in left politics of a kind seldom seen in Hollywood since 1947, beginning with her participation in demonstrations in favor of Native American rights and toward a more overtly political type of filmmaking in the Depression-era social study *They Shoot Horses, Don't They?* (1969). In 1969, through her publicist Steve Jaffe, Fonda met Donald Duncan, a former Green Beret then in the public eye for having quit the service in protest at U.S. policy in Southeast Asia, as well as Mark Lane, a New York–based lawyer well known for his social activism. At a party hosted in early 1970 to celebrate the release of Michelangelo Antonioni's controversial film about youth revolution, *Zabriskie Point*, she met another important antiwar organizer, Fred Gardner, who had acted as script consultant on Antonioni's film, and who would become an important formative influence.

Gardner had served in the U.S. Army in the early 1960s but, deeply opposed to the war in Vietnam, was by 1967 using his experience to help organize dissent among GIs at army bases across the United States as part of what would become known as the "GI movement" against the war. The organizational bedrock of the movement was a network of GI "coffee houses," of which Gardner established the first, the so-called UFO, at Fort Jackson in Columbia, South Carolina, in January 1968.[14] By 1972, over thirty of these coffee houses operated as cafés, bookstores, music venues, and advice bureaus for GIs interested in resisting the war or seeking assistance in deserting. This network, which also extended to U.S. bases in Japan and Germany, would become one of the key concerns of the United States Servicemen's Fund (USSF) established by dissenting GIs to organize, assist, and coordinate resistance to the Vietnam War within the military. The second pillar of the movement was a busy underground industry of as many as three hundred antiwar GI newspapers that mushroomed at U.S. bases around the world from 1968 through 1972, including *FTA* at Fort Knox, *The Fatigue Press* at Fort Hood, *Attitude Check* at Camp Pendleton, *Ultimate Weapon* at Fort Dix, and *Broken Arrow* at Selfridge Air Force Base in Michigan.

As David Cortright has explained, incidents of insubordination and resistance to active duty proliferated among enlistees in the U.S. military during the Vietnam War to an extent not previously known in the nation's history. Opposition to the war grew among enlistees, leading to the formation of coordinated groups such as GIs for Peace at Fort Bliss and GIs United Against the Vietnam War at Fort Jackson. Notwithstanding the historical distrust between the military and the radical left, activists from the Young Socialist Alliance (closely related to the Socialist Workers' Party), the Progressive Labor Party, and the Spartacist League were frequently involved in organizing among the GI population, and very small but significant numbers of active members of such parties were actually enlisted in the army themselves.[15] By the time of the Moratorium protests of late 1969, GIs were regularly taking a prominent part in civilian mass demonstrations against the war, and civilian antiwar activists such as Tom Hayden and Noam Chomsky were addressing meetings of dissenting GIs.

Antiwar activism peaked again with the invasion of Cambodia by U.S. troops in April 1970 and the killings at Kent State University on May 4. By this time, the GI movement was thoroughly embedded wherever U.S. forces served, with the movement's so-called Pacific Counseling Service running offices as far afield as Tokyo, Okinawa, and Quezon City in the Philippines.[16] As noted with alarm by Colonel Robert D. Heinl in his essay "The Collapse of the Armed Forces," published in the *Armed Forces Journal* on June 7, 1971, official studies revealed that at least one in four enlisted personnel took part in "dissident activities" in 1970–71, and up to 55 percent when one included drug taking while on active service.[17] Even in Vietnam, refusal of duty, insubordination, and the "fragging" of officers (i.e., acts of violence including murder) became widespread while reports circulated that the Provisional Revolutionary Government in South Vietnam had issued a decree that its forces would not fire on U.S. soldiers displaying antiwar symbols. As Cortright summarizes:

> American forces were withdrawn [from Vietnam] in 1969 and afterwards because they had ceased to function as an effective fighting force. Richard Nixon brought the troops home not only to accommodate domestic opinion, but to save the armed forces from internal ruin. Stretched beyond their capacity by a prolonged, fiercely fought war in a foreign jungle, lacking domestic political support for their mission, the US armed forces suffered the worst defeat in their history.[18]

The predicament of the GI in the Vietnam War would remain largely absent from narrative fiction film until the late 1970s, when *The Deer Hunter* (1977), *The Boys in Company C* (1978), *Coming Home* (1978; co-scripted by Waldo Salt), and *Apocalypse Now* (1979) drew frank attention to the contradictions and brutality of the war. During the conflict, however, it became one of the key issues around which emerged a counter-cinema of the New Left. On the one hand, a crucial role in justifying the war was played by government-sponsored documentaries such as the Department of Defense's *Why Vietnam?* (1966), numerous prime time TV documentaries, and occasional pro-war Hollywood features such as *The Green Berets* (1968).[19] On the other hand, leftist political filmmakers had to deal with the Vietnam War through "meta-cinematic reflections," as David James has put it, partly because of the need to question the form and ideology of mass media images in favor of the war and partly because of the practical difficulty of gaining direct access to the war and the military given the strict control of such access by the U.S. authorities.[20] Emile de Antonio's *In the Year of the Pig* (1969) consisted of an agit-prop montage of footage of the war and interviews pieced together from archives in East Germany, Hanoi, Prague, and U.S. television news; the homemade aesthetics of extremely low-budget films such as Nick Macdonald's *The Liberal War* (1972) subverted the conventional filmic representation of the war by using paper cut-outs and toy soldiers to achieve a metonymic rather than anthropomorphic figuration of the conflict; and Peter Davis's *Hearts and Minds* (1974), made in 1972, was delayed and almost withdrawn from distribution by Columbia Pictures because of studio concerns about the political and legal ramifications of the film's depiction of U.S. involvement in the war and its advocates. It eventually won the Academy Award for Best Documentary in 1975.

This era witnessed a flourishing of ultra-leftism in American politics in which radical filmmaking collectives such as Newsreel attempted "to build a new society in the lap of the old," as Massimo Teodori has put it, through a sympathetic documentation of the campaigns of students and activists against the war in *San Francisco State: On Strike* (1969) or of the protests of returning Vietnam veterans in *Only the Beginning* (1971).[21] These efforts were analogous to the Old Left cinematic activism of Sam Brody, Leo Selzer, and others who had recorded the hardships of workers and the unemployed poor in the Great Depression for the Film and Photo League. But in the work of Frontier Films and individual masterpieces such as Leo Hurwitz and Paul Strand's *Native Land* (1942), the New Deal had allowed leftist filmmakers access to government support and mainstream exposure, and the Old Left's endorsement of the U.S. war effort in World War II had found expression in propagandistic war films by future blacklistees such as *Action in the North Atlantic* (1943, written by John Howard Lawson), *Destination Tokyo* (1943, written by Albert Maltz), *Thirty Seconds Over Tokyo* (1944, written by Dalton Trumbo), and *Objective, Burma!* (1945, written by Alvah Bessie and Lester Cole).

During the Vietnam War, this pattern was not repeated. Filmmakers aligned with the New Left concentrated their attention neither on official subjects nor on the traditional working class but on disenfranchised social groups such as African Americans, women, students, prisoners, and soldiers whose politics were increasingly radical, if not revolutionary, and who had been historically underrepresented or misrepresented in cinema but who now lent themselves to the mapping of new cinematic terrain. By 1970, as the GI movement emerged as perhaps the most pivotal camp within the antiwar movement as a whole, the GI resister (and the dissenting veteran) came to occupy a particularly influential political position in American society both practically and symbolically, but one that had achieved precious little cinematic representation.

One film that attempted to correct this absence was the antiwar documentary *FTA* (*Fun, Travel, and Adventure*, aka *F . . . the Army*, 1972), which was directed by Francine Parker, produced by Parker, Jane Fonda, and Donald Sutherland, and released in July 1972 as the McGovern-Nixon presidential contest gathered pace. *FTA* typified the new agit-prop tendencies that were central to leftist political filmmaking during the Vietnam War, but it also brought together elements of the Old and New Lefts, radical politics and Hollywood celebrity, in an exceptional, and exceptionally powerful, way. The film's antiwar message relied upon Fonda and Sutherland's conscientious subversion of conventional notions of Hollywood stardom through political activism and culminated in an extended reading by Sutherland from the novel *Johnny Got His Gun* (1939) by Dalton Trumbo, who had been a prominent member of the Hollywood Ten.

As such, *FTA*, more than most films of the era, presented a rebuke to the attempted suppression of leftist political culture in the postwar United States, although the film's release was short and controversial and it has been largely forgotten, unseen, and critically neglected for thirty-five years. Trumbo, who had continued while blacklisted to write successful screenplays, including *Gun Crazy* (1949), *Roman Holiday* (1953), and *The Brave One* (1957), had reemerged in the 1960s with *Spartacus* (1960), *Lonely Are the Brave* (1962), and *The Sandpiper* (1965), the latter three films containing critiques of imperialism, American western mythology, and modern bourgeois society, respectively. Fonda, having become involved with the GI movement, by the middle of 1970 was working almost full-time on antiwar activities, participating in demonstrations, making speeches at coffee houses, and fundraising for veterans' groups and dissenting GIs. That summer, she starred in Alan J. Pakula's *Klute* (1971) in New York City with co-star Sutherland, who emerged in 1970 as a major star in two antiwar films, *M*A*S*H* and *Kelly's Heroes*, and who played the role of Christ in the film adaptation of Trumbo's *Johnny Got His Gun* (1971), directed by Trumbo himself but not a commercial success.

At this time, Fonda and Sutherland became involved with Vietnam Veterans Against the War, which was fast becoming the largest and most public organization of military dissent and one of the key targets of the Nixon administration's expansion of espionage and surveillance against individuals and groups within the United States that would culminate in Watergate. With support from singers David Crosby and Graham Nash, Fonda and Sutherland lent assistance to and raised funds for the organization of the so-called Winter Soldier hearings, held in Detroit, from January 31 to February 2, 1971. These brought veterans together to explain and to investigate the ways in which, as the hearings' publicity stated, "Many of the two million GIs who have served in Vietnam have been forced to employ military tactics which violate Rules of Land Warfare, the Geneva Conventions, and the Nuremberg Charter."[22] This event, captured in the undeservedly neglected film *Winter Soldier*, led in turn to the organization of a traveling antiwar stage show to raise funds and agitate for the movement.

This show, entitled *FTA*, opened to great success at the Haymarket Coffee House near Fort Bragg, Fayetteville, North Carolina, on March 14, 1971. It attracted audiences of 500 each night for three nights before debuting to a civilian audience in a special performance at the NYC Philharmonic Hall. Financially supported by the USSF, the show drew upon the Hollywood celebrity of Fonda and Sutherland as well as other supporters and performers including Peter Boyle, Elliott Gould, Dick Gregory, and Country Joe McDonald.[23] A stage revue of songs and skits about the war and GI life, it presented what Fonda described as a "political vaudeville," aimed squarely at enlistees in order to counter the light-hearted jingoism of the famous United Service Organization (USO) shows then still being regularly hosted for troops by Bob Hope.[24] The loose coalition of stars organized by Fonda and Sutherland attempted to promulgate their ideas in Hollywood under the banner Entertainment Industry for Peace and Justice, a group specifically identified by Colonel Robert Heinl in his "Collapse of the Armed Forces" as an "antiwar show-biz front" claiming over 800 members in the film, TV, and music industries.[25]

The *FTA* film emerged partly as a documentary record of the touring show but also as a study of the dissenting GI and the war itself. Interviewed by Dan Georgakas and Lenny Rubenstein for *Cineaste* in 1975, Fonda explained that her political engagement had led her to ask herself whether her political and artistic interests might best coincide within Hollywood's dominant film culture or with those of a radical group such as Newsreel until in 1970 she had been persuaded by John Watson and Ken Cockrel of the League for Revolutionary Black Workers to stay in Hollywood in order to help reach a larger audience.[26] In an era in which Fonda alternated work in Hollywood on films such as *Klute* with experimental or activist work outside Hollywood in Jean-Luc Godard's *Tout va bien* (1972) and Haskell Wexler's *Introduction to the Enemy* (1974), *FTA* embodied what she saw as a genuinely collective approach to filmmaking in contrast to that of Hollywood but

1.   *FTA*: credit shot of Jane Fonda, Donald Sutherland, and Len Chandler.

resembling that of the Vietnamese film industry which she came to admire during her highly publicized visit to Hanoi in July 1972.[27]

The production of *FTA* brought together a quite unusual array of Hollywood stars and complete unknowns. Directed by Francine Parker, who appears to have directed no other significant films either before or since, it had a script that was co-credited to several individuals, listed in alphabetical order to reflect the informal improvisation of the stage show itself: Michael Alaimo, who had starred in cult sex-exploitation films including Doris Wishman's *Indecent Desires* (1967); Len Chandler, the African American folk-singer and songwriter; Pamela Donegan, a young African American poet; Jane Fonda; Rita Martinson, an African American singer; Robin Menken, the wife of Country Joe McDonald, and a friend of Fonda's by way of the Red Family commune at Berkeley; Holly Near, a protest singer and progressive political activist; Donald Sutherland; and Dalton Trumbo. All these individuals, with the exception of Menken and Trumbo, appear in *FTA* along with Paul Mooney, an African American comedian would go on to success working with Richard Pryor and "Saturday Night Live."

The narrative of the film follows the stage show as it tours a number of cities in the Pacific that were home to U.S. military bases in November and December 1971, from Hawaii to Okinawa and the Philippines, then finishing in Japan.[28] Like other examples of agit-prop political documentary of the era, it rejects the high production values of industrial cinema, combining onstage footage of various live performances of the FTA show, interviews with GIs, marines, and members of the WAF (Women in the Air Force), and frequent cutaways to ethnographic footage of the local people who inhabit the mostly impoverished foreign lands in which the U.S. military is based. This combination, added to which is a selective use of voiceover and archive footage from the war, allows the film to mimic the textual layering typical of official documentaries in favor of the war while undercutting their pretense to factual and ethical authority with heavy doses of irony (as in Donald Sutherland's opening voiceover accompanied by the image of a B-52 bomber in takeoff: "Dreaming of going places, meeting new people, doing exciting things? Ever thought about the Air Force?"). In close-up, young and disillusioned GIs talk frankly to the camera about being "anti-military" or having faced a choice between "either going to jail or coming into the service." These are intercut with handheld close-ups and medium shots of Fonda, Sutherland, and colleagues taken by one camera on stage, another below the stage looking up, and a third in long shot watching from the point of view of the crowd in the auditorium. This cinematographic variety, together with its pacy editing, gives the film a creative instability that is reminiscent of, but more acute than, that of Direct Cinema, especially when we are shown two or three performances of one song or skit edited together as if in one take. Indeed, two of the film's three cinematographers had previously worked in Direct Cinema: Juliana Wang on Drew Associates' *Jazz: The Intimate Art* in 1968 and Eric Saarinen on David and Albert Maysles's and Charlotte Zwerin's *Gimme Shelter* in 1970.[29] Like these films, *FTA* is full of a sense of contingency: Fonda announces that the stage show will be held at 3 P.M. at one venue in order to allow GIs in attendance to return to base at the hour required by their camp commander; on landing in Japan, the cast and crew are unexpectedly detained at the airport by immigration officials and an anxious wait ensues until their visa problems are resolved; at the final performance near Tachikawa Air Force base, Sutherland's performance is rudely interrupted by verbal abuse from an isolated drunken GI objecting to his pacifist message.

However, *FTA* is a far more explicitly partisan affair than the observational mode of Direct Cinema films. As it follows the cast and crew of the FTA show across the Pacific, each geographic stage of the journey is the scene of a particular politically themed exploration: in Hawaii, the emphasis is upon the moral wrong of the war itself, in Okinawa upon the United States as an imperialist power whose military is riddled with racism, in the Philippines, the United States as an imperialist power and a bastion of patriarchy, and in Japan all of these themes together. Thus the film communicates its moral disgust with the war and the social and political status quo that feeds it by means of a careful intensification that gives it a thematic, if not narratological, linearity and conviction.

This is evident in the title of the film itself, *FTA*, whose polite and impolite meanings—"Free the Army" or "Fuck the Army"—are played for comic effect in the film's opening rendition of the "FTA" song by the entire cast in a sequence that ends with raised fists and a unanimous cheer of "Fuck the Army, and the Navy, and the Marines!!!" This is reinforced by the subsequent cut to a rudimentary graphic map of the Pacific region on which a caption explains that the FTA show emerged "in response to the growing movement of American GIs to end the war, U.S. militarism, and military injustice." In the ensuing sequence, a cutaway to footage of the USS *Coral Sea* aircraft carrier, its aircraft, and victims of their bombing sits uncomfortably with Sutherland's factual commentary—"85 planes, 6 million pounds of munitions, 4,500 men. It has dropped more than 800,000 tons of bombs on the people of Indochina." In a series of intimate and emotional segments that run throughout the film, the GI's sense of entrapment and need to communicate is palpable, presented through talking-head interviews with injured young veterans or active service men and women who articulate what they have come to see as the moral and political indefensibility of the war, its military mismanagement, and its physical and psychological cost. These interviews have a solemnity that is effectively balanced by skits from the stage show itself, whose knowing mockery of military authority and competence is warmly received by the crowd.

In this way, *FTA* gets close enough to its subject to provide a critique of the war and the U.S. military, even though it never enters any official institutional spaces of government or the military—in contrast, for example, to the work of the contemporary documentarist Frederick Wiseman who, in *Titicut Follies* (1967), *Law and Order* (1969), and *Basic Training* (1971), exposed institutional repression from the inside. The question of access to and freedom of movement in proscribed spaces is everywhere underlined in *FTA*, as the stage show was never afforded the routine privilege given to official USO shows to mount its performance within the grounds of U.S. military installations but always forced to put on its revue in public auditoriums nearby. In the port of San Diego, 1,500 crew members of the USS *Con-stellation* petitioned their captain for permission to allow *FTA* to be performed on deck, but the request was turned down. Performances in the nearby city then attracted over 4,000 servicemen and women over several nights.[30] As it toured, the show became known for its ability to focus dissent in the ranks. In Hawaii in late November 1971, 50 members of the crew of the USS *Coral Sea* are said to have deserted as a direct result of seeing the show and meeting with the cast. In Japan, where the cast and crew were temporarily detained by airport immigration officials on visa technicalities, their entry was facilitated only with the direct intervention of the Japanese antiwar movement Beheiren and a direct appeal to the Japanese minister for justice. The cast and crew of *FTA* were not permitted to enter Vietnam at all, let alone travel to the combat zone.

With the exception of a short insert of bombing victims at the beginning and of GIs on patrol at the end, very little of the action of the film *FTA* takes place "in country," in the theater of war itself. The victims of the war for whom the film expresses the most outrage—the Vietnamese people—are prominent in their absence from the film in a way that contrasts *FTA* with contemporary documentaries about the war made by the Viet Cong themselves, such as *The Way to the Front* (1969) or with the notable international wave of documentary films sympathetic to their cause, such as Joris Ivens's *The Seventeenth Parallel* (France, 1967), Chris Marker and Jean-Luc Godard's *Loin du Vietnam* (1967), Santiago Alvarez's *Hanoi, Martes 13* (Cuba, 1967), and Walter Heynowski and Gerhard Scheumann's *Pilots in Pajamas* (East Germany, 1968). But what *FTA* cannot show directly it makes up for by analogy in its explicit solidarity with the fight for economic and political rights by the ordinary peoples of the lands it visits. The opening credits of the film announce that it was "made in association with the servicewomen and men stationed on the United States bases of the Pacific Rim together with their friends whose lands they presently occupy." Here the film speaks with a voice typical of the replacement of traditional working class politics by a Third Worldist analysis in the New Left between 1969 and 1972.

The sequence of *FTA* shot in Okinawa begins with a panning close-up of the barbed wire surrounding a U.S. military base, aircraft coming and going, to the banal sound track of American Forces Radio news. As Okinawan workers employed on the base picket it outside, protesting poor working conditions and low pay of thirty cents per hour, Fonda calls on them to understand that "the American GI is not the same as the American government" and Len Chandler strikes up an impromptu performance in the street of "We Shall Not Be Moved." Although the film does not explicitly acknowledge it, the protests by ordinary Okinawans against the U.S. military, filmed in late 1971, take place near the end of a period of transition from U.S. administration of Okinawa, which had begun in 1945, to a return of Okinawa to Japanese control, which took place on May 15, 1972.

The film's empathetic appeal for a recognition of common humanity shared with Okinawans is closely aligned to the film's extended statement of the principles of Black Power in several scenes, intercut with those depicting Okinawans, in which African American marines testify to their experiences of racism in the military and at home and to their reluctance to fight in Vietnam that arises from their sense of commonality with the Vietnamese as oppressed nonwhite peoples. Talking to Len Chandler, one off-duty marine, wearing a beret and Black Panther–style bomber jacket emblazoned with the phrase "Blackness Is A State Of Mind," explains, "More brothers are coming into the service everyday and more brothers are leaving, and the brothers who are leaving are more militant than when they came in . . ."

After Okinawa, that sequence's mixing of Black Power and Third World discourses is complemented in the following sequence at Olongapo in the Philippines by a mixing of Third World and feminist agendas. A scene discussing racism in the U.S. military cuts directly to striking cinéma vérité footage of Filipino pro-democracy demonstrators at the annual Bonifacio Day Parade protesting against the U.S. government's desire to keep the Philippines in a perpetually "semi-feudal" state. One demonstrator explicitly acknowledges a natural "identity of interests" between Filipinos and the American GI against American imperialism. Rows of waving red flags, marchers, pedestrians, traffic, shops, and offices give way to on- and off-duty U.S. service personnel outside the local base, followed by a huge bill-board in the shape of a Coca-Cola bottle beside that passes a traditional horse and cart, leading to shanty towns, and back to the demonstrators, filmed singing in the rain, draped with Esso, Shell, and U.S. flags.

This account of street politics in action is spliced between one vaudeville skit on the FTA stage in which Jane Fonda and Holly Near dance à la Folies Bergère to the tune of "Bomb Another City Today!" and another in which a soldier's wife insists she is pregnant only to be told by the company doctor to "go home and take

2.   *FTA*: shot of Filipino demonstrators draped in the U.S. flag.

two APCs and come back when the swelling goes down." Enlisted sailors explain that at Olongapo a U.S. Navy medical team tests Filipino women in local bars whenever a U.S. ship puts into port, issuing women who are clear of VD with little green badges that they can wear to identify themselves as safe for the American men. Subsequently, in Japan, Fonda, Near, Martinson, and Donegan perform a vaudeville-style call for women's solidarity to an audience composed in large part of visiting enlisted women in the USAF:

> Now I sing this song in the hope that you won't think it's a joke 'cause it's time we all awoke to take a stand. We've been victims all our lives, now it's time we organized and to fight we're gonna need each other's hands. They whistle like a dog and make noises like a hog, heaven knows they've sure got problems, I agree. But they're problems I can't solve 'cause my sanity's evolved and I'm tired of bastards fucking over me!!

Although many commentators have correctly described the decline of political activism on the left in the United States in the 1970s in terms of the splintering of a once mass movement into competing and ultimately irreconcilable voices, in *FTA* a total continuity is posited between a woman's right to control her body and that of a young male GI to refuse to give his body in a futile war. This becomes clear in the final twenty minutes of the film, which take place near Iwakuni Air Force Base in Japan and in which Donald Sutherland's passionate reading from Dalton Trumbo's *Johnny Got His Gun* comes to the fore. Here New Left concerns find a telling resonance in a major Old Left text that revolves around the young protagonist Joe Bonham, a quadruple-amputee in the trenches of World War I, who fights government resistance to have his incapacitated body put on public display as a "piece of meat" in order to make a silent but powerful statement against all war. Sutherland's extended reading from the book is intercut with photographs of faces and bodies wounded and deformed by the Hiroshima atom bombing and with footage of off-duty marines at an *FTA* performance signing an antiwar petition, but the complex textures of the film's visual and aural montage eventually give way to a powerfully simple final image of Sutherland, alone on stage, reading Joe's warning monologue on behalf of the working man against all governments and armies intent on war:

> We are men of peace, we are men who work, and we want no quarrel. But if you destroy our peace, if you take away our work, if you try to range us one against the other, we will know what to do. If you tell us to make the world safe for democracy we will take you seriously and, by God and by Christ, we will make it so. We will use the guns you force upon us, we will use them to defend our very lives, and the menace to our lives does not lie on the other side of a no man's land that was set apart without our consent, it lies within our own boundaries here and now. We have seen it and we know it.

FTA succeeds in displacing the stardom of Sutherland and Fonda by deferring to the universalist, proletarian message of Trumbo's text, and by focusing so much of its attention on a multitude of nameless but important human faces and stories of both GIs and ordinary civilians. These undercut all celebrity while merging with the film's cinéma vérité aesthetics to provide an implicit critique of industrial cinema as a whole. *FTA* thus constitutes an important historical exception to what Todd Gitlin has described as the destruction of real political discourse on the radical left by the distraction of media celebrity and the superficiality of mainstream news reportage.[31]

In the era of the New Left, media, celebrity, and politics were entangled in a qualitatively new way. Leftist activists in the 1930s had to reckon with the power of radio, photography, and the press on a daily basis, but these transformed the content, strategy, and tactics of their politics to a lesser degree. In the late 1940s and 1950s, the high public profile of the Hollywood film industry and its stars was one of the reasons HUAC chose to devote so much of its energy to Hollywood in the first place, with television playing a central role in publicizing its hearings to a national audience with a new kind of immediacy. By the late 1960s, with that decade's dramatically greater media saturation, leaders of the New Left were frequently forced to choose between fleeing celebrity by dropping out of the public eye altogether or, to use Gitlin's phrase, "pyramiding" it—that is, trying to manage the media's creation of celebrity in order to exploit the exposure gained for political purposes.[32]

Although *FTA* bore similarities to Direct Cinema and to New York Newsreel, it was filmed in 35 mm rather than 16 mm and was released through the exploitation film specialists American International Pictures (AIP). Since its foundation in 1954, AIP had become the key player in the youth-oriented, low-budget film industry by producing large volumes of monster movies, horrors, and teenage beach party films, gradually increasing in social topicality in the late 1960s with biker and hippie films such as *The Wild Angels* (1966) and *The Trip* (1967). These gave AIP a relatively progressive profile within American cinema as a whole but also opened up a political tension between AIP's relatively conservative management, led by James H. Nicholson and Samuel Z. Arkoff, and its increasingly liberal creative personnel. For AIP's most important filmmaker, Roger Corman, this tension came to a head with the production of his black comedy of nuclear war and youth revolution, *Gas-s-s-s! Or It Became Necessary to Destroy the World in Order to Save It*, which was released on March 26, 1971, just two weeks after the first *FTA* show. As the United States appeared to decline into ever deeper crisis following the Kent State University killings of May 1970, AIP management became nervous about the political content of their films and refused to give *Gas-s-s-s!* a proper marketing campaign, prompting Corman's departure from the company.[33]

The R-rated *FTA* opened on July 21, 1972, at the Baronet and Forum cinemas in New York, as well as one venue each in Boston and Washington, D.C. It grossed a poor $11,500 in its first week.[34] Reviews were mixed to good, with Roger Greenspun in the *New York Times* complaining that much of the film was "a predictable bore," though its Philippines sequences were "a romantic gesture of extraordinary beauty," and Arthur Knight in *Variety* praising its "superior" cinematography and the "bold intercutting" of its montage.[35] On August 2, 1972, *Variety* reported that "FTA earned a pathetic $7,600 in its second session at the Baronet and Forum and is being pulled," while the *Hollywood Reporter* noted that "American International, acceding to exhibitor pressure and public protests, pulled Jane Fonda's documentary anti-war feature 'FTA' (Free the Army) from its scheduled Los Angeles opening yesterday."[36]

Jane Fonda had started her visit to North Vietnam on July 8, finishing on July 22, the day after *FTA*'s debut. As conservative political criticism of Hollywood reached an intensity not seen in twenty years, Republican senator John Tower of Texas was prominent among those who called for Fonda to be charged with treason.[37] A spokesperson for AIP explained that the company had decided to withdraw the film reluctantly given its poor box office and complaints from movie theater owners. On August 4, AIP head Samuel Z. Arkoff made a public statement in defense of his company's decision, rejecting suggestions that the film had been withdrawn because of protests over Fonda's visit to Hanoi, and insisting in unusually explicit terms that "No one has approached AIP either before or after Ms. Fonda's trip to Hanoi and asked that we stop the distribution of 'FTA.'"[38] Arkoff gave an assurance that AIP planned to re-release the film in the fall when the return of students to college would guarantee a better audience. But that re-release never took place and *FTA* largely disappeared from exhibition and from film history for over thirty years, its marginalization an echo of the suppression of cinematic leftism with which generations of Hollywood filmmakers have had to contend.

14   Red Hollywood

Thom Andersen

New Inquisitions: Books about the Hollywood Blacklist

More than a quarter of the century has passed since Hollywood began its purge of Communists and fellow travelers, but the Hollywood blacklist, as it has come to be known, has not yet passed into history, although it has already had at least three generations of historians. We know what happened, or we can find out easily enough if we are too young to remember. And the meaning of these obsessively remembered events should also be obvious enough. Anti-Communist hysteria produced a senseless, vicious purge whose victims happened to be famous and, in some cases, glamorous or interesting. But do we know how we should regard these victims? Are they martyrs? Or did they to some extent bring their troubles on themselves? They were privileged before they were blacklisted, they were "creative," but were they also artists? And should we then regard their personal loss as a loss to our culture in general, to the art of cinema specifically?

Although these events are not contemporary with us, the arguments are still alive. It is a shard of history that brings to mind the opening words of Christa Wolf's *A Model Childhood*: "What is past is not dead; it is not even past." And a few sentences further on in her novel about forgetting and remembering the recent past of Germany, there is a phrase that could serve as a motto for this essay: "The difficulties haven't even begun."[1] For all the books that have appeared touching on the 1947 hearings of the House Un-American Activities Committee (HUAC) into Communist infiltration of the motion picture industry and its aftermath, there has not been one that seems likely to stand as a definitive study, that could even stand as such at the time of its publication.

Such books seem to come in waves. It is possible to isolate three distinct cycles of interpretation with lulls between each. In the first wave from 1948 to 1956 came the pamphlets. These were partisan works, obviously, written in the belief that their arguments could change people's lives. Only two of these are still read today as history: *Report on Blacklisting* (1956) by John Cogley, commissioned by the Fund for the Republic, which earned Cogley a subpoena from HUAC, and *Part of Our Time* (1955) by Murray Kempton. Both these works came at the end of the cycle, after the crest of the wave, and they are summations of positions that had been evolving since 1947. Both are critical of the blacklist, as were most of the earlier polemics expansive enough to be published by themselves.

But it would be wrong to assume from this apparent consensus that only McCarthyite right-wingers supported the purge of Communists and fellow travelers in Hollywood or in other professions during the fifties. Louis Berg, writing in *Commentary* in November 1952, summarized one of the liberal anti-Communist positions: "A free society may have to tolerate its enemies, but it is not called upon to reward them." There may be jobs for which no political tests or loyalty oaths are appropriate, jobs in which a Communist could do no harm, but the positions in question are among the most prestigious, the most influential in American society. Berg cited the instance of an instructor at Columbia University who had used the prestige of her position to lend credence to the Communist-sponsored charge that the U.S. forces were practicing germ warfare in the Korean War. He could not be so specific about the damage done by Communists in motion pictures or in radio and television, but, "in the cold war, the question of who commands a public forum looms no less large than the possession of air bases and planes in Korea."[2]

This is a perfectly defensible position, always cogently argued under all its variants in the pages of *Commentary* and the *New Leader*, and it is unfortunate, I think, that those survivors from this camp of liberal anti-Communism who have felt called upon during the 1970s and 1980s to defend their politics of the 1950s have been so ambiguous about their positions on the purge of the Communists.

They invoke their opposition to McCarthyism to demonstrate that their hatred of Stalinism did not compromise their commitment to civil liberties; and indeed their journals did run several articles that were critical of McCarthy. But of course, it was possible to criticize McCarthy, the targets of whose attacks were frequently innocent of the charges he brought against them, and still to support a variety of sanctions against the guilty—the Communists and their collaborators. And it is not quite right to say they opposed McCarthyism. Their actual position on McCarthyism was that it didn't exist. In his chilling review of the prison letters of Julius and Ethel Rosenberg for *Commentary*, Robert Warshow noted, "The word 'Communist' never appears except in quotation marks."[3] For analogous reasons the word "McCarthyism" seldom appeared in *Commentary* except in quotation marks. Just as Communism was a phantom to the editors of the Rosenberg letters, McCarthyism was a phantom to the editors and contributors of *Commentary*. "McCarthyism is 90 per cent McCarthy," wrote James Rorty, for once leaving off the quotation marks, in the August 1953 issue of *Commentary*. He expanded a few paragraphs later: "The liberal critics of Senator McCarthy could help [to discredit McCarthy] by dissociating themselves from those who exploit his bad name to attack all investigations of Communism, and who in their own trigger-happy way mow down McCarthy, Jenner, and Velde, without indicating they are aware of the important differences between them. In making him the titular head of 'the forces of McCarthyism' (which they too often identify with all anti-Communist activity, legitimate and illegitimate), they not only reflect unfavorably on their own understanding of the deep national concern over Communism, but inflate McCarthy's importance by ascribing to him an ideology, a national following, and a program, to none of which he can fairly lay claim."[4] This was the standard line in *Commentary* and the

New Leader: criticism of McCarthy was always tempered with a rebuke to those who exploited his recklessness to discredit the cause of anti-Communism.

Another group of anti-Communist liberals was less tough minded than those who wrote for *Commentary*—and perhaps less rigorous in their argumentation—but their position has had a greater influence on present attitudes toward the Hollywood purges. The classic statement of this liberalism is *The Vital Center* by Arthur Schlesinger Jr., published in 1949. At that time the Hollywood blacklist had only claimed a few victims, so Schlesinger was not called upon to produce a verdict on its mature phase. His insistence that Communists be accorded full civil liberties—which do not include, he claimed, the right to work for the government—until their activities "present . . . a clear and present menace," which they did not in 1949, implies at least a formal disapproval. But his assertion that American Communism did not constitute a danger rests on the successes achieved by less formal methods of repression: "It was plainly demonstrated in the United States between 1946 and 1948 that the Communists could be whipped—in the labor movement, in the liberal movement, in the veterans' movement, in the political world—by the traditional democratic methods of debate, identification and exposure."[5] This process of debate, identification, and exposure had led in these organizations to the expulsion of their Communist members (abetted in the case of the labor unions by the Taft-Hartley Act of 1947, which required union officers to sign non-Communist affidavits if their unions were to keep certification rights with the National Labor Relations Board). Would he object, or could he object without sacrificing the consistency of his argument, if identification and exposure of Communists in the movie studios led to similar results?

In any case, Schlesinger made his contempt for the first victims of the Hollywood purge evident enough. The film writers of the Hollywood Left had succumbed to a double corruption—the commercial corruption of Hollywood and the moral and intellectual corruption of the Party. Hollywood had taught them to despise themselves: "The Hollywood writer . . . feels he has sold himself out; he has abandoned his serious work in exchange for large weekly paychecks; and he resents a society which corrupts him (it always seems to be society's fault in these cases)." The Party had taught them to despise their art, to value the slick and the false above their own personal visions: "The larger result has been to create a dangerous inroad upon the moral fabric of American culture. Where direct political control cannot reach, the Communists and their friends have exerted *their* influence toward lowering and softening artistic standards in a pseudo-democratic direction."[6] Once again the indictment of Communist cultural politics is vague, but it is more nuanced than Berg's flat assertion that art is a weapon. Schlesinger then could work up little indignation over the fate of these "film hacks." When "they refused to own up to their political beliefs before a committee of Congress . . . the film industry . . . turned them out into the storm. I do not wish to imply approval of the question asked by the Un-American Activities Committee ['Are you now or have you ever been a member of the Communist Party of the United States?']. I suspect, however, that if the Committee had been asking witnesses whether they were members of the Ku Klux

Klan, the Silver Shirts or the Trotskyites, [John Howard] Lawson and his friends would be overflowing with indignation at the refusal to answer."[7] This is his only comment on the beginnings of the blacklist.

Schlesinger's view of Communist-inspired culture was developed into a narrative account of the rise and fall of Communism in Hollywood by Murray Kempton in the sixth chapter of *Part of Our Time*, which he titled "The Day of the Locust: The Workers' Theater Goes to Hollywood." Kempton had little sympathy for the blacklist. He portrayed it as a craven (and unnecessary) capitulation to the inept posturings of HUAC. But, after all, it's only Hollywood. Kempton accepted the testimony of F. Scott Fitzgerald as definitive: "Everywhere there is, after a moment, either corruption or indifference." And so, "soft, slack Hollywood . . . accepted the political purge which so few really wanted." If not with complete indifference, then with the bemused resignation that is learned from long familiarity with sudden and inexplicable reversals of fortune. HUAC "had forced the industry to choose between its empty affirmations about freedom and the commercial code by which it lived. The choice was inevitable."[8]

If Kempton was contemptuous toward the blacklisters, he had even less sympathy, it seems, for their victims. They are so reduced in his telling of their story that we are not allowed to feel even much pity for them. Of the Hollywood Ten— the first group of witnesses from Hollywood to contest HUAC's right to ask them about their membership in the Communist Party, all of whom were later jailed and blacklisted—he wrote, "They were not very attractive witnesses; their habits were Hollywood's, and long training had reduced their prose to the muddier depths of a Nash-Kelvinator ad." The Communists in Hollywood were third-rate writers, attracted to a third-rate cause and a cheap, vulgar culture. Some had promise once, but that had burned out long before their political trial. In giving up their youthful ambitions to write novels and stage plays, "the Hollywood Communists had not so much violated their essence as found their proper level." Their commitment to the cultural ideals of the Party was not really at odds with their employment: "The aesthetics of Hollywood were, after all, very much like the aesthetics of Josef Stalin." Even the injustice of their fate is turned against them. "They were entombed, most of them, not for being true to themselves but for sitting up too long with their own press releases. . . . [They] did not believe very much and felt a professional compulsion to simulate belief and were burned as finally as if they had been believers." The mortuary imagery at the beginning of this passage reoccurs throughout the essay. John Howard Lawson, the leader of the Hollywood Communists, is introduced with the information that he had "long ceased to interest anyone except grave robbers and the House Committee on UnAmerican Activities." The subtitle of Kempton's book, *Some Ruins and Monuments of the Thirties*, suggested he was writing ancient history. As I read the book, I found myself sometimes startled by the realization that the men he was writing about were still alive, physically at least, in 1955.[9]

For the liberal anti-Communist, Kempton's argument was irresistible, combining as it did reflex anti-Communism and a snobbish disdain for mass culture.

Since the victims of the blacklist had already committed artistic suicide by opting for Hollywood, there was a certain poetic justice in their forced exile from this false Eden.

In fairness to Kempton, it must be noted that he himself later wrote the most acute criticism of *Part of Our Time*. Thirteen years later, in 1968, he wrote,

> Irony [is] the most workmanlike implement for a mind which moves through distaste for the executioner and detachment from the victim. . . . I have . . . worked with irony for a very long while, and only lately have I begun to wonder whether something more—some awareness of horror—must take its place. . . . It can never be more than the refined expression of the very crude and philistine notion that the victim is usually guilty of something. So, in this case, the Hollywood Ten, having been arraigned by the Committee for trying to subvert our culture, are then dismissed by myself for not trying to subvert it enough. . . . The rhetoric of the Hollywood Ten may have been inferior to their cause, as the rhetoric of victims quite often is. But it still ought to be said for them that, in their test, they did what they could with the remaining resources of language and dignity, and that they did better than we.[10]

This self-critique appeared in a review of the next major study of the HUAC Hollywood hearings and the blacklist that followed, the work that began the second cycle of interpretation in the late 1960s, Walter Goodman's *The Committee: The Extraordinary Career of the House Committee on Un-American Activities*. Goodman was clearly indebted to *Part of Our Time*, but his touch was somewhat heavier than Kempton's. Playing a variation on a theme Kempton had also rehearsed, Goodman wrote,

> The Hollywood Ten and their sympathizers pretended to believe that their dismissal from the film capital would result in a disastrous decline in the quality of American movies (not to mention the national plunge into fascism); it was a pardonable conceit, with even less substance than the industry's claim, invoked to repair Hollywood's damaged image, that Movies Are Better Than Ever. In fact, the absence of these writers mattered as little to the quality of America's movies as their presence, and when, at last, Dalton Trumbo was permitted to sign his own name again, it was attached to such extravaganzas as *Spartacus* and *Ben Hur* and *The Sandpiper*.[11]

Trumbo did not write *Ben-Hur*, nor did he receive credit for writing it; that perhaps dubious honor belongs to Karl Tunberg, although a number of more famous writers (Gore Vidal, Christopher Fry, and S. N. Behrman) were reportedly involved. It would presumably complicate Goodman's argument to mention Trumbo's screenplays for *Exodus* or *Lonely Are the Brave*, films that some of his readers might regard as worthwhile. And the apparent substitution of the quasi-biblical epic *Ben-Hur* for *Exodus* lends just the right touch of absurdity to his list. Kempton had also ridiculed the Hollywood Communists with tendentious lists of their screen credits, but he at least got the titles right.

Goodman's tone and his emphasis closely followed Kempton, but the mood of the times had changed. By 1968 the events of the early 1950s seemed incredible, incomprehensible. Somewhere a thread of historical continuity had been broken. The same events are recited, but the story no longer had any meaning. There is still a sense of tragedy in Kempton's account, although it is low mimetic tragedy to be sure. Goodman, on the other hand, tried to present the history of HUAC as spectacle. The epigraph, taken from H. L. Mencken, began "The United States, to my eye, is incomparably the greatest show on earth." And Goodman opened the concluding paragraph of his chapter on the 1947 hearings with these sentences: "The Hollywood hearings brought forward no heroes. The writers, puffed up with a sense of martyrdom, made a burlesque of a Jeffersonian cadre. The producers, exemplified by [Jack] Warner, were like those shrewd, fawning peddlers who appeared in silent films in the days when racial stereotypes were still thought fit for public comedy."[12]

To paraphrase Marx, historiography repeats itself, the first time as melodrama, the second time as burlesque.

Goodman was naturally contemptuous of the claim made by Congressman Vito Marcantonio in the House of Representatives debate on contempt citations against the Hollywood Ten that "the affair [was] another plot of monopoly capitalism,"[13] although in the most literal sense, Marcantonio was prophetically right, as Goodman's own account shows. The decision to deny employment in the movie industry to Communists and to those who refused to testify before the House committee was taken a few days after Marcantonio spoke, at a private meeting attended by fifty representatives of the largest concentrations of capital in the world. Most of the Hollywood producers and studio executives opposed the blacklist; Jack Warner himself had said at the hearings, "I can't for the life of me, figure where men could get together and try in any form, shape, or manner, to deprive a man of a livelihood because of his political beliefs."[14] But, as Goodman put it, "The decisive pressure came from the New York financial interests upon which the studios relied."[15] Before this meeting many in Hollywood had protested the HUAC hearings; after the decision was announced, these protests ceased and everyone fell in line.

Marcantonio may have simplified the issue. But for his overliteralized interpretation Goodman could only substitute a free play of metaphor and analogies. The writers immediately following him searched for a ruling metaphor that could bring a stronger sense of order to their histories. In 1972 the actor Robert Vaughn published a book on the HUAC show business investigations entitled *Only Victims*. His title was borrowed from a speech by Dalton Trumbo, the most successful of the blacklisted screenwriters (before, during, and after his period on the blacklist). Accepting an award from the Writers' Guild, Trumbo had said, "When you who are in your forties or younger look back with curiosity on that dark time, as I think occasionally you should, it will do no good to search for villains or heroes or saints or devils because there were none; there were only victims."[16] One might add, all were victims perhaps, but some were more victimized than others. Of course, if that reservation is added, Trumbo's maxim becomes a tautology.

Apparently it did not occur to Vaughn that in 1972 anyone might disagree with Trumbo. The passage quoted is placed at the head of the text in italics and never referred to again. But that is typical of Vaughn's approach: he did not insist too much on any of the themes developed in the course of his work. His anti-Communism is evident, but it is denatured, almost lifeless. American Communists are extremists of the left who may be rescued from their delusions by a few homilies on the impossibility of violent revolution and a Communist government in the United States. The anti-Communism of Louis Berg and James Rorty was made of sterner stuff. A peculiar book, *Only Victims*—a doctoral dissertation by a famous actor—was revised only slightly for publication. Most of it is devoted to flat chronological summaries of hearings transcripts—its chief defect to those who want interpretation, its major virtue to those who want the record in an accessible form.

If Robert Vaughn's *Only Victims* is the one underwritten history of the Hollywood blacklist, Stefan Kanfer's *A Journal of the Plague Years*, published in 1973, is the most overwritten. Kanfer's title, which asks us to regard the blacklist as some sort of natural disaster, was taken from Defoe, perhaps by way of Kempton who had written in *Part of Our Time* that most of Hollywood regarded its blacklisted colleagues "as victims of one of those plagues which occasionally carry off one's friends and which in Hollywood are familiar misfortunes of nature."[17] And his epigraph came from Camus, from *The Plague*: "No longer were there individual destinies; only a collective destiny, made of plague and the emotions shared by all." Kanfer's own prose created an uneasy amalgam of Kempton (the Moscow Trials "have about them the indecipherable quality of bad foreign cinema") and Raymond Chandler (Clifford Odets "is about as comfortable in Hollywood as a tarantula on a wedding cake," borrowed, if memory serves, from *The Little Sister*). Kanfer enthusiastically repeated all of Kempton's charges against the Hollywood Communists and then offered a vague repudiation of the indictment. "The plague fell upon only one house," he wrote, "and that one the best dwelling, the one that held so much of the era's human potential." The Communists and fellow travelers "did attempt an elevation of the poor, enfranchisement of the damaged and despairing, an awakening of conscience in a world they saw narcotized. If they were strident or philistine, they have paid their dues, paid them at usurious rates."[18] They were owed at least a pardon and a recognition of the wrong that had been done them.

Liberal anti-Communism had done its work too well. In the 1930s, or even in the 1940s, intellectual heroism may have been required to resist the appeals of Stalinism. But by the 1960s anti-Communism had become formulaic. For better or worse, it was the victim of its own success. A younger generation could only wonder why such a pathetic creed as American Communism could have appealed to anyone. The Naked God That Failed was dead. If Communism could no longer be taken seriously as an intellectual and political doctrine, it was impossible to understand the ideas and the passions of those who thought Communists should be purged from American life. The blacklist and the other purges and trials could only be comprehended as a ghastly mistake. To Kanfer it seemed that in 1950s America, the mad doctor Caligari had taken full control of the asylum. A witch hunt, a plague, an inquisition—it was necessary to reach back at least three centuries to find historical analogies that seemed appropriate.

In the 1980s, however, it has become possible to conceive a history of the Hollywood blacklist peopled not only with victims and villains, but with heroes and heroines as well. There have been no revisionist historians eager to restore the reputation of Ayn Rand's "Screen Guide for Americans," the manifesto of the anti-Communist Motion Picture Alliance for the Preservation of American Ideals, or Vincent Hartnett's *Red Channels*, the index of prohibited names for the blacklisters in radio and television. Instead, in this third wave of books, interest has shifted from the inquisitors, the HUAC members, the blacklisters, to their victims, the Communists of Hollywood, and the ex-Communists who became "friendly witnesses."

In 1976 Lillian Hellman had put herself forward as a heroine in her brief memoir of the blacklist era, *Scoundrel Time*. She seemed a likely candidate—an uncooperative witness before the HUAC who had apparently never been a Communist. Goodman, Vaughn, and Kanfer had all praised her conduct as a witness. But in her memoir she manages to give the impression that she failed to join the Party only because she was too snobbish. Dashiell Hammett brought her to meetings in the 1930s, but it didn't take: "In the Hollywood meetings there were seven or eight people. I knew three of them slightly, but the others were something I then called 'unaesthetic.' Certainly the fact that what seemed to be the chairman, or leader, had a habit of tying and untying his shoelaces, making strange cutouts from pieces of yellow pad paper and throwing the cutouts to the floor, took my attention away from what might have been a serious discussion."[19] She did become a leader in the Progressive Party in 1948, but its presidential candidate, Henry Wallace, is made to seem even more disagreeable. Six pages are devoted to the telling of a nasty anecdote about his stinginess. The liberal anti-Communists also let her down by failing to offer support when she was subpoenaed by HUAC. These were people she regarded as her friends. How could they? "Perhaps that, in part, was the penalty of nineteenth-century immigration. The children of timid immigrants are often remarkable people: energetic, intelligent, hardworking; and often they make it so good that they are determined to keep it at any cost."[20] As if their anti-Communism could be dismissed by condemning them as *arrivistes*.

There is in her memoir an irritable, almost solipsistic remoteness, a lack of solidarity, that reminds me of her fellow southerner William Faulkner. I think of Lucas Beauchamp, the aristocratic black man improbably saved from lynching by the protagonist of *Intruder in the Dust*, characterized early in the novel as "apparently not only without friends even in his own race but proud of it."[21] But it is not just Lillian Hellman who assumes this position in her memoirs. Her tone of disappointment and petulant disillusionment is unexpectedly prevalent in political memoirs of the fifties, no matter what the politics of the author. It is, it seems, the authentic voice of the times. It may be found in Alfred Kazin's *New York Jew*, in

Norman Podhoretz's *Making It*, in William Barrett's *The Truants*, in Irving Howe's *A Margin of Hope*. It is especially striking in Kazin's book because it had been preceded by an earlier volume of his memoirs covering the thirties that was as exhilarating as *New York Jew* is gloomy. It is as if the political controversies of the time had marked everyone with a sense of failure, no matter what their position, and no one had been able to find a stance that could be reaffirmed twenty years later with any *élan*. Their attempts to retrace the political arguments of the 1950s are disappointingly thin. They seem caught between a desperate conviction that the ideas that had then exercised them were of overweening importance and a wary suspicion that no one cares anymore and what they did in the 1950s didn't really matter.

Certainly Hellman's political reasoning is unabashedly simplistic. The liberal anti-Communists, she writes, "would have a right to say that I, and many like me, took too long to see what was going on in the Soviet Union. But whatever our mistakes, I do not believe we did our country any harm. And I think they did. They went to too many respectable conferences that turned out not to be under respectable auspices, contributed to and published too many CIA magazines. The step from such capers was straight into the Vietnam War and the days of Nixon."[22] This is a safe alibi for the losers in any political struggle. Of course she and her political allies did their country no harm. They were defeated, purged, and thus in no position to do any harm. What needs to be argued is the harm (or the good) they might have done had they prevailed or at least not been so utterly defeated. And of course their victorious opponents can be held responsible for every consequence of their victory, from the crossing of the 38th parallel to the crossing of the 17th. But it is a giant step from respectable conferences and "too many CIA magazines" (too many is, of course, one: *Encounter*) to Vietnam and Watergate, and if that step was inevitable, we have the right to expect some account of its internal articulations.

Hellman's book was a success, a best seller even, and the liberal anti-Communists she had called to account responded in their traditional journals. Sadly, their response was even more self-righteous than Hellman's book; there was not even the minimal acknowledgment of misjudgments she had offered. In the *New York Times*, Hilton Kramer devoted a column of his usual hand-wringing to *Scoundrel Time*.[23] Nathan Glazer in *Commentary* and Sidney Hook in *Encounter* rehearsed Hellman's long record of collaboration with Communists that she had disingenuously downplayed in *Scoundrel Time*.[24] In *We Must March My Darlings*, published in 1977, Diana Trilling inserted some harsh comments on *Scoundrel Time* into a 1967 essay on liberal anti-Communism. Some of her contentions seem bizarre: she even revives the old charge of a blacklist directed at anti-Communists. And who were the victims of Communist cultural hegemony? She supplies only one name. "Perhaps the outstanding example of how tolerance of whatever furthered the Soviet cause became subsumed in our cultural criteria . . . producing judgments which lingered into the sixties and still obtain today, is the career of George Orwell, a writer of stature who went to Spain in the Spanish Civil War as a Communist sympathizer but who, because of what he learned in that country, left it a radical anti-Communist, which is what he continued to be, and whose reputation has never been allowed to recover."[25]

After rereading this statement scores of times, I still cannot understand what possible meaning it could have that is not evidently false. Orwell was never a Communist sympathizer, although certainly his experience in Spain made anti-Communism a major theme in his political writing. But is it possible to contend that his literary reputation has suffered as a consequence of his anti-Communism?

Trilling may be slightly paranoid, but I feel a certain sympathy for Hellman's critics who found themselves cast as villains in a political melodrama. It is natural that they should resent Hellman's failure to define the political divisions of the times or to explain her positions. I agree that her narrow focus in *Scoundrel Time* is unfortunate. If Hellman had tried to write about her political commitments and her political activities instead of about the persecution they brought on her, she might have created an important work. Few are in a better position to meditate on the failure of the Old Left. Instead she chose to write a morality play that contributes only a few footnotes to our historical understanding of the period.

Still, this choice was apparently the right one for the dominant political culture of the United States in 1976; it was her neglect of politics that made *Scoundrel Time* attractive to readers and reviewers. "She spares us a rehash of the old quarrels— that would be no more than scholasticism," wrote Maureen Howard in the *New York Times Book Review*. And it is praise when Howard notes, "The last thing [Hellman] asks is our support or sympathy for her political positions."[26] The virtue of her book in the minds of these reviewers was its reduction of the complex history of the times to a simple question: "Since when do you have to agree with people to defend them from injustice?"[27]

The culture that welcomed *Scoundrel Time* is the culture of which Richard Sennett wrote in *Authority*, "The moral status of the victim has never been greater or more dangerous than it is now."[28] The ennobling of victimization is dangerous, I think, because it requires the victims to keep in their places to maintain their moral claims. If they revolt they must be defeated if they are to keep our sympathy and indulgence. They must remain victims. When Castro's rebels in Cuba and the Sandinistas in Nicaragua won their revolutions, they immediately forfeited the considerable goodwill their seemingly hopeless struggles against tyranny had earned them in the United States.

This is the culture of whose political thought Robin Blackburn wrote, "Bourgeois sociology only begins to understand modern revolutions in so far as they fail."[29] This dictum may be applied to its dramatic art as well. When it turns to political revolutions for its subject matter, it produces the films *Viva Zapata!* (1952), *The Battle of Algiers* (1967), and *Burn!* (1970), each of which in its own way romanticizes and glorifies revolutionary defeats. *The Battle of Algiers* chose to dramatize the early defeats of the Algerian struggle for national liberation, instead of its later victories, so that our sympathies for the revolutionaries may remain uncomplicated. *Burn!* would have us believe that cunning counter-revolutionaries would rather release the leader of a revolution than execute him, to avoid creating a martyr.

Of course real-life counter-revolutionaries do not subscribe to this romantic ideal-ism about revolution, as the Bolivians demonstrated when they did not hesitate to martyr Che Guevara. *Viva Zapata!* (written by John Steinbeck, directed by Elia Kazan, and released only a few weeks before Kazan appeared as a "friendly wit-ness" before HUAC) went further by having its revolutionary leader actually gain power and then explicitly renounce it. As Kazan himself drew the moral in a public defense of the film, "in his moment of decision this taciturn, untaught leader must have felt, freshly and deeply, the impact of the ancient law: power corrupts. And so he refused power."[30] And so in the Kazan-Steinbeck version, Zapata returned to the righteous path of the true revolutionary: unending, losing struggle.

The moral that Christopher Lehmann-Haupt of the *New York Times* took from *Scoundrel Time* is similar: "The danger is that when big ideas clash, people get trampled."[31] Ideas, like revolutionaries, should stay in their place, which is outside of real life where people can get trampled. *Scoundrel Time* allowed Lehmann-Haupt to forget that Lillian Hellman got trampled because she herself had some traffic with big ideas; for a writer and political activist these ideas were a vocation. But what matters about Hellman to the admirers of *Scoundrel Time* is her martyrdom. If she consented to be more or less than a martyr, she would lose her status as a moral exemplar.

But more substantial works were to follow *Scoundrel Time*. The best is unfortu-nately the most obscure. Nancy Lynn Schwartz died prematurely in 1978 before she could finish *The Hollywood Writers' Wars*, and the work was brought to publication by her mother, Sheila Schwartz, in 1982. Her book followed the appearance of two bigger and more comprehensive works on the blacklist, *The Inquisition in Hollywood* (1980) by Larry Ceplair and Steven Englund, and *Naming Names* (1980) by Victor Navasky. All these writers have benefited from the revisionist spirit of the 1970s. John Cogley and the other contemporary critics of the blacklist were denigrated for relying almost exclusively on anonymous informants. At the beginning of the 1970s Stefan Kanfer found that many of those willing to submit to interviews were still demanding anonymity. But the writers whose books appeared at the beginning of the 1980s talked to people representing all sides of the political battles in Holly-wood; they were able to quote their statements and to attribute the quotations. Thus Schwartz was able to write the first coherent political history of the period relying primarily on the personal recollections of those who lived through it, instead of published sources and the record compiled by HUAC. Her subject is not the blacklist itself, but the political struggles in Hollywood that preceded it, partic-ularly among the screenwriters, who had the most politicized of all the Hollywood guilds. She ended her narrative where most of the others begin, with the HUAC hearings of October 1947. *The Hollywood Writers' War* avoids the hard questions, and it is clearly partisan. Schwartz's sympathies lay with the "progressives," that is, with the less doctrinaire Communists and the more tolerant liberals who were willing to work with them. In a sense her book is a lament over the failure of a postwar Popular Front to develop. The Communists were too confused—it was a period when it seemed they were trying to follow a Left sectarian line with their heads and a Right opportunist line with their hearts—and the liberals were too scared—or perhaps just wearied by past Communist betrayals—for them to form an effective alliance. Despite some sentimental evasions, *The Hollywood Writers' War* is the clearest and most fair-minded account of the Hollywood Left from 1933 to 1947.

The Inquisition in Hollywood, subtitled *Politics in the Film Community, 1930–60*, covers the same ground as Schwartz's book, and more as well. It is the most ambitious and scrupulous work of historical scholarship devoted to the Hollywood blacklist. Ceplair and Englund grappled with the important questions Schwartz avoided posing explicitly. Their answers, I think, give voice to the present consensus, for better or worse, or at least they express an important version of that consensus. Above all, they are willing to attempt to pass judgment on the politics of the Hollywood Communists. They joined the Party because, from 1936 to 1945, "the CPUSA made itself nearly synonymous with serious political engagement." And this political commitment "helped them collectively . . . to display personal resources of solidarity, courage, honor, decency, patience, integrity, and transcendence of which any group could be proud." They also accomplished something. They were unable to advance the demise of capitalism, but they did achieve some of the more modest goals they shared with less radical leftists. They were the "shock troops" of Hollywood progressivism. Without them the Hollywood Left collapsed: "The liberals of the forties and fifties had, on their own, neither the backbone nor the political consciousness to obstruct effectively militant American conservatism." Thus Ceplair and Englund stood on its head the conventional wisdom that pictures liberals as the dupes of Communists in Popular Front organizations: "The Communists played crucial roles in the victory of liberal measures and the defeat of conservative ones, but the Party 'triumphed' only when its interests coincided with the position of the large liberal coalition—as happened during the Popular Front and World War II."[32]

But the Hollywood Communists were not really Communists. At least they did not fit the stereotype of a Communist that prevailed in the 1950s; that is, they were not conspirators, they were not spies, they were not committed to violent revolution. Nor were they Communists as we might understand the term in the 1980s; that is, they were not Marxists. "For in a very real sense, no group, and very few individuals, could be anything but quasi-Communist in America. As an organization, praxis, and ideology, European communism never 'took' in America, even among American Communists, the way it did on the continent of its origins." Most Hollywood Communists "failed to assimilate or even understand Marxism-Leninism. They . . . were courageous American radicals in the Jeffersonian or abolitionist traditions who joined an organization (in this case, the CPUSA) not as a response to class exploitation, but because they regarded it as the most effective means to live out their principles in the twentieth century." And what were the principles that animated their politics? They were "justice, decency, fairness, equality, democratic rights, and (for some) socialism-democratic socialism."[33]

But they were not simply liberals in a hurry. They may have been only quasi-Communists, but they were Stalinists, and Ceplair and Englund presented their own blunted version of the familiar charges against Stalinism: "Communist screenwriters defended the Stalinist regime, accepted the Comintern's policies and about-faces, and criticized enemies and allies alike with an infuriating self-righteousness, superiority, and selective memory which eventually alienated all but the staunchest fellow travelers. As defenders of the Soviet regime the screen artist Reds became apologists for crimes of monstrous dimensions, though they claimed to have known nothing about such crimes, and indeed shouted down, or ignored, those who did."[34]

Perhaps this formulation is worth quibbling over a bit. The Hollywood Communists were not apologists for the crimes of the Soviet regime, nor were other American Communists. They denied that these crimes took place. They did not claim to know nothing of such crimes; they claimed, rather, that the reports of them were untrustworthy products of anti-Soviet propaganda. This distinction between defense and denial may seem trivial and perhaps pernicious if presented to exculpate the American Communist Party of its sins, but I think it is important to bear in mind that in their attitude to the Soviet Union, the American Communists were fools, rather than knaves, although some of them were intemperate and vicious in their efforts to maintain their ignorance and that of their allies.

How could they not have known? For those of us born after 1940, whose beliefs about the Soviet Union were formed after Khrushchev's 1956 speech, which confirmed the worst reports about the Soviet regime under Stalin and settled the essential factual questions about Stalinism, this is a difficult question because we have always known. We have always already known; we have known as we know our own names. But it is a real question, and it is unfortunate that it is so often treated as if it were only rhetorical. For most Americans who wanted to have an opinion about the Soviet Union during the 1930s, it became a question of whether to trust the dispatches of Walter Duranty in the *New York Times* or the distinctly more critical reports of William Henry Chamberlin in the *Christian Science Monitor*. Those who trusted Chamberlin turned out to be right, but the Communists were not the only Americans to have false ideas about the Soviet Union then. Until the end of World War II, one could read denials of Soviet crimes in many journals besides the *Daily Worker*.

But still we can say they were wrong about the Soviet Union, even those of us too young to know for sure whether we would have made the same mistake. The most scathing judgment of the politics of the Hollywood Communists to be found in *The Inquisition in Hollywood* was delivered by Albert Maltz, a leading activist in the Party and one of the Hollywood Ten: "No one I knew in the CP would have stayed in the Party had they known then what they found out later."[35] Since in politics it is sometimes worse to be wrong than to be malevolent, perhaps these defenders of the Soviet Union deserved everything they got, and more.

We can also imagine a more indulgent verdict, one that bases its judgment of a political movement by its responses to immediate concerns, not by its remote alliances. This is the verdict Ceplair and Englund found most sympathetic. Whatever the faults of the Hollywood Communists, these did not justify the purges.

Furthermore, the indictment drawn up against them by the right in the late forties was maliciously wrong. They were not subversives, spies, or conspirators, nor "did they ever try formally to propagandize Hollywood movies in the literal sense of 'subversion,' i.e., to undermine the principles of, or corrupt."[36] This last claim may seem suspiciously narrow, as if broader and more significant questions about these writers' relation to their work were being swept aside. Still I think the general truth of their characterization of the Hollywood Communists must be conceded. Thirty-five years after the beginning of the blacklist, we can say that the American Communists were not Bolsheviks, just as we can say that Joseph McCarthy was not Hitler. The judgments expressed in *The Inquisition in Hollywood* may still be open to question, but the book provides the most thorough account we yet have of the political activities of Hollywood Communists and the activities of their allies and their opponents.

Of the more recent studies, the one that has received the most attention is Victor Navasky's *Naming Names*, but I found it the most disappointing. Navasky is a skillful writer, and he knows where to begin his story, not at the beginning, but at its most dramatic moment: the painful appearance of Larry Parks before HUAC in May 1951. Parks was the first Hollywood witness to admit publicly that he was once a member of the Communist Party, but he begged the committee not to force him into informing on others. However, it was to no avail, and he finally cracked and gave the names of the members of his Party branch to the committee in executive session. It was a sad spectacle, by all accounts. As it turned out, Parks had redeemed neither his honor nor his career. But later witnesses were able to learn from his performance exactly what was demanded and to speak the lines with more conviction. Most of them did save their careers, and some were more successful after their ordeal than they had been before it.

Parks's dilemma allowed Navasky to pose immediately his central question. How had it come to this? Why did American anti-Communism demand victims for "degradation rituals"? And how were men and women able to come to accept that role? Why did they agree to "name names," to become informers? And how should we judge them, and how should we judge those who refused that role?

Like Hellman, Navasky wants us to forget such scholastic matters as ideology and politics and consider questions of morality. He set out to write "less a history than a moral detective story."[37] Navasky has set down the most compelling indictment of the procedures of the House Un-American Activities Committee and the blacklist yet written, and I admire his moral fervor, which exposes the evasions of the ironic mode that prevailed in studies of American Communism from 1955 to 1975. But some of the assumptions and the methods Navasky employed in his detective work trouble me.

The center of the book, both literally and figuratively, is an account of eleven interviews conducted with men and women who had been "friendly witnesses" during HUAC's Hollywood hearings of the fifties, ex-Communists who had given names to the committee. He asked the informers to inform on themselves. He quotes their responses at some length; he tells us that he wanted to let them have their say. "I came to these interviews armed with questions and a tape recorder," he writes. "My questions, however, were designed for more than eliciting specific answers—the idea was to get people talking, to say their say, to free-associate, to open up."[38] He is, we must remember, a detective, not a historian. But whatever opportunity these witnesses are given to have their say, to explain themselves, all of them are finally called to judgment and all judged by the same standard, their willingness to admit guilt. Navasky offers absolution and forgiveness to those who do while condemning those who refused to repudiate their decision to inform.

Daniel Aaron put the matter clearly in his review of *Naming Names*, but he failed to draw what seem to me the obvious conclusions: "Only those who admit they acted badly and regret their capitulation . . . earn his grudging sympathy, but none escapes his disapproval. . . . Although Navasky's arraignment of informers is never shrill or self-righteous, he takes seriously his obligation to expose wrongdoing and to declare, 'Thou art the man.' . . . The detective is also a social physician. 'If there is pain and unpleasantness' in eliciting answers from informers who don't welcome his invitation to unburden themselves, 'that is because lancing a boil means letting the pus out.' The operation is required for the sake of the patient . . . and for the public which needs to be immunized from future contagions. It should be noted in passing that the surgeon goes easy on the anesthetic."[39] I recall similar arguments from the blacklisters to justify their proceedings, but to my knowledge, none of the anti-Communists of the early 1950s, not even McCarthy or Nixon, ever employed such sadistic rhetoric to justify their efforts to immunize the public from the contagion of Communism.

I was surprised that none of the reviewers of *Naming Names* seemed sensitive to what struck me most forcibly about the book, Navasky's inverted mimicking of the efforts of the blacklist ideologues to reduce complex political issues to the ethical question of informing. At least none of the daily and weekly reviewers. Only Eric M. Breindel, in a hostile review—the only one I have seen published in *Commentary*—made these connections: "In effect, [Navasky] appropriates the HUAC test of character, but reverses the Committee's standard of judgment. Willingness to name names remains the test, but in Navasky's world, those who did so are marked as 'guilty,' notwithstanding their special pleas and *ex post facto* ideological rationalizations."

Navasky's focus on the "friendly witnesses" is justified by the form that the purge of Communists in Hollywood took. His demonstration that the informers generally underestimated the harm they did is compelling, but he also exaggerates the effect they had. He claims that the blacklist would not have been possible without the informer, yet the institution of the blacklist antedated the recruitment of the first informers. His argument seems to confuse form with content. Moreover, as Navasky explains more clearly than any earlier historian, HUAC had the names of almost all the Communist Party members in Hollywood from well-placed infiltrators reporting to the Los Angeles Police Department and the Federal Bureau of Investigation. It could have placed them on the stand to expose the Hollywood Communists and let the film industry take its sanctions. In unions and in other professions, more extensive purges of Communists were undertaken without the cooperation of ex-Communist informers.

A Marxist would say that Navasky's approach is idealist. I agree, and I would add that it is also formalist. Neglecting concrete historical analysis, he turned instead for an explanation of the purge to the abstract models of contemporary American social science: Harold Garfinkel's essay on "degradation ceremonies," Daniel Boorstin's concept of "the pseudo-event," Kai Erikson's study of "deviant sanctions," Stanley Milgram's behaviorist experiments on obedience to authority. I am not quite sure how these excursuses into psychological and sociological theory are meant to be taken. Are they offered as full-fledged theoretical explanations or as casual forays into Veblenite satire? Whatever the case may be, they occupy the place where we might expect to find political analysis.

When Navasky turned to the resisters, those who refused to answer the questions of HUAC by invoking their rights under the First or Fifth Amendment, he displayed an almost uncanny knack for missing the point of what his investigations revealed. Hundreds of pages are devoted to explaining why the informers agreed to "name names" and judging their own rationalizations for their actions, but only a few paragraphs to the motives of the resisters. Instead, Navasky constructed a formal case demonstrating that the resisters followed the morally correct path, without reference to the reasons they gave for their actions or to their actual motives. His informer is a frail, confused human being pressured by lawyers, agents, and psychiatrists to betray conscience and friends; his resister is a hero in a bad socialist realist novel.

But, as Breindel noted in his *Commentary* review, it is evident from Navasky's account that political considerations were decisive in most of the subpoenaed witnesses' decisions about how to testify. In Breindel's words, "The witnesses who remained silent were virtually all members of the Communist party (or . . . strict followers of the party line) *at the time of their testimony.*"[40] On the other hand, "nearly every friendly witness had broken with Communism *well before having been summoned to appear.*"[41] Perhaps this truth is so self-evident no one had thought it worth remarking. Or perhaps those who found the HUAC investigations repugnant were embarrassed by the fact that those who refused to cooperate with the committee were overwhelmingly Communists.

One has to read between the lines of Navasky's book to appreciate the primacy of politics in guiding the conduct of witnesses. At one point near the end of the book, on page 409, he finally acknowledged that "doctrinaire Communists . . . were among the fiercest opponents of and organizers against the Committee. No admittedly then-current member of the Communist Party was subpoenaed who failed to take the Fifth Amendment." But there is no estimate of how many witnesses who were not "doctrinaire Communists" took the same path of resistance. It just happened that almost all the resisters given any prominence in *Naming Names* were Communists. I can remember only four exceptions to this rule: Arthur Miller and Lillian Hellman, who as prominent playwrights had careers outside of Hollywood (by Breindel's standards, Hellman would probably qualify as a "strict follower of the party line" at the time of her testimony), and Edward Dmytryk and Robert Rossen, ex-Communists who refused to testify when first subpoenaed but then later relented and were recalled by the committee as friendly witnesses to name more than their share of names.

Most of the informers interviewed in *Naming Names* mentioned their disillusionment with the Communist Party, but Navasky was unable to see that this disenchantment had a decisive influence on them. He refused to entertain any suggestion that their actions may have been principled, insisting that the cause was not Communism, but the First Amendment, the right of free association. He wrote, "To cite one's defection from the CP as a reason to testify before the Committee is to miss the point. The principle at stake was not the well-being of the Communist Party but rather the rights of all Americans and the well-being of the First Amendment. If resistance was required, it was not to protect the Communist Party (except insofar as its rights were violated) so much as to prevent the abuse of power by the state."[42] Apparently almost everyone managed to miss the point; the First Amendment was not a cause for which men and women were willing to sacrifice their careers.

Navasky wanted to make the resisters individual heroes and the informers individual "moral lepers" and leave their politics out of it.[43] His formalist, idealist approach, concentrating on abstract morality and individual psychology, allowed him to mistake secondary psychological influences for determining causes.

Breindel takes another moral from his symptomatic reading of *Naming Names*: "Just about everyone summoned cooperated, save for those who, as Communists, or party sympathizers, were, for the most part, operating under what amounted to an external political discipline." The assumption seems to be that the resisters were therefore not responsible for their actions. The Communist Party told these automatons to sacrifice their careers by taking the Fifth Amendment, just as it "determined what members were permitted to read or write, and for whom they were to vote."[44] For Breindel, being subject to Communist Party discipline is a condition like hypnosis or temporary insanity. Liberal anti-Communists like Breindel are willing to hold Communist Party members individually responsible for every evil deed ever committed in the name of Communism, but when an individual Communist performs a courageous act or takes an admirable position, "external political discipline" serves to discredit it; the hypocritical motives of the Party nullify the good intentions of its individual members. But in truth party discipline is accepted voluntarily. A legislator who votes the line of his party although he does not see its wisdom has not become an automaton and is still personally responsible for his actions. In this instance, when Communists were forced to choose between cooperating with HUAC or following the party line by resisting, there is every reason to believe that party discipline only reinforced the natural inclinations of the resisters. There is no evidence that being asked to plead the Fifth Amendment brought about a crisis of conscience for Party members. None of the "friendly witnesses" interviewed by Navasky had become alienated from the Party because of its response to the HUAC investigations.

It is true of course that a member of an organized political movement must sometimes subordinate his or her beliefs to the collective will of the group and there will be occasions when these compromises seem intolerable. There are times when the only alternatives are to submit or to leave the movement. Even American Communists could always quit. Notwithstanding all the legends about the Party terrorizing defectors from its ranks, the American Communist Party had a membership turnover rate similar to that of other voluntary political organizations in the United States. The CPUSA was never able to impose the tightly disciplined conspiratorial style of its Bolshevik model on its rank-and-file members. What I have read about the political discipline and cohesiveness of American Communists reminds me more of my own experience in a Young Democrats club than of the accounts I have read of the pre-Revolutionary Bolsheviks. Like the Communist screenwriters, we formed caucuses and held faction meetings; we studied parliamentary procedure, and we tried to master it more completely than our opponents had; we learned the patience necessary to sit through long meetings. To the marginally committed occasional meeting-goer we must have seemed pretty obnoxious, as the Communist screenwriters did to some of the apolitical members of the Screen Writers' Guild, but we believed we were simply practicing American democracy.

Breindel wrote of the American Communist Party as if the fantasies of its most doctrinaire leaders had been reality. He countered Lillian Hellman's claim that "the American radicals I met were not violent men" with this argument: "People painstakingly laying the foundations for a mass revolutionary movement are not likely to seem violent; how violent did the Bolshevik exiles appear during their sojourn in Switzerland?"[45] It was on the basis of such fractured syllogisms that the leaders of the American Communist Party were imprisoned under the Smith Act of 1940. The American Communists did not seem like Bolsheviks. The Bolsheviks did not seem like Bolsheviks. Therefore . . . one might add that a butterfly in its larval stage does not look like a butterfly. So for someone who doesn't know much about butterflies, almost anything that doesn't look like a butterfly might turn out to be one.

It happens that the blind spots of Navasky and Breindel are almost reciprocally inverted. Just as Navasky maintains a carefully balanced agnosticism on what Breindel calls "the actual issue of Communism," so Breindel is exceedingly coy about stating his views on "the actual issue of civil liberties" raised by the investigations of HUAC and McCarthy, the blacklist in Hollywood, the prosecution of the leaders of the Communist Party under the Smith Act (for conspiring to advocate or teach the necessity or desirability of forcibly overthrowing the government), and the other measures taken in the purge of Communists in the United States during the late 1940s and 1950s. Nowhere does Breindel express his approval of the HUAC investigations, the Smith Act prosecutions, or the execution of Julius and Ethel Rosenberg, only his disapproval of the critics of these actions.

"The Smith Act, and for that matter the congressional inquiries, may well have represented an abrogation of fundamental constitutional rights," he allows. And he *may* be willing to tell us whether the "may well have" should be dropped if we can convince him we are entitled to ask the question. The Communists disqualified themselves by failing to support the civil liberties of political sects they found odious. Thus their claim that they refused to testify before HUAC to defend the Bill of Rights "came with little grace, let alone sincerity."[46] Since the opportunism of the Communist appeal to civil liberties negates the moral legitimacy of their resistance to HUAC, the question cannot be raised retrospectively by Navasky on their behalf. The dishonesty of the Communist position underlying the conduct of the "unfriendly witnesses" and the others who resisted the purges effectively renders moot the question of whether the measures taken against the Communists and their collaborators at that time did or did not violate fundamental civil liberties. If Navasky's position can be reduced to a schoolyard taunt, squealers are yellow, Breindel's position implicitly rests on another such conversation stopper, who wants to know?

Aaron Katz wrote a letter to *Commentary*, published in its June 1981 issue, in which he accused Breindel of regarding the American Communists as less than human. No, replied Breindel, "the fact that I identified hypocrisy and dishonesty as having informed the behavior of most Communists, fellow travelers, and apologists during the period in question does not mean that I regard Communists as non-people, inhuman."[47] Hypocrisy and dishonesty are eminently human qualities, but Breindel had attributed them to the position of the Communist Party in the abstract, not to individual Party members. Communists are not hypocritical and dishonest as individuals, but only insofar as they incarnate the Party's will. Unlike Navasky, he assumes no distinction needs to be made between personal conduct and the line of the Party. He is being somewhat hypocritical himself when he claims that his strictures applied only to "most Communists, fellow travelers, and apologists," as if they admitted of exceptions. It is writing such as this that has allowed younger historians to regard as an original discovery the idea that Communists are human (see Vivian Gornick's *The Romance of American Communism* [1977] and the film *Seeing Red* [1984] by Julia Reichert and Jim Klein). The distorted absolutism of Breindel's senior colleagues produced the sentimentalism of Navasky as an inevitable reaction.

Navasky assumed that the most significant question about the Hollywood blacklist was the role of the informer, and he has succeeded at least in providing the raw material for an answer. But many equally significant questions remain. The difficulties, as I noted at the beginning, haven't even begun.

Thoughts on Some Un-Answered Questions

To face these difficulties, we must, first of all, reconsider the peculiar role of the House Un-American Activities Committee itself. Hollywood had successfully defied an earlier investigation by a U.S. Senate Subcommittee on War Propaganda in 1941. When the hearings of 1947 were announced, it once again united against the committee, and it seemed poised for another victory over the politicians. The producers indignantly rejected the charge of Communist influence on movie content and denounced the notion of blacklisting suspected Communists as un-American. The Committee for the First Amendment was formed to protest the investigations, enlisting a number of Hollywood's most prominent stars. During the hearings, HUAC failed abjectly in its effort to demonstrate Communist influence on movies, but it did produce Communist Party membership cards for the Hollywood Ten. This documentary evidence of Communist infiltration of Hollywood apparently sufficed to demoralize the liberal opposition to HUAC, although this opposition still had broad public support (a Gallup Poll conducted after the hearings in November 1947 showed the public evenly divided between approval and disapproval of HUAC's investigation). The Committee for the First Amendment disintegrated, and a month after the hearings the producers instituted the blacklist they had so outspokenly condemned earlier.

This chain of events is still difficult to understand. A truce was called, but how was it arranged and what were the terms? The movie industry surrendered its dignity by sacrificing ten employees, but it gained three and a half years of peace. HUAC took an indefinite leave of absence from show business, or rather it created its own when it matched Whittaker Chambers against Alger Hiss in August 1948. In any case its next Hollywood hearings did not take place until March 1951. In the later hearings, HUAC abandoned all pretenses of a general investigation of Communist influence on movies. It worked in harmony with the studios and the unions to purge individual actors, writers, and directors. It was only then that the ritual of naming names and pleading the Fifth began.

HUAC proved itself scrupulous in making accusations of Communist Party membership, but it was inept in its efforts to assess the work of these Party members and Communist fellow travelers in the films they wrote and produced. How is this incompetence to be explained? If HUAC failed to demonstrate Communist influence on movie content, it failed, in my opinion, because it had no intention of making a serious case against the movie industry. Such a direct challenge would have discredited either the studios or the committee; the studios might have been happy to see the committee disgraced, but HUAC did not want to challenge the power of the studios. It only wanted to isolate the union militants who had organized the conference of Studio Unions and the liberals who supported Henry Wallace, and in that it succeeded. So its 1947 investigation was a charade, an elaborate scenographic exercise designed to set off to best advantage its ace in the hole, its smoking gun, the Party cards of the Hollywood Ten.

It is generally assumed that the committee's efforts to investigate film content were feeble because the accusations of Communist influence were baseless. But the committee could have made a much stronger case than it presented. The pro-Soviet distortions in Mission to Moscow were persuasively documented at the time of the film's release, in May 1943, by John Dewey and Suzanne La Follette in the letters columns of the New York Times, by Meyer Schapiro in Partisan Review, and by Manny Farber in the New Republic.[48] Although HUAC made Mission to Moscow the centerpiece of its case against Hollywood, its critique was far milder than many of those that had already appeared in print. While concentrating on wartime pro-Soviet films, the committee ignored the most radical of them all, *Counter-Attack* (directed by Zoltan Korda, 1945), with screenplay by John Howard Lawson. Its thesis that working-class solidarity should outweigh patriotic feelings was far more radical than the conventional war propaganda to be found in Hollywood films. If *Counter-Attack* is not Communist propaganda, then neither is *Battleship Potemkin*.

There is evidence that the committee's failure was self-imposed in the record of its interrogation of Bertolt Brecht. Subpoenaed along with the Hollywood Ten and eight other writers who were finally not called to testify at the 1947 hearings, Brecht became the Hollywood Eleventh, although he had only one movie credit to show for his wartime exile in Hollywood, a story credit on *Hangmen Also Die*, a 1943 United Artists film about the anti-Nazi resistance in Czechoslovakia, directed by Fritz Lang. Brecht was certainly the greatest writer and the most un-American soul ever to appear before the Committee on Un-American Activities, and his testimony is often cited to demonstrate the ineptness of the committee. As soon as Brecht denied Communist Party membership, the committee members seemed to lose interest in him, but their counsel, Robert Stripling, plowed ahead with questions about Brecht's writings from *The Measures Taken* (*Die Massnahme*) to *The Solidarity Song* (*Solidaritätslied*). There were no substantive questions about *Hangmen Also Die*. This neglect of Brecht's Hollywood work seems striking, particularly in light of the discoveries made by James K. Lyon in studying the FBI files on Brecht, discoveries reported in his 1980 book *Bertolt Brecht in America*. According to Lyon these files "included perceptive bits of literary analysis." He quotes one report on *Hangmen Also Die*: "When viewed in the light of previous writings of Bert Brecht, *Hangmen Also Die* takes on something of the complexion of Brecht's education plays in that it emphasizes the conduct required of persons working in an underground movement. In general, the individuals in the story are made to see that their position and even their safety and the safety of their families is completely subordinate to the work of the underground movement. This principle is that which Brecht in his play *The Disciplinary Measure* [*The Measures Taken*] mentioned previously, emphasized."[49]

The collaboration between HUAC and the FBI is well documented, so we may presume the committee had access to this report. That presumption is strengthened by Stripling's emphasis on *The Measures Taken* in his questioning of Brecht and by his apparent reliance on this report's interpretation of the play. He even proposes the idiosyncratic *Disciplinary Measures* as a translation of *Die Massnahme*, although in the translation prepared for HUAC the title was rendered as *The Rule* or *The Doctrine*. But Stripling failed to make the connection with *Hangmen Also Die* sketched out for him in the FBI report. *Hangmen Also Die* is not really a Bertolt Brecht film, since he wrote only the first version of the screenplay, but something of Brecht's vision remains in the film as produced. It is quite un-American in its implicit repudiation of possessive individualism. The Czech resistance in *Hangmen Also Die* is not a bit like the platoons of U.S. soldiers in contemporaneous wartime films. In these carefully integrated cross-sections of Americana, each individual soldier is free to pursue his own selfish ends because internal diversity strengthens the group as a whole, just as free competition brings greater prosperity for all in a capitalist economy. In the Czech resistance of *Hangmen Also Die* (Brecht's title was *Trust the People*), this style of individualism is put to a crueler test and found wanting. Instead of questioning Brecht about the implications of *Hangmen Also Die*, the committee probed him on his German works, and he deflected their inquiries by rejecting the translations read to him. So Brecht befuddled the committee; posterity has remembered their encounter in the terms suggested by Eric Bentley: the "apes . . . had taken to studying the biologist."[50]

If there are still unanswered questions about the slow gestation of the blacklist, about the real intentions of HUAC and the failure of Hollywood to follow its previously announced convictions, about the extent of collaboration between the industry and the committee, there are still more questions about the long twilight of the blacklist. We don't even know when and how the blacklist ended. Or did it ever end for some of its victims? In his recent autobiography, *Hollywood Red*, Lester Cole has contended that some blacklisted writers cleared themselves in the early 1960s by signing secret affidavits that they were no longer Communist Party members. He resisted suggestions that he might clear himself in similar fashion, without making a public statement or undergoing a "degradation ritual," so he remained blacklisted. Perhaps then the blacklist did not fade away, it just went underground. In any case, most of the blacklisted writers who made the strongest comebacks in the sixties and seventies had publicly repudiated their earlier commitment to the Communist Party. Ring Lardner Jr., who won an Academy Award for his *M*A*S*H* screenplay in 1971, had made it clear that he was no longer a Party member in a brief memoir called "My Life on the Blacklist" published in the *Saturday Evening Post* in 1961.[51] In the early 1970s, near the end of his life, Dalton Trumbo, who had become the most prominent of the formerly blacklisted screenwriters, the one who "broke the blacklist" with his credit on *Exodus*, was red-baiting Albert Maltz, another of the Hollywood Ten, in an exchange of letters (published in excerpted form by Navasky in *Naming Names*) on the meaning of the blacklist. Maltz had earlier criticized Trumbo for appearing at the Los Angeles County Museum of Art on the same platform with Michael Blankfort, who had testified before the HUAC twenty years earlier without pleading the First or the Fifth Amendment.[52] The claims of solidarity still ran deep. In response Trumbo recalled that Maltz had also received public honors in circumstances that might be regarded as compromising. "Did you," he asked Maltz, "believe that you spoke for me when . . . you responded to a tribute much more fulsome than mine at the museum by hailing the German Democratic Republic, whose citizens had been so kind to Jews and heretics, as the harbinger of a new era in the history of human freedom and cultural excellence did you, or your audience, truly believe that you were speaking for Dalton Trumbo?"[53]

Certainly we may hope that the German Democratic Republic belongs more to the past than it does to the future, but that is no reason to hold it responsible for the crimes of the Nazis. Trumbo's late conversion to a rhetorical anti-Communism has put him in safe company, however. The almost instinctive anti-Communism to which he lent his voice still obstructs thinking about the actual political and aesthetic positions taken by American Communists during the 1930s and 1940s.

Examples of those positions are revealed by the one episode of Communist "repression" discussed in every history of the Hollywood blacklist, that of Albert Maltz.[54] In February 1946, a year and a half before his testimony to HUAC, Maltz published an article in *New Masses* entitled "What Shall We Ask of Writers?" in which he strongly condemned the literary culture of the Communist movement. He argued against what we would now call "tendency literature," writing intended to support a tactical position; he called it "the political novel." This genre of writing, he claimed, "*usually requires the artificial manipulation of characters* and usually results in shallow writing." For the political novelist, "it is very, very difficult . . . *not* to handle characters in black and white since his objective is to prove a proposition, not to reveal men . . . as they are." As an alternative to "the political novel," Maltz upheld classical realism or "the social novel," which is primarily concerned with "revealing men and society as they are." Instead of manipulating characterization to make his judgments explicit, the social novelist confines himself to an objective, non-ideological critique of the reality presented in his work, he "presents all characters *from their own point of view*, allowing them their own full, human justification for their behavior and attitudes, yet allowing the reader to judge their objective behavior."[55]

Maltz praised a number of contemporary "social novelists" whose political evolution had discredited them for the critics of *New Masses*: Galsworthy, Steinbeck, Richard Wright, James T. Farrell. Maltz reminded his readers that Engels has praised Balzac, a self-proclaimed monarchist and reactionary. Engels has recognized "that a writer may be confused, or even stupid and reactionary in his thinking— and yet, it is possible for him to do good, even great, work as an artist."[56] A writer must be judged by his works, not by the petitions he signs or the committees he joins.

Maltz claimed that the doctrines of left-wing literary criticism had even made his own creative work more difficult. "It has been my conclusion for some time," he wrote, "that much of left-wing artistic activity—both creative and critical—has been restricted, narrowed, turned away from life, sometimes made sterile because the atmosphere and thinking of the literary left wing has been based on a shallow approach." The source of that approach had been a vulgarized interpretation of the phrase "art is a weapon." The doctrine underlying it had been "converted from a profound analytic, historical insight into a vulgar slogan" under whose influence literary works meant to have enduring value were judged as if they were pamphlets, according to "canons of immediate political utility." For Maltz himself, "Communist literary doctrine had become not a useful guide, but a straightjacket," and "in order to write at all," he had found it necessary to repudiate and abandon the notion that art is a weapon.[57]

Maltz's position was attacked for two months in the pages of both *New Masses* and the *Daily Worker* with a violence that must now seem almost inexplicable.

There was a debate, so-called, but the two sides were extremely unequal. All the leading writers and critics then associated with the Communist movement weighed in against him. His defenders were restricted almost entirely to the letters columns, and their tone was mild and apologetic. The same charges were repeated over and over. Maltz had retreated to an anti-Marxist position. He had posited an artificial, idealist division between art and politics, between artist and citizen, in no way sanctioned by Engels's remarks on Balzac. He was an apostle of liquidationism whose position logically demanded the separation of the artist from the Communist movement. He was promoting a new form of reconciliation with Trotskyism. He had gone Hollywood. To some of his detractors, the strengths of Maltz's own novels disproved his new literary doctrines; to others the failings of these same novels demonstrated that these false doctrines had always been implicit in his viewpoint. Some of the harshest criticism came from fellow screenwriters Alvah Bessie and John Howard Lawson, who a year later would be united with Maltz in the Hollywood Ten. Clearly the Communist Party was not ready to abandon its claim on writers and creative artists, the claim that as the vanguard in the struggle for human liberation it deserved the loyalty of all progressive artists. It could still ask of writers their loyalty and obedience, even if fewer and fewer were willing to heed the call.

According to the prevailing standards of American intellectual life, Maltz should have held to his position and suffered whatever ostracism that brought until the tide of fashion shifted in his direction. What he did instead has made "the Maltz affair" a continuing scandal: he changed his mind. After a number of meetings with his Hollywood party colleagues, he wrote a second article, a self-criticism entitled "Moving Forward," published in the April 9 issue of *New Masses* and simultaneously in the *Daily Worker*. This second essay has not received good reviews from the historians. In *The Committee* Walter Goodman gave the consensus opinion its most quotable expression. Maltz's second article, wrote Goodman, "read as though it had been translated direct from the Russian, and it was evident that there was no brighter dream in Albert Maltz's constellation than to be a defendant at a Moscow trial."[58] Certainly Maltz's tone was inappropriately abject: he expressed gratitude for the sharp criticism he had received, and he chastened his defenders for allowing themselves to be misled by his one-sided, non-dialectical approach. "By allowing a subjective concentration upon problems met in my own writing in the past to become a major preoccupation," he confessed, "I produced an article distinguished for its omissions, and succeeded in merging my comments with the unprincipled attacks upon the left that I have always repudiated and combatted."[59] By magnifying the significance of half-truths, he had fallen into "total error"; he had lapsed into revisionism.

For the historians of the blacklist, the moral of this incident is evident enough. In *A Better World* (1982), William L. O'Neill wrote, "Here was Stalinism in action, not the real Stalinism of the blackjack and the labor camp, but the ersatz cultural Stalinism of America."[60] If this is American Stalinism in action, what term would be appropriate for the casually accepted intellectual humiliations screenwriters like

Maltz experienced every day at the studios where they worked? Mayerism? Warnerism? Zanuckism? The story conferences, the chains of rewrites, the memos from producers—these are all certainly more demeaning to artists than the meetings that led to Maltz's "recantation."

Writers more sympathetic to the Communists take their analogies from domestic repression, but their judgments are consistent with those of O'Neill. Nancy Lynn Schwartz wrote, "One of the most tragic aspects of the destruction of the Left in America and in Hollywood was the way in which it countered the growing repressions of government and the press with small repressions of its own."[61]

Forty years later this debate may seem simply tedious and nothing more. It is difficult to write about it today, almost impossible to reanimate the arguments or to rediscover the passions that brought 3,500 people to a forum marking its official conclusion in April 1946. For us the titles given the various responses are enough to condemn them. "No Retreat for the Writer." "Art Is a Weapon." "Reveille for Writers." "The Road to Retreat." But we would be wrong to feel complacent about the supersession of these issues. Certainly no American writer today feels oppressed by party discipline. Yet this negative freedom we share depends on our conceding in advance that our political ideas must be ineffective, that power and truth are strangers. The relation between a writer and a political party is not an issue for us because we cannot imagine a party to which writers might adhere. Maltz's "liquidationism" has achieved a de facto victory.

The notion that any political commitment must stand in the way of a writer's true vocation had become an article of faith in American literary criticism by the end of the 1950s. Thus, in a liberal and authoritative literary history of the 1890s, published in 1966, Larzer Ziff could write, "To be a serious female author in the nineties was to be a writer of stories about women and their demands. The woman novelist was trapped by her affiliations to her sex in precisely the same manner as was the . . . Negro writer in the 1950s trapped by affiliation to his race."[62] It did not occur to Ziff that Henry James might be trapped by affiliation to his sex or to his race or to his class. Of course, a liberal literary historian would no longer regard being female or black as a liability for a writer. But a political commitment not inherited at birth remains suspect.

Writers have reassumed their priestly vocation, but the only external guidance they seek is from an agent or a publisher. Indeed, the cult of the writer as oracle is stronger than ever—and never has it seemed more fatuous. Still we are more than ever aware of the truth of Lenin's dictum quoted against Maltz by Alvah Bessie: "It is impossible to live in a society and yet be free from it."[63] So our writerly freedom can feel like a kind of trap, like one of those enlightened zoos in which the animals are not caged but allowed to roam free in an artificial "habitat." Writers can say anything they like, but (or consequently) they have nothing to say. They may even come to envy (although at the same time they are aware of their bad faith in doing so) those writers in Eastern Europe who know very clearly what they want to say, but are prevented by the state from saying it. Even writers who might find themselves in close agreement on political questions no longer share a common political culture. This is the situation we have inherited from the involution of these post-war debates and from the repressions that invoked them to justify themselves.

If the historians of the blacklist have read Maltz's second essay as the testament of a man broken by psychological pressures, akin to the confessions exacted at the Moscow purge trials in the mid-thirties, they have also taken it for granted that Maltz's original position was correct. "Maltz spoke uncommon sense," wrote Victor Navasky in *Naming Names*.[64] Common or uncommon, it was sense he made in "What Shall We Ask of Writers?"—on that there is general agreement. We may grant that the quality of the debate was not particularly high or that political considerations outweighed strictly literary concerns, but it should be noted that Maltz was not any more sophisticated than his critics. O'Neill ridiculed Maltz's revised view of James T. Farrell, but would he not agree with Maltz's critics that there was a decline in Farrell's work after *Studs Lonigan*?

There was an argument to be made against tendency literature, and in favor of classical realism, but Maltz softened it by claiming that "the social novel" was not only better art, but also better propaganda. He cited as an example Sholokov's *And Quiet Flows the Don* in which the counterrevolutionary Gregor is treated with sympathy. Because we can understand his viewpoint as well as that of the revolutionaries, the political significance of the novel is deepened. But if the social novel turns out to be just a more effective political novel, what becomes of the conflict he posits between the demands of immediate propaganda and those of lasting art? What purpose is served finally by schematic characterization? What we should ask of writers, it seems, is that they write well. In place of party literature, Maltz had nothing to offer but an eclectic humanism, a vague sense that all great art is essentially progressive.

When a group of New York documentary filmmakers had attempted to enlist some of Hollywood's left-wing screenwriters in their efforts to establish a left-wing cinema independent of the Hollywood studios, Maltz rejected their proposals as "economic nonsense."[65] The doctrinaire ideologue John Howard Lawson, the most vehement Hollywood critic of "What Shall We Ask of Writers?" supported them. One of Maltz's defenders later told Nancy Lynn Schwartz, "Albert Maltz was a philosophical idealist. There was not a materialist bone in his body."[66] In other words it was common sense he spoke in his first essay, the common sense that has always set itself against Marxism.

It is not possible to understand why Maltz's first essay produced such an uproar in the Communist Party press without taking into account the political context in which it appeared, but none of the historians who have written about the debate have betrayed the slightest awareness of this context. They assume that the cultural history of the American Communist Party is monolithic, a meaningless series of small repressions, so they already know the meaning of the Maltz affair before they look at it and they are able to see it only insofar as it corresponds to their preconceptions.

Navasky's book, however, can help us to understand the significance the debate had for its participants, but again it is necessary to read between the lines. The help comes from the 1953 HUAC testimony of Leopold Atlas, which Navasky quotes. Atlas was a member of the Communist Party in Hollywood and had attended the meetings that led to Maltz's self-criticism. As a supporter of Maltz's original position, Atlas was disappointed that Maltz came to accept the criticism directed at him. Atlas left the Party, and he appeared before the committee seven years later as a "friendly witness" still able to recall vividly the controversies of early 1946. "When I heard of Maltz's [first] article and read it," he told the committee, "I was enormously pleased. This was not only a further indication to me that the Communist Political Association had honestly broken with the tenets of the Communist Party, but also that Albert Maltz . . . had fought his way clear through to the liberal humanitarian way of thinking and writing."[67]

The Communist Political Association was formed in May 1944 immediately following the formal dissolution of the American Communist Party. This reorientation of the Communist movement in the United States confirmed and institutionalized a wartime move to the right under the leadership of Earl Browder. In 1944 Browder believed that the alliance between the United States and the Soviet Union would carry over after the war into an extended period of peaceful coexistence and that Communists should continue to promote class collaboration, rather than class conflict, in the United States. He believed that the expansive drive of American capitalism into foreign markets was a progressive force and should be supported and encouraged by Communists. In a major speech delivered in December 1943, Browder declared that Communists "must help to remove from the American ruling class the fear of a socialist revolution in the United States in the post-war period."[68] As Maurice Isserman, a scrupulous historian of American Communism, has put it, "Browder had known for many years that he would never lead his party to revolution; now he believed he could accomplish something of equal historical importance by leading his party away from revolution."[69]

However, the Communist Political Association lasted only fourteen months. After an unprecedented public criticism in April 1945 from a leader of the French Communist Party, Jacques Duclos, accusing Browder of liquidationism, opportunism, and revisionism, the leaders of the American party repudiated Browder's policies and reestablished the CPUSA in July 1945. Browder was forced from the leadership when he refused to accept this reversal of his initiatives. He was finally expelled from the Party in February 1946, during the very week Maltz's first essay appeared.

Atlas was confused then about the direction the American Communist movement was taking in 1946, but he was right about Maltz's article: it was a plea for a cultural Browderism. It was read that way not only by Atlas, but also by Maltz's critics in the Daily Worker and New Masses. Maltz supported a cultural policy that would not alienate non-Communist writers; he sought a wide alliance of creative artists based only on a common acceptance of "the great humanist tradition of culture," an alliance like that promoted by the Communists in the Popular Front of the 1930s, like that envisioned by Browder in 1944. The time was not right. In his Daily Worker column "Change the World," Mike Gold reminded Maltz, "The

Communist movement is coming out of . . . a period of Browderism, when Marxism was being liquidated. We grew so broad we lost our own shape and standard. All that was truly Communist and rooted in the masses was being skillfully wrecked by the champions of 'breadth' and Browderism. Now that is over, and we are painfully trying to get back on the Marxist rails of history. The young writers Maltz worries about will never be misled by this return to Marxism. But they would be derailed and damaged if they learned . . . to be as non-political as Albert Maltz tells them they can be."[70] A week earlier the *Daily Worker* that recorded Browder's expulsion from the Party had also reported a general strike in Lancaster, Pennsylvania, and the first major confrontation of the Cold War in Iran. Clearly Browder's predictions of postwar class peace and international coexistence were being refuted. The leaders of the Party might well have felt they had been prescient in rejecting Browder's perspective the previous summer.

Maltz, however, still felt some sympathy for Browder's political line. At least he suggested as much in his one explicit reference to the Duclos critique. He had noted that an emphasis on immediate practical utility had led to novels and plays being "discarded when a change of newspaper headlines occurs." He knew of at least a dozen works of imaginative literature abandoned for this reason and at least one scholarly work: "I even know a historian who read Duclos and announced that he would have to revise completely the book he was engaged upon. But what type of history was this in the first place?"[71] And what type of political party would revise its entire world outlook almost overnight in response to a single schematic critique?

Maltz did not need to enunciate this second question. His critics certainly picked up the implication, although only Alvah Bessie responded specifically to this charge: "Should 'a new headline in the newspapers' cause a writer to rewrite a novel? No—if it is a headline and nothing more. Yes—if the 'headline' involves a fundamental reorientation of human history. So far as the American Communist movement is concerned, the Duclos letter was not a headline."[72]

In truth Maltz had unintentionally strayed into a political battle and found himself in a role he had no wish to play. Like Leopold Atlas, he was unhappy with the Party's new direction, but his disagreement was not so fundamental that he felt compelled to leave. Undoubtedly he hadn't anticipated the effect his February article would have. He was truly embarrassed his criticism had been taken up approvingly by the *New Leader*. He had no desire to become a hero of the anti-Communist left nor was he capable of bringing the debate to a level that would transcend the controversy over Browder. Given the actual choices he faced, his accommodation to the current orthodoxy of the Party was hardly the shameful apostasy the historians of the blacklist have made it out to be.

The final question I want to consider is for me the most significant and it demands more consideration than I can give it here. I hope to return to it in another essay. It does not arise obviously from a comparative review of these historical studies because it involves another point on which there has been consistent unanimity from Kempton and Cogley to Navasky. In *Part of Our Time* Kempton wrote, "When its ordeal was over, Hollywood remained almost as it had been, less some 300 inhabitants. . . . When the Un-American Activities Committee came to root . . . out [the Communists], the one thing none of their worst enemies could say against them was that they had left any permanent impress upon the screen."[73] Kempton's 1955 judgment has become a point of orthodoxy held to consistently by each generation of commentators. Whatever their views on the political, legal, and moral issues raised by the blacklist, they all agree that the films themselves— the films written, produced, and directed by the Hollywood Left and by their antagonists on the right—need not be taken into account.

Some historians of the blacklist have been content to compose variations on Billy Wilder's celebrated witticism about the Hollywood Ten, playing on another title for the group, the Unfriendly Ten: "Two had talent, the others were just unfriendly." In *The Committee* Walter Goodman assumes that Alvah Bessie belongs among the untalented eight: "If there were anything to be said for a blacklist, Bessie's work would say it."[74] This quip has the ring of inevitability. David Thomson later composed a less cautious variation for the entry on Edward Dmytryk in *A Biographical Dictionary of Film*: "There might be a case for a Committee to investigate film-makers capable of rendering the *Bluebeard* story dull."[75] In an article in *Commentary* in 1953, with a cruelty only possible perhaps in a magazine sponsored by the American Jewish Committee, Morris Freedman dismissed the whole generation of Hollywood writers from which the blacklist victims came with one magisterial pronouncement: "The Jews who journeyed West to make movies might better have remained in New York to make dresses."[76]

By the 1970s the cinephobia on which Kempton and Goodman could count had faded. It would no longer do to ridicule the Communists simply for having been vulgar enough to take the movies seriously. But it is still possible to ignore the films they wrote, directed, produced, and starred in. Now, however, this dismissal is offered as a defense of the blacklisted film workers as proof they had not subverted the American cinema. In *A Journal of the Plague Years*, Kanfer writes, "None of the Communists had written a scene more offensive than that of a Russian girl teaching an American how to drive a tractor—and even that had been excised by 20th Century-Fox."[77]

Similar examples are multiplied in the works of Ceplair and Englund, Schwartz, and Navasky. Navasky can even allow himself to write, "John Howard Lawson, who ran the Hollywood branch [of the Communist Party], quickly understood that the collective process of moviemaking precluded the screenwriter, low man on the creative totem pole, from *influencing* [emphasis added] the content of movies."[78] Lawson had once written, "The content of motion pictures is controlled exclusively by producers."[79] Navasky manages to confuse control with influence, yet his nonsensical position is typical rather than exceptional.

There are two questions that need to be borne in mind. Were the films of the blacklist victims *politically* distinctive? Were the films of the blacklist victims *artistically* distinctive? These questions are not independent, and they cannot be entirely disentangled. But we must remember that an answer to one is not necessarily an answer to the other. Surprisingly, none of the histories of the blacklist have addressed either of these questions. The former has been subsumed by a quite different question: Was there Communist propaganda in the films of the blacklist victims? This is a question that cannot be given an unequivocal negative answer, despite the assurances of all the historians, but it is an uninteresting and ahistorical question. It is uninteresting because the term "propaganda" is too crude to be useful in studying the ways in which political ideas are actually expressed in films or in any other mimetic art. It has become nothing more than a term of abuse; it can no longer serve as a conceptual tool for analytic work. The question is ahistorical because none of the blacklist victims conceived of their relation to their work in terms of "propaganda."

The second question—were the films of the blacklist victims artistically distinctive?—has not been posed because the historians of the blacklist do not take Hollywood movies seriously. Committed as it is to the production of ephemeral novelties, Hollywood will always be Hollywood. On the other hand, movie historians are too defensive about their object of study to consider the possibility that its development might have been stunted by a political purge. One can see this defense mechanism at work in a 1982 *Village Voice* column by Andrew Sarris defending the Hollywood cinema of the fifties against Man Stern of the *Boston Phoenix*, who dismissed its products as "clumsy, stodgy, emotionally dishonest . . . timid, hypocritical." Granting that there was some political ugliness in the atmosphere, Sarris can still declare, "I am now of the opinion that the '50s was the greatest of all decades for cinema around the world." The times are past, he announces, "when the most enduring film history can be written by instant sociologists and pop historians."[80] He fills most of the column with a long list of almost three hundred "memorable films" from the 1950s as if to put these sociologists and historians on notice that they have some work to do before they can aspire to write a serious history of the movies. This catalog, which takes the place of argument, may also be taken as a despairing gesture, a sign of his belief that a common ground for dialogue with political historians is impossible.

By the standards of Hollywood, the Hollywood Ten were not untalented, but the standards of Hollywood are not necessarily those that should apply in a critical history. A film producer searches for talent; a critic writing a history searches for genius. The American cinema is notoriously rich in talent, notoriously lacking in genius. I think it can be said that there were no geniuses among the Hollywood Ten, but apparently it is necessary to rehearse the evidence of talent.

The works of Alvah Bessie are no more worthy of suppression than those of Walter Goodman. I haven't seen any of the films written by Samuel Ornitz, so I can't attempt to characterize his work. Most of his credits are for obscure films of the 1930s—perhaps that is enough to condemn him as "untalented."

Herbert Biberman might have passed as untalented in 1947—his credits were also limited to B-movies—but he later directed two remarkable films, *Salt of the Earth* (1954) and *Slaves* (1969). As an independent production written, produced, and directed by filmmakers blacklisted in Hollywood, *Salt of the Earth* became the target of an unprecedented campaign of harassment and abuse. Congressmen denounced it, the star was deported, Pauline Kael wrote a brutal review, and IATSE projectionists refused to project it. It had one theatrical run in New York and then disappeared for fifteen years. *Slaves* was a product of Hollywood's late-1960s liberalism that allowed a number of blacklisted directors a second chance. It is still the only intelligent Marxist film ever produced by a Hollywood studio. By suggesting that the slave system as it existed in the United States had a certain economic rationality, it alienated the American critics who were already waiting for *Roots*. Like *Salt of the Earth*, it was rejected in the United States on political grounds and only received its due in Europe where there was more tolerance for Marxist films.

Lester Cole has become famous (or notorious) in the annals of the blacklist for putting the words of La Passionara, the Spanish Loyalist leader, into the mouth of a football coach at a boys' school, although actually the credit for this minor bit of subversion belongs to Cole's friend Nathanael West.

Cole was the most prolific of the Hollywood Ten, and some of the films he wrote were certainly mediocre. I had regarded him as untalented until I read his autobiography. There I was surprised to learn that the three films of which he is proudest are *The President's Mystery* (1936), *The House of Seven Gables* (1940), and *The Romance of Rosy Ridge* (1947). None of the titles had produced a shock of recognition when I had glanced earlier at his filmography so I hadn't gone out of my way to see them. The lesson is that one cannot judge a screenwriter by glancing at a list of credits; all too often, though, that has been the method of the blacklist historians.

I still have doubts whether any of these three films are artistically distinctive, but *The House of Seven Gables* at least sounds interesting on political grounds. Cole made Holgrave into an active abolitionist and showed antebellum northern capitalists engaged in the illegal slave trade. The film, he claims, was "a radical bombshell." The studio accused Cole and producer Burt Kelly "of writing radical politics into the film and emphasizing them in the shooting," but it was released to good reviews.[81] Cole notes with amusement that none of the reviewers noticed his infidelity to Hawthorne's novel.

Edward Dymtryk has been particularly careless with his reputation. His recantation before HUAC in 1951 has put the films he directed in shadow, and he didn't advance his case by presenting himself as a political dupe and directorial hack in his 1978 autobiography. The two films generally regarded as his best, *The Hidden Room* (1949) and *Give Us This Day* (1949), both made in England while he was still blacklisted in the United States, are now lost. As a director he was unusually sensitive to the political currents around him. As a nominal Communist, he directed some of the best of Hollywood's postwar "social problem" films: *Cornered* (1945), *Till the End of Time* (1946), and *Crossfire* (1947), Hollywood's first tract against anti-Semitism. As a repentant ex-Communist he directed the first manifesto of the therapeutic liberalism of the fifties, *The Sniper* (1952), and one of the most striking expressions of the period's obscurantist reaction, *The Caine Mutiny* (1954). Although his symptomatic importance in the history of this era will always outweigh the artistic significance of his films, I cannot help feeling that he has been underrated as a film director.

Adrian Scott, Dmytryk's favored producer during his Communist period, was clearly one of the most intelligent writer-producers working in Hollywood during the mid-forties; almost every picture he worked on—from *Mr. Lucky* (1943) to *Cross-fire* (1947)—was better than it had any right to be.

Ring Lardner Jr. already had one Academy Award when he appeared before HUAC, an award he shared with Michael Kanin for the screenplay of *Woman of the Year* (1942). He was young enough to come back and win another one in 1971. While he was blacklisted, he wrote one very good novel, *The Ecstasy of Owen Muir* (1954), which could not find a major trade publisher in the United States until 1972.

Albert Maltz's best film was his one collaboration with Lardner, *Cloak and Dagger* (1946). He wrote a few other interesting screenplays, *The Naked City* (1948) and *Two Mules for Sister Sara* (1970), a Clint Eastwood western that offered a parable about the Vietnam War sympathetic to the Vietcong, but his reputation will finally rest on his novels. *The Cross and the Arrow* and *The Underground Stream* will be rediscovered when "proletarian fiction" finally can be read without political prejudice.

John Howard Lawson has become the classic American example of the promising writer destroyed by a commitment to Communism. Murray Kempton sketched the liberal version of this legend in *Part of Our Time*, John Dos Passos offered a more elaborate conservative version in his novel *Most Likely to Succeed*, and Margaret Brenman-Gibson developed a sophisticated psychoanalytic version in her 1981 biography of Clifford Odets. No one would question Lawson's talent, only how much of it was still intact in 1947. The blacklist may have freed him, as it did Biberman and Lardner. He had written three good off-beat war films during World War II, *Counter-Attack* (1945), *Action in the North Atlantic* (1943), and *Sahara* (1943), all of them notable for pro-Soviet sympathies, and Hollywood's single pro-Loyalist film, *Blockade* (1938). *Counter-Attack*, the most radical film of the war, is the only American movie with a Russian Communist as hero, and *Sahara* is one of a handful adapted from a Soviet film. The merchant marine crew of *Action in the North Atlantic* includes one crypto-Communist from Brooklyn who can translate for his mates when their ship finally reaches Murmansk: "Tovarichki—that means 'comrade,' that's good." Lawson's detractors like to point out that as coscenarist of *Algiers* he can also be credited with the line, "Come with me to the casbah." In any case, they argue, his filmscripts do not fulfill the promise he showed as a founder of the New Playwrights Theatre in the 1920s.

After being blacklisted Lawson turned to writing history and criticism. His final work, *Film: The Creative Process*, an attempt to set forth a comprehensive theory of the cinema that appeared in the mid-1960s, seemed dated in its commitment to classical realism and its uncomprehending rejection of Godard and Antonioni—the last gasp of an old and fruitless kind of Marxism. But his pamphlet *Film in the Battle of Ideas* is in my opinion a minor classic of Marxist criticism. It was completely ignored when it was published by a Communist press in 1953, and it is still not as well known as it deserves to be. Were it more widely read, we would be spared a great deal of silliness in writing about Hollywood films of the 1950s.

Dalton Trumbo was one of the most successful and celebrated screenwriters in Hollywood both before and after being blacklisted, but the critics have never shared the producers' enthusiasm for his work. The publication of his selected correspondence in 1970 gave rise to the melancholy speculation that he had saved his best writing for bill collectors, plumbers, and other small businessmen. But as more and more of his pseudonymous credits have come to light, it has become apparent that his best work was done while he was on the blacklist. *Gun Crazy* (1949), *The Prowler* (1951), and *He Ran All the Way* (1951) are good enough for us to forgive his more lucrative ventures.

The Ten were only the first wave of blacklist victims. In the 1950s there were hundreds more. Many of those caught in the second and third wave of the blacklist were members of a younger generation whose first film credits dated from the late forties. Since all the histories of the blacklist assume that whatever possibilities there were for left-wing filmmaking in Hollywood must have ended with the black-listing of the Hollywood Ten in 1947, the work of this new generation is not taken into account when the effect of the blacklist on the Hollywood cinema is assessed. But the films made by Robert Rossen, Abraham Polonsky, Joseph Losey, Jules Dassin, John Berry, and Cyril Endfield between 1947 and 1951 are the most significant achievements of the victims of the Hollywood blacklist.

I believe that these men and their artistic fellow travelers created a new genre of Hollywood films in the late 1940s, between the first HUAC hearings of October 1947 and the second of May 1951. It has not been recognized as such because its development was cut off prematurely when the blacklist was extended beyond its first victims in 1951. I have been tempted to give it a name, although I would be relieved if no one should adopt it. Because this genre grew out of the body of films that have come retrospectively to be called film noir and because it may be distinguished from the earlier noir by its greater psychological and social realism, I will call the genre film gris. The term seems appropriate because we have been taught to associate Communism with drabness and greyness, and these films are often drab and depressing and almost always photographed in black-and-white.

I count thirteen films as composing this genre: Robert Rossen's *Body and Soul* (1947), Abraham Polonsky's *Force of Evil* (1948), Jules Dassin's *Thieves' Highway* (1949) and *Night and the City* (1950), Nicholas Ray's *They Live by Night* (1949) and *Knock on Any Door* (1949), John Huston's *We Were Strangers* (1949) and *The Asphalt Jungle* (1950), Michael Curtiz's *The Breaking Point* (1950), Joseph Losey's *The Lawless* (1950) and *The Prowler* (1951), Cyril Endfield's *Try and Get Me* (1951), and John Berry's *He Ran All the Way* (1951). There may be others I have not seen. This is not a large body of work, but most classic film genres are smaller than we assume them to be. My attribution of these films to their directors is no more than a shorthand expedient; the concept of director as author is too simplistic for the kind of film history I want to propose. In some instances the contribution of a writer or an actor is more significant. But it is necessary to break with histories of the blacklist that consider only screenwriters, and that tendency has been accentuated in the most recent wave of histories. In claiming that these films constitute a genre, I am claiming they deserve a more sustained attention than I can give them here. I shall limit myself to a few preliminary remarks, which I hope will at least suggest that a history of the blacklist must take account of the films made by its victims and that a history of the Hollywood cinema must register the displacements brought about by the blacklist even if it restricts itself to textual evidence, that is, to the films themselves.

The first axiom of film gris is John Garfield. Garfield was the first "method actor" to become a Hollywood star, and he remains the greatest, in my opinion. But I also happen to agree with Julie Burchill's characterization of Garfield: "The most beautiful and talented actor ever to have lived."[82] When I write that John Garfield is an axiom, I mean it in the same sense in which Michel Mourlet once wrote, "Charlton Heston is an axiom. By himself alone he constitutes a tragedy, and his presence in any film whatsoever suffices to create beauty." Mourlet's remarks on Heston achieved a certain notoriety in the Anglo-American film world when Richard Roud quoted them in *Sight and Sound* as his most extreme example of the deliriums of French film criticism.[83] That was in 1960 when *Cahiers du Cinéma* was a safe target for ridicule. Twenty years later it is possible to recognize at least a half-truth in Mourlet's abject hagiography: Charlton Heston was more important than critics were willing to recognize. With his midcult sobriety and his safely conservative politics, he incarnated perfectly the values of mid-1950s American cinema.

Just as Heston perfectly represented America's Protestant middle class, even when portraying Moses in *The Ten Commandments*, John Garfield managed to embody in his screen persona a group that had never before appeared in American films, the Jewish working class. He remains an exemplary figure—above all perhaps because he was fated to live out in his own life his archetypal film role: a kid from the streets of the slums, ambitious, talented, sensitive but tough, fighting his way up only to discover that success doesn't mean the end of moral choice. Garfield had a special knack for projecting brashness and vulnerability at the same time. In her biography of Odets, Margaret Brenman-Gibson relates an anecdote that provides a clue to the psychic source of this ability. The principal of P.S. 45 in the Bronx cured Garfield's chronic truancy by appealing to him on behalf of the flowerbed Garfield inadvertently trampled as he leaped over the wall. "Son, don't you know those flowers have a right to live, too?" the principal Angelo Patri told Garfield, and after that he stayed in school.[84]

Garfield starred in the films that defined and inaugurated the film gris genre, and it was his power as a movie star that allowed them to be made. He had come to Hollywood in 1938 after establishing himself as a stage actor with the Group Theatre in Clifford Odets's *Awake and Sing*. Odets then wrote *Golden Boy* for Garfield, but Harold Clurman insisted on casting Luther Adler in the lead role, consigning Garfield to a bit part as a comic relief cab driver. So Garfield was in a receptive mood when an offer of a movie contract came from the Warner brothers. He was not pleased, however, that they insisted he change his name—his stage name Jules Garfield sounded too Jewish to the Warners. Still it was fortunate that he began his career at Warner Bros. Whatever Jack Warner told HUAC in 1947, his studio had a lasting commitment to the "social problem film" and the Warners were Holly-wood's leading "premature anti-fascists." While MGM supported the war effort by celebrating the stoic courage of the English bourgeoisie in films like *Mrs. Miniver*, Warners carried on the celluloid war with the same lurid characters, drawn from the depths of the lumpenproletariat who had populated their films of the 1930s.

At any other studio Garfield's special gifts would have been wasted. But he resented the studio system that allowed him no choice over the films in which he appeared. When Warner Bros. refused to loan him to Columbia for the film version of *Golden Boy* and he lost another chance at the role Clifford Odets had written for him, he took the first of nine suspensions without pay for refusing an assigned project. When his Warners contract expired after seven years, Garfield didn't give any serious thought to a renewal. He immediately formed his own production company with producer Bob Roberts.

For their first venture, Garfield gave his favorite writer from Warner Bros., Robert Rossen, his first opportunity to direct. The film was *Body and Soul*, a prize-fighting movie with an original screenplay by an unknown writer named Abraham Polonsky, which brought the street poetry Odets had synthesized in his plays of the thirties into the American cinema for the first time. It ended with Garfield's most famous line, "What can they do, kill me? Everybody dies." It was the first film gris. The following year Polonsky wrote and directed Garfield's second independent film, *Force of Evil*, adapted from Ira Wolfert's novel about the numbers racket, *Tucker's People*. Polonsky's dialogue in *Force of Evil* is even more stylized than it had been in *Body and Soul*. It becomes a kind of vernacular blank verse, and it is spoken with an uncanny feeling for its rhythms by Garfield, Thomas Gomez, and Beatrice Pearson. Both these films have received eloquent praise, but their thematic originality has not been appreciated.

Polonsky called Wolfert's novel an autopsy on capitalism, and the characterization fits both of the films he made with Garfield. That was something new in Hollywood. The left-wing "social problem" films of the 1930s, like the social documentaries of that period, were protests against vestiges of feudalism in American society; the most frequent targets were sharecropping, contract prison labor, and forms of peonage based on racism. The only critique of capitalism in the American cinema came from the radical right, in the films of Frank Capra and King Vidor. *Body and Soul* and *Force of Evil* are both set on the margins of American society, but they implicate the entire system of capitalism in their criticisms. Again a comment on Wolfert's novel provides an apt description of the films. In her review for the *Nation*, Diana Trilling wrote, "If [Wolfert] writes about gangsterism, it is as an aspect of our whole predatory economic structure, and at least by implication his novel is as much a novel of legitimate American business methods and business people as it is of racketeering. . . . What Mr. Wolfert is saying is that gangsters are little different from their legitimate brothers, they have the same amount of principle and are driven by the same fears and insecurities, 'cutting the world to measure as they can and cutting themselves to measure where they have to.'"[85]

I have never believed that organized crime could be portrayed to serve as an interesting metaphor for business enterprise. Marx's critique of Proudhon convinced me that property is *not* theft. But the point in these two films is not that property is theft, rather that theft is property. In other words, *Body and Soul* and *Force of Evil* do not advance a claim that business is criminal, only that criminality can be businesslike. The businesses dissected in these two films just happen to be illegal. Thus the films can offer a critique of capitalism in the guise of an exposé of crime. In both films, despite the bleakness in their vision of American capitalism, there is a sense of exhilaration in the work itself, as if the filmmakers felt liberated by the knowledge that this critique could finally be expressed openly.

Why had it taken so long? The filmmakers who created film gris were Browderite Communists and left-liberals. During the war they had enthusiastically made patriotic films, and at the beginning of 1945 they had shared Browder's optimism about the postwar world. Anything seemed possible if the energies harnessed to win the war could be utilized to build a better society. It took more than Duclos's critique of Browder to convince them they were wrong. But by 1947 Henry Wallace, the most prominent representative of these "progressives" in mainstream politics, had been forced out of Truman's administration; the Taft-Hartley Act had been passed; and the Truman Doctrine had been announced in March 1947 to justify America's first major postwar counterinsurgency campaign in Greece. By 1947 the new line of the American Communist Party corresponded to a general sentiment on the left. This feeling was recalled by Joseph Losey in an interview with Michel Ciment in the late 1970s: "The conflicts and optimism of the thirties made it difficult to accept the brutality and the degradation of the end of the forties. . . . But after Hiroshima, after the death of Roosevelt, after the investigations, only then did one begin to understand the complete unreality of the American dream."[86]

The unreality of the American dream is a constant theme in film gris. In Losey's film *The Prowler* and in Endfield's *Try and Get Me*, this disillusionment produced chilling portrayals of the psychological injuries of class. The unsympathetic protagonist of *The Prowler*, Webb Garwood (Van Heflin), is a uniformed cop who feels he has been cheated out of the good life. He lost his college athletic scholarship because he got into an argument with the coach over playing time. "Just another of my lousy breaks," he says. "If it hadn't been for that, I would have my four years of college. I would have had a nice soft job at one of those big bond houses." He could have been "one of those guys who shows up around ten in the morning after having a big argument with himself over whether he'll drive the station wagon today or the convertible." His vision of upward mobility has gone sour, and he is drifting through life as "just another cop." After rejecting the stolid working-class values of his father ("My old man's idea of success was a buck-twenty an hour, union-scale"), he has nothing to rely on but cynicism and envy. He has one dream left: to own a motor court in Las Vegas. "Even when you're sleeping," he notes, "it's making money for you." To get his motel, he is able to plan and execute a bold and intricate seduction and murder plot. In *Try and Get Me*, Jerry Slocum (Lloyd Bridges) begins on the other side of the law as a petty stick-up man, but he

is driven by the same sense of *ressentiment*. He teams up with an unemployed veteran to kidnap the richest young man in town, Donald Miller, and he carries out
the kidnapping as a private class war. As he drives Miller to his death, he can't resist
admiring Miller's suit and asking where he bought it. After Miller imperiously
announces that he goes to a tailor "back East," Slocum responds, "You rich guys
sure know how to treat yourselves." Such an acknowledgment of class envy had
not appeared before in Hollywood films and it would not again. If the American
dream could go this far wrong, the dream was empty to begin with.

At the end of *Try and Get Me*, Slocum and his partner are captured and then
lynched, in the most unrelenting and disturbing scene of mob violence I have ever
seen in a Hollywood movie. On one level it is a remarkable tour de force of action
filmmaking, like the battle scenes Endfield directed in *Zulu* fourteen years later, but
it is conceived without the compromises that generally soften lynching scenes in
Hollywood movies. The crowd is implacable, the forces of order demoralized and
ineffectual; the liberals who might be counted on to dissuade the mob with a
noble speech can only watch helplessly. The lynch mob itself is composed to
implicate the film's audience. Endfield avoids the grotesque types who usually pre-
dominate in a Hollywood lynch mob. He places at the front of the mob a number
of clean-cut young men wearing college sweatshirts. Film reviewers had complained
with some justice about the sudden last-reel reversals that so often transformed the
social problem films of the 1930s and 1940s from bleak tragedies to sentimental,
ameliorative fantasies, but they found the bleakness of *Try and Get Me* no more
appealing. In the *New York Times*, Bosley Crowther noted that the thesis of Endfield's
film was humane, but he felt it was not "constructively advanced." There was nothing positive about the film: "Unfortunately, the arguments are so doleful and negative in this film that they offer no demonstration of correction and even hope."[87]

Lynching was an important theme in film gris—Losey had treated it somewhat
more conventionally the year before in *The Lawless*. It is as if the future victims of
the blacklist were creating presumptive allegories of their own impending fates
(just as those who favored cooperation with HUAC began to make films presenting
informers in a sympathetic light). Some of the writers who were blacklisted could
still earn a diminished income by selling pseudonymous scripts to independent
production companies. Directors, however, had to be physically present during the
shooting of a film to practice their craft. If they wanted to continue making films,
their only choice was exile. Joseph Losey and Cyril Endfield moved to England,
Jules Dassin and John Berry to France. Only Losey may have ultimately benefited
from this forced relocation. Eventually he found in Europe greater freedom to pursue his vision of filmmaking, but even Losey had a blighted career; as Gilles Jacob
wrote in 1966, "The prime Losey hero is Losey himself, who seems destined to be
remembered less for his mutilated body of work—a sort of dress rehearsal for an
ideal film which never materializes—than for his intellectual journeying in search
of a style."[88] Endfield managed to direct a few good films in England, most notably
Hell Drivers (1957) and *Zulu* (1964). Dassin was able to adapt some of Hollywood's
most reliable genres to a European context before succumbing to a schematic

classicism. John Berry was the youngest of the blacklist victims; he was only thirty-three when he directed John Garfield's last film, *He Ran All the Way*. He was able to work only sporadically in France, and then only in unpromising genre films. He returned to Hollywood in the seventies, and he directed *The Bad News Bears Go to Japan* when he was sixty-one.

But it was the blacklisted actors who suffered the most. Their craft is particularly resistant to transplantation. For a number of them the blacklist meant a literal death. In a 1941 version of *The Sea Wolf*, Robert Rossen had given John Garfield the line, "There's a price no man will pay to keep on living." In *Body and Soul*, he plays a boxer who allows himself to be convinced he should throw a bout but fights back when he isn't allowed to lose with dignity. His manager betrays him once too often, and he discovers he has to resist. These are two of the most striking of the fictional premonitions of Garfield's encounter with HUAC. He was subpoenaed to testify in the second round of HUAC's Hollywood investigations in April 1951. He was already finding it difficult to get good parts because he was "too controversial"; producers who would have hired him a year or two earlier were now telling agents, "find me a John Garfield type." He said he felt like a baseball player when everybody on the team knows he's going to be traded. Although there is no evidence Garfield was ever a member of the Communist Party, he had associated closely with Communists since the beginning of his career. He had hired Communists to write and direct the films he produced.

He thought he could save his career and avoid naming names by denouncing Communism while claiming he had never known any live Communists. "I think [Communism] is a subversive movement and is a tyranny and is a dictatorship and is against democracy," he told the committee. He even suggested that the Communist Party should be outlawed. But he insisted that he had never known any Party members. This testimony was received with considerable skepticism. Archer Winsten, the *New York Post* film critic, helpfully pointed out that no one could have lived in New York during the 1930s without knowing a single Communist. (True enough, one imagines, but Winsten's logic suggests that the committee could have subpoenaed everyone who lived in New York and asked them which of their neighbors were Communists.) There were rumors that the committee was pondering a perjury indictment. No new parts were coming; obviously Garfield had not been "cleared." More disturbingly, old friends from the Group Theatre such as Clifford Odets, Elia Kazan, and Lee J. Cobb, who had advised Garfield against testifying and then accused him of betraying the cause in which they all believed, were now going farther than he had by giving the committee the names of other old friends. Garfield gave hints he was preparing to follow their lead. But his heart wouldn't let him. It stopped first. Garfield died of a coronary thrombosis on May 20, 1952.

Clifford Odets wrote the official obituary, the one printed in the *New York Times*, but fresh from his testimony before HUAC, he couldn't say what blacklist victim Abraharn Polonsky did: "He said he hated Communists, he hated Communism, he was an American. He told the committee what it wanted to hear. But he wouldn't say the one thing that would keep him from walking down his old neighborhood block. Nobody could say, 'Hey, there's the fucking stool pigeon.' "[89]

In the long run, Andrew Sarris's judgment is certainly correct: "The Hollywood blacklist of the '50s was an undeniably obscene ritual, and many talented people were damaged and destroyed thereby. The fact remains that a great deal of interesting work was made before, during, and after the blacklist."[90] In other words, it is futile to speculate about what might have been. Where can such speculation end? If there had been no blacklist. . . . There would have been no blacklist if the rage that animates John Garfield's best work had been suppressed in any of the usual ways. And there were many others in Hollywood who kept alive the knowledge that nobody lives forever. Finally, it would be an injustice to those who were blacklisted to say they did nothing to deserve it. A history of the blacklist must first of all be worthy of them. That is not so easy. As a reminder of the difficulties to be faced, we might bear in mind Walter Benjamin's sixth thesis on the philosophy of history: "To articulate the past historically does not mean to recognize it 'the way it really was.' It means to seize hold of a memory as it flashes up at a moment of danger. . . . The danger affects both the content of the tradition and its receivers. The same threat hangs over both: becoming a tool of the ruling class. . . . To fan the spark of hope that exists in the past, the historian must be firmly convinced that *even the dead* will not be safe from the enemy if he wins. And this enemy has not ceased to be victorious."[91]

Afterword

Thom Andersen

The republication of "Red Hollywood" after twenty years is for me a somewhat melancholy occasion. I always regarded it as a preliminary text, a historiographical prelude to the definitive study of the Hollywood blacklist I would one day write. But that day never quite arrived, although my interests in the questions I posed there never waned.

I have returned to these questions a number of times in the past two decades, and these subsequent works have been enriched by collaboration with my friend Noël Burch. In 1986 we began to dream about making a film that would prove that the victims of the blacklist had created a distinctive and significant body of film work, a claim advanced too circumspectly in "Red Hollywood." We never could raise the money for the film (although we received grants for research from the Ohio Arts Council and the Center for New Television), so we produced a cheap video version in the summer of 1995. We called it *Red Hollywood*. It was shown at a lot of film festivals and almost nowhere else.

While we were struggling to produce the movie, we put together a book published by the Presses de la Sorbonne Nouvelle in 1994, titled *Les Communistes de Hollywood: Autre chose que des martyrs*. In English that would be something like *The Communists of Hollywood: Not Just Martyrs* (shorter, but less elegant). It included "Red Hollywood" in French translation, which I had revised and abridged (having already come to regard its passages on the film work of the Hollywood Ten as excessively ignorant), along with three other texts. One of these was an essay I wrote for the catalogue of the 1991 Rotterdam Film Festival to accompany a retrospective program organized by Bernard Eisenschitz that he called "Nicholas Ray in Context." I was able to develop my account of film gris and write about some of the earliest films written by the future blacklist victims: *The Public Enemy* (1931), *Hell's Highway* (1932), and *Success at Any Price* (1934). Noël Burch contributed an essay on the feminism of the Hollywood Communists, its strengths and limitations, and together we compiled and annotated a list of what we then regarded as their most significant films. We briefly tried to find an American publisher for this book, but we retreated at the first signs of resistance. It began to seem inadequate to us, and the videotape *Red Hollywood* expressed more pointedly what we most wanted to say.

Occasionally the video inspired a film programmer to schedule a series of films written or directed by blacklist victims. The most ambitious of these programs gave us an opportunity to recontextualize all our previous work on the Hollywood blacklist. For a program he titled "Blacklisted: Movies by the Hollywood Blacklist Victims," Hans Hurch, the director of the Viennale (the Vienna International Film Festival), allowed us to pick the thirty-nine films that were screened at the Austrian Film Museum throughout the month of October 2000 and to contribute as much as we wanted to the catalogue edited by Andreas Ungerböck. Noël revised the essay he wrote for *Les Communistes de Hollywood*, and I wrote an introductory essay and brief commentaries on three of the more obscure films in the program: *Way Down South* (1939), *I Stole a Million* (1939), and *Shakedown* (1950). All in all, this catalogue is a valuable document, quite apart from our contributions, and I wish it were more easily accessible.

So all my work on the blacklist is fugitive and ephemeral, beginning with "Red Hollywood" itself, which was out of place in an anthology of critical essays and interviews on fine arts with the absurdly generic title *Literature and the Visual Arts in Contemporary Society*, published ironically by the press of an institution, the Ohio State University, that had just fired me in a political purge. After "Red Hollywood," there is a videotape without a commercial distributor, a book published by an obscure French academic press culled primarily from work that had appeared previously, and contributions to two film festival catalogues.

The promise of "Red Hollywood" remains unfulfilled then, but Noël and I have managed to demonstrate, again and again, that it would be an injustice to those who were blacklisted to say they did nothing to deserve it (to quote one of the last sentences of "Red Hollywood"). The Hollywood Communists did leave a permanent impress upon the screen, and not only in the thirteen films I singled out in "Red Hollywood" as constituting film gris. Of course, film noir provided a fertile terrain for depicting the pathologies of class relations in capitalist society, and I still think that some of the films I cited are among the most significant achievements of the blacklist victims. Today I would add to the list at least four films I didn't know then: *Road House* (1948), written by Edward Chodorov; *Not Wanted* (1949), Ida Lupino's first directorial effort, co-written by Lupino and Paul Jarrico; *Quicksand* (1950), directed by Irving Pichel; and *Shakedown* (1950), co-written by Alfred Lewis Levitt. *Quicksand* featured an avaricious blonde whose lust for a mink coat leads the amiable working-class hero into a downward spiral of crime and desperation, but the other three feature male predators for whom women are purely and simply objects to exploit.

I might also add the 1950s British noir films of Cy Endfield and Joseph Losey. In these still obscure and underrated films, Endfield and Losey laid the groundwork for the resurgence of British cinema in the 1960s. I could also mention a noir western, *The Man from Colorado* (1948), co-written by Ben Maddow. In my view, it is the only Hollywood western that systematically subverts the conservative ethos of the genre. (The anti-blacklist westerns *High Noon* and *Johnny Guitar* exploit the implicit aristocratic bias of the genre to position their heroes as potential victims of a populist hysteria.)

Finally, two exceptional films released in 1939 appear in retrospect to anticipate both film noir and film gris. In *I Stole a Million*, written by fellow traveler Nathanael

West from a story outline by Lester Cole, a tough but guileless cab driver falls into a life of crime when he is victimized by a credit scam (much like the hero in *Quicksand*). *Back Door to Heaven*, written by John Bright and Robert Tasker from a story by Christian socialist director William K. Howard, traces the stories of four childhood friends for whom class is destiny. The poorest and noblest of the group, Frankie Rogers, faces bleaker prospects than any later film noir hero, but he maintains an almost saintly equanimity in the face of any setback, even a death sentence for a crime he didn't commit. Because in this movie injustice is a given, there is no need to dwell on the cruelty and irony of fate. The tone is very different from forties film noir, in which self-pity is a pervasive sentiment.

Two sympathetic critics of "Red Hollywood" have proposed some other films that I might have included. In *Something More Than Night: Film Noir in Its Contexts*, James Naremore posits a "left-wing school or community" of filmmakers who "often gave a social-realist spin to familiar noirish plots."[1] He writes perceptively about *Force of Evil*, *The Sound of Fury*, and *The Asphalt Jungle*. He carefully analyzes the contradictions and evasions of a film I omitted, Edward Dmytryk's *Crossfire* (1947), confirming, I believe, the summary criticism Noël and I offered in *Les Communistes de Hollywood*: "The anti-racist message is subverted by the codes of the genre and by an authoritarian tone that prefigures the fifties."[2] But Naremore shows that the censorship imposed by RKO and the Production Code Administration also weakened its message, and he concludes, "Despite its many compromises and concessions to censorship, *Crossfire* mounted a strong attack on domestic fascism."[3]

More briefly, Naremore cites seven other films that may be placed in the vicinity of film gris. Three of these may also be regarded as critiques of domestic fascism. Following Brecht, if only dimly, John Huston's *Key Largo* (1948) suggests an affinity between Nazi tyrants and Hollywood gangsters. Set in a penitentiary that may be regarded as a microcosm of an authoritarian society, Jules Dassin's *Brute Force* (1947) is clearly an anti-fascist allegory, but I still find it sentimental and overwrought. Robert Rossen's *All the King's Men* (1949) traces the rise and fall of a southern demagogue with fascist tendencies—modeled on Huey Long—from the viewpoint of a disillusioned follower. The contempt for the people evident in this film is disturbing, and it brought harsh criticism from the Communist press, hastening Rossen's disengagement from the Party and his eventual apostasy before the House Un-American Activities Committee.

I have fewer reservations about the other four films he mentions. Joseph Losey's *M* (1951) is a creditable, underrated transposition of Lang's film from Berlin to Los Angeles, in which the association between the criminal underworld and monopoly capital is even more evident than in the original. Naremore calls it "documentary-style."[4] Losey's film gives that impression because it features the most striking location photography of any Los Angeles noir film before *Kiss Me Deadly* (Robert Aldrich, the director of *Kiss Me Deadly*, was Losey's assistant on *M*). Edgar Ulmer's *Ruthless* (1948), co-written by blacklist victims Alvah Bessie and Gordon Kahn along with S. K. Lauren, is a low-rent version of *Citizen Kane*, a review of a tycoon's life told in flashbacks. It is certainly less flamboyant than *Kane*, but it is perhaps more sophisticated in its delineation of capitalist competition and more complex in the characterization of its protagonist. Noël would include Joseph H. Lewis's *Gun Crazy* (1949), co-written by Dalton Trumbo, in what he calls *film noir de gauche* for its definitive treatment of America's exceptionalist fascination with firearms. He would also include Nicholas Ray's *In a Lonely Place*, one of the few examples of film noir that offers a critique of male narcissism. In his early films, Ray was especially sensitive to the empty ceremonies of masculinity and the falseness of proscribed sexual roles.

So much for film gris. I'm not attached to the term or the concept, as I suggested in "Red Hollywood." I wrote then, "I would be relieved if no one adopted it." I implied it was advanced half in jest, an ironic play on the stereotyped association of Communism with drabness, an association I despised as the arrogant boast of a complacent consumerism. I had in mind noir films in which a social critique carries more weight then a psychological diagnosis. In film gris, work, class, money, and sometimes race are dramatic issues for the characters, just as they are for us in our lives outside the movies. But like film noir, the term film gris can't be defined so that any film can be definitively placed inside or outside its borders. There are always marginal cases. For example, *The Strange Love of Martha Ivers*, written by Robert Rossen, is a film about class and capitalism, contrasting solid working-class values against the decadence of the bourgeoisie, but the plot turns on a classically Freudian primal scene and its misogyny is evident.

Not Wanted is a more interesting borderline case. Is it a noir film or a woman's picture? The heroine's troubles are overdetermined by poverty, an unsympathetic American Gothic family, and unrequited love. The story is simple: seduced and abandoned by an itinerant jazz pianist, small-town waitress Sally Kelton (Sally Forrest) gives birth to a child she can't keep and goes mad from the loss and guilt. Her seducer, portrayed brilliantly by future blacklist victim Leo Penn, is perhaps the first hipster in Hollywood movies: cynical, rootless, self-absorbed. Her would-be savior is the relentlessly cheerful manager of a self-service gas station who gives her a job and falls in love with her, but he has a prosthetic calf that is evidently stigmatic of an impotence that he assuages by playing with an elaborate model train set. In the end, he must chase Sally across a bridge spanning the Los Angeles railroad yards to find redemption and reconciliation. Jarrico disowned the film, except for the remarkable monologue Sally addresses to her newborn child, which we quoted in *Red Hollywood*. Couldn't you take care of yourself while I'm at work? she asks the infant. "Wash your own diapers and feed yourself? Fix your own bottle?" Perhaps Jarrico found its portrait of masculine irresponsibility and immaturity— which may be attributed to Lupino—too discomforting. In my introduction to the Viennale catalogue, I called *Not Wanted* "the great masterpiece of Hollywood Freudian-Marxist neorealism."[5] I'd say anything to rescue this film from the unjust neglect that has been its fate, but I do believe it reveals the promise and possibilities of an American neorealism that was prematurely cut off by the blacklist. Like Rossellini's films of the early fifties, it is a drama of perception: Sally experiences a world that is indifferent to her and an everyday reality that is unbearable.

Of course, I should acknowledge that film gris as I have defined it need not be the exclusive province of blacklist victims. In "Red Hollywood," I mentioned *The Breaking Point* although only its star, John Garfield, was a victim of the blacklist (and he was never a Communist Party member). Although neither director Michael Curtiz nor screenwriter Ranald MacDougall were blacklist victims, it is, I remain convinced, one of the strongest films in the genre, especially for its bitterly ironic treatment of racism in an era when disavowal of the real racial problems prevailed.

Nothing is made of the racial differences between charter boat captain Harry Morgan (Garfield) and his gentle black first mate Wesley Park (Juano Hernandez), although their characters play against racial stereotypes, until the very end of the film. Then as Morgan strives desperately to hang onto his boat and his way of life, he allows it to be used by four racetrack robbers as a getaway vessel, knowing that they will kill him if he can't kill them first. Although he is badly wounded, he does manage to kill the robbers, but not before they kill Wesley and throw his body overboard. A crowd gathers to meet the Coast Guard cutter that brings Morgan back to shore, and it drifts away when the ambulance takes him to the hospital. Nobody notices Wesley Park's young son in the crowd. In the last shot, the boy is alone on the pier waiting for a father who will never return. Nobody else has noticed that the first mate is missing. Nobody comes to console the boy. Father and son are both invisible men.

I included another Garfield film, *We Were Strangers*, directed by John Huston and written by Trotskyist Peter Viertel, although I only dimly remembered it, primarily because of the hysterical denunciations it inspired in the Los Angeles press. The reviewer for the *Hollywood Reporter* called it "Red propaganda." But he was wrong. In its treatment of revolutionary struggle in Latin America, *We Were Strangers* is as conservative as *Viva Zapata!* It is set safely in the past: 1933, Cuba, in the final days of the Machado dictatorship. In orthodox noir fashion, Garfield's band of revolutionaries is doomed not only to failure but also to moral compromise: they target and assassinate the most humane of the government's leaders in a misguided, almost absurd plot to blow up his more venal colleagues at his funeral. To atone for his ruthless but ineffectual plotting, Garfield must die, bravely but futilely. *We Were Strangers* demonstrates once again that Hollywood can represent revolutionary struggles only insofar as they fail.

Of course, a focus on film gris provides an excessively narrow perspective on the film work of the blacklist victims. Noël and I tried to broaden this perspective in our movie *Red Hollywood* and in our book *Les Communistes de Hollywood*. In *Red Hollywood*, we presented excerpts from 44 films written or directed by blacklist victims or former Communists. We tried to let the films speak for themselves, without extensive commentaries, and we didn't claim our survey was exhaustive. However, we did make an effort to suggest the distinctiveness (and sometimes the distinction) of the work created by the blacklist victims not only in film noir, but also in the social problem film, the woman's film, as well as in explicitly political films such as *Blockade* (1938). In *Les Communistes de Hollywood*, we offered brief commentaries on 128 films. We watched many more, but we didn't try to see every available film directed or written by a blacklist victim. When the reviews and plot summaries indicated a routine effort, we passed.

On the other hand, Paul Buhle and Dave Wagner apparently did set out to see everything. After only fourteen years of research, they published four books in three years (from 2001 to 2003) on the film work of the blacklist victims, some 1,318 pages in all. Their work is exhaustive (although they somehow forgot *Shakedown* and *The Story on Page One* [1959], the second and final film directed by Clifford Odets) and arguably overreaching. They claim that "the collective contribution of these artists to popular filmmaking was astonishing." Their output "contains a surprising number . . . of the best films Hollywood ever made."[6]

Is this then the definitive study I never wrote? I think it is fair to characterize their work as controversial, but unfortunately the controversy has not been very edifying. Most reviews have been favorable, but their measured praise was always mixed with certain reservations so they have been overshadowed by a few notably vituperative responses.

The strangest of these responses are two pseudonymous letters (signed "Martin Brady") published in the nominally left-wing film magazine *Cineaste* that alternate between recitals of small errors (real, imagined, and questionable) and hyperbolic denunciations that are widely disproportionate to the detailed criticisms offered. The first letter, a response to a sympathetic review by James Naremore of Buhle and Wagner's first book, *A Very Dangerous Citizen: Abraham Lincoln Polonsky and the Hollywood Left*, ended by demanding that the book "ought to be recalled like any defective product and buyers refunded their money."[7] When *Cineaste* published a moderately favorable review of *Hide in Plain Sight: The Hollywood Blacklistees in Film and Television, 1950–2002*, the third book in their blacklist quartet, he responded with even more acrimony (this book by "the demented duo" should be "recalled—and pulped") and also took the editors to task for not paying sufficient heed to his earlier letter and "persisting in lending credence to these con men by continually drawing respectful attention to their pernicious efforts—which will poison libraries and corrupt credulous readers and researchers for years to come."[8]

Remarkably, the editors responded with a qualified endorsement of his position. The "litany of errors" produced by "Martin Brady" (which they accepted uncritically) raised serious doubts about the value of *Hide in Plain Sight*, and they weren't troubled about his motives: "As far as we can see, he is a merely an aggrieved film buff who is mightily perturbed by sloppy scholarship."

Moreover, they concluded, "We feel it our duty to warn our readers that Buhle and Wagner's latest book, *Blacklisted: The Film Lover's Guide to the Hollywood Blacklist* [a directory of films with contributions by blacklist victims, listed in alphabetical order], is likewise awash in significant factual errors and numerous misinterpretations." None of these significant errors or misinterpretations is specified. Okay, I found a few errors without searching too hard. A single film has two separate titles on the same page. Is it *The Jolson Story* or *The Al Jolson Story*? They write that Lana Turner plays the wife of the accused man in *They Won't Forget* (1937);

actually she plays the murder victim. They write that Jeanne Cagney plays Mickey Rooney's spurned girl friend in *Quicksand*; actually she plays the temptress who lures him away. Some of the movie summaries are muddled, but I wouldn't characterize them as misinterpretations. I do disagree with many of their critical judgments. I would say that their taste is midcult. They dismiss *Johnny Guitar*, and they overpraise *The Majestic*, *The Way We Were*, and *High Noon* ("an uncompromised . . . masterpiece"). Still their perspective enables them to write originally and provocatively about the most familiar films they treat. *Blacklisted* deserved a review from *Cineaste*, not a one-sentence dismissal.

Furthermore, the editors' insistence that "Martin Brady" has no hidden axe to grind seems to me astonishingly naïve. The tone of his letters is too hysterical for someone who is just an aggrieved film fan. The work of Buhle and Wagner is needlessly, inexplicably sloppy, but concentrated attention to scholarly precision from reviewers is almost always selective—and partisan. The errors of Los Angeles historian Mike Davis became a scandal when he published *Ecology of Fear* (he was almost literally driven out of town), but the more egregious errors of his friend and fellow historian Kevin Starr have passed unnoticed. Why? Davis's books divide; Starr's unite. Davis is writing history that challenges the reader's preconceptions, while Starr is writing consensus history that flatters the reader's sense of enlightened liberalism.

Like Buhle and Wagner, Davis and Starr both write too much (although it would be churlish to demand they curtail their production). But even those of us who write too little are not immune to sloppiness. When the University of California Press sent the English manuscript of *Les Communistes de Hollywood* out for review, one hostile critic noted that we had spelled the surname of Orson Welles "Wells." He concluded that a writer who doesn't know how to spell the name of our most famous director couldn't be trusted to get anything right. I thought that one typographical error didn't invalidate our whole book, but maybe it was a symptom of larger flaws.

There are also errors in the published text of "Red Hollywood" caused by carelessness rather than ignorance. It took me twenty years to realize that a reference to the Conference of Studio Unions appeared as "the conference of Studio Unions." Larry Ceplair, coauthor with Steven Englund of *The Inquisition in Hollywood*, one of the books surveyed in my essay, pointed out to me a more significant error, which rightfully aggrieved him. In retracing how Albert Maltz ran afoul of the Communist Party's cultural arbiters in 1946 and was persuaded to accept their new orthodoxy, I wrote, "It is not possible to understand why Maltz's first essay produced such an uproar in the Communist party press without taking into account the political context in which it appeared, but none of the historians who have written about the debate have betrayed the slightest awareness of this context." In fact, *The Inquisition in Hollywood* provides a thorough treatment of this context (the removal of Earl Browder as party chief), and my account follows it quite closely. This lapse convinced Ceplair that my whole article was unreliable. I suspect he resented more than this single error: although I characterized *The Inquisition in*

Hollywood as "the most ambitious and scrupulous work of historical scholarship devoted to the Hollywood Blacklist," I didn't really do justice to their book. Mostly I argued with it, quibbling, as I put it, about some of their judgments. Blinded by their superficial treatment of the blacklist victims' film work, I refused to acknowledge *The Inquisition in Hollywood* as a fundamental advance in blacklist studies, still dominated when Ceplair and Englund began their work by a stale anti-Communism that had degenerated from outrage to irony to cynicism. So Ceplair was right to be indignant (and yet I still feel miffed by his exclusion of *Red Hollywood* from his survey of blacklist documentaries in the new preface written for the 2003 paperback edition of *The Inquisition in Hollywood*).

My own objections to the work of Ronald Radosh and Allis Radosh in *Red Star Over Hollywood* (2005) turn on errors that might be regarded as minor by a sympathetic reader, but to me they betray a lack of interest in movies that fatally undermines the basic argument of the book. The major innovation in their indictment of Hollywood Communists is a revival of the charge that they propagandized and subverted the screen. The primary exhibit is *Mission to Moscow* (1943), but they made me wonder if they had actually looked at the film. They insist that Walter Huston played Stalin, although he had the lead role: Joseph Davies, American ambassador to the Soviet Union from 1936 to 1938 and the author of the book on which the film is based. Stalin had only a bit part in the film, and he was played by Manart Kippen, an actor chosen for his physical resemblance to the Soviet leader. In any case, *Mission to Moscow* is a dubious example for their thesis since the pro-Soviet slant of the film comes directly from the book by Davies, who was certainly not a Communist. They try to skirt this inconvenient reality by inflating the role of Jay Leyda, a "now-forgotten [not by some of us] Communist" who as technical advisor "suggested changes that would deeply affect the political content of the film."[9] The three changes they cite are trivial, at best, but they fail to notice that none of his three suggestions was followed in the film.

These errors, which I suppose are significant, are not surprising from writers who characterize *The Public Enemy* as a "detective thriller," who identify William Bendix as the actor playing O'Hara in *Action in the North Atlantic* (it was Alan Hale; Bendix wasn't in the film), who believe that Fritz Lang's 1938 film *You and Me* was never produced, who refer to Pietro di Donato's novel *Christ in Concrete* (the literary source for Edward Dmytryk's film *Give Us This Day*) as a play. They even manage to substitute an awkward paraphrase for one of the most famous lines in the history of Hollywood movies. At the end of John Ford's *The Man Who Shot Liberty Valance*, a newspaper editor declares, "When the legend becomes fact, print the legend." Although Ford's film has just shown us the fact, not the legend, this line has come to be taken as his credo. The Radoshes call it "John Ford's maxim," but in their version it reads, "When there is a conflict between the truth and the myth, print the myth."[10]

On the other hand, I can forgive the errors in Buhle and Wagner's work because I am in basic sympathy with their project, and I feel more comfortable with it because they are unapologetic film fans. I should add that the more serious charges made against their work do not stand up to scrutiny. They have been accused of exaggerating the political significance of the films they treat: crudely put, as it generally is, they mimic the red hunters of the 1950s but reverse their value judgments. In *salon.com* (June 4, 2002), Michelle Goldberg wrote, "Joseph McCarthy and the bottom-feeding red-baiters of the House Un-American Activities Committee (HUAC) saw signs of subversion in even the most anodyne Hollywood product. Most observers have interpreted their inability to view art as anything but a conduit for politics as symptomatic of their fascist philistinism. . . . Yet if the authors of *Radical Hollywood* are correct, the House Un-American Activities Committee was on to something. Not that authors Paul Buhle . . . and Dave Wagner . . . apologize for McCarthyism. Quite the opposite—they celebrate cinema leftists as the soul of old Hollywood, makers of the most moral and complex movies in history." And Richard Schickel, reviewing *Radical Hollywood* in the *Los Angeles Times Book Review*, wrote, "No less than HUAC, Paul Buhle and Dave Wagner see, albeit happily, Reds under all the beds who were far more influential than they or we ever imagined. One can only guess at the glee with which this book would have been greeted by HUAC's investigators had it been published, say, in 1950."[11]

Never mind that Senator Joseph McCarthy had no part in the congressional investigations of the Hollywood motion picture industry. Never mind that HUAC never analyzed the content of movies in which blacklist victims had a hand, limiting itself to a few potshots at Hollywood's wartime pro-Soviet films, which Buhle and Wagner rightfully disdain. In *Blacklisted*, they call *Mission to Moscow* "the all-time stinker of apologies-for-Stalinism films." Actually, they are cautious in their claims and judgments. Their most general claims seem modest enough: "Nearly all of the [blacklist] victims were, in our considered view, quietly heroic, their film contributions interesting, however much their higher cinematic aspirations remained unrealized."[12]

Buhle and Wagner set out first of all to overturn Billy Wilder's often quoted judgment on the Hollywood Ten (aka the Unfriendly Ten for their belligerent responses to HUAC): "Only two of them have talent. The rest are just unfriendly." Reading Buhle and Wagner's work gives the impression that Hollywood's Communists and ex-Communists had more than their share of talent. I might suspect a pro-Communist bias in their praise of *Holiday*, adapted by Communist screenwriters Donald Ogden Stewart and Sidney Buchman from a play by Philip Barry, as "one of the best screwball comedies of all time," but Leonard Maltin agrees with them.[13] They also admire *Casablanca* more than I do, but they are not exactly alone. The Writers' Guild of America in April 2006 voted its screenplay, co-written by blacklist victim Howard Koch, the best ever.

But they can also be quite critical. While Carl Foreman's *High Noon* is a masterpiece, his script for *The Victors* (1963) is "drifty and stilted."[14] I can't dispute their judgment of *The Victors* (I haven't seen it), but I would dispute their dismissal of Nicholas Ray's *Johnny Guitar* and Herbert Biberman's *Slaves* (1969), although the appreciation Noël and I feel for Biberman's Marxist interpretation of the slave system is not widely shared. They discuss *Johnny Guitar* in both *Blacklisted* and *Hide in Plain Sight*. In *Blacklisted*, they write, "The allegorical interpretation, alas, sustains interest longer than the film."[15] In *Hide in Plain Sight*, they assert that this interpretation is mistaken: "This oddity became an auteur favorite when the French critics mistakenly interpreted it as an allegory about McCarthyism and the blacklist."[16] Yet one scene, at least, is as explicit as blacklist allegories ever got. When the ranchers interrogate the young outlaw Turkey, they are clearly bent on a witch hunt and they make him the same offer HUAC proposed to its subpoenaed ex-Communist witnesses: he can clear himself by naming others. "Just tell us she was one of you, Turkey, and you can go free," Emma exhorts him.

As their treatment of *Johnny Guitar* suggests, the political claims they make are generally quite conservative. There is a strain of utopianism in the lavish praise they bestow on some films, such as *The Wizard of Oz* and *Citizen Kane*, which Michelle Goldberg ridicules as wild-eyed fantasy, but I believe this fulsomeness is an excusable response to the cynical dismissal of Hollywood movies that has served in the past to discredit all the work of the blacklist victims. With other films, she ignores their criticisms. For example, she asserts that in their synopsis of *Angels with Dirty Faces* (1938), "they just call the film left-wing and leave it at that." But they criticize the film for upholding "one of the most reactionary institutions in contemporary American life, the [Catholic] Church," which it certainly does, and the left-wing content they detect is rather mild: "For all that apparent weakness, *Angels* still had the gritty feel of a Lower East Side neighborhood, with its tenement and street life, and the hope of a redemption more than personal."[17]

Schickel doesn't dispute any of the claims they make for specific films. Instead, he argues that they are guilty of "overstating the importance of the communists and their allies in film history and underplaying the significance of those less formally committed to ideology." Most of the "socially conscientious" films of the 1930s and 1940s were made by non-Communists, so it is still possible to claim that "the Communist left . . . did not appreciably or subversively affect the content of American films during the popular front decade (from the mid-'30s to the mid-'40s)." Communists contributed to a few films that he regards as great (*The Public Enemy* and *Mr. Smith Goes to Washington*), but non-Communists created similar films, and more of them. His judgment is colored by his loathing for the blacklist victims and their politics, which no argument could overcome, but it is nearly tautological, in any case. Take away any 500 films from the totality of Hollywood's production, and the history of American cinema will look roughly the same if the perspective is remote enough. Move closer, and a single film, such as *Force of Evil*, looms large.

The real problems in Buhle and Wagner's work lie elsewhere. First of all, there is the often slipshod writing, which even sympathetic critics have noted. Let me cite just one sentence, taken not quite at random, a characterization of a 1954 Eddie Constantine vehicle John Berry directed during his French exile: "*Ça va barder*, a tramp steamer of a film carrying a strange cargo of French left-wing existentialism, crypto-Marxism American-style and low-budget popular culture, could also be called the representative project of the exiled devotees of high modernism in urgent need of ready cash."[18] And it's a tramp steamer of a sentence. Every noun needs unpacking, and an adjective or two hardly suffices. A sentence or perhaps a paragraph is required. It confuses more than it illuminates, and it is symptomatic of a more significant flaw: except in their first book, the biography of Polonsky, Buhle and Wagner don't allow themselves enough space to analyze or even summarize adequately any of the films they treat. *The Sound of Fury*, a masterpiece of the Hollywood left, gets two paragraphs in *Radical Hollywood*, three short paragraphs in *Blacklisted*, and passing mention in their other two books. It is accorded roughly the same importance as *Ça va barder*—or *National Velvet*. Trying to cover the entire range of the blacklist victims' film work, they lose sight of what is most important and distinctive in it. The forest does disappear behind a multitude of trees.

The real originality of their work also gets lost. They have created an obsessive, idiosyncratic monument of film scholarship, but they have tried to pass it off as middlebrow film history, affecting the breezy journalistic style of populist film criticism. Near the beginning of *Hide in Plain Sight*, they acknowledge that they didn't anticipate some of the critical responses to *Radical Hollywood*: the "often indirectly expressed" fear that its "real purpose was to perturb and replace the established narrative of the history of Hollywood." Yet the presence of so many Communist sympathizers in Hollywood during the 1930s and 1940s seems anomalous, today more than ever, and some of their work is hard to assimilate into any standard view of Hollywood history. How could a thorough survey of this work not threaten the established history? They do suggest the need for a new theoretical underpinning to understand this history, but it remains ineffable: "Somewhere in this part of the story awaiting further discovery is one of the founding secrets of popular culture itself."[19]

Perhaps we should regard their work, despite its massiveness, as another prelude. They have compiled an inventory of the film work of Hollywood's Communists and ex-Communists, and now we can begin to make sense of it. Can we ever get it right? There are a few more models today than there were twenty years ago. We should take note of the example provided by Michael Denning in his book *The Cultural Front* (1996), a history of Popular Front culture in the United States from its beginnings in 1934 to its destruction by the Hollywood blacklist and related purges. He manages to write a synoptic history, delineating the scope of Popular Front culture, while bringing sustained attention to a few key works and episodes of struggle. He pointedly rejects what he calls "a fetishization of [Communist] party membership"[20] in cultural histories of the Popular Front as necessarily reductionist, and I have contributed my share to this reductionism. I believed that isolating the work of the blacklist victims was necessary when I wrote "Red Hollywood," and I believe it is still useful today, but with the work of Buhle and Wagner, we can move beyond that concentration and place the work in a broader context.

More recently, I felt encouraged by the treatment of the blacklist in David Thomson's history of Hollywood, *The Whole Equation* (2005). He gets it right. He places responsibility for the blacklist where it belongs, with the studios, not with the congressional investigators or "finks like Elia Kazan." His judgment on the blacklist does not trivialize it. I could quote a number of similar passages, but here is one: "By 1947, the history of Hollywood cannot be judged properly without considering the malaise of the United States. What happens in the crisis called the blacklist is an opting for false security over real thinking, and a preference for money over ideas or openness. . . . In other words, there were forces in America, business and political, that felt the danger of too many open, critical movies. We have not yet reversed that trend."[21]

What was lost? He mentions two directors, Abraham Polonsky and Joseph Losey, who might have created a different kind of cinema had they been allowed to continue working in Hollywood during the 1950s. There were many other losses that historians have barely begun to inventory. For me, the great loss was the marginalization of neorealism in American cinema. I mentioned *Not Wanted* as an example of this emerging neorealism, but it wouldn't have been possible five years later. From 1950 to 1953, Ida Lupino directed five more independent features, each with neorealist elements, and then her Filmakers company collapsed when it could no longer secure studio distribution for its films. These films aren't masterpieces, and they aren't as provocative politically as *Not Wanted* (after Jarrico, she avoided prominent leftist collaborators), but they depict the journeys and struggles of ordinary, vulnerable people patiently and observantly, with an open sense of life naturally unfolding.

Blacklist victims did contribute to most of the strongest Hollywood neorealist films. Hugo Butler co-wrote *The Southerner* (1945) with its director Jean Renoir. Paul Jarrico co-wrote *The Search* (1948), directed by Fred Zinnemann. Jules Dassin directed *Thieves' Highway* (1949). Ben Barzman wrote *Give Us This Day* (1949), directed in England by Edward Dmytryk before his recantation. Carl Foreman wrote *The Men* (1950), directed by Zinnemann.

Hollywood neorealism died when they were silenced. As movies turned away from social criticism, they turned away from location shooting. Realistic depictions of working-class lives disappeared. The movies reverted to displacement in representing class relations. The disappearance of neorealism is made manifest in one film: *Clash by Night* (1952), directed by Fritz Lang, adapted from a Clifford Odets play by Alfred Hayes, one-time Communist poet, scriptwriter for Rossellini's *Paisan* and Zinnemann's *Teresa* (1951), Hollywood's most self-conscious approximation of Italian Neo-Realism. At the beginning of the film, Mae Doyle walks through a small fishing village, suitcase in hand, from the train to her old home. Peggy walks out of the San Xavier Fish Packing plant with her co-workers at the end of their shift and meets her boyfriend Joe Doyle. They walk to his house where Mae is waiting on the porch. After this beautiful open air prologue, the film moves to studio interiors, and it turns stagy and leaden, redeemed only partially by Lang's merciless deployment of medium shots.

Neorealism went underground—notably with *Salt of the Earth* in 1953, the last hurrah of the Hollywood Communists, but also in a few films by Morris Engel, Irving Lerner, John Cassavetes, Sidney Meyers, Joseph Strick, Kent Mackenzie, Paul Wendkos, and Denis Sanders—until the unexpected popular success of Cassavetes's *Faces* (1968) brought it back into the mainstream. But that is another story.

Acknowledgments

We wish to thank the editors of *Film Studies: An International Review* for permission to publish revised versions of the essays by Jeff Smith, Erica Sheen, Brian Neve, and Peter Stanfield that first appeared in winter 2005. This issue contains additional work on the blacklist and television by Steve Neale, on Adrian Scott by Jennifer Langdon-Teclaw, on Sinatra and postwar liberalism by Karen McNally, and interviews with Cy Endfield and Albert Ruben. Copies of this issue of *Film Studies* can be obtained from Manchester University Press, Oxford Road, Manchester M13 9NR, United Kingdom.

The editors of this volume would like to thank Leslie Mitchner and Alicia Nadkarni for their help and support.

Notes

INTRODUCTION

1. These books include Patrick McGilligan and Paul Buhle, eds., *Tender Comrades: A Backstory of the Hollywood Blacklist* (New York: St. Martin's Press, 1997); Paul Buhle and Dave Wagner, *A Very Dangerous Citizen: Abraham Polonsky and the Hollywood Left* (Berkeley: University of California Press, 2001); Paul Buhle and Dave Wagner, *Radical Hollywood: The Untold Story Behind America's Favorite Movies* (New York: New Press, 2002); Paul Buhle and Dave Wagner, *Hide in Plain Sight: The Hollywood Blacklistees in Film and Television, 1950–2002* (New York: Palgrave Macmillan, 2003); and Paul Buhle and Dave Wagner, *Blacklisted: The Film Lover's Guide to the Hollywood Blacklist* (New York: Palgrave Macmillan, 2003). In his afterword to "Red Hollywood," published in this volume, Thom Andersen considers some of the problems raised by the scholarship of Buhle and company. For further discussion, see Ralph Luker's article "Paul Buhle Strikes Out," *History News Network*, *http://hnn.us/articles/7088.html* (September 20, 2004).

2. Other notable studies on the Hollywood blacklist generation include Gordon Kahn, *Hollywood on Trial* (New York: Boni & Gaer, 1948); Robert Vaughn, *Only Victims: A Study of Show Business Blacklisting* (New York: Putnam, 1972); Victor S. Navasky, *Naming Names* (New York: Hill & Wang, 1980), Bernard F. Dick, *Radical Innocence: A Critical Study of the Hollywood Ten* (Lexington: University Press of Kentucky, 1989), and Brian Neve, *Film and Politics in America: A Social Tradition* (London: Routledge, 1992). Also worth consulting is the growing body of blacklistee memoirs, including: Alvah Bessie, *Inquisition in Eden* (New York: Macmillan, 1965); Lester Cole, *Hollywood Red: The Autobiography of Lester Cole* (Palo Alto: Ramparts Press, 1981); Edward Dmytryk, *Odd Man Out: A Memoir of the Hollywood Ten* (Carbondale: Southern Illinois University Press, 1996); Walter Bernstein, *Inside Out: A Memoir of the Blacklist* (New York: Knopf, 1996); Bernard Gordon, *Hollywood Exile, or How I Learned to Love the Blacklist* (Austin: University of Texas Press, 1999); Ring Lardner Jr., *I'd Hate Myself in the Morning: A Memoir* (New York: Thunder's Mouth Press/Nation Books, 2000); Jean Rouverol, *Refugees From Hollywood: A Journal of the Blacklist Years* (Albuquerque: University of New Mexico Press, 2000); Norma Barzman, *The Red and the Blacklist: The Intimate Memoir of a Hollywood Expatriate* (New York: Thunder's Mouth Press/Nation Books, 2003); and Bernard Gordon, *The Gordon File: A Screenwriter Recalls Twenty Years of FBI Surveillance* (Austin: University of Texas Press, 2004). Studies of individual filmmakers include: Peter Hanson, *Dalton Trumbo, Hollywood Rebel: A Critical Survey and Filmography* (Jefferson, N.C.: McFarland, 2001); Gerald Horne, *The Final Victim of the Blacklist: John Howard Lawson, Dean of the Hollywood Ten* (Berkeley: University of California Press, 2006), and Brian Neve, *Elia Kazan: The Cinema of an American Outsider* (London: I. B. Tauris, 2008).

3. J. Edgar Hoover, testimony before HUAC, March 26, 1947. From *Cold War Experience; Episode 6: Reds*, CNN interactive website, http://www.cnn.com/SPECIALS/cold.war/episodes/06/documents/hoover/. Ring Lardner Jr., one of the Hollywood Ten screenwriters, offers a contrasting view of these radical artists' political motivations: "Many of us had entered our profession with hopes, which we still harboured in various degrees, that the great new medium of motion pictures would be a force for change, not in the crude way that such a thing might have been conceived in the Soviet world, but in the sense of allowing us to portray some of the not so beautiful realities of modern life and to gently illuminate areas of possible improvement." Lardner, *I'd Hate Myself in the Morning*, 7.

4. Larry Ceplair and Steve Englund, *The Inquisition in Hollywood: Politics in the Film Community, 1930–60* (Urbana: University of Illinois Press, 2003), 126.

5. Ibid., 126.

6. Ibid., 180.

7. The generalized and suppositional nature of alleged textual subversion is well captured by the HUAC testimony of right-wing actor Adolphe Menjou: "I believe that under certain circumstances a Communistic director, a Communistic writer, or a Communistic actor, even if he were under orders from the head of the studio not to inject Communism or un-Americanism or subversion into pictures, could easily subvert that order, under the proper circumstances, by a look, by an inflection, by a change in the voice, I think it could be easily done. I have never seen it done, but I think it could be done." Quoted in Kahn, *Hollywood on Trial*, 135.

8. J. Edgar Hoover, testimony before HUAC.

9. Quoted in Ceplair and Englund, *The Inquisition in Hollywood*, 322. Three decades later, Lawson's Hollywood Ten comrade Lester Cole proposed a more nuanced account of such political influence: "Was it possible for a Marxist . . . to make a creative contribution to films, aside from trade-union work? For years, of course, our opponents claimed we sought to subvert the industry and the country by 'sneaking in' lines of revolutionary propaganda. The truth is that if anyone were foolish enough to try something that silly it would immediately be discovered and eliminated. The other truth is that 'politics' are expressed in every film. An escapist 'entertainment' is political to the degree that it denies the existing social realities and, as in the film *The President's Mystery*, I sought to inject such reality when the subject called for it. My politics, pro-union and pro-socialist, were never 'injected' into films, yet I believe often the feelings were represented in attitudes of the characters. In future films this became more evident, but by then it was historically more acceptable." Cole, *Hollywood Red*, 159.

10. Dan Georgakas, "Hollywood Blacklist," in *Encyclopedia of the American Left*, ed. Buhle, and Georgakas (Urbana: University of Illinois Press, 1992). From http://www.english.upenn.edu/~afilreis/50s/blacklist.html.

11. Walter Bernstein, *Inside Out: A Memoir of the Blacklist* (Cambridge, Mass.: Da Capo Press, 2000), 7.

12. Thom Andersen, "Red Hollywood," in *Literature and the Visual Arts in Contemporary Society*, ed. Suzanne Ferguson and Barbara Groseclose (Columbus: Ohio State University Press, 1985), 141–196. Reprinted in this volume.

13. David Bordwell, *Making Meaning: Inference and Rhetoric in the Interpretation of Cinema* (Cambridge, Mass.: Harvard University Press, 1989).

14. Brenda Murphy, *Congressional Theatre: Dramatizing McCarthyism on Stage, Film, and Television* (Cambridge: Cambridge University Press, 1999), 259.

15. Budd Schulberg, interview with Brian Neve, Westhampton Beach, N.Y., October 13, 2004.

16. In his chapter on the films of Robert Rossen, Brian Neve briefly discusses a story treatment Rossen produced in 1943 that was partly based on the zoot suit riots.

17. Raymond Borde and Etienne Chaumeton, *Panorama du Film Noir Americain, 1941–1953* (San Francisco: City Light Books, 2002), 5–7.

18. Quoted in Michael S. Ybarra, "Blacklist Whitewash," *New Republic* (January 5 and 12, 1998), 23.

19. Quoted in Ceplair and Englund, *The Inquisition in Hollywood*, 242.

20. See, for example, Ronald Radosh and Joyce Milton, *The Rosenberg File* (New Haven: Yale University Press, 1997); Ronald Radosh, *Commies: A Journey Through the Old Left, the New Left and the Leftover Left* (New York: Encounter Books, 2001); Ronald and Allis Radosh, *Red Star Over Hollywood: The Film Colony's Long Romance with the Left* (New York: Encounter Books, 2005); Ronald Radosh, *Divided They Fell: The Demise of the Democratic Party, 1964–1996* (New York: Free Press, 1998); and Ronald Radosh and Harvey Klehr, *The Amerasia Spy Case: Prelude to McCarthyism* (Chapel Hill: University of North Carolina Press, 1996).

21. Michael Denning, *The Cultural Front: The Laboring of American Culture in the Twentieth Century* (London and New York: Verso, 1998).

22. American Civil Liberties Union, "Surveillance Under the USA Patriot Act," *http://www.aclu.org/safefree/general/17326res20030403*.html (April 3, 2003).

23. To build Murrow up as a heroic defender of free speech, and to hone a workable narrative from a more dispersed series of events, Clooney's film inevitably simplifies the tortuous procedures that led to McCarthy's downfall. For a lively snapshot of the unraveling of McCarthy's red-baiting adventure, see Richard M. Fried, *Nightmare in Red: The McCarthy Era in Perspective* (New York: Oxford University Press, 1991), 120–143.

24. Clooney had earlier starred in *Three Kings* (1999), an action-adventure film that offered a jaundiced account of U.S. participation in the 1991 Gulf War. The same year as *Good Night, and Good Luck*, he also starred in *Syriana*, which offered a sober indictment of the corrupt machinations of the U.S.-dominated oil industry.

25. Quoted in Emma Brookes, " 'I've Learned to Fight,' " *Guardian* (February, 10, 2006).

CHAPTER I — ARE YOU NOW OR HAVE YOUR EVER BEEN A CHRISTIAN?

I would like to thank William Paul, John Belton, Lea Jacobs, Julie D'Acci, Ben Singer, and Kelley Conway for their earlier comments on this essay. I would also like to thank T. J. Plunk, Chris Dart, John Stadler, Brad Boyd, Matt Traverso, Patrick McCollough, and Elizabeth Schaefer for their help in analyzing the strengths and weaknesses of reception theory.

1. Stephen King, *Danse Macabre* (New York: Berkeley Books, 1983), 130.

2. Ismail Xavier, "Historical Allegory," *A Companion to Film Theory*, ed. Toby Miller and Robert Stam (Malden, Mass.: Blackwell), 354.

3. For representative examples of this type of scholarship, see Leger Grindon, *Shadows on the Past: Studies in the Historical Fiction Film* (Philadelphia: Temple University Press, 1994), 88–90; John Belton, *American Cinema/American Culture* (New York: McGraw-Hill, 1994), 247; Maria Wyke, *Projecting the Past: Ancient Rome, Cinema, and History* (New York: Routledge, 1997), 142–146; Anthony Miller, "*Julius Caesar* in the Cold War: The Houseman-Mankiewicz Film," *Literature/Film Quarterly* 28, no. 2 (2000): 95–100; Mark Jancovich, "The Purest Knight of All: Nation, History, and Representation in *El Cid*," *Cinema Journal* 40, no.1 (Fall 2000): 79–103; Bruce Babington and Peter William Evans, *Biblical Epics: Sacred Narrative in the Hollywood Cinema* (New York: Manchester University Press, 1993), 210–213.

4. See Philip L. Gianos, *Politics and Politicians in American Film* (Westport: Praeger, 1998), 23–24.

5. David Bordwell, *Making Meaning: Inference and Rhetoric in the Interpretation of Cinema* (Cambridge: Harvard University Press, 1989). See especially pp. 105–128 and 195–201.

6. Belton, *American Cinema/American Culture*, 247.

7. Tiberius's speech is quoted in Babington and Evans, *Biblical Epics*, 211.

8. Xavier, "Historical Allegory," 337.

9. See Philip Dunne, *Take Two: A Life in Movies and Politics* (New York: McGraw-Hill, 1980), 253–256.

10. For more on the political shifts in Hollywood after World War II, see Larry Ceplair and Steven Englund, *The Inquisition in Hollywood: Politics in the Film Community, 1930–1960* (Berkeley: University of California Press, 1979), 200–253.

11. Quoted in Eric Bentley, ed., *Thirty Years of Treason* (New York: Viking Press, 1971), 333. Interestingly, Parks's testimony was released to the public in 1953, the same year as *The Robe*'s debut.

12. Quoted in Gordon Kahn, *Hollywood on Trial: The Story of the Ten Who Were Indicted* (New York: Boni and Gaer, 1948), 84.

13. Bernard F. Dick, *Radical Innocence: A Critical Study of the Hollywood Ten* (Lexington: University Press of Kentucky, 1989), 92.

14. Lloyd C. Douglas, *The Robe* (Boston: Houghton Mifflin, 1942), 351.

15. I should note that Lela Rogers's reference to *Tender Comrade* was made during her initial testimony before HUAC in the spring of 1947, but was not included in the more famous hearings that were conducted in October. For more, see Victor Navasky, *Naming Names* (New York: Penguin Books, 1980), 79.

16. Albert Maltz, First Draft Screenplay of *The Robe*, dated August 21, 1945, Box 7, Folder 6, US Mss 17AN, Wisconsin Center for Film and Theatre Research, State Historical Society Library, Madison, Wisconsin.

17. Ibid.

18. Ibid.

19. Ibid.

20. Ibid.

21. Philip Dunne, *The Robe*, Final Screenplay, August 13, 1952, Twentieth Century Fox Collection, Special Arts Library, University of California at Los Angeles.

22. Memo from Albert Maltz to Frank Ross, December 27, 1945, Box 7, Folder 6, Albert Maltz Collection.

23. Conference Memo from Darryl Zanuck to Philip Dunne and Frank Ross, July 25, 1952, Twentieth Century Fox Collection.

24. Ibid.

25. It is worth noting, however, that Zanuck's biographer, George Custen, argues that Zanuck was personally opposed to the blacklist even if he never publicly spoke out against it. Perhaps the best example of Zanuck's opposition was his work behind the scenes to adapt Albert Maltz's *The Journey of Simon McKeever* after the screenwriter was blacklisted. Zanuck made an agreement with Jules Dassin to film *McKeever* with John Huston doing the screenplay and Walter Huston starring. For his part, Dassin said that he would take care of Maltz and would tell no one about the project until Zanuck had secured it with Fox. Shortly thereafter, Maltz went public with the news of the project and declared to the *Hollywood Reporter* that the film of *McKeever* was in a prime position to break the blacklist. After Maltz's gaffe, Zanuck canceled the production and denied to Fox management that he knew anything about it. See Custen's *Twentieth Century's Fox: Darryl F. Zanuck and the Culture of Hollywood* (New York: Basic Books, 1997), 312–313.

26. Philip Dunne, *The Robe*, Writer's working script, June 26, 1952, Twentieth Century Fox Collection.

27. Quoted in Custen, *Twentieth Century's Fox*, 315.

28. Wyke, *Projecting the Past*, 28–29.

29. Philip T. Hartung, "The Screen," *Commonweal*, October 9, 1953, 12–13.

30. "'Robe' an Undertaking of Many Problems," *Motion Picture Herald*, July 7, 1945, in *The Robe*, clippings file, Margaret Herrick Center for Motion Picture Research, Academy of Motion Picture Arts and Sciences, Beverly Hills, California.

31. "Ross and Anderson Confer On 'Robe' Prod.," *Hollywood Reporter*, June 8, 1948; and "Ross to Produce 'Robe' in 1949," *Motion Picture Herald*, June 12, 1948, in *The Robe*, clippings file, Margaret Herrick Center.

32. "Howard McClay," *Los Angeles Daily News*, 26 August 1952, in *The Robe*, clippings file, Margaret Herrick Center.

33. Ibid.

34. Janet Staiger, *Interpreting Films: Studies in the Historical Reception of American Cinema* (Princeton: Princeton University Press, 1992), 34.

35. Ibid., 33.

36. Ibid., 46.

37. Ibid., 47.

38. Jason Mittell, *Genre and Television: From Cop Shows to Cartoons in American Culture* (New York: Routledge, 2004), 2-19.

39. Ibid., 56-93.

40. Michael Barrier, *Hollywood Cartoons: American Animation in its Golden Age* (New York: Oxford University Press, 1999).

41. Albert Maltz's research notes for *The Robe*, undated, Box 7, Folder 6, Albert Maltz Collection.

42. W. Cleon Skousen, *The Naked Communist* (Salt Lake City: Ensign Publishing Company, 1958), 343.

43. Ibid., 346.

44. See, for example, David Nelson Duke's *In the Trenches With Jesus and Marx: Henry F. Ward and the Struggle for Social Justice* (Tuscaloosa: University of Alabama Press, 2003); and Mark L. Kleinman, *A World of Hope, A World of Fear: Henry A. Wallace, Reinhold Neibuhr, and American Liberalism* (Columbus: Ohio State University Press, 2000).

45. Albert Maltz, "The American Artist and the American Tradition," Speech at the Hotel Astor, March 16, 1948, Box 15, Folder 2, Albert Maltz Collection.

CHAPTER 2 — UN-AMERICAN: DMYTRYK, ROSSELLINI, AND *CHRIST IN CONCRETE*

1. Richard Maltby, "Made for Each Other: the Melodrama of Hollywood and the House Committee on Un-American Activities, 1947," in *Cinema, Politics and Society in America*, ed. Philip Davies and Brian Neve (Manchester: Manchester University Press, 1981), 76.

2. Ibid., 78, 77.

3. Dan Georgakas, "The Hollywood Reds: 50 Years Later," *American Communist History* 2, no. 1 (2003): 63.

4. See John Lewis, " 'We Do Not Ask You to Condone This': How the Blacklist Saved Hollywood," *Cinema Journal* 39, no. 2 (2000): 5, for the argument that HUAC was "a first step" in the transformation of the industry from the entrepreneurial studio mode of production characterized by a high degree of relative creative autonomy into a corporatist conglomerate system subject to increasingly interventionist political pressure.

5. I refer to it throughout this discussion as *Christ in Concrete* because that is the title under which it has been made available on DVD.

6. Edward Dmytryk, *Odd Man Out: A Memoir of the Hollywood Ten* (Carbondale: Southern Illinois University Press, 1996), 154.

7. Maltby, "Made for Each Other," 76.

8. Peter Bondanella, *Hollywood Italians: Dagos, Palookas, Romeos, Wise Guys, and Sopranos* (New York: Continuum, 2004), 29-34. My emphasis.

9. Howard K. Smith used the phrase "terrestrial paradise" to describe the status of postwar America as a destination for Italian immigrants in *The State of Europe* (New York: Knopf, 1949), 198-219.

10. Tullio Kezich, "The Venice Festival 1950," *Hollywood Quarterly* 5, no. 4 (1951): 373.

11. Stephen Gundle, *Between Hollywood and Moscow: the Italian Communists and the Challenge of Mass Culture 1943–1991* (Durham, N.C.: Duke University Press, 2001), 66.

12. Robert Shaw, "New Horizons in Hollywood," *Public Opinion Quarterly* 10, no. 1 (1946): 72, 75.

13. Ibid, 76.

14. Ibid.

15. Roberto Rossellini, "A Few Words about Neo-Realism," in *Springtime in Italy: A Reader on Neo-Realism*, ed. and trans. David Overbey (London: Talisman Books, 1978), 89.

16. Kezich, "The Venice Festival 1950," 377.

17. Maltby, "Made for Each Other," 81–82.

18. Lewis, " 'We Do Not Ask You to Condone This,' " 5.

19. Robin W. Winks, *Cloak and Gown: Scholars in America's Secret War 1939–1961* (New Haven: Yale University Press, 1996).

20. William H. Epstein, "Counter-Intelligence: Cold-War Criticism and Eighteenth-Century Studies" *ELH* 57, no. 1 (1990).

21. Maltby, "Made for Each Other," 81.

22. Dmytryk, *Odd Man Out*, 92.

23. See the "passage in Borges" with which Michel Foucault begins his account of "the order of things" in *The Order of Things* (London: Tavistock, 1974).

24. "All the people who took the First and Fifth Amendments after us knew something we had not known, namely that they would not work for years": Dalton Trumbo in Victor Navasky, *Naming Names* (New York: Viking, 1980), 393.

25. Accompanying notes, *Christ in Concrete* (All Day Entertainment, 2004).

26. Dmytryk, *Odd Man Out*, 97–98.

27. In their conversation included as an "additional feature" on the All Day Entertainment DVD, Pietro di Donato's son Peter and film scholar Bill Wasserzeiher suggest that Visconti had also been considered, but documentation shows that the negotiations with Rossellini reached the option stage. Di Donato worked as the principle translator for the English language release of *Rome Open City*.

28. Gerald Meyer, "Italian Americans and the American Communist Party," in *The Lost World of Italian-American Radicalism: Politics, Labor, and Culture*, ed. P. Cannistraro and G. Meyer (Westport, Conn.: Praeger, 2003), 220.

29. Ibid., 216.

30. For an account of the strategic interests served by this partnership see Kaeten Mistry, "The Partnership between the Democrazia Cristiana and the United States 1947–8," *49th. Parallel: An Interdisciplinary Journal of North American Studies* 14 (2004).

31. See Mario Del Pero, "The United States and 'Psychological Warfare' in Italy 1948–1955," *Journal of American History* 87, no. 4 (2001). For a full account of the activities

involved see William Blum, *Killing Hope: US Military and CIA Interventions since World War II* (Montreal, Black Rose, 1998), esp. chap. 2.

32. Philip V. Cannistraro and Gerald Meyer, "Introduction," in *The Lost World of Italian-American Radicalism: Politics, Labor, and Culture*, 25–26.

33. Del Pero, "The United States and 'Psychological Warfare' in Italy 1948–1955," 1.

34. Geir Lundestad, "How (Not) to Study the Origins of the Cold War," in *Reviewing the Cold War: Approaches, Interpretations, Theory*, ed. Odd Arne Westad (London, Portland: Frank Cass 2000), 72.

35. Enzo Ungari with Donald Ranvaud, *Bertolucci by Bertolucci* (London: Plexus, 1982), 21.

36. Steve Neale, "Art Cinema as Institution," *Screen* 22, no. 1 (1981): 14.

37. Overbey, *Springtime in Italy: A Reader on Neo-Realism*, 100.

38. Ibid., 95.

39. Ibid., 100, 102.

40. Geoffrey Nowell-Smith, "North and South, East and West: Rossellini and Politics," in *Roberto Rossellini: Magician of the Real*, ed. D. Forgacs, S. Lutton, and G. Nowell-Smith (London: BFI, 2000), 9.

41. Ellen Draper, "'Controversy Has Probably Forever Destroyed the Context': *The Miracle* and Movie Censorship in America in the Fifties," *Velvet Light Trap* 25 (1990): 72. Rossellini also records these attacks in Overbey, *Springtime in Italy: A Reader on Neo-Realism*, 109.

42. Draper, "'Controversy Has Probably Forever Destroyed the Context,'" 70.

43. Thomas H. Guback, *The International Film Industry* (Bloomington: Indiana University Press, 1969), cited in ibid., 76.

44. "Legislative Inquiry into Political Activity: First Amendment Immunity from Committee Interrogation," *Yale Law Journal* 65, no. 8 (1956): 1182–1183.

CHAPTER 3 — "A LIVING PART OF THE CLASS STRUGGLE"

Versions of this chapter were delivered at the 2005 conference of the Society for Cinema and Media Studies in London and the 2005 conference of SERCIA at the University of Rennes. I would like to thank both the organizers and audiences of each event. My attendance at the SCMS conference was made possible by support from the Humanities Research Center of the University of Sussex. I would also like to thank the many other individuals who helped me with information and materials that enabled me to research and complete this chapter, including Theo Caldwell and David A. Mellor, who helped me identity some of the paintings discussed here; my co-panelists and co-editors Steve Neale, Peter Stanfield, and Brian Neve; Janet Moat of the BFI, who allowed me to consult materials in the Joseph Losey Collection; Alex Krutnik, for his computer aided wizardry; but most of all Catherine Morris for incisive copyediting and much more, and to Jessica Morris for putting up with this crazy journey into Mexicanidad.

1. To be more precise, the films were released between September 1947, when HUAC launched its first high-profile investigation of Communist influence in Hollywood, and the beginning of the second and more devastating round of hearings in 1951.

2. Thom Andersen, "Red Hollywood," in *Literature and the Visual Arts in Contemporary Society*, ed. Suzanne Ferguson and Barbara Groseclose (Columbus: Ohio State University Press, 1985), 141–196 (reprinted in this volume).

3. Details of these films are taken from respective entries in the American Film Institute (AFI) catalogue, *http://afi.chadwyck.com*.

4. This low-budget B-comedy thriller was directed by soon-to-be-blacklisted Bernard Vorhaus. See the interview with Vorhaus in *Tender Comrades: A Backstory of the Hollywood Blacklist*, ed. Patrick McGilligan and Paul Buhle (New York: St. Martin's Press, 1997), 657–681.

5. The film was co-scripted by soon-to-be-blacklisted comedy specialist Allen Boretz. See the interview with Boretz in McGilligan and Buhle, *Tender Comrades*, 112–127.

6. Such reuse of paintings persists for quite some time: besides appearing together in *In a Lonely Place*, for example, *La Mousmé* and Renoir's *La Loge* also adorn the apartment of artist-prostitute Hallie Gerard (Capucine) in the 1962 Columbia co-production *Walk on the Wild Side*.

7. *La Fille du déjeuner* also decorates the apartment of Anne Treadwell (Judith Andersen) in the 1944 Twentieth Century Fox film *Laura*. Recycling of this order was a standard practice in Hollywood productions and could involve the reuse of stories, sets, and songs. For example, songs initially used in *Gilda* (1946) are repeated across the Columbia films *Dead Reckoning, In a Lonely Place,* and *The Big Heat*, while the latter two films also use the same set of check curtains.

8. There is also a brief glimpse of *The Flower Carrier* within the 1953 thriller *Count the Hours*, an independent production distributed through RKO, where it decorates the apartment of socialite Paula Mitchener (Dolores Moran). Like *Bury Me Dead*, this film was co-scripted by left-winger Karen deWolf, who would be blacklisted soon afterward.

9. Leon Trotsky wrote his letter to *Partisan Review* on June 18, 1938. It was republished as part of "Art and Politics in Our Epoch," *Fourth International* 11:2 (March–April 1950), 61–64.

10. According to Bertram Wolfe, Rivera's work first made an impression in the United States in 1915, when some of his Parisian paintings were exhibited in New York at Marius de Zayas's small Fifth Avenue gallery. Zayas exhibited further Rivera paintings in subsequent years. The painter's reputation north of the border increased substantially from 1924 onward, when his mural work began to attract highbrow attention. See Bertram D. Wolfe, *The Fabulous Life of Diego Rivera* (New York: Cooper Square Press, 2000), 278–279. Articles on Rivera began to appear in North American newspapers and periodicals from 1924, and a succession of U.S. artists traveled to Mexico to watch him at work on his murals. A 1929 issue of the journal *Creative Art* was dedicated to Rivera's work and a lavishly illustrated book was devoted to his murals. See Francis V. O'Connor, "The Influence of Diego Rivera on the Art of the United States during the 1930s and After," Detroit Institute of Arts, *Diego Rivera: A Retrospective* (New York: W. W. Norton, 1986), 161.

11. Wolfe, *The Fabulous Life*, 144.

12. Ida Rodriguez-Prampolini, "Rivera's Concept of History," Detroit Institute of Arts, *Diego Rivera: A Retrospective*, 131–132. The manifesto was originally published as a broadside in Mexico City in 1922, and was republished in June 1924 in *El Machete*, no. 7 (Barcelona).

13. Quoted in Hayden Herrera, *Frida: The Biography of Frida Kahlo* (New York: Harper and Row, 1983), 82–83.

14. Diego Rivera, with Gladys March, *My Art, My Life: An Autobiography* (New York: Dover Publications, 1991), 66.

15. Rodriguez-Prampolini, "Rivera's Concept of History," 132.

16. One source of friction was Rivera's growing disenchantment with Stalinist doctrine, which began during his ten-month visit to the Soviet Union in 1927–28. For an account of this visit, see Wolfe, *The Fabulous Life*, 212–224.

17. From 1930 on, Rivera affiliated himself progressively with the heretical Communism of the exiled Leon Trotsky. Rivera petitioned the government to grant Trotsky asylum in Mexico, and accommodated him for several years in one of his own residences. The Communist Party also chastised him as an "opportunist" for accepting commissions from Yankee millionaires. Patrick Marnham, *Dreaming with His Eyes Open: A Life of Diego Rivera* (London: Bloomsbury, 1999), 248.

18. "Rivera's New Sociological Frescoes of New York Are Acclaimed," *Art Digest*, January 15, 1932, 5. This was only the second single-artist exhibition mounted by the museum, the first being devoted to Henri Matisse.

19. He also accepted several commissions for easel works from North American patrons.

20. Quoted in Herrera, *Frida Kahlo*, 116.

21. Quoted in Prampolini, "Rivera's Concept of History," 135.

22. Herrera, *Frida Kahlo*, 115.

23. For accounts of the controversy sparked by the Detroit murals, see "Field Notes: Men, Machines, and Murals—Detroit," *American Magazine of Art* 26, no. 5 (May 1933): 254; Diego Rivera: "Dynamic Detroit—an Interpretation," *Creative Art* (April 1933): 289–295; "Will Detroit, Like Mohammed II, Whitewash Its Rivera Murals," *Art Digest* (April 1, 1933); and "Rivera Again," *Art Digest* (May 15, 1933): 41, 49.

24. A lively re-creation of the construction and destruction of the Rockefeller mural can be found in Tim Robbins's filmic homage to the Popular Front, *Cradle Will Rock* (1999).

25. "Rivera Again," 41.

26. Linda Downs, "Introduction," Detroit Institute of Arts, *Diego Rivera: A Retrospective*, 18.

27. "Rivera Again," 41.

28. See Downs, "Introduction," 18.

29. "We repudiate the so-called easel art and all such art which springs from ultra-intellectual circles, for it is essentially aristocratic. We hail the monumental expression of art because such art is public property." Manifesto of the Syndicate of Technical Workers, Painters and Sculptors, quoted in Herrera, *Frida: The Biography of Frida Kahlo*, 82–83.

30. See Pete Hamill, *Diego Rivera* (New York: Harry N. Abrams, 2002), 172, and Andrea Kettenmann, *Rivera* (Köln & New York: Taschen, 2003), 80. Rita Eder says of Rivera's 1950s society commissions: "These works are those of an artist who now painted "bourgeois pictures for the bourgeoisie," showing us "a kind of X-ray image of a new class at

the very moment it was coming into existence, a class that acquired wealth through the onset of industrialization, and employed 'the Mexican' as a cosmetic element, a facial paint which was the exclusive fashion of filmstars, politician's wives and a few intellectuals." Rita Eder, "The Portraits of Diego Rivera," Detroit Institute of Arts, *Diego Rivera: A Retrospective,* 199.

31. See Anthony W. Lee, *Painting on the Left: Diego Rivera, Radical Politics and San Francisco* (Berkeley: University of California Press, 1999), 48–56, and Bertram Wolfe, *The Fabulous Life,* 282–284.

32. The painting was initially known as *The Flower Vendor.* See Detroit Institute of Arts, *Diego Rivera: A Retrospective,* 91.

33. Ibid., 343.

34. Tom Milne, ed., *Losey on Losey* (London: Secker & Warburg, 1967), 76. The film had a troubled production history. According to the entry in the American Film Institute catalogue, the film passed through numerous scripted versions and was assigned to various directors (including Losey, John Cromwell, and Nicholas Ray) and stars (including Barbara Bel Geddes, Jane Greer, Merle Oberon, Robert Young, Glenn Ford, and Paul Lukas). Robert Stevenson eventually directed it, with Robert Ryan, Laraine Day, Janis Carter, John Agar, and Thomas Gomez starring. See *The Woman on Pier 13,* AFI catalogue entry. For a useful account of the film's convoluted production history, including discussion of its various script drafts, see Daniel J. Leab, "How Red Was My Valley: Hollywood, the Cold War Film, and *I Married a Communist,*" *Journal of Contemporary History* 19 (1984): 59–88. Leab's archival research casts doubt upon the validity of Losey's (highly influential) claim that the film was used by Howard Hughes as a loyalty test.

35. Anthony W. Lee, *Painting on the Left,* 220–221.

36. To emphasize further the deadly consequences of flirting with radical politics, Brad himself is ultimately shot dead by Vanning's henchmen—soon after he kills the Communist ringleader with a grappling iron.

37. Milne, *Losey on Losey,* 76.

38. Eisenschitz claims that RKO studio head Howard Hughes considered numerous other directors for the project after Ray bowed out. Bernard Eisenschitz, *Nicholas Ray: An American Journey* (London: Faber & Faber, 1993), 125.

39. Sam Spiegel and John Huston purchased the story, originally titled *The Cost of Living,* for production at Columbia Pictures in 1949 (*Daily Variety,* August 9, 1949, 8). They obtained the story from German writers Robert Thoeren and Hans Wilhelm, and Huston allegedly did some polishing of the screenplay as well. See Natasha Fraser-Cavassoni, *Sam Spiegel: The Biography of a Hollywood Legend* (London: Time-Warner, 2004), 120–122. The film was eventually made by Horizon Pictures (through the banner of Eagle Productions), an independent company set up by Spiegel and Huston in 1948, and was released through United Artists. The film had a tight shooting schedule of twenty-four days but was actually completed a few days early owing to painstaking planning by Losey and his crew. See Darr Smith, *Daily News,* April 13, 1950, in "Scrapbook," Item no. 5a, BFI Joseph Losey Collection. *The Prowler* was one of four films Losey made within a year in which

"he shaved four to seven days from each of his scheduled production days." Milton Epstein, "Hollywood Vine-Yard," *Film Daily*, July 3, 1950, in "Scrapbook," Item no. 5a, BFI Joseph Losey Collection. The two stars, Van Heflin and Evelyn Keyes, were both on loan from major Hollywood companies. At the time, Keyes was in dispute with Columbia Pictures, and was loaned to several other companies as a means of serving out her contract.

40. Losey admits that he "used Trumbo's voice for the radio voice as a kind of protest." Michel Ciment, *Conversations with Losey* (London: Methuen, 1985), 103.

41. Jean Rouverol, *Refugees from Hollywood: A Journal of the Blacklist Years* (Albuquerque: University of New Mexico Press, 2000), 41.

42. The *Hollywood Reporter* described the film as "a mystery melodrama in the high tension vein of *Double Indemnity* and *Sorry, Wrong Number*" (April 25, 1951), 4. Although he has expressed great admiration for *Double Indemnity*, Losey denies that it consciously influenced him. See Ciment, *Conversations with Losey*, 106. *The Prowler* could also be viewed as part of a cycle of rogue cop films—including *Where the Sidewalk Ends* (1950), *The Big Heat* (1953), *Pushover* (1954), *Rogue Cop* (1954), and *Touch of Evil* (1958)—that emerged in reaction against the glorification of law enforcement agencies in semi-documentary crime thrillers such as *The House on 92nd Street* (1945), *Trapped* (1949), and the anti-Communist *Walk East on Beacon!* (1952). See Frank Krutnik, *In a Lonely Street, Film Noir, Genre, Masculinity* (London: Routledge, 1991), 191–193, and also Rebecca Prime's chapter in this volume.

43. Ciment, *Conversations with Losey*, 100.

44. "Scrapbook," Joseph Losey Collection, British Film Institute.

45. *The Prowler*, AFI catalogue entry. The PCA also objected later to the film's publicity campaign, which included a picture of Evelyn Keyes draped in a towel.

46. Review of *The Prowler*, *Boxoffice* (May 5, 1951), 1255.

47. Review of *The Prowler*, *Variety* (April 25, 1951), 6.

48. Ciment, *Conversations with Losey*, 104.

49. The director's script copy held in the BFI Joseph Losey Collection confirms the importance of this speech, which receives particular attention during the repeated rewrites of the film's final act. The version used in the film derives from a script revision dated April 19, 1950. This replaced a less punchy version used in a revised scene written three days earlier, in which Garwood tries to justify himself as follows: "What I did is done every day. Every day of my life. I've seen it. Those guys who live on Lakeview—*your* street—how did they get there? . . . And the guys in the University Clubs—who are they? . . . Doctors who split fees—lawyers who take bribes—politicians who can buy votes . . . and why? . . . All for *one* reason—all for the same reason—a buck! What have I done that they don't do? . . ." Alongside this version of the speech, Losey has scrawled in pencil: "Much too reduced." *The Prowler*, Annotated Script (Item no. 3), The Joseph Losey Collection, BFI.

50. James Leahy, *The Cinema of Joseph Losey* (London and New York: Zwemmer/Barnes, 1967), 43.

51. *The Prowler*, Annotated Script, 2.

52. Ciment, *Conversations with Losey*, 104–105. Hubley also worked as Losey's design consultant on *The Boy with Green Hair* (1948), *The Lawless* (1949), and *M* (1951), as well as on the 1947 stage production of Bertolt Brecht's *Galileo*.

53. *The Prowler*, Annotated Script, "Staff List."

54. *Variety*, review of *The Prowler*, 6.

55. Significantly enough, the coach identifies Garwood's failing as his inability to work as a team player. *The Flower Carrier*, by contrast, depicts two people working closely together as a team.

56. Quoted in Leahy, *Cinema of Joseph Losey*, 41.

57. Dana Polan, *In a Lonely Place* (London: BFI, 1993), 46. In 1947 Bogart and his business manager A. Morgan Maree signed a long-term contract for one picture per year with journalist and producer Mark Hellinger. When Hellinger died in December 1947 Bogart bought up his stock and formed Santana Pictures with Maree and writer-producer Robert Lord. Santana made five films in six years, all distributed by Columbia; *In a Lonely Place* was the third film from the company. See A. M. Sperber and Eric Lax, *Bogart* (London: Phoenix Books, 1998), 420–421, and Jeffrey Meyers, *Bogart: A Life in Hollywood* (London: Andre Deutsch, 1997), 235–236.

58. For more on the Committee for the First Amendment, see Larry Ceplair and Steve Englund, *The Inquisition in Hollywood: Politics in the Film Community, 1930–60* (Urbana: University of Illinois Press, 2003), 275–290.

59. See Sperber and Lax, *Bogart*, 354–88, and Meyers, *Bogart*, 202–203.

60. See Meyers, *Bogart*, 198, and Ceplair and Englund, *Inquisition in Hollywood*, 150, 157.

61. Meyers, *Bogart*, 199.

62. See ibid., 211–215, and Ceplair and Englund, *Inquisition in Hollywood*, 289–291.

63. Eisenschitz, *Nicholas Ray*, 23–72.

64. Ibid., 27.

65. Ibid., 124.

66. Ibid., 27.

67. Ibid., 116.

68. Polan, *In a Lonely Place*, 35.

69. V. F. Perkins, "*In a Lonely Place*," in *The Movie Book of Film Noir*, ed. Ian Cameron (London: Studio Vista, 1992), 224.

70. James W. Palmer, "*In a Lonely Place*: Paranoia in the Dream Factory," *Film/Literature Quarterly* 13, no. 3 (1985): 205.

71. Ibid., 204–205.

72. Ibid., 205.

73. Dorothy B. Hughes, *In a Lonely Place* (Harpenden: No Exit Press, 1990), 14. I would like to thank Pete Stanfield for bringing the relevance of this passage to my attention.

74. As Dana Polan points out, the film romance is initially developed in a manner evoking Hollywood's screwball comedies of the 1930s. Polan, *In a Lonely Place*, 16–18.

75. Ibid., 37.

76. Ibid., 10. For further discussion of film and novel, see Polan, *In a Lonely Place*, 26–28.

77. A further justification for the inclusion of a painting by Van Gogh may be the kinship he shares with Dix Steele as a tortured artist. But where Van Gogh directed violence against himself, Dix repeatedly commits acts of violence against others.

78. For feminist readings of *La Loge*, see Albert Boime, "Maria Deraismes and Eva Gonzalès: A Feminist Critique of *Une Loge aux Théâtre des Italiens*," *Woman's Art Journal* 15, no. 2 (Fall 1994/Winter 1995): 31–37, and Tamar Garb, "Gender and Representation," *Modernity and Modernism: French Painting in the Nineteenth Century* (New Haven: Yale University Press, 1993), 219–290.

79. Dix is only prevented from killing Laurel by the last-minute intervention of a telephone call from the police, which ironically enough exonerates him of Mildred's murder.

80. Polan, *In a Lonely Place*, 36.

81. The kiss, the strangulation, and the scenes with her masseuse Martha (Ruth Gillette) all point toward a masochistic streak in Laurel that encourages her submission to violence and domination.

82. The other character that the film connects to *The Flower Carrier* is Dix's loyal agent, Mel Lippman. Art Smith, who plays this role, was blacklisted in 1952 after being named before HUAC by Nicholas Ray's friend and mentor, Elia Kazan. See Victor Navasky, *Naming Names* (New York: Hill and Wang, 2003), 201. Mel and Laurel are the two people with the greatest love and respect for Dix, and he lashes out with violence at both of them.

83. This is also true of another film that uses *The Flower Carrier*. Made outside the period I am discussing here, the 1957 United Artists release *Crime of Passion* illustrates the legacy of Rivera's painting as a signifier of exploited labor. It is associated with the feisty Kathy Ferguson (Barbara Stanwyck), who swaps her exciting job on a big city newspaper for a frustrating existence as a suburban housewife. It is also worth noting that two Rivera paintings crop up in the signature film of the Hollywood Left, *Body and Soul* (1947); see the chapter in this volume by Peter Stanfield.

84. For example, from the 1920s on Rivera's work revealed an increasing dedication to the promise of a Pan-American art that was distinct from, and opposed to, the European colonial heritage. The brown-skinned peasant laborers of *The Flower Carrier* contrast emphatically with the often upscale white Americans who have purchased this decorously "primitive" image for their lavish homes.

CHAPTER 4 — A MONARCH FOR THE MILLIONS

1. Richard Keenan, "*The Set-Up/Champion* Controversy: Fight Films Go to Court," *American Screen Classics* 2, no. 6 (July 1978): 40–42.

2. See Leger Grindon, "Body and Soul: The Structure of Meaning in the Boxing Film Genre," *Cinema Journal* 35, no. 4 (Summer 1996): 54–69.

3. See, for example, Sean McCann, *Gumshoe America: Hard-Boiled Crime Fiction and the Rise and Fall of New Deal Liberalism* (Durham, N.C.: Duke University Press, 2000).

4. Paul Buhle and Dave Wagner, *A Very Dangerous Citizen: Abraham Lincoln Polonsky and the Hollywood Left* (Berkeley: University of California Press, 2001), 108–117.

5. Thom Andersen, "Red Hollywood," in *Literature and the Visual Arts in Contemporary Society*, ed. Suzanne Ferguson and Barbara Groseclose (Columbus: Ohio State University Press, 1985), 141–196. Reprinted in this volume.

6. Garfield and his producer Roberts had originally planned *Body and Soul* to be an account of the life of Barney Ross, an ex-marine and world lightweight champion in 1933 and 1935. What drew Garfield and Roberts to Ross's story was the self-evident fit with Garfield's screen persona—street tough, New York prizefighter, and ex-soldier (Garfield was 4F, but had played military personnel in a number of wartime films, notably in *The Pride of the Marines*, 1945). Ross's biography would eventually be filmed in 1957 as *Monkey on My Back*. The film, however, showed little interest in Ross's boxing or military story, preferring to exploit the drug angle (Ross had become a drug addict following his time in the army) in a bid to capitalize on the recent notoriety of *The Man with the Golden Arm* (1956). Coincidentally, John Garfield and his producer Bob Roberts had originally optioned the screen rights for Nelson Algren's novel. Furthermore, Cameron Mitchell in *Monkey on My Back* overtly recalls Garfield in both style and performance. The actor Dane Clark also drew upon Garfield for inspiration in the derivative boxing movie *Whiplash*, confirming Warner Bros.' intention to use him as a replacement for their departed star.

7. Allen Bodner, *When Boxing Was a Jewish Sport* (Westport, Conn.: Praeger, 1997), 117. Baer's biography on the International Boxing Hall of Fame web site records that he had a Jewish grandfather: http://www.ibhof.com/baer.htm.

8. Jeffrey T. Sammons, *Beyond the Ring: The Role of Boxing in American Society* (Urbana: University of Illinois Press, 1988), 92.

9. See Bodner, *When Boxing Was a Jewish Sport*.

10. Ibid., 57.

11. Odets appeared before HUAC in executive session in April 1952, and gave public testimony in May 1952.

12. Eric Mottram, "Introduction," to Clifford Odets, *Golden Boy, Awake and Sing!, The Big Knife* (Harmondsworth: Penguin, 1963), 19.

13. Other critics have also made the link between the two plays; see for instance G. Weales, *Odets: The Playwright* (London: Methuen, 1985), 162, and Gabriel Miller, *Clifford Odets* (New York: Continuum, 1989), 62–93.

14. The preeminent left-wing dramatist of the age, Bertolt Brecht, had also shown some interest in boxing. In 1926 he began production on what was to be an unfinished work called *The Human Fighting-Machine*, a collaboration with the then-German middleweight champion Paul Samon-Korner. Brecht's aesthetic interest in boxing was for its formal properties: the ring as a theatrical space, the "hard seats and bright lights," and an audience "smoking and observing," rather than, as with Odets, for its potential thematic interest. See John Willett, *The Theatre of Bertolt Brecht* (London: Methuen, 1977), 71, 146–148.

15. Miller, *Clifford Odets*, 65–66.

16. John Lahr, "Waiting for Odets," *Lincoln Center Theater Review* 42 (Spring 2006): 18.

17. Irving Shulman, *The Square Trap* (New York: Popular Library, 1953), 74.

18. Ibid., 165.

19. Ibid., 76.

20. *The Hollywood Reporter* (August 20, 1952), 3.

21. When *The Big Knife* opened in New Haven in January 1949, its star was John Garfield. In 1952 Garfield would star in the revival of *Golden Boy*; he had been Odets's first choice for the role when the play debuted in 1937, though Luther Adler got the part. Garfield was also Columbia's first choice for the lead in its film adaptation of *Golden Boy*, but Warner Bros., who had Garfield under exclusive contract, refused Columbia's advances. See Robert Nott, *He Ran All The Way: The Life of John Garfield* (New York: Limelight Editions, 2003), 119. Eighteen months before *The Big Knife*'s debut, *Body and Soul* opened in New York; the film reconfirmed Garfield as a star of the first order. Garfield had earlier portrayed a boxer in *They Made Me a Criminal* (1939), in which his character is framed for murder and he goes on the lam, ending up on a ranch in Arizona with the Dead End Kids. It was one performance, among many, that helped establish Garfield's onscreen proletarian persona. The critic for the *New Yorker* took note of his performance: "There is nothing noisy, stagy, or showy about him. One can find hundreds such along Sixth Avenue, spelling out the signs in front of the employment agencies." Cited in Robert Sklar, *City Boys: Cagney, Bogart, Garfield* (Princeton, N.J.: Princeton University Press, 1992), 90.

22. For a contemporary analysis of this "slippage" see Henry Popkin, "The Vanishing Jew of Our Popular Culture: The Little Man Who Is No Longer There," *Commentary* 14, no. 1 (1952): 46–55.

23. Her sculptures are described as "surrealist" in the published screenplay, Abraham Polonsky, *Body and Soul: The Critical Edition* (Northridge: California State University, Northridge, 2002), 38.

24. Joyce Carol Oates, *On Boxing* (London: Bloomsbury, 1987), 26.

25. A. J. Liebling, *Sweet Science* (London: Sportsman's Book Club, 1958), 9.

26. Ibid., 241–243.

27. W. C. Heinz, *The Professional* (New York: DaCapo, 2001), 87.

28. W.C. Heinz, *Once They Heard Cheers* (New York: Doubleday, 1979), 257–258.

29. Rich Cohen, *Tough Jews* (New York: Simon and Schuster, 1998), 156.

30. Quoted in Gordon Burn, "The Games Writers Play," *Guardian Review* (October 9, 2004), 5.

31. Susan J. Douglas, *Listening In: Radio and the American Imagination* (Minneapolis: University of Minnesota Press, 1999), 63.

32. Ibid., 199–200.

33. Ibid., 208.

34. Review collected in the *Body and Soul* clipping file, Margaret Herrick Library, AMPAS.

35. Nott, *He Ran All The Way*, 198.

36. Polonsky, *Body and Soul*, 18.

37. Buhle and Wagner, *A Very Dangerous Citizen*, 113, 109.

38. *The Hollywood Reporter* (August 13, 1947).

39. *Variety* (August 13, 1947).

40. *Daily Variety* (August 13, 1947).

41. Sammons, *Beyond the Ring*, xv.

42. Oates, *On Boxing*, 13.

43. Marcus Klein, *Foreigners: The Making of American Literature: 1900–1940* (Chicago: University of Chicago Press, 1981), 201.

44. Ibid., 215.

45. Ibid., 184.

46. Ibid., 226.

47. Stanley Ellin, *Dreadful Summit* (New York: Lion Books, 1950).

48. Ellin's characterization of the singer is based upon Billie Holiday. When the boy approaches her outside the club he uses the same lines as those given to him in the film, except Ellin has him say "nigger." In the novel the singer's response is to spit at him. Stanley Ellin, *Dreadful Summit* (Harmondsworth: Penguin, 1964), 80–83.

49. Liebling, *Sweet Science*, 8–9.

50. Ibid.

51. Heinz, *Once They Heard Cheers*, 248.

52. Sammons, *Beyond the Ring*, 131. Wednesday night fights were sponsored by Pabst Blue Ribbon beer, Friday night fights by Gillette razor blades. "By 1952 experts reported that the ranks of professional boxers had been depleted by 50% and 'town fight nights' had been wiped out." Ibid., 149.

53. Ibid., 134.

54. Ibid., 133.

55. Cited in Russell Sullivan, *Rocky Marciano: The Rock of His Times* (Urbana: University of Illinois Press, 2002), 208.

56. In *He Ran All the Way*, 318, Nott notes that Odets wrote a television boxing drama "Leather Dollar" starring Robert Blake for the "Richard Boone Show" (1963–64). However, I cannot find this episode listed elsewhere. Nevertheless, progressive sentiments are ably expressed in the television boxing drama "Viva Paco!" an episode in the "Johnny Staccato" series (1959–60), which generally had a strong Popular Front accent. Paco is a Puerto Rican contender for the championship, a symbol for his people. Staccato tells it this way: "Compared to Chinatown, the Lower East Side, Greenwich Village, Spanish Harlem was brand new. The 100s and 1000s of people there added a new rhythm to the city; it's American alright, but with an Afro-Cuban beat. And to these people, Paco was a great hero—a symbol of success in the new country." A fictional incident in Benny Leonard's career is

used in "Fight for the Title," a 1957 episode from "Telephone Time" (1956–58). The boxing film *Roaring City* (1951) was designed to be cut into two after the completion of its theatrical run and sold as episodes of "Danger Zone". There are, I have no doubt, many more examples of television boxing dramas.

57. See Sullivan, *Rocky Marciano*, 203–204.

58. Marciano's biographer makes the argument that Rocky was the last of the great heavyweights at a time when boxing meant something to the American public. Ali, on the other hand, "was a political and social force that transcended his sport (and all sports for that matter). His individual brilliance and charisma did not restore the kingdom of heavyweight championship boxing but merely obscured the fact that it had crumbled years before." Sullivan, *Rocky Marciano*, 210.

CHAPTER 5 — THE VIOLENT POETRY OF THE TIMES

1. Eduardo Obregón Pagán, *Murder at the Sleepy Lagoon: Zoot Suits, Race, and Riot in Wartime L.A.* (Chapel Hill: University of North Carolina Press, 2003), 91.

2. *Los Angeles Times*, January 7–9, 1943.

3. Pagán, *Murder at the Sleepy Lagoon*, 73.

4. *Los Angeles Times*, January 13, 1943.

5. *Los Angeles Times*, June 7, 1943.

6. *Los Angeles Times*, June 11, 1943.

7. Citizen's Committee for the Defense of Mexican-American Youth, *The Sleepy Lagoon Case* (Los Angeles, 1943), 7.

8. Guy Endore, *Sleepy Lagoon Mystery* (Los Angeles: Sleepy Lagoon Defense Committee, 1944), 7.

9. Ibid., 18.

10. Ibid., 26.

11. Citizen's Committee, *The Sleepy Lagoon Case*, 7.

12. Endore, *Sleepy Lagoon Mystery*, 13.

13. Pagán, *Murder at the Sleepy Lagoon*, 224.

14. Endore, *Sleepy Lagoon Mystery*, 13.

15. Pagán, *Murder at the Sleepy Lagoon*, 222–223.

16. Ibid., 195.

17. Philip Dunne, *Take Two: A Life in Movies and Politics* (New York: Limelight Editions, 1980), 194.

18. John Huston, *An Open Book* (New York: Alfred A. Knopf, 1980), 133.

19. A. M. Sperber and Eric Lax, *Bogart* (New York: William Morrow, 1997), 386.

20. Huston, *An Open Book*, 133.

21. Nancy Lynn Schwartz, completed by Sheila Schwartz, *The Hollywood Writers' Wars* (New York: Alfred A. Knopf, 1982), 281.

22. Sperber and Lax, *Bogart*, 397.

23. Huston, *An Open Book*, 215.

24. David F. Prindle, *The Politics of Glamour: Ideology and Democracy in the Screen Actors Guild* (Madison: University of Wisconsin Press, 1988), 60.

25. Dunne, *Take Two*, 213.

26. Ibid., 212.

27. Ibid., 214 and 221.

28. *Variety*, May 15, 1946.

29. Tom Flinn, "Screenwriter Daniel Mainwaring Discusses 'Out of the Past,'" *Velvet Light Trap* 10 (Fall 1973): 44.

30. Geoffrey Homes, "New Study of Migratory Workers in California," *New York Times*, March 5, 1950.

31. Ibid.

32. William Boddy, "Daniel Mainwaring (Geoffrey Homes)," *American Screenwriters*, 2nd ser., ed. Randall Clark (Detroit: Gale Research Company, 1986), 209, and Flinn, "Screenwriter Daniel Mainwaring," 44.

33. Flinn, "Screenwriter Daniel Mainwaring," 44.

34. Michel Ciment, *Conversations with Losey* (New York: Methuen, 1985), 94.

35. Pierre Rissient, "Daniel Mainwaring," *Film Dope* 38 (December 1987): 16.

36. The filmography in *American Screenwriter* lists twenty films in that period. The Internet Movie Database lists twenty-three. The two lists don't entirely overlap.

37. Flinn, "Screenwriter Daniel Mainwaring," 45.

38. Boddy, "Daniel Mainwaring (Geoffrey Homes)," 209.

39. Ibid.

40. *Variety*, February 19, 1947.

41. Flinn, "Screenwriter Daniel Mainwaring," 44, and Boddy, "Daniel Mainwaring (Geoffrey Homes)," 211.

42. Ciment, *Conversations with Losey*, 79, 82.

43. Ibid., 94.

44. Boddy, "Daniel Mainwaring (Geoffrey Homes)," 211.

45. Ciment, *Conversations with Losey*, 93.

46. Ibid., 92.

47. Boddy, "Daniel Mainwaring (Geoffrey Homes)," 211.

48. Joseph Breen to Luigi Luraschi, October 5, 1949, PCA File on *The Lawless*, Margaret Herrick Library.

49. Joseph Breen to Luigi Luraschi, November 22, 1949, PCA File on *The Lawless*, Margaret Herrick Library.

50. James Leahy, *The Cinema of Joseph Losey* (New York: A. S. Barnes, 1967), 35.

51. Ciment, *Conversations with Losey*, 52–54.

52. David Caute, *Joseph Losey: A Revenge on Life* (New York: Oxford University Press, 1994), 55.

53. Ibid., 56.

54. Ibid., 100.

55. Ibid., 100–108.

56. Pagán, *Murder at the Sleepy Lagoon*, 163.

57. AFI Catalogue for *The Lawless*.

58. Tom Milne, ed., *Time Out Film Guide*, 3rd ed. (New York: Penguin Books, 1993), 393.

59. "Movie News," *New York Herald-Tribune*, May 16, 1950.

60. Bosley Crowther, *New York Times*, June 23, 1950.

61. *Variety*, April 12, 1950.

62. Howard Barnes, *New York Herald-Tribune*, June 23, 1950.

63. Caute, *Joseph Losey*, 102.

64. Foster Hirsch, *Joseph Losey* (Boston: Twayne Publishers, 1980), 39.

CHAPTER 6 — DARK PASSAGES

1. Duke Ellington quoted in Krin Gabbard, *Jammin' in the Margins: Jazz and the American Cinema* (Chicago: University of Chicago Press, 1996), 192.

2. David Hadju, *Lush Life: A Biography of Billy Strayhorn* (New York: Farrar, Strauss Giroux, 1996), 188.

3. Lionel Trilling, *The Liberal Imagination* (1950; reprint, New York: Scribner's, 1976), xiv. On the literary aesthetics of the new liberalism more generally, see Thomas Schaub, *American Fiction in the Cold War* (Madison: University of Wisconsin Press, 1991).

4. Peter Bogdanovich, *Who the Devil Made It: Conversations with Legendary Film Directors* (New York: Ballantine, 1998), 635, 633, 631.

5. Ellington, interview, liner notes, *Anatomy of a Murder: Music by Duke Ellington, from the Soundtrack of the Motion Picture* (1959; reissue, New York: Sony Music Entertainment, 1999), 32.

6. Dean Bingham, *Acting Male: Masculinities in the Films of James Stewart, Jack Nicholson, and Clint Eastwood* (New Brunswick, N.J.: Rutgers University Press, 1994), 91.

7. On Ellington and the Popular Front, see Michael Denning, *The Cultural Front: The Laboring of American Culture in the Twentieth Century* (New York: Verso, 1997), 309–318.

8. Sidney Finkelstein, *Jazz: A People's Music* (New York: Citadel, 1948), 263, 230, 231.

9. Piazza, quoted in Gabbard, *Jammin,'* 189.

10. Wynton Marsalis, "Music by Duke Ellington," liner notes, *Anatomy of a Murder*, 16; Gabbard, *Jammin*, 187–188.

11. Though his aims were distorted by studio editing, Welles carefully specified his film's Latin jazz theme. The music should be "Afro-Cuban" and not "the usual 'rancheros' and 'mariachi' numbers," Welles requested—precisely, it appears, for the way that, in sacrificing local authenticity, the music would emphasize a cosmopolitan excitement that, like the marriage of Susie and Mike Vargas, escaped the bigotry of small-town Texas. Welles, quoted in David Butler, *Jazz Noir: Listening to Music from Phantom Lady to The Last Seduction* (New York: Praeger, 2002), 106.

12. Ibid., xiv.

13. On the film's artful use of its title theme, see the superb discussion in Peter Stanfield, *Body and Soul: Jazz, Blues, and Race in American Film, 1927–63* (Urbana: University of Illinois Press, 2005), 151–156.

14. For a thorough and critical review of the various, inconsistent, and unsatisfactory efforts to define film noir, see Steve Neale, *Genre and Hollywood* (New York: Routledge, 2000), 151–178. Neale convincingly demonstrates that, "as a single phenomenon, noir . . . never existed" (173). For the purposes of this essay, however, whether or not it is possible to identify a distinctive kind or style of noir film is unimportant. It is enough to note, rather, that crime thrillers of the forties and fifties employed jazz in a set of consistent ways that used the symbolic resonance of popular music to relate stories of crime and violence to the larger social tensions they dramatized.

15. On jazz's relation to film noir's arguable expressionist fascination with violence, death, and sexuality, see Robert G. Porfirio, "Dark Jazz: Music in the Film Noir," *Film Noir Reader 2*, ed. Alain Silver and James Ursini (New York: Limelight, 1999), 177–187.

16. On *Blue Dahlia* as an exemplary film noir highlighting gender issues raised by postwar integration, see Frank Krutnik, *In a Lonely Street: Film Noir, Genre, Masculinity* (New York: Routledge, 1991), 65–71.

17. See, e.g., Butler, *Jazz Noir*, 69.

18. Kathryn Kalinak, *Settling the Score: Music and the Classical Hollywood Film* (Madison: University of Wisconsin Press, 1992), 167. For an excellent survey of some of the diverse meanings to which Hollywood jazz could be put, and of its racial and political implications, see Stanfield, *Body and Soul*.

19. As Leighton Grist notes, Tourneur used the same low-key lighting for both women, in contrast to the high-key lighting used in the scenes featuring masculine control. Grist, "Out of the Past, a. k. a., Build My Gallows High," *The Book of Film Noir*, ed. Ian Cameron (New York: Continuum, 1993), 208. And, indeed, in her command to Jeff that he "be very sure that there isn't even a little bit of love left for" Kathie, and in her explanation that "you have to go all the way to find" it, Ann virtually demands Jeff's fatal return to Kathie's command.

20. See the useful discussion in J. P. Telotte, *Voices in the Dark: The Narrative Patterns of Film Noir* (Urbana: University of Illinois Press, 1989), 54, 199.

21. An illuminating comparison figure might be seen in the role played by Shorty Polaski (Joseph Pevney), Charley Davis's childhood friend in *Body and Soul*. In his trajectory from overconfident hustler to angry populist, Shorty anticipates Charley's transformation and,

in his death, warns of the danger Charley faces. Interestingly, although he will be killed after being beaten by a gangster, Shorty dies because he stumbles into the street and is run down by a passing car. The moment allows us to think both that Shorty, betrayed by his friend, has lost the will to live, and, analogously, that cut off from the neighborhood associations that sheltered him, he has become vulnerable to urban accident. As in *DOA* the corrupt city is inseparable from the city ruled by chance. Counterintuitive though that association may seem, it is consistent with the fact that only corruption introduces an element of chance into Charley's bouts.

22. Paula Rabinowitz, *Black & White & Noir: America's Pulp Modernism* (New York: Columbia University Press, 2002), 61.

23. Carmichael is a particularly resonant figure here because of the way his music and his career dramatized jazz's potential to communicate across racial boundaries. From early in his career, Carmichael was renowned for his "love of black musical and vocal idioms." During the late twenties he was identified in the popular press as a "Negro Blues composer." His enthusiasm for the Cotton Club and Ellington, whom he called "the king of jazz," was also noted. See Richard M. Sudhalter, *Stardust Melody: The Life and Music of Hoagy Carmichael* (New York: Oxford University Press, 2002), 149.

24. On this second order narrative as a reestablishment of patriarchal authority, see Krutnik, *In a Lonely Street*, 114–123; for the claim that it is a bad-faith "insurance against nothingness" otherwise registered in the Swede's confrontation with mortality, see Oliver Harris, "Film Noir Fascination: Outside History, but Historically So," *Cinema Journal* 43, no. 1 (Fall 2003): 3–24.

25. On the role of singing women in film noir and their challenge to both "masculine autonomy" and "the sadistic course of narrative," see Adrienne L. McLean, " 'It's Only That I Do What I Love and Love What I Do': 'Film Noir' and the Musical Woman," *Cinema Journal* 33, no. 1 (1993): 3–16, 4, 7.

26. On the prevalence of that ideology in Hollywood filmmaking during the war, see Lary May, "Making the American Consensus: The Narrative of Conversion and Subversion in World War II Films," in *The War in American Culture: Society and Consciousness during World War II*, ed. Lewis A. Erenburg and Susan E. Hirsch (Chicago: University of Chicago Press, 1996), 79, 71–103.

27. Paul Buhle and David Wagner, *Radical Hollywood: The Untold Story Behind America's Favorite Movies* (New York: New Press, 2002), xvi, 360; David Reid and Jayne L. Walker, "Strange Pursuit: Cornell Woolrich and the Abandoned City of the Forties," in *Shades of Noir: A Reader*, ed. Joan Copjec (New York: Verso, 1993), 86; for a more nuanced discussion, seeing much of noir as reflecting a reaction of the Hollywood Left to the blacklist and the decline of social democratic hopes, see James Naremore, *More than Night: Film Noir and Its Contexts* (Berkeley: University of California Press, 1998), 123–135.

28. See, e.g., Richard Slotkin, "Unit Pride: Ethnic Platoons and the Myths of American Nationality," *American Literary History* 13, no. 3 (2001): 469–498. Both *The Killers* and Siodmak's subsequent *Cry of the City* (1948) also thematized the era's preoccupation with ethnic assimilation. But those two earlier films both featured the white ethnics (Italians, Jews,

Irish) of the eastern industrial cities—a population the New Deal and, still more signifi-cantly, World War II had successfully recast as the heart of a new cultural and political order. *Criss Cross*'s turn to California and its much more cautious allusion to the region's Hispanic minority thus raised a different set of issues.

29. For a more detailed discussion of the negative characterization of Ramirez and a thorough comparison of the way *Criss Cross* both resembles and differs from *The Killers*, see Michael Walker, "Robert Siodmak," in *The Book of Film Noir*, 139–145.

30. Alain Silver, "Criss Cross," in *Film Noir: An Encyclopedic Reference to the American Style* rev. and expanded ed., ed. Alain Silver and Elizabeth Ward (New York: Overlook Press, 1988), 72. As Krutnik notes, *The Killers* does not introduce Kitty by showing Swede's view of her but, in an awkward shot that distances the viewer from Swede's perspective, shows him transfixed by her as he is watched in turn by his girlfriend. In effect, the scene encour-ages the viewer to take Reardon's perspective on Swede's self-destructive passion. Krut-nik, *In a Lonely Street*, 114.

31. Silver, "Criss Cross," 72.

32. Stanfield, *Body and Soul*, 148–150; Naremore, *Something More than Night*, 118.

33. Saverio Giovacchini, *Hollywood Modernism: Film and Politics in the Age of the New Deal* (Philadelphia: Temple University Press, 2001), 195–198.

34. Telotte, *Voices in the Dark*, 127.

35. Stanfield, *Body and Soul*, 159–172; Will Straw, "Urban Confidential: The Lurid City of the 1950s" in *The Cinematic City*, ed. David B. Clarke (London: Routledge, 1997), 110–128; the difference between the B-girl played by Gloria Grahame in *Crossfire* and the similar role she took in *The Big Heat* is instructive here—since in the latter case her sexual trans-gressions, dramatized by her cruel disfigurement, are only redeemed by her death. In *Crossfire*, she is forced to undergo the humiliation of an interview with the police, but suf-fers no worse fate.

36. The other character most sympathetic to Dix is his agent Mel Lippman, played by Ray's old friend from radical theater, the soon-to-be blacklisted actor Art Smith. Though Mel probes Dix's private life, as do all the film's main characters, he also intuitively shrugs off the authority of the law, offering to spirit Dix to Mexico even if he has killed Mildred. The most affectionate and intimate conversation between the two men occurs signifi-cantly neither in Dix's home nor in the public space of the restaurant where they often meet, but in the covert space of the restaurant's men's room.

37. Dana Polan, *In a Lonely Place* (London: BFI Publishing), 54.

38. See, e.g., Michael Warner, *Publics and Counterpublics* (Cambridge, Mass.: MIT Press, 2005).

39. See the valuable discussion in Butler, *Jazz Noir*, 131–137; Butler suggests that in its combination of Hamilton's on-screen "diegetic" performance and Elmer Bernstein's jazz score, *Sweet Smell of Success* demonstrates a confusion about whether jazz represents a sleazy metropolis or disciplined artistry. But it would surely be more accurate to say that this is a deft contrast rather than unintended confusion. Calling on two related but distinct

musical styles, the film casts the hard bop combo and the big band theme music in a dialectical conflict, emphasizing two counterpoised kinds of music and by extension two aspects of postwar urban life—with the freedom and artistry of hard bop defended against the sleaze and demagoguery associated with Bernstein's big band score. A similar, but reversed structure can be seen in *Odds Against Tomorrow* (1959, dir. Robert Wise, screenplay Abraham Polonsky). There the passion of a blues performed in a nightclub by Johnny (Sidney Poitier) is made to seem expressive of his anger at being trapped by the exploitative labor relations of the mob-controlled nightclub industry. But that diegetic performance is all but explicitly contrasted to the meditative modern jazz score composed by John Lewis, which, in its extensive use during long shots that place the film's isolated characters in stark environments that dwarf them, is implicitly aligned with a narratorial perspective whose knowledge and wisdom exceeds the limits of the characters. Coincidentally, both films focus on the dangers of bigotry and implicitly cast their anti-racist stance against what by contrast appears an outworn populism. In *Odds Against Tomorrow*, the straitened circumstances of the ex-cop Burke (James Begley) and the background of Earle Slater (Robert Ryan) among impoverished tenant farmers turns out to be less significant than Slater's resentment and racism. Similarly, in its anti-populist concern about demagoguery, *Sweet Smell* resembles *Dark Passage* and *In a Lonely Place*, films often placed in the noir canon that stand out for their absence of any intimation of class exploitation. So, too, *Anatomy of a Murder* alludes to the class backgrounds of its major characters, but prefers to see them as sources of differing cultural styles and views its implicitly working class characters as the representatives of the most robust and dangerous social forces.

CHAPTER 7 — DOCUMENTARY REALISM AND THE POSTWAR LEFT

Acknowledgments: Many thanks to Robert Read for research assistance.

1. Epigraph from Noel Meadow, "The Documentary Film Era," *Screen Writer* 2, no. 2 (1946): 32. Meadow, whose original name was Leon Blumenfeld, began staging his own plays at the Ninety-second Street YMHA in New York in 1926, at the age of eighteen. In the early 1930s, he wrote celebrity gossip columns for such magazines and tabloid newspapers as *Broadway Magazine*, *Hot-Cha*, *Scandal*, *Broadway Tattler*, and *Broadway Brevities*, while producing more plays and hosting radio broadcasts.

2. See, for example, "Screen News Here and in Hollywood," *New York Times*, April 20, 1942, 17; "Of Local Origin," *New York Times*, September 7, 1943, 20; "Of Local Origin," *New York Times*, June 10, 1944, 12.

3. On Meadow's distribution of films see the various advertisements in the *Screen Writer*, but also "News of the Screen," *New York Times*, July 24, 1946, 24; "Of Local Origin," *New York Times*, September 25, 1948, 11.

4. Michael Denning, *The Cultural Front* (London: Verso, 1997).

5. This period in the history of the *Screen Writer* is described in Larry Ceplair and Steven Englund, *The Inquisition in Hollywood: Politics in the Film Community, 1930–1960* (Berkeley: University of California Press, 1983), 250. From 1943 to 1946, Noel Meadow was an associate editor of the New York–based trade paper *Writers Journal*, assuming the position of

managing editor in 1946. (*Writers Journal* seems to have ceased publication in 1949, shortly after a change in management which saw Meadow's name disappear from its masthead.)

6. See Noel Meadow and Harold L. Ober, "Adults Not Admitted," *Screen Writer* 2, no. 6 (1946): 21; for a fuller discussion of *The House That I Live In*, see Art Simon's chapter in this volume.

7. Wesley F. Pratzner, "What Has Happened to the Documentary Film?" *Public Opinion Quarterly* 11, no. 3 (1947): 397.

8. See, for example, William Lafferty, "A Reappraisal of the Semi-Documentary Film in Hollywood, 1945–1948," *Velvet Light Trap* 20 (1983): 22–26; and Steven N. Lipkin, "Real Emotional Logic: Persuasive Strategies in Docudrama," *Cinema Journal* 38, no. 4 (1999): 68–85.

9. The articles in the series, all by Herb Tank, are the following: "New Documentary Look in Hollywood," *Daily Worker*, March 16, 1948, 12; "Today's Films: More on Hollywood Documentary Style," *Daily Worker*, March 18, 1948, 12; "Today's Films: Holly'd On-the-Spot films conceal truth," *Daily Worker*, March 19, 1948, 12.

10. This characterization of the *Daily Worker* is based on my own observation, but see, for further confirmation and discussion, Henry D. Fetter, "The Party Line and the Color Line: The American Communist Party, the Daily Worker, and Jackie Robinson," *Journal of Sport History* 28, no. 3 (2003): 375–402.

11. See, in order of mention, "Cagney Spy Thriller Goes Haywire After Fine Start," *Daily Worker*, January 20, 1947, 11; " 'Call Northside 777' Factual News Yarn," *Daily Worker*, February 19, 1948, 12; " 'T-Men'—Tough, Exciting Movie," *Daily Worker*, January 23, 1948, 12; " 'Kiss of Death' is Tough, Skilful Melodrama," *Daily Worker*, September 8, 1947, 11; " 'The Naked City' Good Job, Well Done," *Daily Worker*, March 5, 1948, 12.

12. "Today's Film: 'Call Northside 777' Factual News Yarn," *Daily Worker*, February 19, 1948, 12.

13. "T-Men'—Tough, Exciting Movie," 12.

14. "Fox to Make Film on Russian Spying," *New York Times*, April 10, 1947, 35.

15. "PCA Blasts *Iron Curtain*," *Daily Worker*, February 23, 1948, 12.

16. "Stars Speak Up for the Bill of Rights," *Daily Worker*, March 16, 1948, 12.

17. "New Documentary Look in Hollywood," 12.

18. Ibid.

19. "More on Hollywood Documentary Style," 12.

20. Ibid.

21. "Today's Films: Holly'd On-the-Spot Films Conceal Truth," 12.

22. See " 'The Naked City' Good Job Well Done" and "New Documentary Look in Hollywood."

23. " 'The *Iron Curtain*,' Anti-Communist Film, Has Premiere Here at the Roxy Theatre," *New York Times*, May 13, 1948, 31; " 'The *Iron Curtain*': New Roxy Film Poses a Question: Is It Being Raised or Lowered?" *New York Times*, May 16, 1948, X1.

24. "Zanuck Defends 'The *Iron Curtain*,'" *New York Times*, May 30, 1948, X5.

25. "Today's Film: '*Iron Curtain*' Drops on Roxy," *Daily Worker*, May 13, 1948, 12.

26. "Nation-Wide Picketing of '*Iron Curtain*,'" *Daily Worker*, May 21, 1948, 12.

27. Milton Krims, "*Iron Curtain* Diary," *Screen Writer* 4, no. 3 (1948): 1–15, 32.

28. Tony Bennett, "Museums, Cultural Objecthood, and the Governance of the Social," *Cultural Studies* 19, no. 5 (2005): 521–547.

29. See, for example, Parker Tyler, "Documentary Technique in Film Fiction," *American Quarterly* 1 (1949): 99–115; and Joseph P. Brinton, J.P., "Subjective Camera or Subjective Audience?" *Hollywood Quarterly* 2 (1947): 359–366.

30. See Lester Koenig, "Back from the Wars," *Screen Writer* 1 (1945): 23–29; Robert Shaw, "New Horizons in Hollywood," *Public Opinion Quarterly* 10, no. 1 (1946): 71–77.

31. "Today's Films: Holly'd On-the-Spot Films Conceal Truth," 12.

32. See, among many other denunciations of the brutality of postwar cinema, John Houseman, "Today's Hero: A Review," *Hollywood Quarterly* 2 (1947): 161–163. Official condemnation of the postwar brute-cult may be found in V. J. Jerome, *Culture in a Changing World: A Marxist Approach* (New York: New Century Publications, 1947), especially pages 26–30. See, as well, the useful discussion of Jerome in Andrew Hemingway, *Artists on the Left: American Artists and the Communist Movement, 1926–1956* (New Haven: Yale University Press, 2002).

33. See, again, Shaw, "New Horizons in Hollywood."

34. Koenig, "Back from the Wars."

35. Frank Krutnik, *In a Lonely Street: Film Noir, Genre, Masculinity* (London: Routledge, 1991), 204.

36. Jay Richards Kennedy, "An Approach to Pictures," *Screen Writer* 3, no. 1 (1947): 6.

37. "An Approach to Pictures," 6.

38. Ibid., 7.

39. Ibid. This recalls the possibly apocryphal statement by Columbia studio head Harry Cohn, to the effect that a documentary film was a film without women; if there was one woman in a film, it was a semi-documentary.

40. In fact, the flatness of Dick Powell's performance in *To The Ends of the Earth* (as *Assigned to Treasury* was known upon its release) differed little from the stoic, hardboiled tone of so many of his postwar roles. The film itself offers a richly varied series of picturesque, orientalizing settings, from Shanghai to Cuba and Egypt, and a set of secondary, villainous characters more typical of a Mr. Moto film than of other postwar semi-documentaries.

41. Siegfried Kracauer, "Those Movies with a Message," *Harper's* 196, no. 1176 (May 1948): 568.

42. Tyler, "Documentary Technique in Film Fiction," 115.

43. "By Way of Report," *New York Times*, November 12, 1961, X7.

CHAPTER 8 — CLOAKED IN COMPROMISE

Epigraph: Jean Paul Marquet, "Le Vrai Dassin: de *La Cité sans voiles* au *Rififi chez les hommes*," *Positif* (November 1955): 70; my translation.

1. James Agee, "The Naked City," *Time*, March 22, 1948.

2. Daily Production Report, Mark Hellinger Productions (October 21, 1947), Box 15: Folder 19, Mark Hellinger Collection, University of Southern California Library.

3. Jules Dassin, telephone interview with author, March 23, 2006.

4. Edward Dimendberg makes this observation in his discussion of *The Naked City*'s use of urban space. See Edward Dimendberg, *Film Noir and the Spaces of Modernity* (Cambridge, Mass.: Harvard University Press, 2004), 72–73. An exception, noted by Dimendberg, is Carl Richardson's detailed account of *The Naked City*'s production, which situates the film in relation to its political and cultural context to some degree. See Carl Richardson, *Autopsy: An Element of Realism in Film Noir* (Metuchen, N.J.: Scarecrow Press, 1992), 106–107.

5. In his contribution to this volume, Will Straw discusses an alternate history for the semi-documentary. In a series of articles published in the *Daily Worker* in 1948, film critic Herb Tank revises the conventional narrative of the semi-documentary's genesis, tracing its roots beyond the war to the social documentaries of the 1930s. As Straw observes, situating the cycle within this longer history provides a shift in emphasis away from the war and toward "more longstanding political continuities. Within this longer view, the wartime documentary became a temporary, imperfect expression of the progressive search for truth, rather than its most perfect achievement." See Will Straw, "Documentary Realism and the Postwar Left," in this volume.

6. See Thomas Doherty, "Documenting the 1940s," in *Boom and Bust: The American Cinema in the 1940s*, ed. Thomas Schatz (New York: Scribner, 1997), 417.

7. For an in-depth account of the postwar economic circumstances (including the increased price of film stock and the shortage of soundstages due to the rise of independent production) that may have predisposed the studios to the semi-documentary, see William Lafferty, "A Reappraisal of the Semi-Documentary in Hollywood, 1945–1948," in *Velvet Light Trap* 20 (Summer 1983): 22–26. MGM's decision to open its own low-budget, semi-documentary unit was precipitated "by a steady dwindling of the profits under the old system of operation since the end of the war." See Thomas F. Brady, "Old Order Changes: Metro Adopts Topical Films and Signs de Rochemont," *New York Times*, February 8, 1948, 5.

8. "*The House on 92nd Street* Terrific Drama. 20th's First 'Living Journalism' Pic," *Hollywood Review*, September 17, 1945. Quoted in Haden R. Guest, "The Police Procedural Film: Law and Order in the American Cinema, 1930–1960" (Ph.D. diss., University of California, Los Angeles, 2005), 108. Guest, whose study situates the postwar semi-documentary within the broader continuum of the police procedural film, notes that *The House on 92nd Street* is not without antecedents. Anatole Litvak's *Confessions of a Nazi Spy* (Warner Bros., 1939) uses newsreel-style voiceover narration in addition to documentary footage, including scenes from Leni Riefenstahl's *Triumph of the Will* (1934). See Guest, "The Police Procedural Film," 118.

9. Thomas M. Pryor, "Blazing a Trail. Feature Film on FBI Will Be a Blend of Factual and Entertainment Techniques," *New York Times*, April 1, 1945, 3.

10. Guest, "The Police Procedural Film," 124.

11. Quoted in ibid., 125.

12. A number of semi-documentary crime films were produced after 1948: *The Port of New York* (Eagle-Lion, 1949, dir. Benedek,), *Panic in the Streets* (Fox, 1950, dir. Kazan), and *Walk East on Beacon!* (Columbia, 1952, dir. Werker).

13. Raymond Borde and Etienne Chaumeton, *Panorama du Film Noir Américain, 1941–1953* (Paris: Flammarion, 1988), 18 (my translation).

14. Thomas M. Pryor, "The House on 92nd Street," *New York Times*, September 27, 1945, 24; Edwin Schallert, "Spies' Activities Vividly Shown in Superthriller," *Los Angeles Times*, October 19, 1945, 8. Writing in 1955, Jean Paul Marquet suggests that the implicit ideological purpose of the semi-documentary was to support the nascent Cold War-era surveillance state. " 'Don't worry,' it tells us, 'you can see you're well-protected.' But we can't help hearing instead 'Watch out, don't protest, you're being watched.' " See Marquet, "Le Vrai Dassin," 69; my translation.

15. In its review of *The Naked City*, the American Communist Party's *Daily Worker* praised the film's unglamorous look and concern for the poor, criticizing only its failure to probe beneath "surface effects" for their underlying causes. See Straw, "Documentary Realism," in this volume.

16. Bosley Crowther, "Fact or Fiction? Hollywood Manifests Confusion in Using 'Documentary Technique," *New York Times*, March 9, 1947, 1.

17. Robert Hatch, "The New Realism," *New Republic*, March 8, 1948.

18. Thomas F. Brady, "Hollywood Notes: Foy Quits as Studio Head to Make Own Films—The Documentary Fad Grows," *New York Times*, April 11, 1948, 5.

19. Lary May, "Movie Star Politics: The Screen Actor's Guild, Cultural Conversion, and the Hollywood Red Scare," in *Recasting America: Culture and Politics in the Age of Cold War*, ed. Lary May (Chicago: University of Chicago Press, 1989), 127.

20. See Guest, "The Police Procedural Film," 132.

21. Perhaps because of the public's evident appetite for these new "hard-hitting" social dramas, Hollywood's conservative turn was gradual. During the first half of 1947, 21 percent of Hollywood films fit the Production Code Administration's "social problem" category, the first time this genre was represented in significant numbers. Despite the activities of HUAC, this percentage didn't decline precipitously, but leveled off at 16.5 percent in 1948 and 1949. However, by 1950 only 9.5 percent of Hollywood's productions were dealing with social issues, a percentage that would remain the average for the first half of the 1950s. See Brian Neve, *Film and Politics in America: A Social Tradition* (London: Routledge, 2000), 84–85. For more on liberal productions during this period, see also Thom Anderson, "Red Hollywood," in this volume.

22. See Philip K. Scheuer, "Movie Realism at Peak in 1948. But Signs Begin to Hint That Crust of Postwar Hardness is Cracking," *Los Angeles Times*, December 26, 1948,

D1. Thomas Doherty also notes the impact of the war on film technicians, arguing that the "climate-controlled environment of the soundstage, deemed essential for quality lighting, sound, and set design, was a frustrating constraint for men who had weathered artillery bombardment and automatic weapons fire." See Doherty, "Documenting the 1940s," 417.

23. Bosley Crowther, "Open City. A Powerful New Film From Italy Points a Line of European Approach," *New York Times*, March 3, 1946, 1. See also Lee Morris, "Open City Has Spirit That Makes a Movie—and a People—Great," *Philadelphia Sunday Record*, [n.d.], *Rome: Open City*, Clipping File, AMPAS.

24. The *New York Times* observed that "Distributors, who in pre-war days, wouldn't go around the corner to see an Italian picture much less undertake to sell one, now are frantically scrambling to get their hands on anything coming out of Italy." See Thomas M. Pryor, "Foreign Films Become Big Business," *New York Times*, February 8, 1948, 5.

25. Bosley Crowther, "How Italy Resisted," *New York Times*, February 26, 1947, 32. See also Crowther, "Open City," March 3, 1946, 1.

26. Morris, *Rome: Open City* Clipping File, AMPAS.

27. Like Dassin, Elia Kazan suggests that the films of Rossellini, De Sica, and so on influenced his approach to the semi-documentary. Discussing *Panic in the Streets* (1950), he offers this assessment: "It was our neo-realism, exactly at the same time as *Paisà*, but of course in no way as good as *Paisà*." See Michel Ciment, ed., *Kazan on Kazan* (New York: Viking, 1974), 56.

28. Lino Miccichè quoted in Mira Liehm, *Passion and Defiance: Film in Italy from 1942 to the Present* (Berkeley: University of California Press, 1984), 129.

29. André Bazin, "An Aesthetic of Reality: Neo-Realism," in *What Is Cinema?*, ed. Hugh Gray, vol. 2 (Berkeley: University of California Press, 1972), 20–21.

30. See Malvin Wald, "Afterword," in *The Naked City: A Screenplay by Malvin Wald and Albert Maltz*, ed. Matthew J. Bruccoli (Carbondale and Edwardsville: Southern Illinois University Press, 1979), 136–137; see also Jim Bishop, *The Mark Hellinger Story: A Biography of Broadway and Hollywood* (New York: Appleton-Century-Crofts, 1952), 329; see also Cynthia Grenier, "Jules Dassin," *Sight and Sound* 22, no.3 (Winter 1957–58): 142, and Claude Chabrol and François Truffaut, "Entretien avec Jules Dassin (1)," *Cahiers du Cinéma*, no. 46 (April 1955): 6.

31. Wald, "Afterword," 137.

32. Ibid., 141–142. The documentary influence extends to Wald's use of narration which, as Sarah Kozloff notes, more closely resembles the "quieter, more lyrical style" associated with the Grierson school of British documentary than the "pontificating from on high" so common in other semi-documentaries. See "Humanizing 'The Voice of God': Narration in *The Naked City*," *Cinema Journal* 23, no. 4 (Summer 1984), 43.

33. According to Wald, Hellinger was frightened by the documentary form; like many producers of the period, Hellinger had never seen a documentary film, let alone a documentary script. Malvin Wald, telephone interview with author, March 2, 2006.

34. The *New York Times* notes the continuity between Hellinger's admiration for the NYPD and *The Naked City*'s subject matter: "None of us, knowing Mark's interests and his

brand of hero worship, were surprised to find [*The Naked City*] is mainly about the police force and its efficiency in solving crime." See Bosley Crowther, "Tales of Two Cities," *New York Times*, March 14, 1948, 1.

35. Christopher P. Wilson, *Cop Knowledge: Police Power and Cultural Narrative in Twentieth-Century America* (Chicago: University of Chicago Press, 2000), 77.

36. Bishop, *The Mark Hellinger Story*, 311.

37. Jules Dassin, telephone interview with author, March 23, 2006.

38. See "Jules Dassin, Interview by Patrick McGilligan," in Patrick McGilligan and Paul Buhle, *Tender Comrades: A Backstory of the Hollywood Blacklist* (New York: St. Martin's Press, 1997), 202.

39. Ibid., 207.

40. Hellinger let Dassin have a say in the casting of *Brute Force*, which features a number of his friends from the Actors Lab, including Hume Cronyn, Jeff Corey, and Roman Bohnen. Dassin describes Hellinger's approach as very hands-off; "His attitude was 'You're the director—go make the film." Jules Dassin, telephone interview with author, March 23, 2006. See also McGilligan, "Jules Dassin, Interview by Patrick McGilligan," 207.

41. Letter from Robert E. Kopp to Mark Hellinger (April 8, 1947), Box 1, Mark Hellinger Collection, University of Southern California Library.

42. Grenier, "Jules Dassin," 142. Wald claims that Dassin loved the screenplay, exclaiming, "We're going to make history!" See Nate Nichols, "Naked Truth," *New Times Los Angeles*, March 28–April 3, 2002, 19.

43. Jules Dassin, telephone interview with author, March 23, 2006.

44. See Christian Viviani, "Jules Dassin: Décidé à être un héros," *Positif*, no. 466 (December 1999): 95. See also Tom Charity, "Red Nightmare," *Time Out London* 7–12 (August 2002): 78.

45. Jules Dassin, telephone interview with author, March 23, 2006.

46. Viviani, "Jules Dassin: Décidé à être un héros," 95.

47. In a 1978 interview with *Cineaste*, Dassin makes this reference to his experience making *The Naked City*: "I was able to achieve more when I got out of their sight. . . . They didn't know what I was doing." See Dan Georgakas and Petros Anastasopoulos, "A Dream of Passion: An Interview with Jules Dassin," *Cineaste* 9, no. 1 (Fall 1978): 23.

48. "When *The Naked City* came along, I was so relieved." See Charity, "Red Nightmare," 78.

49. Despite the clear imbalance between Maltz's and Wald's contributions to the film, Hellinger insisted on giving them joint credit for the screenplay the better to capitalize on Maltz's renown. Malvin Wald, telephone interview with author, March 2, 2006. A comparison of Wald's script dated April 2, 1947, and Maltz's version dated April 7, 1947, suggests that Maltz's contributions were primarily to the film's introductory narration. See "Malvin Wald, *Homicide*" (April 2, 1947), Box 15: 13, Mark Hellinger Collection, University of Southern California Library, and Albert Maltz, "*Homicide*: Production Notes for Mark

Hellinger" (April 7, 1947), Box 15: 12, Mark Hellinger Collection, University of Southern California Library.

50. In an article published in the *New Masses* in 1946, Maltz suggested that the conception of art as a political weapon had become a literary "straightjacket" to socially conscious writers. His views prompted a schism within the Hollywood Communist Party and, under intense pressure, Maltz eventually recanted his position. See Barbara Zheutlin and David Talbot, *Creative Differences: Profiles of Hollywood Dissidents* (Boston: South End Press, 1978) 32–33.

51. Albert Maltz, *"Homicide*: Production Notes for Mark Hellinger" (April 7, 1947), Box 15: 12, Mark Hellinger Collection, University of Southern California Library.

52. Jules Dassin, telephone interview with author, March 23, 2006.

53. Virginia Wright, *Daily News*, March 15, 1948.

54. See John Francis Lane, "I See Dassin Make 'The Law,'" *Films and Filming*, September 4, 1958, 28–29, 34.

55. Jules Dassin, telephone interview with author, March 23, 2006. See also Lane, "I See Dassin Make 'The Law.'"

56. Herb A. Lightman, "'The Naked City' Tribute in Celluloid," *American Cinematographer* 29, no. 5 (May 1948): 179. See also Wilson, *Cop Knowledge*, 70.

57. Douglas Gilbert, "And Crowds Flock to Toss In the Color," *World Telegram*, [n.d.], *The Naked City* Clipping File, AMPAS.

58. Wright, Daily *News*, March 15, 1948. Hellinger had even hoped to film a scene with New York's police commissioner, who would tell the audience "honestly and sincerely that, no matter how big a case may seem, it's just another job to the police force," but was not able to secure Mayor William O'Dwyer's approval. Letter to William O'Dwyer from Mark Hellinger (June 16, 1947), Box 15: 9, Mark Hellinger Collection, University of Southern California Library.

59. Daily Production Report, Mark Hellinger Productions (October 21, 1947), Box 15: 19, Mark Hellinger Collection, University of Southern California Library.

60. In numerous interviews, Dassin indicates that he was closely involved with the film's editing. In 1955, he told the *Cahiers du Cinéma* that he worked on the editing "for ten weeks, day and night," and in 1977, he told Andrew Horton that Hellinger had promised him final cut. However, in 2006, he told me that he spent the "least amount of time in the cutting room" on *The Naked City* than on any of his films (Dassin, telephone interview). See Chabrol and Truffaut, "Entretien avec Jules Dassin," 7; see also Andrew Horton, "Jules Dassin: A Multi-National Filmmaker Considered," *Film Criticism* 7, no. 3 (Spring 1984): 24.

61. Jules Dassin, telephone interview with author, March 23, 2006. See also Viviani, "Jules Dassin: Décidé à être un héros," 95.

62. Jules Dassin, telephone interview with author, March 23, 2006.

63. Ibid. Dassin overstates his case, as the film still contains many vivid images of New York's working class and immigrant poor, particularly in the scenes filmed on location in Manhattan's Lower East Side. The film also retains a definite sense of class consciousness.

Its opening montage juxtaposes images of the working class (a man sleeping in a hot tenement apartment; a woman cleaning an office building; a man operating machinery) with those of wealthy New Yorkers enjoying the city's night life; the deadpan voiceover—"And while some people work, others are rounding off an evening of relaxation"—drives the point home. Throughout the film, New York's geography provides a medium for class commentary; it's clear what it means to have "Park Avenue friends" or to live in the suburbs of Jackson Heights.

64. The scene with the Hotel Progress was not used because Universal's legal department was unable to secure clearance from the owner. This decision was made early in the film's production and reported to Dassin's production manager, Gil Kurland, which raises the question of whether Dassin is being disingenuous when he bemoans the scene's absence from the film's final cut. "Interoffice Memo from Jim Pratt to Mark Hellinger" (June 25, 1947), Box 15: 6, Mark Hellinger Collection, University of Southern California Library.

65. In the missing dialogue, Lieutenant Muldoon ascribes social causes to the murdered girl's death:

When you think it over, I guess it was everybody's fault. People get so pounded and pounded in this life. It's a jungle, a city like this. Eight million people struggling for life, for food, for air, for a bit of happiness. Seems like there ain't enough of everything to go around . . . and so sometimes it breaks out in . . . violence.

"Homicide," undated script revisions, Box 15: 16, Mark Hellinger Collection, University of Southern California Library.

66. Frank McFadden (July 3, 1947), Box 442: 14096, Universal Collection, University of Southern California Library. Dassin assured me that this was pure fiction. Jules Dassin, telephone interview with author, March 23, 2006.

67. Frank McFadden (September 3, 1947), Box 544: 18144, Universal Collection, University of Southern California Library.

68. "New York Is the Star of 'Naked City.' Hellinger's Last Film Is Manhattan Melodrama," Cue, February 14, 1948.

69. Jacquelyn Judge, "Shooting The Naked City," Photography 1 (Winter 1947), Box 501: 14811, Universal Collection, University of Southern California Library; Alva Winston, "Photographing 'Naked City.' Problems Were Realism and Lighting," Home Movies (June), Box 501: 14811, Universal Collection, University of Southern California Library; Herb A. Lightman, "The Naked City.' Tribute in Celluloid," American Cinematographer 29, no. 5 (May 1948); Mayor William O'Dwyer, "Our Town," Modern Screen (January), Box 510: 14811, Universal Collection, University of Southern California Library; "New York Stars in a Movie," Screen Guide (March 1948), Box 501: 14811, Universal Collection, University of Southern California Library; "The Naked City," Movies (November), Box 501: 14811, Universal Collection, University of Southern California Library; "East Side, West Side," Movie Play (May 1948), Box 501: 14811, Universal Collection, University of Southern California Library.

70. Quoted in Irving Hoffman, "Critics Hail 'Naked City' as Tribute to New York," Hollywood Reporter, March 8, 1948.

71. "Thanks to the actuality filming of much of its action in New York, a definite parochial fascination is liberally assured all the way and the seams in a none-too-good who-dunnit are rather cleverly concealed." See Bosley Crowther, "Naked City,' Mark Hellinger's Final Film, at Capitol—Fitzgerald Heads Cast," *New York Times*, March 5, 1948, 17.

72. This is not true of French reviews of *The Naked City*, which refer to Italian Neo-Realism with notable consistency. See Jean H. Roy, "La cité sans voiles," *Temps Modernes*, no. 45 (July 1949): 190–191; Jean-Pierre Vivet, *Combat*, May 17, 1949, quoted in *Jules Dassin*, ed. Fabien Siclier and Jacques Levy (Paris: Editions Edilig, 1984), 18.

73. Wright, *Daily News*, March 15, 1948.

CHAPTER 9 — THE PROGRESSIVE PRODUCER IN THE STUDIO SYSTEM

Epigraph: Typescript funeral eulogy, n.d., Paxton Biographical File, Academy of Motion Picture Arts and Sciences (AMPAS), Los Angeles, California.

1. Scott never wrote publicly about when or why he joined the CPUSA, though there is little doubt that he was a member. Norma Barzman, screenwriter and one of Scott's closest friends, remembers that he was in the Party at the same time as her husband, Ben, who joined in 1939. Scott's FBI file, however, dates the beginning of his Party involvement to the early 1940s. Norma Barzman, interview with author, April 1999; Barzman, interview with Larry Ceplair, in *Tender Comrades: A Backstory of the Hollywood Blacklist*, ed. Patrick McGilligan and Paul Buhle (New York: St. Martin's Press, 1997), 5. See also Larry Ceplair and Steven Englund, *The Inquisition in Hollywood: Politics in the Film Community, 1930–1960* (Berkeley: University of California Press, 1979), 116, and Bernard F. Dick, *Radical Innocence: A Critical Study of the Hollywood Ten* (Lexington: University Press of Kentucky, 1989), 122–123.

2. John Paxton to Keith Kelly and Clay Steinman, July 1977, in Paxton Bio File, AMPAS.

3. Barzman, interview with author, April 1999; Brian Neve, *Film and Politics in America: A Social Tradition* (New York: Routledge, 1992), 87.

4. In addition to his work on progressive feature films, Scott was a founding member of the Motion Picture Guild, an independent group dedicated to making socially relevant documentaries and shorts. Ceplair and Englund, *Inquisition*, 116; Dick, *Radical Innocence*, 122–123.

5. Thomas Schatz, *The Genius of the System: Hollywood Filmmaking in the Studio Era* (New York: Pantheon, 1988), 12.

6. Recent studies reevaluating the role of the producer in the studio system include George F. Custen, *Twentieth Century's Fox: Darryl F. Zanuck and the Culture of Hollywood* (New York: Basic Books, 1997) and Matthew Bernstein, *Walter Wanger: Hollywood Independent* (Berkeley: University of California Press, 1994).

7. Scott's perception was shared by John Houseman, who himself straddled the roles of producer and actor: "Beginning in the late twenties with talking pictures and ending with the dissolution of the major studios in the mid-sixties, the producer was, in fact, the key figure in the California filmmaking structure." John Houseman, *Front and Center* (New York: Simon and Schuster, 1979), 117.

8. Barzman, interview with author, April 1999; Joan Scott, interview with author, April 1999.

9. Richard Jewell, interview with author, July 20, 2004; Jewell, *The RKO Story* (London: Octopus Books, 1982), 140–142.

10. David Bordwell, Janet Staiger, and Kristin Thompson, *The Classical Hollywood Cinema: Film Style and Mode of Production to 1960* (New York: Columbia University Press, 1985), 328.

11. Sid Rogell is credited as executive producer on a number of Scott's early films, including *Murder, My Sweet* and *Deadline at Dawn*, though not on *My Pal Wolf*, a "kiddie flick" that was Scott's first foray as a producer. Lower-budget films generally attracted less studio oversight, which may explain Scott's solo credit on *My Pal Wolf*. However, the extent of Rogell's contributions as executive producer is unclear, since a 1945 article in the trade press noted that Scott and his collaborators "were left alone in the making of *Murder, My Sweet*. It was their baby and they were free to do with it as they chose." Article by David Hanna, n.p., July 19, 1945, in Scott Papers, American Heritage Center, University of Wyoming-Laramie.

12. Paxton had been one of Scott's closest friends since they worked together at *Stage*; his other credited work of the 1940s included *My Pal Wolf* and *Crack-Up*. Dmytryk moved from editing to directing in the late 1930s; his major credits at RKO included *Behind the Rising Sun*, *Hitler's Children*, and *Tender Comrade*, which had catapulted him onto RKO's A-list of directors in 1944. Scott's major work apart from Paxton and Dmytryk included *Deadline at Dawn*, scripted by Clifford Odets and directed by Harold Clurman, both denizens of the Group Theatre, and *The Boy with Green Hair*.

13. Marsha Hunt, interview with Glenn Lovell, in *Tender Comrades*, 318.

14. On Thalberg the man and the myth, see Neal Gabler, *An Empire of Their Own: How the Jews Invented Hollywood* (New York: Anchor Books/Doubleday, 1988), 218–236.

15. Barzman, interview with author, April 1999; Betsy Blair Reisz, interview with Patrick McGilligan, in *Tender Comrades*, 551; Bruce Cook, *Dalton Trumbo* (New York: Charles Scribner's Sons, 1977), 281.

16. Article by David Hanna [no date, no source], Scott Papers.

17. Ceplair and Englund, *Inquisition*, 6.

18. Paxton to Keith Kelly and Clay Steinman, n.d. [July 1977], in Paxton Bio File, AMPAS.

19. Alfred Lewis Levitt, interview by Larry Ceplair, in *Tender Comrades*, 453.

20. Typescript funeral eulogy, n.d., Paxton Bio File, AMPAS.

21. Edward Dmytryk, *It's a Hell of a Life but Not a Bad Living: A Hollywood Memoir* (New York: Times Books, 1978), 69; Dick, *Radical Innocence*, 144–145.

22. Originally an actor and playwright, Wexley worked at every major Hollywood studio, writing gritty gangster films like *The Roaring Twenties* (1939) as well as two powerful anti-fascist dramas: *Confessions of a Nazi Spy* (1939) and *Hangmen Also Die* (1943). An ardent Communist, Wexley was active in left politics, working on the defense of the Scottsboro Boys (about whom he wrote another successful play, *They Shall Not Die*), Upton Sinclair's 1934 EPIC campaign, and the volatile strikes by the Conference of Studio Unions in the

1940s. John Wexley, interview with Patrick McGilligan and Ken Mate, in *Tender Comrades*, 699–715.

23. Wexley, interview in *Tender Comrades*, 716; Ceplair and Englund, *Inquisition*, 314. The RKO Script Files at UCLA contain Wexley's planning notes and incomplete first draft, dated December 28, 1944.

24. William Appleman Williams, *The Tragedy of American Diplomacy* (New York: Dell Publishing, 1962), 162–200; Michael E. Birdwell, *Celluloid Soldiers: Warner Bros.'s Campaign against Nazism* (New York: New York University Press, 1999), 22–23; and "Nazi Propaganda in America," *Look*, December 31, 1940, 15.

25. RKO memo from William Gordon to William Dozier and telegram from Dorsey to Gordon, February 8, 1945, both in Scott Papers.

26. Wexley, screenplay notes on *Cornered*, RKO Script Files, UCLA.

27. Dozier to Scott, April 3, 1945; Crow to Dozier, April 24, 1945, Scott Papers.

28. Crow to Dozier, April 24, 1945, Scott Papers.

29. As a Communist writer, Wexley was particularly vulnerable to charges of propagandizing. Nevertheless, the overlap between "radical" and "mainstream" perceptions of fascism during this period is striking. In many ways, Wexley's script is a shining example of the Office of War Information (OWI) guidelines for representing the anti-fascist struggle. For example, Wexley dramatized the Allied forces as engaged in a "people's war," showing a unified front of Canadians, French, and South Americans working to defeat fascism. He also dramatized that the foes of democracy were not simply the Germans, Italians, or Japanese, but included anyone with anti-democratic tendencies, from fifth columnists and saboteurs to the uncommitted and pessimistic. Wexley, *Cornered* Screenplay, RKO Script Files, UCLA.

30. Wexley, interview in *Tender Comrades*, 716; Ceplair and Englund, *Inquisition*, 315; Edward Dmytryk, *Odd Man Out: A Memoir of the Hollywood Ten* (Carbondale: Southern Illinois University Press, 1996), 19.

31. Quotations taken from the final filmed version of *Cornered* (RKO, 1945).

32. Dmytryk described him as "reliable, nonpolitical John Paxton," an interesting statement in this context, since Paxton—though not a Party member—was far from nonpolitical. According to Norma Barzman, Paxton was sympathetic liberal, even a "fellow traveler," who agreed with most Communist positions "straight down the line." Dmytryk, *Odd Man Out*, 19; Barzman, interview with author, April 1999. See also taped interview with John Paxton, 1977; my thanks to Sarah Jane Paxton for lending me the tape.

33. Ceplair and Englund, *Inquisition*, 315.

34. "Luther Adler," "Morris Carnovsky," and "Walter Slezak," in *The Film Encyclopedia*, ed. Ephraim Katz (New York: Perigree Books, 1979), 12, 209, 1066. See also Wendy Smith, *Real Life Drama: The Group Theatre and America, 1931–1940* (New York: Alfred A. Knopf, 1990).

35. J. D. Marshall, "The Greeks Had Another Word for It, Meaning—Exaltation," in *Blueprint in Babylon* (Tempe, Ariz.: Phoenix House, 1987), 263.

36. Peter Rathvon to Scott, July 30, 1946, Scott Papers.

37. Robert Murphy, "Rank's Attempt on the American Market," in James Curran and Vincent Porter, *British Cinema History* (Totowa, N.J.: Barnes & Noble Books, 1982), 177–178.

38. Scott to Rathvon, n.d., [before July 26], Scott Papers.

39. Scott to Rathvon, July 17, 1946, Scott Papers.

40. Rathvon to Scott, July 15, 1946, Scott Papers.

41. Paxton to William Pomeranz, SWG, June 24, 1946, Scott Papers.

42. Robert Murphy, *Realism and Tinsel: Cinema and Society in Britain, 1939–1948* (London: Routledge, 1989), 220.

43. Scott to Harry (?), June 24, 1946; Paxton to William Pomeranz, SWG, June 24, 1946, Scott Papers.

44. Ceplair and Englund, *Inquisition*, 212–221. See also Mike Nielsen and Gene Mailes, *Hollywood's Other Blacklist: Union Struggles in the Studio System* (London: British Film Institute, 1995), and Gerald Horne, *Class Struggle in Hollywood, 1930–1950: Moguls, Mobsters, Stars, Reds, and Trade Unionists* (Austin: University of Texas Press, 2001).

45. Scott to Rathvon, n.d. [July 1946]; Paxton to William Pomeranz, SWG, June 24, 1946, Scott Papers.

46. This revised agreement, however, still excluded those American workers who were affiliated with IATSE, as Scott regretfully explained to an RKO worker who planned to join the production unit in England later that summer. Scott to Harry (?), June 24, 1946; Paxton to Pomeranz, SWG, June 24, 1946, Scott Papers.

47. Scott to Rathvon, n.d. [July 1946]; Rathvon to Scott, July 26, 1946, Scott Papers.

48. Robert Sparks to Scott, September 27, 1946, Scott Papers.

49. Jack Votion to Scott, May 27, 1947, Scott Papers.

50. Scott to Rathvon, n.d. [July 1946], Scott Papers

51. Scott to Leon Goldberg, December 26, 1946, Scott Papers.

52. Ceplair and Englund, *Inquisition*, 222–225.

53. Scott to Goldberg, December 26, 1946, Scott Papers.

54. Though the ACT's George Elvin had indeed cabled CSU leader Herb Sorrell, he challenged IATSE's interpretation of the cable as a public pledge of support for the CSU or the strike, insisting that the ACT had simply followed "normal Trade Union practices" in instructing its members "not to handle work which would otherwise have been handled by a Company whose workers are engaged in a Trade dispute." George Elvin to Scott, February 11, 1947; Goldberg to Roy Brewer, January 8, 1947; Goldberg to Scott, January 14, 1947, Scott Papers.

55. Scott to Elvin, January 27, 1947; Scott to Elvin, February 8, 1947, Scott Papers.

56. Leon Goldberg to Rathvon, August 8, 1947, Scott Papers.

57. John Gossage to Scott, July 8, 1947, Scott Papers.

58. Scott to Gossage, July 24, 1947, Scott Papers.

59. Scott to Gossage, July 24, 1947, Scott Papers.

60. Scott, Draft notes for "You Can't Do That," n.d. [Spring-Summer 1947], Scott Papers.

61. Scott, "You Can't Do That," in *Thought Control in the U.S.A.: The Collected Proceedings of the Conference of the Subject of Thought Control in the U.S., called by the Hollywood Arts, Sciences and Professions Council, PCA, July 9–13, 1947*, ed. Harold J. Salemson (Los Angeles: Progressive Citizens of America, 1947), 324.

62. Joseph Breen to William Gordon, July 17, 1945, *Crossfire* Production File, Production Code Administration Records, AMPAS.

63. Scott, typescript of "Some of My Worst Friends," 1, Scott Papers.

64. Paxton to Keith Kelly and Clay Steinman, n.d. [July 1977], in Paxton Bio File, AMPAS.

65. Scott, "You Can't Do That," 328.

66. Paxton, Letter to the Editor, February 27, 1980, Paxton Bio File, AMPAS.

67. Scott, "You Can't Do That," 330.

68. Thomas F. Brady, "Hollywood Buzzes," n.d., Schary Papers, State Historical Society of Wisconsin; David Platt, "*Crossfire* Box Office Terrific, Says Variety," *Daily Worker*, August 1, 1947, Scott papers; Scott, typescript of "Some of My Worst Friends," Scott Papers; Virginia Wright, *Los Angeles Daily News*, March 20, 1948, Scott Papers; Affidavit of Adrian Scott in Opposition to Motion for Summary Judgment, U.S. District Court, Southern District of California, Central Division, n.d., Kenny-Morris Papers, State Historical Society of Wisconsin; Dick, *Radical Innocence*, 133–134; Neve, *Film and Politics in America*, 99.

69. Scott to Charles Katz, typed notes in preparation for civil suits, n.d.

70. Ibid.

71. RKO's anticipated gross for *Crossfire* was between $2,000,000 and $2,400,000 in domestic distribution alone, quite an achievement considering the picture's final cost of under $600,000. Scott to Charles Katz, typed notes in preparation for civil suits, n.d.; Scott to Bill [last name unknown], December 3, 1947; Scott to George Elvin, December 11, 1947, all in Scott papers.

72. David Caute, *The Great Fear: The Anti-Communist Purge under Truman and Eisenhower* (New York: Simon and Schuster, 1978), 500.

CHAPTER 10 — *THE HOUSE I LIVE IN*

1. Letter from Frank Sinatra to Albert Maltz dated August 31, 1945, Albert Maltz Papers, Box 5, Folder 13, Wisconsin Center for Film and Theater Research, Wisconsin State Historical Society, Madison, Wisconsin. My thanks to Steve Berndt for his research assistance with this essay.

2. See Alan Wald, *Exiles from a Future Time: The Forging of the Mid-Twentieth-Century Literary Left* (Chapel Hill: University of North Carolina Press, 2002), and Barbara Foley, *Radical Representations: Politics and Form in U.S. Proletarian Fiction, 1929–1941* (Durham, N.C.: Duke University Press, 1993). For the most comprehensive account of the Popular Front

see, of course, Michael Denning, *The Cultural Front: The Laboring of American Culture in the Twentieth Century* (London: Verso, 1996).

3. Some recent scholarship does discuss Maltz's work but in the context of a larger discussion of proletarian fiction. The same can be said for discussions of his film work. It is usually considered within the broader subject of the Hollywood Ten or the work of the Hollywood Left generally. The Twayne Authors Series devoted a volume to Maltz. See Jack Salzman, *Albert Maltz* (Boston: Twayne, 1978). See also Barbara Zheutlin and David Talbot, "Albert Maltz: Portrait of a Hollywood Dissident," *Cineaste* 8, no. 3 (1978).

4. Maltz asked that his name be removed from *The Beguiled*. *A Tale of One January* was published in England in 1966 by Calder and Boyers but never by an American publisher. Maltz published a limited number of copies himself in 1971.

5. Albert Maltz, "What Shall We Ask of Writers?" *New Masses*, February 12, 1946, 19.

6. Ibid.

7. Letter from Louis Harap to Joseph North, Maltz Papers, Box 5, Folder 15, Wisconsin Center for Film and Theater Research.

8. Letter from Albert Maltz to Mike Gold, Maltz Papers, Box 5, Folder 15, Wisconsin Center for Film and Theater Research.

9. For a more thorough account of the affair and a sensitive interpretation of Maltz's actions see Salzman, *Albert Maltz*, 85–95.

10. Albert Maltz, "The Citizen Writer in Retrospect," transcript of oral history conducted in 1975, 1976, 1978, and 1979 by Joel Gardner. Collection 300/197. Department of Special Collections, Young Research Library, University of California, Los Angeles, 574.

11. Ibid., 576.

12. Albert Maltz, *The Citizen Writer* (New York: International Publishers, 1950), 17.

13. Maltz, "The Citizen Writer in Retrospect," 10–11.

14. These are the contributors as described on the cover of the pamphlet. It also told readers that proceeds would be given to exiled anti-fascist writers.

15. *"We Hold These Truths . . ."* (New York: League of American Writers, 1939), 19.

16. Ibid., 19.

17. "To All People of Good Will," *Equality*, May 1939, 5.

18. "Equality Is Not Divisble," *Equality*, May 1939, 16.

19. James W. Ford, *Anti-Semitism and the Struggle for Democracy* (New York: National Council of Jewish Communists, 1939), 11.

20. Gerald Meyer, "Frank Sinatra: The Popular Front and an American Icon," *Science & Society* 66, no. 3 (Fall 2002): 311–335.

21. In her biography of Sinatra, Kitty Kelley claims the singer's press agents George Evans and Frank Keller convinced Sinatra to do the film. She also cites Keller and Evans as promoting Sinatra's emerging social conscience, in part to deflect criticism of the star after bad publicity with regard to his USO tour appearance in 1945. Kitty Kelley, *His Way: The*

Unauthorized Biography of Frank Sinatra (New York: Bantam, 1978), 116. Kelley's dating is wrong, however, since Sinatra was already associated with the struggle against race prejudice by 1944. As for the origins of the film project, I have relied on the account given by Maltz in his UCLA Oral History.

22. I am not suggesting that Maltz hijacked the film at this point or that he was not also concerned about race prejudice. But given Maltz's account of the origins of the film, it does seem striking that what began as a vehicle for Sinatra's anti-racism ended up being a warning against anti-Semitism. My thanks to Kevin Walter for his cogent suggestions on this point.

23. Students of the Old Left will be familiar with both men. Robinson was among the movement's most important songwriters, having composed "The Ballad for Americans" and "Joe Hill." Meeropol, who wrote under the pseudonym Lewis Allan, composed the ballad made famous by Billie Holiday, "Strange Fruit." He and his wife, Anne, adopted the children of Julius and Ethel Rosenberg after the parents were executed.

24. Earl Robinson, *Ballad of an American: The Autobiography of Earl Robinson* (Lanham, Md.: Scarecrow Press, 1998), 152.

25. Ibid., 155.

26. The *Daily Worker* did its part in promoting the film. Twice in November of 1945 it published a still from the film without any accompanying article. Captions for both photos ascribe authorship to Maltz. See issues of the *Daily Worker* for November 9 and 23, 1945, 11.

27. *The Cross and the Arrow*, published in 1944, was Maltz's second novel and had received considerable critical praise.

28. Limited access to the film has probably prevented most scholars from quoting its dialogue correctly. From the first reviews by *Time* and the *Daily Worker* to more recent scholarship, not a single one I have come across accurately quotes the film's dialogue.

29. Denning, *The Cultural Front*, 125.

30. Four shots from this sequence appear to have been lifted directly from Howard Hawks's 1943 film *Air Force*. *The House I Live In* echoes the Hawks film in so far as *Air Force* ends with a successful attack of a Japanese fleet and features a heroic Irish pilot who leaves behind a wife and child when killed in action.

31. In Michael Selzer, ed., *"Kike!" A Documentary History of Anti-Semitism in America* (New York: World Publishing, 1972), 191.

32. According to Edward Shapiro, "World War II was the great watershed in the history of American Jewish identity. Military service broadened the cultural perspective of Jewish servicemen, and American Jewry emerged from the struggle convinced that they were no longer an exotic ethnic and religious minority but an integral part of American culture." Edward Shapiro, *A Time for Healing: American Jewry Since World War II* (Baltimore: Johns Hopkins University Press, 1992), 15. Along similar lines, Deborah Dash Moore has written, "The war would make Jews visible, not as objects of scorn or hatred, but as subjects participating in American culture, politics and survival." Deborah Dash Moore, *GI Jews: How World War II Changed a Generation* (Cambridge, Mass.: Harvard University Press, 2004), 21.

33. As Patricia Erens has pointed out, the Hollywood war films that centered on the platoon often included a Jewish character. Patricia Erens, *The Jew in American Cinema* (Bloomington: Indiana University Press, 1984), 171.

34. It is the case that during the late thirties, major Jewish organizations cloaked their response to the Nazi threat in language that depicted Hitler as anti-American and not strictly anti-Jew. As Felicia Herman has argued in her work on the Jewish community's relationship to Hollywood and its representation of Nazism, agencies such as the American Jewish Committee and the Anti-Defamation League discouraged highly visible, Jewish-identified protests against the Nazis. "Instead, believing that the Nazis could only be defeated by broad-based American antipathy for Nazi methods and beliefs and that most Americans would not be sympathetic to the particular concerns of Jews, they sought to universalize Nazi ideology and to propose it as a threat to American democracy as a whole." Thus, the strategy that emerges as dominant in fighting domestic anti-Semitism in the postwar years did have roots among Jewish organizations during the height of the Popular Front period. Felicia Herman, "Hollywood, Nazism, and the Jews, 1933–1941," *American Jewish History* 89, no. 1 (March 2001): 64.

35. Stuart Svonkin, *Jews Against Prejudice: American Jews and the Fight for Civil Liberties* (New York: Columbia University Press, 1997), 18. The AJC stated its position clearly in its annual report from 1945: "Our basic philosophy is the same now as it has always been: namely, that anti-Semitism is an American problem and not just a Jewish problem." *Annual Report 1945* (New York: American Jewish Committee, 1945), 28.

36. For a thorough discussion of this movement see Svonkin, *Jews Against Prejudice*.

37. Leonard Dinnerstein, "Anti-Semitism Exposed and Attacked, 1945–1950," *American Jewish History*, September 1981, 134.

38. Memorandum from Dorothy Nathan, October 18, 1945. Papers of the American Jewish Committee, Gen. 10, Box 227. AJC Papers are located in the YIVO Collection at the Center for Jewish History in New York City.

39. Memo from Julius Cohen to Dorothy Nathan, Papers of the American Jewish Committee, Gen. 10, Box 227.

40. AJC Papers, Gen. 10, Box 168. Educators subsequently attempted to study the effect of the film. On December 16, 1946, a sample of New York University students were asked to gauge their responses to the film and to a documentary short titled *Don't Be a Sucker*. Students pressed green and red buttons to record their positive and negative reactions as the film was screened. In the discussion that followed, students characterized the film as soothing, at times sentimental, subtle, and not overly propagandistic. See "Report of Audience Reaction to Showings of Films," in AJC Papers, Gen 10, Box 168.

41. Paul Buhle and Dave Wagner, *Blacklisted: The Film Lover's Guide to the Hollywood Blacklist* (New York: Palgrave Macmillan, 2003), 102.

42. The victimized child is also wearing a beanie at the beginning of the scene. It is not a yarmulke but its allusion to one is fairly clear.

43. David Platt, "Sinatra's Stirring Tolerance Film 'The House I Live In,'" *Daily Worker*, November 8, 1945, 11.

44. For a remarkable example of the song being read out of context see Steven E. Schoenherr, "Teaching with Audiovisual Documents: Resources in the National Archives," *The History Teacher*, July 1977, 387. In an essay devoted to informing history teachers about the resources available at the National Archives, Schoenherr tells his reader the song documents "the conservatism that characterized American life in the 1940's and 1950's." Unaware that the song was the product of the left, Schoenherr claims it illustrates a period "dominated by a resurgent faith in traditional American values."

45. Thomas Cripps, "Racial Ambiguities in American Propaganda Movies," in *Film and Radio Propaganda in World War II,* ed. K.R.M. Short (Knoxville: University of Tennessee Press, 1983), 136. Echoing Cripps, readers and conference respondents with whom I have shared this work often ask for an accounting of why Maltz composed the gang with all white youth. If Sinatra sings, "All races and religions, that's America to me," why is there no black child present here? My answer is: How could there be? The gang represents the opposite of the ideal imagined by Abe Meeropol's lyrics. Given Maltz's sensitivity to the struggles of black America, why would he enlist a black child in a pack of anti-Semites? While Maltz chose to frame his script with these two songs, Meeropol's lyrics clearly did not dictate its contents. Nothing I have come across indicates whether Maltz or LeRoy chose to omit the song's second refrain with its explicit reference to integration. Sinatra may well have sung this refrain at live performances. Even Paul Robeson, who also performed the song at many concerts, did not always include these lyrics. On his *Ballad for Americans* collection (1958), Robeson sings half of the first refrain and half of the second but, like Sinatra, does not sing "The house I live in, my neighbors white and black."

46. "Movies Have a Job to Do," in AJC Papers, Gen. 10, Box 168.

47. Transcript of "How to Get in Good with Hitler," dated December 4, 1944. AJC Papers, Gen. 10, Box 168.

48. *Time*, October 1, 1945, 61.

49. Meyer, "Frank Sinatra," 322. See also Jon Wiener, *Professors, Politics and Pop* (New York: Verso, 1991), 263–269.

50. *Time*, November 12, 1945.

51. This reading of the film was suggested to me by Teresa Podlesney.

52. Gertrude Stoughton, "Start Little United Nations After Learning Value of Cooperation," *Daily Worker*, November, 9, 1945, 11.

53. Letter from Albert Maltz to Frank Sinatra dated September 24, 1945, Albert Maltz Papers, Box 5, Folder 15, Wisconsin Center for Film and Theater Research, Wisconsin State Historical Society.

54. After enumerating those rights against which "Congress can not advance," Maltz told his audience, "I submit humbly but earnestly that it is time once again that Americans understand this fully." Maltz, *The Citizen Writer*, 28.

55. Ibid., 23.

56. Ibid., 23–24.

57. Maltz, "The Citizen Writer in Retrospect," 867.

CHAPTER 11 — RED HOLLYWOOD IN TRANSITION

1. Thom Andersen, "Red Hollywood," in *Literature and the Visual Arts in Contemporary Society*, ed. Suzanne Ferguson and Barbara Groseclose (Columbus: Ohio State University Press, 1985), 183–191. Reprinted in this volume.

2. See Paul Buhle and Dave Wagner, *Hide in Plain Sight: The Hollywood Blacklistees in Film and Television, 1950–2002* (London: Palgrave Macmillan, 2003); Paul Bulhe and Dave Wagner, *Radical Hollywood* (New York: New Press, 2002); Patrick McGilligan and Paul Buhle, *Tender Comrades: A Backstory of the Hollywood Blacklist* (New York: St. Martins Press, 1997); Dan Georgakas, "The Hollywood Reds: Fifty Years Later," *American Communist History* 2 (2003): 63–76; Brian Neve, *Film and Politics in America: A Social Tradition* (London: Routledge, 1992); Lary May, *The Big Tomorrow: Hollywood and the Politics of the American Way* (Chicago: University of Chicago Press, 2000); Arthur Eckstein, "The Hollywood Ten in History and Memory," *Film History* 16 (2004): 424–436.

3. On Rossen see Alan Casty, *The Films of Robert Rossen* (New York: Museum of Modern Art, 1969); Brooks Atkinson, *New York Times*, November 1, 1935.

4. Outline treatment, October 3, 1936, United Artists Collection, Wisconsin Center for Film and Television Research, Madison, Wisconsin (UA/Wisconsin); Edelman to Wallis, July 23, 1936, Warner Bros. collection, University of Southern California (WB/USC); Brian Neve, "The Screenwriter and the Social Problem Film, 1936–38: The Case of Robert Rossen at Warner Brothers," *Film & History* 14 (1984): 2–13.

5. Warner to Wallis, February 22, 1937, WB/USC; *Daily Worker*, April 14, 1937, 7.

6. McGilligan and Buhle, *Tender Comrades*, 33.

7. *New York Times*, August 11, 1938: 13; *Daily Worker*, June 2, 1943: 7.

8. Mark Hellinger memo, July 15, 1958, Edelman to Hal Wallis, August 3, 1938, WB/USC.

9. *New York Times*, October 7, 1939; undated clipping, *Daily Worker*, UA/Wisconsin; Richard Maltby, *Harmless Entertainment: Hollywood and the Ideology of Consensus* (Metuchen, N.J.: Scarecrow Press, 1983).

10. Edward G. Robinson, with Leonard Spiegelgass, *All My Yesterdays: An Autobiography* (New York: Hawthorn Books, 1973), 218; first Rossen draft screenplay, September 17, 1940, UA/Wisconsin; for the final screenplay see Rocco Fumento and Tony Williams, eds., *Jack London's "The Sea Wolf," a Screenplay by Robert Rossen* (Carbondale: Southern Illinois University Press, 1998).

11. Joseph I. Breen to Jack Warner, December 19, 1940, WB/USC.

12. Clayton R. Koppes and Gregory D. Black, *Hollywood Goes to War: How Politics, Profits, and Propaganda Shaped World War II Movies* (New York: Free Press, 1987), 82–112.

13. *Daily Worker*, April 12, 1943, 7; Nancy Lynn Schwartz, *The Hollywood Writers' Wars* (New York: Alfred A. Knopf, 1982), 189; Paul Trivers, "Hollywood Writers Move Up," *New Masses* 48 (September 14, 1943): 20.

14. Contract information, Robert Rossen, Warner Bros. collection, Princeton University Library.

15. Rossen testimony, May 7, 1953, *Hearing before the Committee on Un-American Activities, House of Representatives*, 83rd Congress, First Session, Washington D.C., 1953, 1490; Rossen, "An Approach to Character, 1943," *Proceedings of Writers Congress, Sponsored by Hollywood Writers Mobilisation and University of California* (Berkeley, 1944), 61–67; Rossen, "The Blood of the Lamb," October 19, 1943, WB/Wisconsin.

16. Rossen, "New Characters for the Screen," *New Masses* 50 (January 18, 1944): 18–19; Karl Holton to H. Lissauer, Warners Research Department, July 17, 1943, WB/Wisconsin; Koppes and Black, *Hollywood Goes to War*, 131–132.

17. Bright in McGilligan and Buhle, *Tender Comrades*, 153; Warner's testimony, *Hearings before the Committee on Un-American Activities, House of Representatives*, Washington D.C., October 20, 1947, WB/USC; telegram to Jack and Harry Warner, signed by Milestone, Rossen, Dalton Trumbo, John Howard Lawson, John Garfield, John Wexley, and others, October 8, 1945, WB/USC.

18. Lewis Milestone collection, AMPAS.

19. Ibid.

20. Rossen, "Love Lies Bleeding," September 21, 1945, Kirk Douglas collection, UA/Wisconsin.

21. Production Code Administration file on *The Strange Love of Martha Ivers*, Motion Picture Association of America collection, AMPAS.

22. Farber, quoted in Casty, *Films of Robert Rossen*, 11; MPAPAI reference to *The Strange Love of Martha Ivers* in *Conference on the Subject of Thought Control in the United States*, ed. Harold J. Salemson, July 9–13, 1947, 309.

23. Adrian Scott memo in Larry Ceplair and Steven Englund, *The Inquisition in Hollywood, Politics in the Film Community, 1930–1960* (Berkeley: University of California Press, 1983), 451–454.

24. Rossen testimony, May 7, 1953, on the letter from Jacques Duclos that signaled the postwar change in Communist Party strategy, directed from Moscow, 1489–1490; Alvah Bessie, *Inquisition in Eden* (New York: Macmillan, 1965), 63.

25. Tavernier introduction to film, BBC2, February 6, 1988.

26. Budd Schulberg interview with the author, October 13, 2004.

27. Abraham Polonsky interview with the author, August 20, 1988; Robert Parrish, *Growing Up in Hollywood* (London: Bodley Head, 1976), 193–195.

28. Peter Valenti, in John Schultheiss, ed., *Abraham Polonsky's "Body and Soul": The Critical Edition* (Northridge: California State University, Northridge, 2002), 307.

29. Robert Sklar, *City Boys, Cagney, Bogart, Garfield* (Princeton, N.J.: Princeton University Press, 1992), 186; Edwin. T. Arnold and Eugene L. Miller, eds., *Robert Aldrich Interviews* (Jackson: University Press of Mississippi, 2004), 97.

30. Details of contract, *Film Index* 11 (1971): 115.

31. *Hollywood Reporter*, December 2, 1947, cited in Joseph Foster, "Entertainment Only," *New Masses* 66 (1948): 21–22.

32. Richard Collins, testimony, April 12, 1951, *Hearings*, Washington, 1951, 240; Martin Gottfried, *Arthur Miller, His Life and Work* (Cambridge, Mass.: Da Capo, 2003), 111; Bernard F. Dick, *The Merchant Prince of Poverty Row, Harry Cohn of Columbia Pictures* (Lexington: University Press of Kentucky, 1993), 169.

33. Parrish, *Growing Up in Hollywood*, 200–206.

34. R. Borde and E. Chaumeton, *A Panorama of American Film Noir 1941–1953* (San Francisco: City Lights, 2002), 116–117; P. Dubuisson Castille, "Red Scare and Film Noir: The Hollywood Adaptation of Robert Penn Warren's *All the King's Men*," *Southern Quarterly* 33 (1995): 173.

35. Edward Dmytryk, *It's a Hell of a Life But Not a Bad Living* (New York: Times Books, 1978), 115; Ring Lardner Jr., in Schwartz, *Hollywood Writers' Wars*, 170.

36. *Hollywood Reporter*, November 4, 1949, and Rotha, "Storm in a Tea Cup," *Public Opinion*, April 28, 1950, in microfiche for *All the King's Men*, British Film Institute Library, London.

37. M. Augspurger, "Heading West: *All the King's Men* and Robert Rossen's Search for the Ideal," *Southern Quarterly* 39 (2001): 62–64.

38. Rossen testimony, May 7, 1953, 1454–99; Brian Neve, "An Interview with Cy Endfield," *Film Studies* 7 (Winter 2005): 125. on Rossen's passport.

CHAPTER 12 — SWASHBUCKLING, SAPPHIRE, AND SALT

I would like to thank the AHRB Centre for British Film and Television Studies and the British Academy for funding aspects of this research, as well as Norma Barzman, Tim Hunter, Sonya Marks, Peggy Phillips, and Albert Ruben for answering my queries, and Michael Eaton, Barbara Hall, James Marshall, Brian Neve, Joanna Rapf, and Jeffrey Richards for their interest and help.

1. For further details on the production and distribution of these series, see Steve Neale, "Transatlantic Ventures and *Robin Hood*," in *ITV Cultures: Independent Television Over Fifty Years*, ed. Catherine Johnson and Rob Turnock (Maidenhead: Open University Press, 2005), 73–97, and "Adventure, Exchange and Identity: British, American, and Un-American Involvement in Costume Adventure TV Series and Films in the Postwar Era," in *Trading Culture: Global Traffic and Local Cultures in Film and Television*, ed. Sylvia Harvey (Luton: John Libbey Press, 2006), 175–189.

2. Brian Taves, *The Romance of Adventure: The Genre of Historical Adventure Movies* (Jackson: University Press of Mississippi, 1993), 73–80.

3. There is some uncertainty as to when all thirty-nine episodes of "Sword of Freedom" were first shown in Britain. Listings in the *TV Times* indicate that transmission in the London region began in January 1958. However, only thirty-two episodes appear to have been broadcast by the end of 1962, even though 1961 is the year normally given as the end of its initial run (see http://www.screenonline.org.uk/tv/id/1136195).

4. Neale, "Transatlantic Ventures and *Robin Hood*," and Neale, "Adventure, Exchange and Identity."

5. Larry Ceplair and Steven Englund, *The Inquisition in Hollywood: Politics in the Film Community, 1930–1960* (Garden City, N.Y.: Doubleday, 1980), 405.

6. Norma Barzman, *The Red and the Blacklist: The Intimate Memoir of a Hollywood Expatriate* (New York: Nation Press, 2003), 260; Walter Bernstein, *Inside Out: A Memoir of the Blacklist* (New York: Knopf, 1996), 245–249; Paul Buhle and Dave Wagner, *Hide in Plain Sight: The Hollywood Blacklistees in Film and Television, 1950–2002* (New York: Palgrave Macmillan, 2003), 42, 86–88, 264; Bernard Dick, *Radical Innocence: A Critical Study of the Hollywood Ten* (Lexington: University Press of Kentucky, 1989), 177–178; Bernard Gordon, *Hollywood Exile, Or How I Learned to Love the Blacklist* (Austin: University of Texas Press, 1999) 62, 87; Howard Koch, *As Time Goes By: Memoirs of a Writer* (New York: Harcourt Brace Jovanovich, 1979), 202; Ring Lardner Jr., *I'd Hate Myself in the Morning: A Memoir* (New York: Nation Books, 2000), 140–142; Patrick McGilligan and Paul Buhle, *Tender Comrades: A Backstory of the Hollywood Blacklist* (New York: St. Martin's Press, 1997), 16, 437, 595; Louis Marks, "Hood Winked," *The Listener*, January 18, 1990, 8–9; Peggy Phillips, *My Brother's Keeper* (San Jose: Writer's Club Press, 2002), 145–147, 163–164; Maurice Rapf, *Back Lot: Growing Up with the Movies* (Lanham, Md.: Scarecrow Press, 1999), David Robb, "Naming the Right Names: Amending the Hollywood Blacklist," *Cineaste* 22, no. 2 (1996): 28; Jean Rouverol, *Refugees from Hollywood: A Journal of the Blacklist Years* (Albuquerque: University of New Mexico Press, 2000), 203–204.

7. The Ian McLellan Hunter Collection (IMHC), Ring Lardner Jr. Collection (RLJC), and Robert Lees and Fred Rinaldo Collection (RLFRC), Margaret Herrick Library, Academy of Motion Picture Arts and Sciences (MHL-AMPAS), the Waldo Salt Papers (WSP), Arts Library Special Collections, Charles E. Young Research Library, UCLA (ALSC-UCLA) and the Adrian Scott Papers (ASP), American Heritage Center, University of Wyoming–Laramie. It should be noted that RLJC was housed in ALSC–UCLA when I first began this research, that IMHC is not yet fully catalogued, and thus that the box and folder numbers cited in this article are provisional. Most of the documents and letters I have drawn on are indexed as "TV Correspondence, 1955–1956."

8. For more information on *Colonel March*, see Bernstein, *Inside Out*, 245–249, Neale, "Transatlantic Ventures and *Robin Hood*," 86, and Steve Neale, "Swashbucklers and Sitcoms, Cowboys and Crime, Nurses, Just Men and Defenders: Blacklisted Writers and TV in the 1950s and 1960s," *Film Studies* 7 (2006): 93.

9. Koch to Lardner and Hunter, January 26, February 11, February 26, March 14, 1955, and memo from Koch to Weinstein, February 7, 1955, IMHC, Box 4, Folder 17.

10. *Variety* estimated the cost per episode of "Sword of Freedom" at $25,000 ("Cost-Chart: Syndicated Film Series," July 31, 1957, 80). This compares with its estimate of $32,000 for "Robin Hood," $32,500 for "Sir Lancelot," and $27,500 for "The Buccaneers" ("Estimated Weekly Network TV Program Costs," November 21, 1956, 26). Its review of the opening episode described it as "a poorly-produced swashbuckler marred by a generally mediocre tone and a story of the same description" ("Syndication Review," November 13, 1957, 54).

11. "Ivanhoe" was produced by Columbia Screen Gems, "William Tell" by ITP, and "Sir Francis Drake" by ITC. "Richard the Lionheart" was produced by the Danziger Brothers

(Edward J. and Harry Lee) for their company, Danziger Productions. For further details, see Neale, "Adventure, Exchange and Identity."

12. Dave Rogers and S. J. Gillis, *The Rogers & Gillis Guide to ITC* (Shrewsbury: SJG Communication Services, 1997), 81–86, http/www.78rpm.co.uk/tv4.htm. Letters to and from Weinstein and Lardner and Hunter, IMHC, Box 4, Folder 17, indicate that "The Four Just Men," along with topics, titles, and subjects such as Sanders of the River, Marco Polo, D'Artagnan, Kubla Khan, François Villon, Lloyd's of London, Bow Street, Zorro, and The Rebels (which was to center on a revolutionary Quaker in the Restoration era), was being considered as the basis for a series as early as the summer of 1956. It should also be noted that Sapphire planned another series called "The Highwayman," for which Waldo Salt wrote outlines for at least two episodes, "The Indiscreet Timepiece" and "The Distiller's Apprentice" (WSP, Box 60, Folder 2). These episodes were never filmed and the series was aborted. However, a pilot entitled "The Chimneysweep" was filmed and transmitted in the UK on June 14, 1958. It was directed by Robert Day and co-starred Adrienne Corri, both of them Sapphire regulars. See "100 Pilots," *Variety*, March 6, 1957, 103; "Telepix On Adventure Kick," *Variety*, January 30, 1957; "Flock of New Telefilm Series Set In Britain," *Variety*, February 20, 1957, 29; "Official Gears for '57–'58," *Variety*, March 6, 1957, 24; Ruben to Salt, March 28, 1957; and Salt to Ruben, April 3, 1957, WSP Box 80, Folder 47, and Hunter to Lardner, May 28, 1957, RLJC, Box 9, Folder 119.

13. See Neale, "Swashbucklers and Sitcoms," 98.

14. *Variety* estimated the cost per episode of "The Four Just Men" at $50,000 ("'Four Just Men' Hot on Sales Front, But How Do You Turn a Profit?" August 12, 1959, 31). Lavish spending on "The Four Just Men" and an overstretching of Sapphire's financial resources appears to have coincided with Weinstein's marriage to lawyer and businessman Jonathan Fisher in 1958. The ensuing crisis led to the sale of Walton Studios as well as to the demise of Sapphire and "The Four Just Men" (*Evening Standard*, January 17, 1961, 11; January 18, 1961, 12; *Times*, January 16, 1961, 6; March 21, 1961, 19; April 25, 1961, 8; April 27, 1961, 6).

15. Hal Hackett, "When Knighthood Was in Flower on TV Film," *Variety*, January 9, 1957, 103; Lardner, *I'd Hate Myself in the Morning*, 140.

16. Lardner, *I'd Hate Myself in the Morning*, 142.

17. "An Interview with Albert Ruben by David Marc," *Film Studies* 7 (Winter 2006): 108.

18. Dick, *Radical Innocence*, 178.

19. IMHC, Box 4, Folder 17. Most of the correspondence to and from Hunter and Lardner is addressed to or signed "WSFT." A letter from Ruben dated May 6, 1956, in the same folder makes it clear that "WS" stood for "Will Scarlett" and "FT," "Friar Tuck."

20. Lardner and Hunter to Ruben, April 15, 1957, RLJC, Box 9, Folder 119. This folder contains a letter from Lardner to Matti Salo dated September 17, 1984, which states that checks to Hunter "were made out to Samuel B. West and mine to Oliver Skene."

21. An email from Ruben to the author on June 19, 2002, indicates that the "contact process was 2-way. Sometimes we reached out. Sometimes we were contacted. Sometimes writers we were working with recommended colleagues." The multiple use of pseudonyms by a number of different writers clearly dovetails with Lardner's account (as

quoted in Robb, "Naming the Right Names," 28) of the use made of pseudonyms by writers based in the United States: "We had pseudonyms that we used just for the purposes of getting money. We had to open bank accounts under these assumed names, and transferred our Social Security numbers to our assumed name. We had to put different names on the scripts because we didn't want to call attention to any one name." Complementing the use by the same writers of different pseudonyms, the use of the same pseudonyms by different writers would have helped further disguise their identity. Documents and letters in IMHC and RLJC indicate that Cooper Associates and Daniel Sandomire of Greenman, Shea, Sandomire, and Zimet handled payments and provided legal and financial advice. Sandomire also acted as an additional point of contact between Lardner and Hunter and Weinstein and Sapphire.

22. Letters to Lardner and Hunter from Ruben on August 8 and from Lardner and Hunter to Ruben on August 14, 1956 (IMHC, Box 4, Folder 17), indicate that Phillips was used as a front. An undated listing of "Skene-West episode titles" (RLJC, Box 9, Folder 119) indicates that Lardner and Hunter wrote "Secret Mission," and thus that in this instance Smart acted a front as well. It should be noted that Phillips and Smart both wrote or had already written scripts in their own right for television programs of various kinds. It is therefore likely that they wrote at least some of the episodes of "Robin Hood" and Sapphire's other series for which they were credited.

23. RLJC, Box 9, Folder 120.

24. Anne Green was a blacklisted writer who mostly wrote for radio. She was married to Howard Koch. In Koch, *As Time Goes By*, 201, 202, it is noted that she used Anne Rodney as a pseudonym and that she wrote episodes for "Robin Hood." In Neale, "Swashbucklers and Sitcoms," I erroneously refer to her real name as Janet Green.

25. Barzman, *The Red and the Blacklist*, 260, recalls that she wrote three episodes of "Robin Hood" with Mischa Altman, though she does not specify which ones. In a letter to the author dated November 8, 2002, she recalls that she co-wrote an episode about Eleanor of Aquitaine and the raising of ransom money for King Richard, and that "Hannah used the names Ring and Ian were using." "Queen Eleanor," which is credited to Eric Heath, fits her description, but so does "The Traitor," which is about the transportation of ransom money and which is credited to Norma Shannon and Ralph Smart, a possible pseudonym and front for Barzman and Altman, respectively.

26. Although Eric Heath was one of the regular pseudonyms used by Lardner and Hunter, a letter to Ruben from Scott and Rinaldo dated June 6, 1956 (ASP, Box 6, Folder 9), indicates that "The Alchemist" was written by them.

27. In McGilligan and Buhle, *Tender Comrades*, 437, Lees claimed that he wrote "four *Robin Hood* episodes, all with gag names on the credits, like Cecil B. Humphrey Smythe or Alfred Leslie Higginbottom." Neither of these names appears on the "Robin Hood" credits. The nearest equivalents are C. Douglas Phipps, who is credited with writing "The Vandals," and Milton S. Schlesinger, who is credited with writing "The Bandit of Brittany," "Flight from France," and "Too Many Earls." Schlesinger was a pseudonym for Maurice Rapf and Sam Moore, as detailed in note 32 below. There are versions of scripts

for four episodes of "Robin Hood" in RLFRC: "The Charter" (Box 10, Folders 130–132), "The Imposter" (Box 10, Folders 136–140), "The Grand Ball" (Box 10, Folders 133–135), which was never produced, and "The Rivals" (Box 11, Folder 153), which is incorrectly indexed as an episode of "Sir Lancelot," and which was credited to Leslie Poynton, a pseudonym usually used by Adrian Scott and Fred Rinaldo, but not by Lees. According to the listings in RLJC, "The Imposter" was the original title of "Too Many Robins." The episode actually entitled "The Imposters" was credited to Norman Best, which is specified in the list of "Writers Involved in Rerun Settlement with Official Films" and confirmed in another listing as a pseudonym for Norman Kahn. This list also cites S. B. Wells as a pseudonym for Arnaud D'Usseau, Arthur Dales as a pseudonym for Howard Dimsdale, John Ridgely (as well as Leslie Ponyton) as a pseudonym for Adrian Scott and Fred Rinaldo, Clare Thorne as a pseudonym for Janet Stevenson, and Robert Newman as a pseudonym or front for Arnold Manoff.

28. WSP contains outlines and scripts for ten episodes of "Robin Hood" (Box 60, Folders 2 and 3). Two of these episodes, "The Robber Baron" and "The Walking Trees of Sherwood," were never filmed. Of the others, four were credited to Neil R. Collins, one to John Dyson, and two to Arthur Behr.

29. See note 22.

30. See notes 22 and 25.

31. See note 27.

32. Rapf, *Back Lot*, 193, notes that he and Sam Moore wrote "The Bandit of Brittany" and "Flight from France," though he does not mention "Too Many Earls," which is credited, like them, to Milton S. Schlesinger, and which is confirmed as an episode they wrote in the listings in RLJC.

33. See note 27.

34. Ibid.

35. Ibid.

36. Ibid.

37. Ibid.

38. Ibid.

39. Ibid.

40. The fourth series of "Robin Hood" was for the most part scripted by young British writers, among them Louis Marks and Leon Griffiths. It should be noted in this context that Griffiths had been an active supporter of Communism in the early 1950s, having worked for Budapest radio and as a drama critic and reporter for the *Daily Worker*.

41. IMHC, Box 4, Folder 4.

42. See letters and telegrams to and from Ruben and Lardner and Hunter, February 9, 16, 25, March 6, and April 26, 1956, IMHC, Box 4, Folder 17.

43. There are versions of scripts for "The Adventures of Sir Lancelot" in IMHC, Box 12, Folder 5, and Box 13, Folders 1 and 4.

44. *Lancelot's* "amiable and lighthearted approach to . . . the melodrama" (Scott to Ruben, May 17, 1956, IMHC, Box 4, Folder 17) was a point of contention and in practice proved hard to achieve.

45. Ruben to Lardner and Hunter, May 6, 1956, IMHC, Box 4, Folder 17.

46. Ibid. Partly for this reason, partly because it was anticipated that TV programs in the United States might soon be transmitted in color, a number of early episodes of "Sir Lancelot" were filmed in color, an option that was considered for "The Buccaneers" too (Ruben to Lardner and Hunter, October 25, 1955, IMHC, Box 4, Folder 2).

47. In *On My Way to the Theater* (New York: Macmillan, 1972), 192, 195, Hy Kraft recalls that he wrote "three or four segments" for Weinstein's TV series, and that his pseudonym was Harold Kent. "Roman Wall" is one of two episodes of "Sir Lancelot" with this name on its credits. However, there is a copy of an invoice from Hunter for payment of the script of "Roman Wall" in IMHC, Box 4, Folder 47. Whether he and Lardner wrote the script or whether he was claiming payment on Kraft's behalf remains unclear.

48. Memo from Ruben to Lardner, Hunter and Koch, June 16, 1955, Lardner and Hunter to Ruben, June 20, 1955, IHMC, Box 4, Folder 2.

49. Lardner and Hunter to Ruben, March 27, 1956, Ruben to Lardner and Hunter, March 30, 1956, Lardner to script editor Kathryn Dawes, May 5, 1956, IMHC, Box 4, Folder 17; Hunter to Salt, April 27, 1956, WSP, Box 80, Folder 4.

50. Salt to Dawes, November 9, 1956, WSP, Box 120, Folder 3. (This folder contains a number of letters on the new format and an extensive set of research notes).

51. WSP, Box 61, Folder 5 and Box 80, Folder 47. The former contains outlines and scripts, the latter a letter from Salt to Dawes dated July 27, 1956, listing episodes, outlines, and scripts with their authors' initials.

52. Weinstein to Lardner and Hunter, May 25, 1956, IMHC, Box 4, Folder 17. Wilson's authorship of this episode is confirmed in Lardner to Hunter, June 30, 1959, RLJC, Box 4, Folder 119. There is a copy of the script in the Michael Wilson Papers, ALSP-UCLA, Box 4, Folder 4.

53. There is a script for an episode entitled "Steer by the Southern Cross" in WSP Box 61, Folder 5, which bears a number of similarities to "Slave Ship." There is also a script for "Unholy Alliance," which was never filmed.

54. "Terence Moore" was a pseudonym used by Lardner and Hunter and by Salt and Perl. I have been unable to identify who wrote this particular episode.

55. One of the listings in RLJC attributes "Cutlass Wedding" and "Mistress Higgins' Treasure," among others, to Nancy Reals. According to the list of "Writers Involved in Rerun Settlement with Official Films," Nancy Reals was a fictional person with a New York address used by Salt, Perl, and Lampell for the purposes of correspondence. All the other episodes listed under this name in the untitled listing were written by Lampell, so it seems likely that he wrote these episodes too. However, a letter from Arthur Behrstock (Waldo Salt) to Albert Ruben (May 17, 1957, WSP, Box 80, Folder 47) refers to "Reels" [sic] as "AP," Arnold Perl, so authorship of these episodes remains, for the moment, unclear.

56. One of the listings in RLJC attributes authorship of "Flip and Jenny" and "The Decoy" to Joel Carpenter, a pseudonym used by Arnold Manoff since the early 1950s (Neale, "Transatlantic Ventures and *Robin Hood*," 85–86).

57. See note 54.

58. Ruben to Hunter, October 18, 1956, IMHC, Box 4, Folder 8.

59. There are copies of scripts of all these episodes in IMHC, Box 8, Folder 2.

60. There are copies of outlines and scripts for all the episodes listed here in WSP, Box 75, Folder 6.

61. A letter from script editor Sonya Marks dated February 26, 1957, in IMHC, Box 8, Folder 6, which refers to copies of "Westerby's scripts 'The Winged Victory' and 'The Duke.'" Westerby was a London-born screenwriter who worked in Hollywood. However, as noted above, "Winged Victory," an episode of "Sir Lancelot," was written by Adrian Scott. It is therefore possible that Westerby, who was based, like Scott, in Los Angeles, acted as a front for him, though I have not been able to confirm this from other sources.

62. It is probably no more than a coincidence that he wrote an early draft of the script for the 1952 film version. See John Lenihan, "English Classics for Cold War America: MGM's *Kim*" (1950), "Ivanhoe" (1952), *Julius Caesar* (1953)," *Journal of Popular Film and Television* 20, no. 3 (1992): 45–47.

63. WSP, Box 66, Folder 2. The outline is dated May 7, 1956.

64. For a listing of these novels, see http://textbook-authors.abebooks.co.uk/Author/43434/Berenberg+Benedict.htm.

65. WSP, Box 75, Folder 3.

66. http://www.starmdb.com/STAR-B/200510/Ben-Berenberg-66649.htm http://www.mrlucky.com/html/music/rev46.htm and http://www.nationarchive.com/Summaries/v265i0002_19htm.

67. WSP, Box 66, Folders 2 and 3. These scripts are numbered (Programs 12, 16, 29, and 13, respectively) rather than titled, but can be easily identified on the basis of their content.

68. Program 20, WSP, Box 66, Folder 3.

69. Program 15, WSP, Box 66, Folder 2.

70. See note 27 for S. B. Wells as a pseudonym for D'Usseau.

71. For further recent histories, see Paul Buhle and Dave Wagner, *Hide in Plain Sight: The Hollywood Blacklistees in Film and Television* (New York: Palgrave Macmillan, 2003), Neale, "Swashbucklers and Sitcoms," and J. Schultheiss and M. Schaubert, eds., *"You Are There" Teleplays: The Critical Edition* (Northridge: Center for Communication Studies, California University, 1997). While this essay was in press, I was informed that Michael Sayers, a refugee from McCarthyism, wrote episodes of "Robin Hood" under the pseudonym Michael Connor. Michael Connor is credited as writing "The Frightened Tailor," "The Black Five," "Sybella," and "Pepper." My thanks to Sean Sayers for providing me with this information.

CHAPTER 13 — HOLLYWOOD, THE NEW LEFT, AND *FTA*

1. Larry Ceplair and Steven Englund, *The Inquisition in Hollywood: Politics in the Film Community, 1930–1960* (Champaign: University of Illinois Press, 2003), 407.

2. Ibid., 408.

3. Ibid., 420.

4. "D'Inzillo Says Walsh Uses Commie Smear, Echoing Roy Brewer's '54 Line," *Variety*, July 12, 1972, 3.

5. See Christopher Lasch, *The Agony of the American Left* (New York: Andre Deutsch, 1970), 180.

6. See Todd Gitlin, *The Sixties: Years of Hope, Days of Rage* (New York: Bantam, 1987), 125; Staughton Lynd, "The Prospects of the New Left," in *Failure of a Dream? Essays in the History of American Socialism*, ed. John H. M. Laslett and Seymour Martin Lipset (Garden City, N.Y.: Anchor, 1974), 714.

7. See Mark Shiel, "The American New Wave, Part 1: 1967–1970" and "The American New Wave, Part 2: 1970–1975," in *Contemporary American Cinema*, ed. Michael Hammond and Linda Ruth Williams (New York: McGraw-Hill, 2006), 51–68, 136–153.

8. See Robert Sam Anson, *McGovern: A Biography* (New York: Holt, Rinehart and Winston, 1972), 239–240; Theodore H. White, *The Making of the President 1972* (London: Jonathan Cape, 1973), 115–119.

9. Mitchell, quoted in Jon Wiener, *Professors, Politics and Pop* (London: Verso, 1991), 321; McGovern, quoted in White, *Making of the President 1972*, 43.

10. See "All-Star Concert Set for McGovern," *Hollywood Reporter*, April 6, 1972, 1; "McGovern Concert Gross is $300,000," *Hollywood Reporter*, April 13, 1972, 3.

11. Gary Crowdus, *Cineaste* 6, no. 4 (1975): 1. See also the chapter on Jane Fonda in *Creative Differences: Profiles of Hollywood Dissidents*, ed. Barbara Zheutlin and David Talbot (Boston: South End Press, 1978), 131–143.

12. Ibid.

13. Mary Hershberger, *Jane Fonda's War: A Political Biography of an Antiwar Icon* (New York: New Press, 2005), 4; Dan Georgakas and Lenny Rubenstein, "'I Prefer Films that Strengthen People': An Interview with Jane Fonda," *Cineaste* 6, no. 4 (1975): 9.

14. See Fred Gardner, "Hollywood Confidential: Part I," in *Viet Nam Generation Journal & Newsletter* 3, no. 3 (November 1991), hosted by the Sixties Project, Institute of Advanced Technology in the Humanities at the University of Virginia at Charlottesville, http://lists.village.virginia.edu/sixties/HTML_docs/Texts/Narrative/Gardner_Hollywood_1.html.

15. Matthew Rinaldi, "The Olive-Drab Rebels: Military Organizing during the Vietnam Era," *Radical America* 8, no. 3 (May–June 1974): 17–32.

16. David Cortright, *Soldiers in Revolt: GI Resistance during the Vietnam War* (Chicago: Haymarket Books, 2005), 78.

17. Robert D. Heinl, "The Collapse of the Armed Forces," *Armed Forces Journal*, June 7, 1971, 30–38.

18. Cortright, *Soldiers in Revolt*, 261.

19. David James, *Allegories of Cinema: American Film in the Sixties* (Princeton, N.J.: Princeton University Press, 1989), 202.

20. Ibid., 196.

21. Massimo Teodori, ed., *The New Left: A Documentary History* (London: Jonathan Cape, 1970).

22. Quoted in Hershberger, *Jane Fonda's War*, 31.

23. "Left Face," *New Republic*, March 13, 1971, 9; James T. Wooten, "500 GIs at Debut of Antiwar Show," *New York Times*, March 15, 1971, 9; Cortright, *Soldiers in Revolt*, 78.

24. Fonda, interviewed by journalists in the film *FTA*; see also "Hope Reminiscent," *Newsweek*, January 10, 1966, 41; also Fonda, *My Life So Far* (New York: Random House), 272–275.

25. Heinl, "The Collapse of the Armed Forces."

26. Georgakas and Rubenstein, "I Prefer Films that Strengthen People," 3.

27. Ibid., 7.

28. Arthur Knight, "'FTA' Goes to War against Army," *Variety*, July 11, 1972, 3.

29. On Juliana Wang, see Alexis Krasilovsky, *Women Behind the Camera: Conversations with Camerawomen* (Westport, Conn.: Greenwood Press, 1997), 14–17.

30. Cortright, *Soldiers in Revolt*, 111.

31. Todd Gitlin, *The Whole World Is Watching: Mass Media in the Making and Unmaking of the New Left* (Berkeley: University of California Press, 1980), 177–178.

32. Ibid., 166.

33. Roger Corman, American Film Institute Seminar proceedings, October 16, 1970, American Film Institute, Louis B. Mayer Library, n.p.; Digby Diehl, "The Simenon of Cinema," *Show* 1, no. 5 (May 1970): 30.

34. This was in comparison to what *Variety* called a "promising" $58,100 for *Joe Kidd* (1972) and $37,500 for AIP's *Boxcar Bertha* (1972). *Variety*, July 12, 1972, 24; *Variety*, July 26, 1972, 8–9; Will Tusher, "AIP Pulls 'FTA' in LA; Fonda's Visit to Hanoi Is Catalyst," *Hollywood Reporter*, August 3, 1972, 1, 3.

35. "Jane Fonda's FTA Show Now a Film," *New York Times*, July 22, 1972, 14; Arthur Knight, "'FTA' Goes to War against Army," 3.

36. *Variety*, August 2, 1972, 8–9; Tusher, "AIP Pulls 'FTA' in LA," 1.

37. Tusher, "AIP Pulls 'FTA' in LA," 3.

38. "AIP Firm on 'FTA'; Arkoff Denies Any Pressure to Dump," *Hollywood Reporter*, August 4, 1972, 1, 19.

CHAPTER 14 — RED HOLLYWOOD

1. Christa Wolf, *A Model Childhood*, trans. Ursule Molinaro and Hedwig Rappolt (New York: Farrar, Straus, and Giroux, 1980), 3.

2. Louis Berg, "How End the Panic in Radio-TV?" *Commentary* 14 (October 1952): 322, 324.

3. Robert Warshow, "The 'Idealism' of Julius and Ethel Rosenberg," *Commentary* 16 (November 1953): 415.

4. James Rorty, "The Anti-Communism of Senator McCarthy," *Commentary* 15 (August 1953): 127. In 1953, when Republicans controlled the Eighty-third Congress, William Jenner was chairman of the Internal Security Subcommittee of the Senate Judiciary Committee, and Harold Velde was chairman of the House Committee on Un-American Activities.

5. Arthur Schlesinger Jr., *The Vital Center: The Politics of Freedom* (Boston: Houghton Mifflin, 1949), 210.

6. Ibid., 125–126.

7. Ibid., 125.

8. Murray Kempton, *Part of Our Time: Some Ruins and Monuments of the Thirties* (New York: Simon & Schuster, 1955), 184, 206, 209.

9. Ibid., 204, 197, 196–197, 183, 184.

10. Murray Kempton, "The Limits of Irony," *New Republic* (April 15, 1968): 28, 30, 34.

11. Walter Goodman, *The Committee: The Extraordinary Career of the House Committee on Un-American Activities* (New York: Farrar, Strauss and Giroux, 1968), 224.

12. Ibid., 224–225.

13. Ibid., 221–222. An abridged version of Marcantonio's statement against the contempt citations is reprinted in Annette T. Rubinstein, ed., *I Vote My Conscience: Debates, Speeches and Writings of Vito Marcantonio* (New York: Vito Marcantonio Memorial, 1956): 236–238. Incidentally, Goodman's characterization of Marcantonio's statement is tendentious and misleading.

14. Quoted in Goodman, *The Committee*, 217.

15. Ibid., 218.

16. Quoted in Robert Vaughn, *Only Victims: A Study of Show Business Blacklisting* (New York: Proscenium, 1972), 14. The full text of Trumbo's address has been published as a postscript in Helen Manfull, ed., *Additional Dialogue: Letters of Dalton Trumbo, 1942–1968* (New York: Evans, 1970), 569–570.

17. Kempton, "The Limits of Irony," 182.

18. Stefan Kanfer, *A Journal of the Plague Years* (New York: Atheneum, 1973), 29, 26, 36, 38.

19. Hellman, *Scoundrel Time* (Boston: Little, Brown, 1976), 43–44.

20. Ibid., 40–41.

21. William Faulkner, *Intruder in the Dust* (New York: Signet, 1948), 23.

22. Hellman, *Scoundrel Time*, 154–155.

23. Hilton Kramer, "The Blacklist and the Cold War," *New York Times*, October 3, 1976, section 2:1, 16–17.

24. Nathan Glazer, "An Answer to Lillian Hellman," *Commentary* 61 (June 1976): 36–39; Sidney Hook, "Lillian Hellman's *Scoundrel Time*," *Encounter* 48 (February 1977): 82–91.

25. Diana Trilling, "Liberal Anti-Communism Revisited," in *We Must March My Darlings* (New York: Harcourt, Brace, Jovanovich, 1977), 53.

26. Maureen Howard, review of *Scoundrel Time*, *New York Times Book Review*, April 25, 1976: 2.

27. Hellman, *Scoundrel Time*, 85.

28. Richard Sennett, *Authority* (New York: W. W. Norton, 1980), 149.

29. Robin Blackburn, "A Brief Guide to Bourgeois Ideology," in *Student Power/Problems, Diagnosis, Action*, ed. Alexander Cockburn and Robin Blackburn (Baltimore: Penguin, 1969), 187.

30. Elia Kazan, "Letters to the Editors," *Saturday Review*, April 5, 1952, 22.

31. Christopher Lehmann-Haupt, "Going One's Own Way," *New York Times*, April 15, 1976: 31.

32. Larry Ceplair and Steven Englund, *The Inquisition in Hollywood: Politics in the Film Community, 1930–60* (Garden City, N.Y.: Doubleday, 1980), 48, 77, 51, 152, 79.

33. Ibid., 75.

34. Ibid., 239.

35. Quoted in ibid., 242.

36. Ibid., 243.

37. Victor Navasky, *Naming Names* (New York: Viking Press, 1980), xv.

38. Ibid., 224.

39. Daniel Aaron, "Informing on the Informers," *New York Review of Books*, December 4, 1980: 6.

40. Eric M. Breindel, "The Communists and the Committee," *Commentary* 71 (January 1981): 50.

41. Ibid.

42. Navasky, *Naming Names*, 306.

43. Ibid., 426.

44. Breindel, "The Communists and the Committee," 50, 51.

45. Ibid., 48.

46. Ibid., 51.

47. Eric M. Breindel, response to Aaron Katz, *Commentary* 71 (June 1981): 22.

48. Dewey and La Follette, "Several Faults Are Found in 'Mission to Moscow' Film," *New York Times*, May 9, 1943, sec. 4: 8; Meyer Schapiro, "Film Chronicle," *Partisan Review* 10 (May–June 1943): 275–278; Manny Farber, "Mishmash," *New Republic*, May 10, 1943: 636. For a very thorough account of the controversy surrounding the production of *Mission to Moscow*, see David Culbert's introduction to the published screenplay, "The Feature Film as Official Propaganda," in Culbert, ed., *Mission to Moscow* (Madison: University of Wisconsin Press, 1980), 11–41.

49. James K. Lyon, *Bertolt Brecht in America* (Princeton: Princeton University Press, 1980), 71.

50. Eric Bentley, ed., *Thirty Years of Treason: Excerpts from Hearings before the House Committee on Un-American Activities* (New York: Viking Press, 1971), 206. Brecht's testimony is printed on pages 207–224.

51. Ring Lardner Jr., "My Life on the Blacklist," *Saturday Evening Post*, October 14, 1961: 38–44.

52. Blankfort was not a "friendly witness" as the term is generally understood, that is, he did not identify any of his Hollywood colleagues as Communist Party members, but I think he can be fairly characterized as a supine one. He was called as a witness before HUAC in 1952 because he had been identified as a Communist by Louis Budenz, editor of the *Daily Worker* in the thirties. Blankfort denied he had ever been a party member and insisted he had always been anti-Communist despite a long record of association with Communist front organizations. He repudiated or apologized for most of these commitments, including his opposition to the committee itself. Consequently, he found himself trapped in exchanges like this one, about the theater criticism he wrote for the *Daily Worker* in the thirties. Committee counsel Frank S. Tavenner Jr. was questioning him about an essay written in 1934 on a play called *The Stevedore*:

> TAVENNER: In the second column appears these words: "There are no stock Mammies or night-club jazz babies or comic butlers, or any other of the false characters which colored actors or actresses are called on to play in bourgeois theater." Will you tell the Committee what you meant by "bourgeois theater"?
>
> BLANKFORT: The whole French theater of the nineteenth century has been called, in many histories, not necessarily left wing, the theater of the bourgeoisie.
>
> TAVENNER: Was that not the stereotyped language of the Communist Party in referring to anything which was not Communist?
>
> BLANKFORT: The word "bourgeois" goes back long before the Communists took it as a stereotype.
>
> CONGRESSMAN HAROLD H. VELDE: Do you still use the term "bourgeoisie"?
>
> BLANKFORT: I don't, no, Sir.
>
> VELDE: Do you recall when you stopped using it, or any of the other well-known Communist terms?
>
> BLANKFORT: No, Sir, I don't recall.

This exchange is quoted in Bentley, *Thirty Years of Treason*, 468.

53. Quoted in Navasky, *Naming Names*, 395–396.

54. The "Maltz affair" (or even sometimes "l'affaire Maltz") is discussed in Kempton, *Part of Our Time*, 200–202; Goodman, *The Committee*, 213–214; Kanfer, *A Journal of the Plague Years*, 32–33; Nancy Lynn Schwartz, *The Hollywood Writers' Wars* (New York: Knopf, 1982), 235–237; Ceplair and Englund, *The Inquisition in Hollywood*, 233–237; and Navasky,

Naming Names, 287–302. It figures equally prominently in histories of the Communist Party that cover the postwar period: Irving Howe and Lewis Coser, *The American Communist Party* (Boston: Beacon Press, 1957), 316–317; David A. Shannon, *The Decline of American Communism* (New York: Harcourt, Brace & World, 1959), 56–57; Joseph R. Starobin, *American Communism in Crisis, 1943–1957* (Cambridge, Mass.: Harvard University Press, 1972), 135–138. It is also treated briefly by William L. O'Neill in his study of attitudes toward the Soviet Union on the non-Communist left in the United States, *A Better World—The Great Schism: Stalinism and the American Intellectuals* (New York: Simon & Schuster, 1982), 248.

55. Albert Maltz, "What Shall We Ask of Writers?" *New Masses*, February 12, 1946: 22.

56. Ibid., 20.

57. Ibid., 19, 20.

58. Goodman, *The Committee*, 214.

59. Albert Maltz, "Moving Forward," *New Masses*, April 9, 1946: 9.

60. O'Neill, *A Better World*, 248.

61. Schwartz, *The Hollywood Writers' Wars*, 235.

62. Larzer Ziff, *The American 1890s: Life and Times of a Lost Generation* (New York: Viking Press, 1966), 283.

63. Quoted in Alvah Bessie, "What Is Freedom for Writers?" *New Masses*, March 12, 1946: 10.

64. Navasky, *Naming Names*, 288.

65. Quoted in Ceplair and Englund, *The Inquisition in Hollywood*, 73.

66. Screenwriter Fred Rinaldo, quoted in Schwartz, *The Hollywood Writers' Wars*, 237.

67. Quoted in Navasky, *Naming Names*, 290.

68. Quoted in Maurice Isserman, *Which Side Were You On? The American Communist Party during the Second World War* (Middletown, Conn.: Wesleyan University Press, 1982), 186.

69. Ibid.

70. Gold, "Albert Maltz and Plain Speaking," *Daily Worker* (February 23, 1946): 6.

71. Maltz, "What Shall We Ask of Writers?" 22.

72. Bessie, "What Is Freedom for Writers?" 9.

73. Kempton, *Part of Our Time*, 182.

74. Goodman, *The Committee*, 215.

75. David Thomson, *A Biographical Dictionary of Film* (New York: William Morrow, 1976), 141.

76. Morris Freedman, "New England and Hollywood," *Commentary* 16 (October 1953): 392.

77. Kanfer, *A Journal of the Plague Years*, 141.

78. Navasky, *Naming Names*, 78.

79. Quoted in Ceplair and Englund, *The Inquisition in Hollywood*, 322.

80. Andrew Sarris, "A Few Kind Words for the '50s," *Village Voice*, September 14, 1982: 47.

81. Lester Cole, *Hollywood Red* (Palo Alto, Calif.: Ramparts Press, 1981), 172–173.

82. Julie Burchill, "Red Stars," *The Face*, no. 24 (April 1982): 47.

83. Quoted in Richard Roud, "The French Line," *Sight and Sound* 29 (Autumn 1960): 171.

84. Margaret Brenman-Gibson, *Clifford Odets, American Playwright: The Years from 1906 to 1940* (New York: Atheneum, 1981), 244. A slightly different version of this story is told in Larry Swindell's biography of Garfield, *Body and Soul* (New York: William Morrow, 1975), 15–16.

85. Diana Trilling, "Fiction in Review," *Nation*, June 26, 1943: 899.

86. Michel Ciment, *Le livre de Losey* (Paris, Editions Stock, 1979), 126–127.

87. Bosley Crowther, review of *Try and Get Me*, *New York Times*, May 7, 1951: 22.

88. Gilles Jacob, "Joseph Losey, or The Camera Calls," *Sight and Sound* 35 (Spring 1966): 62.

89. Quoted in Navasky, *Naming Names*, xix.

90. Sarris, "A Few Kind Words for the '50s," 47.

91. Walter Benjamin, "Theses on the Philosophy of History," in *Illuminations*, trans. Harry Zohn (New York: Schocken, 1968), 257. Translation modified.

AFTERWORD

1. James Naremore, *Something More Than Night: Film Noir and Its Contexts* (Berkeley: University of California Press, 1998), 124–125.

2. Thom Andersen and Noël Burch, *Les Communistes de Hollywood: Autre chose que des martyrs* (Paris: Presses de la Sorbonne Nouvelle, 1994), 147.

3. Naremore, *Something More Than Night*, 122.

4. Ibid., 125. For an intelligent detailed analysis of Losey's M, see James Morrison, *Passport to Hollywood: Hollywood Films, European Directors* (Albany: State University of New York Press, 1998), 148–164.

5. Thom Andersen, "Blacklisted," in *Blacklisted: Movies by the Hollywood Blacklist Victims* (Wien: Viennale, 2000), 14.

6. Paul Buhle and Dave Wagner, *Blacklisted: The Film Lover's Guide to the Hollywood Blacklist* (New York: Palgrave Macmillan, 2003), ix.

7. "Polonsky Hagiography Replete with Flimsy Critical Commentary and Shoddy Film Scholarship," *Cineaste* 27, no. 2 (Spring 2002): 59.

8. "A Litany of Errors," *Cineaste* 29, no. 3 (Summer 2004): 68–69.

9. Ronald Radosh and Allis Radosh, *Red Star Over Hollywood: The Film Colony's Long Romance with the Left* (San Francisco: Encounter Books, 2005), 100 and 102.

10. Ibid., 242.

11. Schickel, *Los Angeles Times Book Review*, June 2, 2002, R2.

12. Paul Buhle and Dave Wagner, *Radical Hollywood: The Untold Story Behind America's Favorite Movies* (New York: New Press, 2002), xii.

13. Buhle and Wagner, *Blacklisted*, 99.

14. Paul Buhle and Dave Wagner, *Hide in Plain Sight: The Hollywood Blacklistees in Film and Television, 1950–2002* (New York: Palgrave Macmillan, 2003), 165.

15. Ibid., 115.

16. Ibid., 114.

17. Ibid., 169.

18. Ibid., 139.

19. Ibid., xix, xx.

20. Michael Denning, *The Cultural Front: The Laboring of American Culture in the Twentieth Century* (London and New York: Verso, 1996), xviii.

21. David Thomson, *The Whole Equation: A History of Hollywood* (New York: Alfred A. Knopf, 2005), 274.

Notes on the Contributors

THOM ANDERSEN teaches film and video composition at the California Institute of the Arts. His films include *Melting, Olivia's Place, Eadweard Muybridge, Zoopraxographer* (1975), and *Los Angeles Plays Itself* (2003). His work with Noël Burch on the history of the Hollywood blacklist and the filmic writing of its victims has produced the book *Les Communistes de Hollywood: Autre chose que des martyrs* (1994) and the videotape *Red Hollywood* (1995).

DOUG DIBBERN is a PhD candidate in the Cinema Studies department at New York University. He is writing a dissertation about leftists in Hollywood during the McCarthy period.

JENNIFER LANGDON-TECLAW is a writer and teacher based in Chicago and northern California. She has taught courses in history, gender and women's studies, popular culture, and creative nonfiction, most recently at the University of Illinois at Chicago. Her research on Adrian Scott and the politics of film production and reception in 1940s Hollywood won the American Historical Association's Gutenberg "<e>" Prize and will be published as a digital book by Columbia University Press in 2007.

FRANK KRUTNIK teaches film at the University of Sussex. He has published the books *In a Lonely Street: Film Noir, Genre, Masculinity* (1991), *Popular Film and Television Comedy* (coauthored with Steve Neale, 1990), and *Inventing Jerry Lewis* (2000) and has edited *Hollywood Comedians: The Film Reader* (2003). He is currently working on a new book on film noir.

SEAN MCCANN, an associate professor of English and American Studies at Wesleyan University, is the author of *Gumshoe America: Hardboiled Crime Fiction and the Rise and Fall of New Deal Liberalism* (2000). He is currently at work on a book titled *The Anti-liberal Imagination: American Literature and Presidential Government*.

STEVE NEALE is a professor of Film Studies at Exeter University. He is the author of *Genre and Hollywood* (2000), editor of *Genre and Contemporary Hollywood* (2002) and co-editor of *Contemporary Hollywood Cinema* (1998). He has published on the blacklistees and television in the *Historical Journal of Film, Radio and Television* (2003) and *Film Studies* (2005).

BRIAN NEVE is a senior lecturer in the Department of European Studies at Bath University. He is the author of *Film and Politics in America: A Social Tradition* (1992) and *Elia Kazan: The Cinema of an American Outsider* (2007), as well as of numerous journal articles and book chapters on aspects of film, film history, and film politics. He teaches on the University of Bath's MA film programme.

REBECCA PRIME is a Ph.D. candidate in the Department of Film, Television, and Digital Media at the University of California, Los Angeles, where she is writing a dissertation on blacklisted American filmmakers in Europe. Her other research interests include early ethnographic cinema and transnational cinema. Her work has appeared in the journals *Post Script* and *Film Quarterly* and is included in *Filmic Folklores* (University of Utah Press, forthcoming).

ERICA SHEEN is a visiting fellow in film in the Department of English and Related Literatures at the University of York. Previous publications on Cold War Hollywood include articles and chapters on Disney and the widescreen biblical epic.

MARK SHIEL is a lecturer in Film Studies at King's College London, where he specializes in post–WWII American cinema and cinema and the city. He is the author of Italian *Neorealism: Rebuilding the Cinematic City* (Wallflower Press / Columbia University Press, 2005) and co-editor of *Screening the City* (Verso, 2003) and *Cinema and the City: Film and Urban Societies in a Global Context* (Blackwell, 2001).

ART SIMON is an associate professor of Film Studies in the English Department at Montclair State University. He has also taught as a visiting professor in Cinema Studies at New York University. He is the author of *Dangerous Knowledge: The JFK Assassination in Art and Film* (1996). New research focuses on the relationship between Hollywood and the American Jewish community at mid-century. He is currently writing about *Crossfire* in the context of debates around domestic anti-Semitism and Jewish postwar identity.

JEFF SMITH is a professor of Film Studies in the Communication Arts Department of the University of Wisconsin–Madison and the author of *The Sounds of Commerce: Marketing Popular Film Music* (1998). His previous work on the Hollywood blacklist includes " 'A Good Business Proposition': Dalton Trumbo, *Spartacus*, and the End of the Blacklist," in *Controlling Hollywood: Censorship and Regulation in the Studio Era* (2000).

PETER STANFIELD is a reader in Film Studies at the University of Kent and the author of *Body & Soul: Jazz & Blues in American Film, 1927–63* (2005), *Horse Opera: The Strange History of the Singing Cowboy* (2002), *Hollywood, Westerns and the 1930s: The Lost Trail* (2001), and joint-editor of *Mob Culture: Hidden Histories of the American Gangster Film* (2005). He is currently working on a book entitled *Maximum Movies*.

WILL STRAW teaches in the Department of Art History and Communications Studies at McGill University in Montreal, Canada. He is the author of *Cyanide and Sin: Visualizing Crime in 50s America* (2006), and of the forthcoming *Popular Music: Scenes and Sensibilities* (2007). He has published over fifty articles on film, music, and urban culture. Dr. Straw's current research centers on New York tabloid newspaper culture of the late 1920s and early 1930s.

Index

Bishop, Jim, 147

"Black, Brown, and Beige" (Ellington production), 116

Blackburn, Robert, 234

blacklist: alleged, against anti-Communists, 233; annotated bibliography, 225–243; antedates informers, 239; artistic merits of films by victims of, 254–257; broken by Preminger with *Exodus*, 114; end of, 210; film allegories of, 6, 8, 21–24, 28, 34; historiography of, and Writers' Guild of America, 13; Kempton unsympathetic to, 228; long twilight of, 246; Schlesinger on beginnings of, 227–28; second and third wave, 257; Zanuck's opposition to, 283n.25

"Blacklisted: Movies by the Hollywood Blacklist Victims" (Viennale program), 265

Black Panther Party, 211

Black Power, 211, 212, 220–221

Blair [Reisz], Betsy, 155

Blake, Robert, 295n.56

Blankfort, Michael, 246, 333n.52

blaxploitation thrillers, 212

Blockade, 256, 268

Blood of the Lamb (Marked Children), 189

Blue Dahlia, 118, 299n.16

Blues in the Night, 13, 188, 189

Blumenfeld, Leon, *see* Meadows, Noel

Bodner, Allen, 81

Body and Soul, 8, 13, 80–81, 81, 84, 85, 86–87, 88, 89–90, 91, 118, 184, 192, 194–195, 257, 259, 260, 262, 292n.83, 293n.6, 299n.13, 299–300n.21

The Body Beautiful (Rossen play), 184

Boetticher, Budd, 102

Bogart, Humphrey, 17; *Dark Passage*, 126; Hellinger and Santana Pictures, 291n.57; "How to Get in Good with Hitler," 180; *In a Lonely Place*, 75, 75–77, 127; *Knock on Any Door*, 71; *Marked Woman*, 185; and 1947 HUAC hearings, 101; *They Live By Night*, 70–71; *To Have and Have Not*, 121

Bohnen, Roman, 308n.40

"Bomb Another City Today" (song), 221

Bondanella, Peter, 41

Boomerang!, 10, 132, 133, 136, 139, 141, 144

Boorstein, Daniel, 240

Borde, Raymond, 11, 144, 196

Border Incident, 102

Bordwell, David, 5

Boretz, Allen, 287n.5

boxer-as-artist analogy, 86–87

boxing: champion as spokesman for tolerance, 181; as metaphor for labor-capital struggle, 88–89; and organized crime, 94; televised, 95–96, 295n.52

boxing films, 8–9, 79–96

Boyle, Peter, 212, 217

The Boys in Company C, 214

The Boy with Green Hair, 155, 167, 291n.52, 312n.12

Bradford, William, 37

Brady, Martin (pseud.), 269, 270

The Brave Bulls, 197

The Brave One, 14, 216

Breakdown, 80

The Breaking Point, 257, 268

Brecht, Bertolt, 104, 105, 245–246, 291n.52, 293n.14

Breen, Joseph, 62, 103–104

Breen Office, *see* Production Code Administration (PCA)

Breindel, Eric M., 239, 240, 241, 242–243

Brenman-Gibson, Margaret, 256, 258

Brent, George, 185

Brewer, Roy, 164

The Brick Foxhole, see Cornered

Bridges, Lloyd, 260

Bright, John, 189, 266

British Documentary Movement, 10

Brody, Sam, 215

Broken Arrow (film), 6

Broken Arrow (GI newspaper), 213

Brooklyn Jewish Community Council, 178

Brooks, Hadda, 127

Browder, Earl, 251, 260; Browderism, cultural, 251–252

Brown, Harry, 189

Bruskin, Perry, 70

brute-cult, of postwar cinema, 139, 304n.32. *See also* violence

Brute Force, 80, 266, 308n.40

Bryant, William Cullen, 171

Bryan, William Jennings, 20

"The Buccaneers" (TV series), 14, 198, 200, 201, 204, *206*, *207*, 206–208, 323n.10, 327n.46

Buchalter, Louis "Lepke," 87

Buchman, Sidney, 105, 140, 272

Budenz, Louis, 333n.52

Buhle, Paul, 3, 16, 80–81, 89–90, 179, 269, 271–274

Build My Gallows High (Mainwaring novel), 102

The Bullfighter and the Lady, 102

Buñuel, Luis, 130

Burchill, Julie, 258

Burch, Noël, 16, 264, 265, 266, 267, 268, 272

Burn!, 234–235

Burnett, W. R., 122

Burns, Hamish Hamilton, 205. *See also* Moore, Sam; Rapf, Maurice; Rinaldo, Fred; Scott, Adrian